PEARSON

WORD STUDY

JANE ERVIN

ELWELL • MURRAY • KUCIA

ACKNOWLEDGMENTS

DESIGN
Judi DeSouter, Michele Episcopo, Denise Ingrassia, Aggie Jaspon, Diedre Mitchel,
Karolyn Necco, Ruth Otey, Siok-Tin Sodbinow, Terry Taylor, Deborah Walkoczy

EXECUTIVE EDITOR
Ronne Kaufman

EDITORIAL DEVELOPMENT
Brown Publishing Network

CREATIVE DIRECTOR
Doug Bates

PROJECT EDITORS
Leslie Feierstone-Barna, Nancy Ellis,
Beth Fernald, Donna Garzinsky,
Betsy Niles

MANUFACTURING & INVENTORY PLANNING
Karen Sota, Danielle Duchamp

PRODUCT MANAGER
Christine A. McArtor

PRODUCTION
Julie Ryan, Helen Wetherill

ART DIRECTORS
Rosanne Guararra, Elaine Sandersen

ELECTRONIC PUBLISHING DIRECTOR
Sandy Kerr

IMAGE SERVICES MANAGER
Sandy Gregg

COMPOSITION
Desktop Media, Devost Design, Hester Hull Associates, Caragraphics

LAYOUT AND PRODUCTION
Deena Uglione, Terri Shema
Larry Berkowitz, Peter Herrmann, Rachel Avenia-Prol, Pat Carlone, Diane Fristachi, Mary Jean Jones,
Chris Otazo, Andrea Schultz, Nancy Simmons, Dave Simoskevitz, Melinda Judson, Diana Rudio,
Murray Levine, Johanna Moroch, Sarah Balogh, Ruth Leine, Jennifer Peal

ILLUSTRATION CREDITS
Terry Taylor: p.3o, 31o, 61o, 87o, 121o, 167o; Elise Mills: p.4;
Mary Keefe: p. 32, 62, 88, 142; Chris Reed: p. 122, 168; Peter Fasolino: bulletin board frames

PHOTO CREDITS
Photo credits appear on pages 209–210, which constitute an extension of this copyright page.

IMAGE SERVICES
Barbara Haugh
Photographers: John Paul Endress; Michael Gaffney, Michael Provost;
Image Research: Leslie Laguna, Betsy Levin
Digital Photographers: John Serafin, Bob Grieza, Douglas Carney; Stylists: Judy Mahoney, Debbie Gaffney

REDUCED STUDENT PAGES
Pearson gratefully acknowledges the following for the use of copyrighted materials: "Cricket"
Copyright © 1991 by X.J. Kennedy. First appeared in The Kite That Braved Old Orchard Beach, published
by Margaret K. McElderry Books. Reprinted by permission of Curtis Brown, Ltd.

Previous copyright © 1998, 1995, 1991, 1988, 1982, 1976, 1970, 1966, 1963, 1958.

ISBN-13: 978-1-4284-3102-7
ISBN-10:   1-4284-3102-0

Printed in the United States of America

1-800-321-3106
www.pearsonlearning.com

CONTENTS

Plurals, Possessives, Contractions, Syllables

UNIT 5

Prefixes, Roots, Syllables

UNIT 6

Synonyms, Antonyms, Homonyms, Dictionary Skills

UNIT 7

Unit 1

Short and Long Vowels, Hard and Soft c and g, Blends, Consonant Digraphs, Syllables

Student Performance Objectives

In Unit 1, students will be developing skill in recognizing and distinguishing among consonant and vowel sounds, consonant blends, consonant digraphs, and syllables. As students learn to apply these phonics and word study skills, they will be able to

◆ Distinguish among short and long vowel sounds

◆ Distinguish between the hard and soft sounds of *c* and *g*

◆ Distinguish among consonant blends and consonant digraphs

◆ Recognize the number of syllables in words

Contents

Assessment Strategy Overview

Throughout Unit 1, assess students' ability to read and write words with short and long vowel sounds, hard and soft c and g, blends, consonant digraphs, and multiple syllables. There are various ways to assess students' progress. You may also want to encourage students to evaluate their own work and to participate in setting goals for their own learning.

FORMAL ASSESSMENT

The Unit 1 Pretest on pages 3e–3f helps to assess a student's knowledge at the beginning of the unit and to plan instruction.

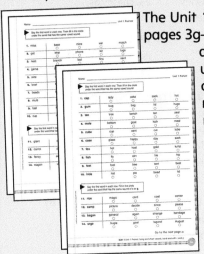

The Unit 1 Posttest on pages 3g–3h helps to assess mastery of unit objectives and to plan for reteaching, if necessary.

PORTFOLIO ASSESSMENT

Portfolio This logo appears throughout the teaching plans. It signals opportunities for collecting students' work for individual portfolios. You may also want to collect the following pages.

❖ Unit 1 Pretest and Posttest, pages 3e–3h

❖ Unit 1 Reading & Writing, pages 19–20, 27–28

❖ Unit 1 Checkup, pages 29–30

INFORMAL ASSESSMENT

The Reading & Writing pages and Unit Checkup in the student book are an effective means of evaluating students' performance.

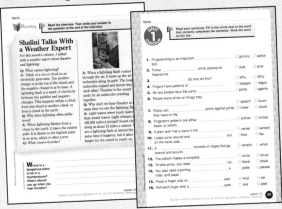

STUDENT PROGRESS CHECKLIST

Use the checklist on page 3i to record students' progress. You may want to cut the sections apart to place each student's checklist in his or her portfolio.

Skill	Reading & Writing Pages	Unit Checkup
Short and Long Vowels	19–20,	29–30
Hard and Soft c and g	19–20	29–30
Blends	19–20	29–30
Consonant Digraphs	27–28	29–30
Syllables	27–28	29–30

Administering and Evaluating the

Pretest and Posttest

DIRECTIONS

To help you assess student's progress in learning Unit 1 skills, tests are available on pages 3e–3h. Administer the Pretest before students begin the unit. The results of the Pretest will help you identify a student's strengths and needs in advance, allowing you to structure lesson plans to meet individual needs. Administer the Posttest to assess students' overall mastery of skills taught in the unit and to identify specific areas that will require reteaching.

PERFORMANCE ASSESSMENT PROFILE

The following chart will help you identify specific skills as they appear on the tests and enable you to identify and record specific information about an individual's or the class's performance on the tests.

Depending on the results of the tests, refer to the Reteaching column for lesson-plan pages where you can find activities that will be useful for meeting individual needs or for daily word study practice.

ANSWER KEYS

Unit 1 Pretest, page 3e (BLM 1)

1. sack
2. bug
3. bench
4. goat
5. tube
6. day
7. hot
8. hip
9. bee
10. pie
11. center
12. picture
13. again
14. legend

Unit 1 Pretest, page 3f (BLM 2)

15. crown
16. slide
17. scarecrow
18. tusk

19. chain
20. wishes
21. then
22. whistle
23. chemical

24. 2
25. 3
26. 2
27. 1
28. 3
29. 1
30. 2
31. 3

Unit 1 Posttest, page 3g (BLM 3)

1. win
2. stop
3. sent
4. brake
5. dive
6. go
7. seal
8. tune
9. lamp
10. bunny
11. giraffe
12. cute
13. since
14. leg

Unit 1 Posttest, page 3h (BLM 4)

15. trail
16. glove
17. skip
18. trunk

19. shoulder
20. nothing
21. cheer
22. feather
23. whimper

24. 2
25. 1
26. 2
27. 3
28. 1
29. 3
30. 3
31. 2

PERFORMANCE ASSESSMENT PROFILE

Skill	Pretest Questions	Posttest Questions	Reteaching: Focus on All Learners	Reteaching: Daily Word Study Practice
Short and Long Vowels	1–10	1–10	5–8, 19–20	196
Hard and Soft *c* and *g*	11–14	11–14	9–12, 19–20	196–197
Consonant Blends	15–18	15–18	13–20	197
Consonant Digraphs	19–23	19–23	21–24, 27–28	197–198
Syllables	24–31	24–31	25–28	208

▶ Say the first word in each row. Then fill in the circle under the word that has the same vowel sound.

1. cap	lady ○	cake ○	sack ○	hot ○
2. gum	bug ○	bag ○	lid ○	huge ○
3. ten	tree ○	bench ○	tan ○	seal ○
4. mole	bottom ○	goat ○	lock ○	meal ○
5. cube	cup ○	cent ○	cut ○	tube ○
6. case	glass ○	happy ○	day ○	sack ○
7. fox	hot ○	host ○	gold ○	lump ○
8. fish	fly ○	elm ○	file ○	hip ○
9. feet	foot ○	bee ○	tent ○	best ○
10. hide	hid ○	pie ○	bead ○	lid ○

▶ Say the first word in each row. Fill in the circle under the word that has the same sound of **c** or **g**.

11. rice	magic ○	card ○	coat ○	center ○
12. camp	picture ○	decide ○	since ○	peace ○
13. began	general ○	again ○	strange ○	bandage ○
14. urge	bugle ○	goal ○	legend ○	August ○

Go to the next page.→

BLM 1 Unit 1 Pretest: Long and short vowels, hard and soft c and g

3e

> ▶ Say the first word in each row. Fill in the circle next to the word that has the same sound as the blend underlined in the first word.

15.	crow	○ cow	○ sled	○ crown	○ clown
16.	slip	○ slide	○ snip	○ stripe	○ drip
17.	scarf	○ surf	○ scarecrow	○ snug	○ slam
18.	mask	○ mast	○ tusk	○ tent	○ stomp

> ▶ Say the first word in each row. Then fill in the circle under the word that has the same sound as the consonant digraph underlined in the first word.

19. coach	cash ○	chain ○	thorn ○	wheel ○
20. shape	whip ○	other ○	wishes ○	chop ○
21. either	wheat ○	sheep ○	teacher ○	then ○
22. while	child ○	whistle ○	crashes ○	brother ○
23. chorus	shuttle ○	chemical ○	cheese ○	catch ○

> ▶ Write 1, 2, or 3 to show the number of syllables in each word.

24. brother ____   28. chemistry ____

25. orchestra ____   29. porch ____

26. thirty ____   30. whistle ____

27. which ____   31. architect ____

Possible score on Unit 1 Pretest is 31. Number correct _____

BLM 2 Unit 1 Pretest: Consonant blends and digraphs, syllables

> ► Say the first word in each row. Then fill in the circle under the word that has the same vowel sound.

1. miss	base ○	mice ○	win ○	match ○
2. got	stop ○	phone ○	let ○	tugs ○
3. nest	branch ○	last ○	fins ○	sent ○
4. game	brake ○	grind ○	seem ○	gift ○
5. size	June ○	sift ○	sale ○	dive ○
6. boat	base ○	go ○	like ○	spot ○
7. beads	bone ○	vase ○	seal ○	best ○
8. mule	mail ○	tune ○	team ○	make ○
9. fast	lamp ○	fade ○	fun ○	hope ○
10. cup	cape ○	bunny ○	cap ○	flute ○

> ► Say the first word in each row. Then fill in the circle under the word that has the same sound of **c** or **g**.

11. giant	count ○	great ○	giraffe ○	again ○
12. carrot	pencil ○	cute ○	center ○	grace ○
13. fancy	second ○	garden ○	since ○	danger ○
14. wagon	village ○	leg ○	certain ○	general ○

Go to the next page.→

▶ Say the first word in each row. Fill in the circle next to the word that has the same sound as the blend underlined in the first word.

15. <u>tr</u>ain	○ rain	○ trail	○ tail	○ frail
16. <u>gl</u>ue	○ grew	○ glove	○ sled	○ true
17. <u>sk</u>ate	○ slid	○ snake	○ skip	○ late
18. sku<u>nk</u>	○ skate	○ tusk	○ stump	○ trunk

▶ Say the first word in each row. Fill in the circle under the word that has the same sound as the consonant digraph underlined in the first word.

19. fini<u>sh</u>	fetch ○	shoulder ○	scheme ○	whistle ○
20. <u>th</u>ank	nothing ○	where ○	touch ○	chair ○
21. rea<u>ch</u>	when ○	leash ○	them ○	cheer ○
22. mo<u>th</u>er	fast ○	feather ○	most ○	watch ○
23. <u>wh</u>y	whimper ○	they ○	shy ○	child ○

▶ Write **1, 2,** or **3** to show the number of syllables in each word.

24. Thursday ____   **28.** splash ____

25. through ____   **29.** anywhere ____

26. orchard ____   **30.** skeleton ____

27. microscope ____   **31.** whether ____

Possible score on Unit 1 Posttest is 31. Number correct _____

BLM 4 Unit 1 Posttest: Consonant blends and digraphs, syllables

Student Progress Checklist

Make as many copies as needed to use for a class list. For individual portfolio use, cut apart each student's section. As indicated by the code, color in boxes next to skills satisfactorily assessed and mark an X by those requiring reteaching. Marked boxes can later be colored in to indicate mastery.

STUDENT PROGRESS CHECKLIST
Code: ■ Satisfactory   ☒ Needs Reteaching

Student: _____ _____ Pretest Score: _____ Posttest Score: _____	**Skills** ❑ Short Vowels ❑ Long Vowels ❑ Hard and Soft *c* ❑ Hard and Soft *g* ❑ Consonant Digraphs ❑ Syllables ❑ Consonant Blends	**Comments / Learning Goals**
Student: _____ _____ Pretest Score: _____ Posttest Score: _____	**Skills** ❑ Short Vowels ❑ Long Vowels ❑ Hard and Soft *c* ❑ Hard and Soft *g* ❑ Consonant Digraphs ❑ Syllables ❑ Consonant Blends	**Comments / Learning Goals**
Student: _____ _____ Pretest Score: _____ Posttest Score: _____	**Skills** ❑ Short Vowels ❑ Long Vowels ❑ Hard and Soft *c* ❑ Hard and Soft *g* ❑ Consonant Digraphs ❑ Syllables ❑ Consonant Blends	**Comments / Learning Goals**

Spelling Connections

INTRODUCTION

The Unit Word List is a comprehensive list of spelling words drawn from this unit. The words are grouped by phonemic elements studied throughout the unit. To incorporate spelling into your word study program, use the activity in the Curriculum Connections section of each teaching plan. The spelling lessons utilize the following approach for each word study element.

1. Administer a pretest of all words that have not yet been introduced. Dictation sentences are provided.

2. Provide practice.

3. Reassess. Dictation sentences are provided.

A final test is provided at the end of the unit on page 30.

DIRECTIONS

Make a copy of Blackline Master 6 for each student. After administering the pretest for each phonemic element, give students a copy of the appropriate word list.

Students can work with a partner to practice spelling the words orally and identifying the phonemic element in each word. You may want to challenge students to add to the list other words with the phonemic element. Students can also write words of their own on *My Own Word List* (see Blackline Master 6).

Students may store their list words in envelopes or plastic zipper bags in their books or notebooks. You may want to suggest that students keep a spelling notebook, listing words with similar elements. Another idea is to build word walls with students and display them in the classroom. Each section of the wall can focus on words with a single word study element. The walls will become a good resource for spelling when students are writing.

UNIT WORD LIST

Long and Short Vowels

luck	ant
gentle	six
top	cube
jeep	fine
rake	cone

Hard and Soft *c* and *g*

cane
rice
go
huge

Blends with *r, l* and *s*

black	spoon
fly	skunk
plants	snake
spring	storm
train	swim
drum	sled
string	

Final Blends

drink	print
wasp	vest
stamp	hand
mask	

Digraphs *sh, th, wh, ch*

shoulder	chef
thing	chemist
wheel	
chipmunk	

Name _____

 Spelling   UNIT 1 WORD LIST

Hard and Soft c and g	Blends with r, l and s		Long and Short Vowels	
cane	black	spoon	luck	ant
rice	fly	skunk	gentle	six
go	plants	snake	top	cube
huge	spring	storm	jeep	fine
	train	swim	rake	cone
	drum	sled		
	string			

Final Blends	Digraphs sh, th, wh, ch	My Own Word List
drink	shoulder	
wasp	thing	
stamp	wheel	
mask	chipmunk	
print	chef	
vest	chemist	
hand		

Word Study Games, Activities, and Technology

The following collection of ideas offers a variety of opportunities to reinforce word study skills while actively engaging students. The games, activities, and technology suggestions can easily be adapted to meet the needs of your group of learners. They vary in approach so as to consider students' different learning styles.

● WORD SCAVENGER HUNTS

Divide the class into small groups. Have students work together to identify names of classroom objects that have one syllable. Then have them identify names of objects that have two or three syllables. Have each group keep separate lists of the one-, two-, and three-syllable words.

Variation: Challenge students to list names of objects that begin with consonant blends or consonant digraphs.

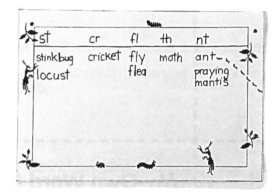

▲ BUG COLLECTIONS

Have students brainstorm a list of insect names. Then have them sort the names into categories of consonant blends and consonant digraphs. Have students tally the number of names for each category. Help students record the data in a class chart.

Variation: Have students compile a list of insect names with a specified number of syllables.

◆ GUESS MY WORD

Have partners create lists of ten words that contain a phonemic element, such as consonant blends. When both partners are familiar with the list, one partner writes one of the words on a piece of paper and tapes the card on the other partner's back. The second partner tries to guess the word by asking questions such as *Does my word contain an* r- *consonant blend? Is it the* dr *blend? Is the blend at the beginning of the word?* Partners get a point for each correctly guessed word.

■ FOUR-SQUARE

Mark off four squares on the floor or pavement with masking tape or chalk. One student stands in each square. Choose a consonant blend, such as *st*. The first player says a word that begins with *st* and bounces a rubber ball to another student. The player who catches the ball says a different *st* word and bounces the ball to another player. Players who say an incorrect word are out of the game. Play continues until only one player remains.

Variations: Four-Square can be played using any phonemic element, such as long and short vowels, consonant digraphs, or hard and soft *g* and *c*. In Syllable Four-Square, players say a word before bouncing the ball to another player. The receiving player must count the number of syllables in the word and let the ball bounce exactly the number of times before catching it.

Make flip books that feature consonant blends. As the letter pages are flipped, each new word that is formed is read.

● RIDDLE ME THIS

Have pairs of students challenge each other with riddles based on words that contain a phonetic element, such as consonant blends. Students can earn one point for each riddle correctly answered. Some examples are *What* ch *word is a science? (chemistry)* and *What amusement has both a hard and a soft c in it? (circus)*.

▲ CONSONANT-BLEND BINGO

Provide students with blank bingo game boards and markers for covering. Have students fill the board by randomly writing the letters making up consonant blends in the spaces, or have them write words given by you. The words you choose may already appear on a word wall in your classroom. To play, call out a word slowly and have students repeat it. They can cover the letters of the consonant blend heard in the word or the word itself, whatever the case may be. Play until someone calls out *Bingo*!

◆ SLAP!

Have partners use index cards to create two identical decks of word cards using words with the consonant digraphs *sh, th, wh,* and *ch*. Each partner holds a shuffled deck face down and turns cards face up one at a time. Players continue turning cards until they come to a matched pair. The first player to slap the matching pair and say the name of the consonant digraph in the words (for example, *CH*! for *chair* and *chair*) gets the pair. The first player to run out of cards loses.

Variations: Students can make decks of cards for consonant blends, hard and soft *g* and *c,* or long and short vowels. For a very challenging version, students can match the number of syllables in the words rather than matching the words themselves.

■ PICTURE THIS

Have small groups make word cards for words having a common phonemic element— for example, consonant digraphs. One student chooses a word card and writes the consonant digraph in that word on the chalkboard. He or she then draws a picture representing the chosen word, and the team tries to guess the word. Two groups can compete against each other by trying to guess their words from the picture in the least amount of time.

✳ PHONEMIC SEARCH

Have pairs of children brainstorm lists of words with a certain phonemic element, for example, hard and soft *g* and *c*. Give them sheets of graph paper and have them make up word search puzzles containing each of the words on their lists. Partners exchange their puzzles and race to see who can complete his or her puzzle first.

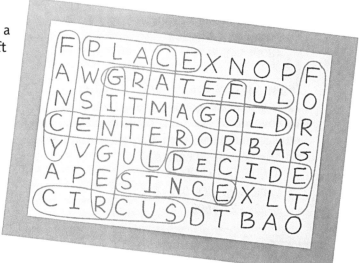

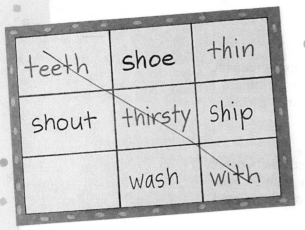

● CONSONANT DIGRAPH TIC-TAC-TOE

Show students how to draw nine-square grid playing boards. Each player chooses a different consonant digraph: *sh, th, wh,* or *ch.* Players take turns making moves, each saying a word that contains his or her chosen consonant digraph and writing the word in one of the squares on the grid. Players can play additional games by drawing new grids and choosing different consonant digraphs.

Variations: This game may be adapted to practice other phonemic elements, such as hard and soft *c* and *g* or consonant blends. Players may also choose one-, two-, or three-syllable words to play.

▲ OPEN WORD SORTS

Provide a set of word cards featuring words with long and short vowels. Students can work in pairs to read the words and decide how to sort them. They may sort by category, word length, initial letter, vowel sound, or rhyming elements. To conclude the activity, sort the words by vowel and read together with the group. These words could be added to an already existing word wall.

Variation: Provide word cards with different consonant blends, consonant digraphs, or hard and soft *g* and *c.*

◆ FERRIS WHEEL

Use Blackline Master 7 to make a game board featuring words with consonant blends. Distribute copies of the game board and have students cut out the circles at the bottom of the page. The object of the game is to make as many words as possible. Players take turns choosing a circle to place in the center of the Ferris wheel and writing down all the words that can be made from combining the blends on the Ferris wheel seats with the phonogram in the middle. The player with the most words after all of the circles have been played wins.

Technology

The following software products are designed to provide practice in spelling.

Reading Blaster 2000   Six- to nine-year-olds help Blaster characters solve problems in a space-age game show that highlights phonics, vocabulary, and reading comprehension.
** Davidson & Associates, Inc.
   19840 Pioneer Avenue
   Torrance, CA 90503
   (800) 545-7677

Super Solvers Spellbound!   Children ages 7 to 12 can practice spelling words (which can be customized by teachers) through playing several educational games including a spelling bee.
** The Learning Company
   1 Athenaeum Street
   Cambridge, MA 02142
   (800) 227-5609

Merriam-Webster's Dictionary for Kids
Children can use this online dictionary to find the meanings of 20,000 words and play a variety of word games.
** Mindscape
   88 Roland Way
   Novato, CA 94945
   (800) 234-3088

Name _____

Cut out the phonogram circles at the bottom of the page. Place each one in the center of the Ferris wheel. Write a list of words that combine the phonogram with the blends on the seats.

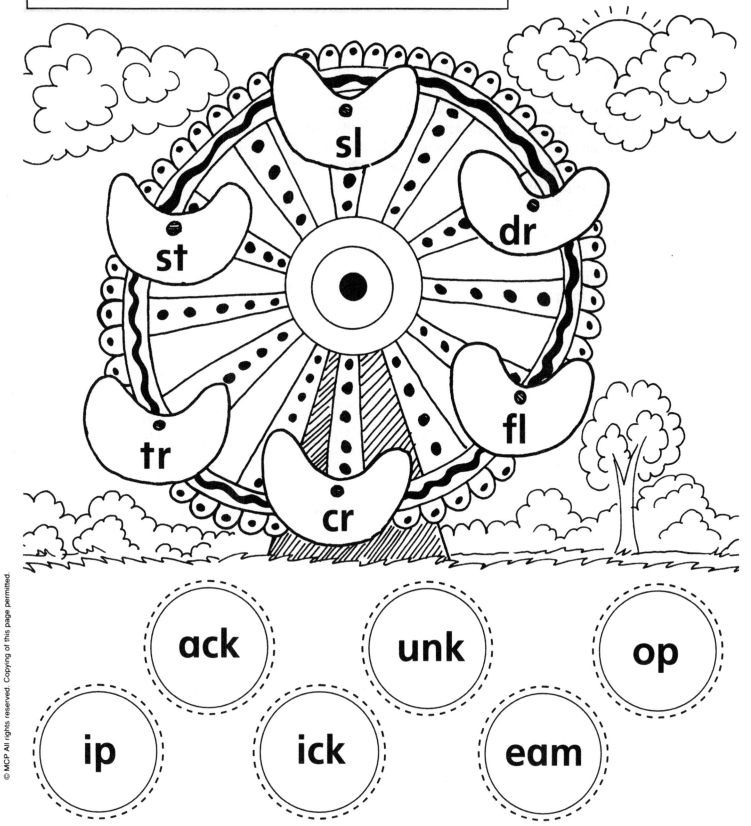

ack

unk

op

ip

ick

eam

Home Connection

A letter is available to be sent home at the beginning of Unit 1. This letter informs family members that students will be learning to read and write words with long and short vowel sounds, the hard and soft sounds of *c* and *g*, consonant blends, and consonant digraphs. The suggested home activity focuses on looking through newspapers and magazines to find words with the sounds and spellings studied in this unit. This activity promotes interaction between student and family members while supporting students' learning of reading and writing words. A Book Corner feature suggests books family members can look for in a local library and enjoy reading together. A letter is also available in Spanish on page 3q.

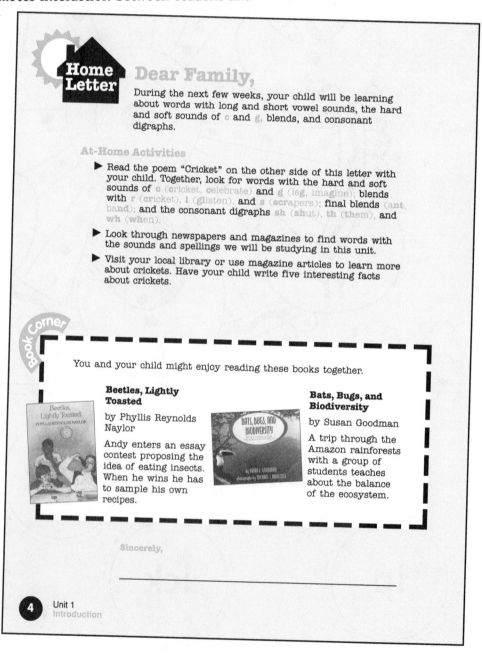

Home Letter

Dear Family,

During the next few weeks, your child will be learning about words with long and short vowel sounds, the hard and soft sounds of c and g, blends, and consonant digraphs.

At-Home Activities

▶ Read the poem "Cricket" on the other side of this letter with your child. Together, look for words with the hard and soft sounds of c (cricket, celebrate) and g (leg, imagine); blends with r (cricket), l (glisten), and s (scrapers); final blends (ant, band); and the consonant digraphs sh (shut), th (them), and wh (when).

▶ Look through newspapers and magazines to find words with the sounds and spellings we will be studying in this unit.

▶ Visit your local library or use magazine articles to learn more about crickets. Have your child write five interesting facts about crickets.

Book Corner

You and your child might enjoy reading these books together.

Beetles, Lightly Toasted

by Phyllis Reynolds Naylor

Andy enters an essay contest proposing the idea of eating insects. When he wins he has to sample his own recipes.

Bats, Bugs, and Biodiversity

by Susan Goodman

A trip through the Amazon rainforests with a group of students teaches about the balance of the ecosystem.

Sincerely,

_____

Carta para la casa

Estimada familia,

Durante las próximas semanas, su hijo/a estará aprendiendo palabras en inglés con sonido de vocal corta y larga, los sonidos de la **c** y la **g** fuerte y suave, combinaciones de consonantes y digramas de consonantes (o consonantes dobles).

Actividades para hacer en casa

▶ Lean el poema "Cricket" en la página 3 del libro de su hijo/a. Juntos, busquen palabras con los sonidos fuertes y suaves de la **c**: **cricket** (**grillo**), **celebrate** (**celebrar**); y de la **g**: **leg** (**pierna**), **imagine** (**imagina**); combinaciones de consonantes con **r**: **cricket** (**grillo**); **l**: **glisten** (**resplandece**); y **s**: **scrapers** (**raspadores**); combinaciones de consonantes finales: **ant** (**hormiga**), **band** (**banda**); y digramas de consonantes: **sh**, **shut** (**cerrado**), **th**, **them** (**ellos**) y **wh**, **when** (**cuando**).

▶ Busquen en periódicos y revistas palabras con los sonidos y la ortografía que vamos a estudiar en esta unidad.

▶ Visiten la biblioteca de su localidad o usen artículos de revistas para aprender más acerca de los grillos, saltamontes o chapulines. Pídanle a su hijo/a que escriba cinco datos interesantes acerca de ellos.

Rincón del libro

Su hijo/a y ustedes pueden disfrutar juntos de la lectura de estos libros. Búsquenlos en la biblioteca de su localidad.

Beetles, Lightly Toasted
por Phyllis Reynolds Naylor

Andy se inscribe en un concurso de escritura, proponiendo la idea de comer insectos. Cuando gana, ¡se ve forzado a probar sus propias recetas!

Bats, Bugs, and Biodiversity
por Susan Goodman

Este libro relata una travesía por la selva del Amazonas con un grupo de alumnos que describe el equilibrio del ecosistema.

Atentamente,_____

Unit 1

Pages 3–4

Short and Long Vowels, Hard and Soft c and g, Blends, Consonant Digraphs, Syllables

ASSESSING PRIOR KNOWLEDGE

To assess students' prior knowledge of short and long vowels, hard and soft *c* and *g*, blends, consonant digraphs, and syllables, use the pretests on pages 3e–3f.

Unit Focus

USING THE PAGE

- Read the poem "Cricket" aloud for students. Then invite students to read along with you as you read the poem again and visualize what the cricket looks like and what it's doing.

- **Critical Thinking** Have students read the questions at the bottom of page 3 and discuss their responses.

BUILDING A CONTEXT

- Ask students to find in the first verse a word with a short vowel sound and a word with a long vowel sound.

- Write the words *celebrate* and *cricket*, and ask which has the sound of *s* and which has the sound of *k* at the beginning. Explain that these are the hard and soft sounds of *c*.

- Write and say *just*. Circle *st*. Explain that this is a blend, two consonants together that can be heard when saying the words.

- Write *sh, ch, th,* and *wh*. Tell students that they are called digraphs and stand for one sound in a word. Have students find a word in the poem with each digraph.

- Reread the first verse of "Cricket" and ask students to count the beats. Tell them that each beat is a syllable.

UNIT OPENER ACTIVITIES

CRICKET FACTS

Ask a volunteer to read the poem. Provide a picture of a cricket, and ask students to talk about what they see. Then talk about how crickets and other animals are adapted to their habitat and climate. Encourage students to share facts they know about other insects or animals.

WHAT IF . . . ?

What if horses were four inches tall? What if zebras laid eggs? Invite students to use their imaginations and write three "What if . . ." questions about animals. Then have them exchange questions with a classmate and make up funny answers to each other's questions.

ANIMALS GOOD AND BAD

In several cultures around the world, crickets are cherished. They are thought to bring good luck. Have students make two lists of animals: those they like and those they dislike. Let them compare their lists in small groups and discuss them.

Home Letter

Dear Family,

During the next few weeks, your child will be learning about words with long and short vowel sounds, the hard and soft sounds of c and g, blends, and consonant digraphs.

At-Home Activities

▶ Read the poem "Cricket" on the other side of this letter with your child. Together, look for words with the hard and soft sounds of c (cricket, celebrate) and g (leg, imagine); blends with r (cricket), l (glisten), and s (scrapers); final blends (ant, band); and the consonant digraphs sh (shut), th (them), and wh (when).

▶ Look through newspapers and magazines to find words with the sounds and spellings we will be studying in this unit.

▶ Visit your local library or use magazine articles to learn more about crickets. Have your child write five interesting facts about crickets.

You and your child might enjoy reading these books together.

Beetles, Lightly Toasted

by Phyllis Reynolds Naylor

Andy enters an essay contest proposing the idea of eating insects. When he wins he has to sample his own recipes.

Bats, Bugs, and Biodiversity

by Susan Goodman

A trip through the Amazon rainforests with a group of students teaches about the balance of the ecosystem.

Sincerely,

_____

BULLETIN BOARD

Have each student browse through nature books and then draw and label a picture of an especially strange-looking real animal. Post the pictures on a bulletin board with the title "It Takes All Kinds," and talk about the wonderful diversity of living things on Earth.

HOME CONNECTIONS

● The Home Letter on page 4 is intended to acquaint family members with the word study skills students will be studying in the unit. Students can tear out page 4 and take it home. Suggest that they complete the activities with a family member and look for the books pictured on page 4 in the library to read together.

● The Home Letter can also be found on page 3q in Spanish.

CURRICULUM CONNECTIONS

WRITING

Portfolio Have each student choose an animal and imagine that they are like their animal in some way. Ask them to write a poem like "Cricket," telling what it would be like.

SCIENCE

Materials: reference books on animal communication

Humans talk to other humans; crickets chirp to crickets. Have pairs of students use reference books to find out how animals communicate with others in their species. Students can either make a booklet of what they learned or give an oral presentation.

MATH

The temperature in summer can be calculated by counting a cricket's chirps and using this formula: Count the number of chirps in one minute. Subtract 40, divide the result by 4, and add 50. That's the temperature in degrees Fahrenheit. Have students do the math backwards to figure out how many times per minute a cricket would chirp if the temperature were 70 degrees (120 times), 95 degrees (220 times), and 102 degrees (248 times).

Lesson 1
Pages 5–6

Short Vowels

INFORMAL ASSESSMENT OBJECTIVES

Can students

- ✔ identify words that have short vowel sounds?
- ✔ match words that have the same short vowel sound?
- ✔ demonstrate reading comprehension by choosing words to complete sentences?

Lesson Focus

INTRODUCING THE SKILL

- Ask students to name the vowels. Then say the words *tap, let, fin, hot,* and *up.* Ask students what kind of vowel sounds they hear. Encourage students to name the vowel in each word.

- Call on volunteers to write the words *tap, let, fin, hot,* and *up* on the board. Help students conclude that if a word or syllable has only one vowel and the vowel comes at the beginning or between two consonants, the vowel usually stands for the short sound.

- Ask students to suggest more short vowel words and to describe how the words illustrate the short vowel rule.

USING THE PAGES

- Make sure students understand what to do on pages 5 and 6. After they have completed the pages, encourage pairs to discuss what they learned about short vowel sounds.

- **Critical Thinking** Have students share their response to the questions at the bottom of page 6.

Look at the pictures in each row. Circle the pictures whose names have the same vowel sound as the first picture. Then write the name of each picture you circled.

> **RULE**
> If a word or syllable has only one vowel and it comes at the beginning or between two consonants, the vowel usually stands for the short sound.
>
> **a**x   l**u**ck

1   fan   **a**   nest   ant   cat   hand

2   gift   **i**   six   pin   ram   bib

3   duck   **u**   bug   ham   sun   bus

4   mop   **o**   block   box   top   bell

5   egg   **e**   bed   bag   jet   hen

Lesson 1
Short vowels   **5**

FOCUS ON ALL LEARNERS

ENGLISH LANGUAGE LEARNERS/ESL

Build background for the story on page 6 by asking students what they know about baseball or softball games. Display a bat, ball, and glove, if available, to prompt the discussion. Encourage students to share games they have played.

VISUAL LEARNERS

LARGE GROUP   Write the following incomplete words on the board: *c__p, h__t, st__ck, b__t, b__g, p__g, l__mp.* Invite volunteers to choose one item, add a vowel, and write the completed word on the board. See how many short vowel words the class can list for each item.

KINESTHETIC LEARNERS

SMALL GROUP   **Materials:** index cards, marker

Prepare five word cards for each short vowel sound. Post *a, e, i, o, u* in different places around the room. Deal the word cards, one to each student. At a signal, students go to the posted vowel in their words. Reshuffle and play again.

▶ Read each sentence. Fill in the circle next to the word that correctly completes the sentence. Write the word on the line.

1. Our school team earned a ___spot___ in the tournament.
   ● spot ○ pots ○ speed

2. We rode the team ___bus___ to the game.
   ○ fuss ● bus ○ ban

3. We ___sat___ in the stands to watch.
   ○ cat ● sat ○ cut

4. Jesse is at ___bat___.
   ○ cap ○ bet ● bat

5. It's a base ___hit___!
   ○ sit ○ hot ● hit

6. We cheer as Jesse ___tags___ first base.
   ● tags ○ tugs ○ rags

7. The pitcher squints in the ___sun___.
   ○ fun ○ fad ● sun

8. Katie misses the first ___pitch___.
   ● pitch ○ witch ○ hatch

9. She ___rests___ for a minute.
   ○ reads ○ bests ● rests

10. The pitcher winds ___up___ and throws.
    ● up ○ at ○ but

11. Katie swings at a ___fast___ ball.
    ○ fist ● fast ○ flag

12. The bat connects with a ___crack___.
    ● crack ○ creek ○ stack

13. It's a home ___run___!
    ● run ○ runt ○ ran

14. Our team ___wins___ the game.
    ○ pans ○ pins ● wins

15. We ___stand___ to cheer.
    ○ plant ● stand ○ stack

16. Everyone ___hugs___ each other.
    ● hugs ○ bags ○ bugs

17. We are all so ___happy___.
    ○ handy ○ bunny ● happy

18. We will ___have___ a party to celebrate.
    ○ hit ● have ○ lamp

Critical Thinking

What game are the children watching? What clues are in the story?

6 Lesson 1
Review short vowels

See Daily Word Study Practice, page 196.

AUDITORY/VISUAL LEARNERS

SMALL GROUP

Materials: index cards, marker

Prepare short vowel word cards. Player 1 draws a card and says the word. If Player 2 can name the vowel sound, he or she draws and reads the next card. If not, play passes to Player 3. When all cards are used, the player with the most cards wins.

GIFTED LEARNERS

Challenge pairs of students to think of five one-syllable words, each of which contain a different short vowel sound. Then have them use the five words in a sentence.

LEARNERS WHO NEED EXTRA SUPPORT

Say these word pairs: *bat, bait; seat, set; pin, pine; hop, hope; cute, cut.* Have students read each word pair and identify the word with a short vowel sound. See Daily Word Study Practice, page 196.

CURRICULUM CONNECTIONS ✳ ● ◆ ● ● ●

SPELLING

The following sentences can be used as a pretest for spelling words that have short and long vowels, hard and soft *g* and *c*, and blends with *r* and *l*.

1. **luck** I wish you good **luck** on your test.
2. **gentle** Mom has a **gentle** voice.
3. **top** I keep my brush on **top** of the dresser.
4. **jeep** The soldier parked the green **jeep**.
5. **cane** Grandpa walks with a **cane**.
6. **rice** Chicken with **rice** is my favorite meal.
7. **go** Let's all **go** for a long hike.
8. **huge** I'm full because I ate a **huge** dinner.
9. **black** The white Dalmatian has **black** spots.
10. **spring** A **spring** closes the screen door.

WRITING

Portfolio Have students write a short narrative about a game or competition, using as many words with short vowels as they can.

MATH

On chart paper, make a short vowel pictograph with five columns, each headed with a vowel letter. Have students cut pictures from magazines of items whose names have short vowel sounds spelled with that vowel letter (*hat, pen, ship, pond, skunk*). When a few dozen pictures have been gathered, have students tape each in the appropriate column.

LANGUAGE ARTS

Challenge teams to write a silly story using as many short vowel words as possible: for example, *Ted and his big black dog got on the bus to go to the sub shop . . .* Set a time limit.

Technology

AstroWord Short Vowels: *a, i;* Short Vowels: *i, o;* Short Vowels: *e, u.* © 1998 Silver Burdett Ginn Inc. Division of Simon & Schuster.

6

Lesson 2

Pages 7–8

Long Vowels

Lesson Focus

INTRODUCING THE SKILL

- Write *can, pin, set,* and *ran* on the board and have students identify the short vowels. Then write *cane, pine, seat,* and *rain* and have students identify the vowels that were added. *(e, e, a, i)* Have them describe how the additions changed the vowel sounds.

- Help students note that in a one-syllable word, such as *seat*, with two vowels, the first vowel usually stands for the long sound and the second vowel is silent. Ask which vowels are silent in *cane, pine,* and *rain*.

- Then say *go* and *cupid*. Have students identify the long vowel sounds. Write the word on the board and explain that if a word or a syllable has one vowel at the end, the vowel usually stands for the long sound.

USING THE PAGES

- Read aloud the rules on page 7.

- After students have completed pages 7 and 8, have them discuss how they know if a word has a long vowel sound.

- **Critical Thinking** Have students discuss the teamwork between a guide dog and a blind person.

7

Name _____

> Study the rules. Then say the name of each picture. Write the name of the picture on the line.

RULES

Long Vowel Rule 1 If a one-syllable word has two vowels, the first vowel usually stands for the long sound and the second vowel is silent.

rain   kite   cane   jeep

Long Vowel Rule 2 If a word or syllable has one vowel and it comes at the end of the word or syllable, the vowel usually stands for the long sound.

we   go   cupid   pony

1	2	3
bone	five	tape
4	5	6
heel	cube	radio
7	8	9
seal	rake	key
10	11	12
vase	cone	tune

Lesson 2
Long vowels **7**

FOCUS ON ALL LEARNERS

ENGLISH LANGUAGE LEARNERS/ESL

To build background for the story on page 8, ask students if they know what a guide dog is. Have students speculate how a dog might be able to help a blind person go places.

VISUAL LEARNERS

INDIVIDUAL Have students write a one-paragraph silly story using as many one-syllable long vowel words as they can. Have them share their stories with a partner, who will then identify the long vowel words by circling them.

AUDITORY/KINESTHETIC LEARNERS

LARGE GROUP Have students stand with their arms to their sides. Read the words below. When students hear a long vowel sound, they extend their arms out as far as they will go. Try these words: *tea, hide, can, tip, tape, cub, cube, met, meet, fine, six, mop, five, vote.*

Read each sentence. Circle the word that correctly completes the sentence. Write it on the line.

As you read, think of different ways a guide dog and a blind person work together as a team.

Critical Thinking

1. My neighbor June is _____blind_____ .   bleed   (blind)
2. _____June_____ has a guide dog named Duke.   (June)   Jeep
3. Several _____breeds_____ can become guide dogs.   brides   (breeds)
4. _____These_____ include boxers and retrievers.   Tries   (These)
5. German shepherds are _____fine_____ guide dogs.   (fine)   feet
6. Duke is a golden _____retriever_____ .   (retriever)   rival
7. June and Duke walk each _____day_____ .   die   (day)
8. _____Duke_____ wears a harness.   (Duke)   Duck
9. June _____holds_____ it firmly.   hides   (holds)
10. Duke walks first and _____leads_____ the way.   (leads)   rides
11. Duke stops at each curb and _____waits_____ .   writes   (waits)
12. He does not _____go_____ until he is told.   tea   (go)
13. June might _____say_____ , "Right."   (say)   sue
14. Then Duke goes on his _____way_____ .   why   (way)
15. Duke has been well _____trained_____ .   (trained)   tried
16. His training lasted _____five_____ months.   fate   (five)
17. I _____like_____ to see Duke with June.   lake   (like)
18. They make a good _____team_____ !   tame   (team)

8   Lesson 2
Review long vowels

AUDITORY/VISUAL LEARNERS

PARTNER   Write *st(a)in, ch(e)ap, pr(i)ce, r(o)be,* and *t(u)be* on the board with blanks for the letters in parentheses. Have pairs fill in each missing vowel and use the word in a sentence. Ask them to create similar puzzles with long vowel words for others to solve.

GIFTED LEARNERS

Materials: several storybooks

Invite students to hunt through books for words with the same long vowel sound, such as *comb, rose, loan, rainbow, soul, spoken,* and *doe.* Then have them group the words by spelling pattern.

LEARNERS WHO NEED EXTRA SUPPORT

Help students complete page 7. Have them identify each picture and repeat the word making the vowel as long as they can (*booooooooooone*). See Daily Word Study Practice, page 196.

CURRICULUM CONNECTIONS

SPELLING

Have students watch as you write on the board one spelling word. Immediately erase the word and have students silently write it from memory. If you wish, increase the challenge by writing and erasing two words at a time. Spelling words: *cane, luck, spring, rice, gentle, top, go, huge, jeep, black.*

WRITING

Portfolio Have students wear blindfolds for five minutes and pay careful attention to the world around them. Then suggest that they write a short poem about what they heard, felt, and smelled while blindfolded or about what it might be like to be blind. Encourage them to use as many long vowel words as they can in their poems.

SOCIAL STUDIES

Suggest that students find out about other aids for disabled persons—Braille, American Sign Language, closed captioning, "hearing ear" dogs and other animals trained to help, computers that "speak" for people who cannot, or motorized wheelchairs. Ask students to share what they learned with the class.

MUSIC

Portfolio Encourage students to write a song about the life of a guide dog, using a familiar melody such as "Down in the Valley" ("Oh, I am a guide dog; My master can't see . . .") or making up their own tune. Help them get started by brainstorming lists of long vowel words that rhyme (*wait, date, gate, late*) with the class. Provide time for students to teach their songs to the class.

Technology   **AstroWord** Long Vowels: *a, i;* Long Vowels: *i, o;* Long Vowels: *e, u.* © 1998 Silver Burdett Ginn Inc. Division of Simon & Schuster.

Lesson 3
Pages 9–10

Hard and Soft *c* and *g*

INFORMAL ASSESSMENT OBJECTIVES

Can students

- associate pictures with words that have the hard or soft *c* sound?
- identify the hard and soft *g* sound in words?

Lesson Focus

INTRODUCING THE SKILLS

- Say the words *cake* and *center*. Have students repeat the sound they hear at the beginning of each word. Then ask volunteers to write the words on the board. Help students identify the hard and soft sounds of *c* in *cake* and *center*.

- Explain that when *c* is followed by *e*, *i*, or *y*, *c* is usually soft and has the sound of *s*. Otherwise, *c* has a hard sound, or /k/. Have students apply the rule to the words *record* and *pencil*.

- Follow the same procedure, using *go* and *gentle*, to identify the hard and soft sounds of *g*. Explain that when *g* is followed by *e*, *i*, or *y*, the *g* is usually soft and has the sound of *j*. Otherwise, *g* has a hard sound. Write *gum* and *ginger* on the board and call on volunteers to apply the rule.

USING THE PAGES

- Explain that the word bank on page 9 is to be used for both exercises.

- When students have completed pages 9 and 10, call on a volunteer to summarize what he or she has learned about hard and soft *c* and *g*.

9

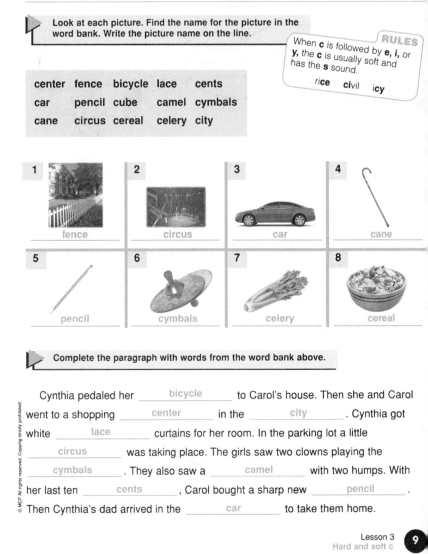

Name _____

▶ Look at each picture. Find the name for the picture in the word bank. Write the picture name on the line.

RULES
When **c** is followed by **e, i,** or **y**, the **c** is usually soft and has the **s** sound.
rice   civil   icy

center	fence	bicycle	lace	cents
car	pencil	cube	camel	cymbals
cane	circus	cereal	celery	city

1	2	3	4
fence	circus	car	cane
5	6	7	8
pencil	cymbals	celery	cereal

▶ Complete the paragraph with words from the word bank above.

Cynthia pedaled her _____bicycle_____ to Carol's house. Then she and Carol went to a shopping _____center_____ in the _____city_____. Cynthia got white _____lace_____ curtains for her room. In the parking lot a little _____circus_____ was taking place. The girls saw two clowns playing the _____cymbals_____. They also saw a _____camel_____ with two humps. With her last ten _____cents_____, Carol bought a sharp new _____pencil_____. Then Cynthia's dad arrived in the _____car_____ to take them home.

FOCUS ON ALL LEARNERS

ENGLISH LANGUAGE LEARNERS/ESL

Before students begin working, read the words in the box on page 9 and the words in items 1–15 on page 10 with students to be sure they are pronouncing the words correctly.

VISUAL LEARNERS

PARTNER   **Materials:** index cards, markers

Give pairs of students 16 cards. Have them write four words each with soft *c*, hard *c*, soft *g*, and hard *g*. Then have them shuffle the cards and use them to play *c* and *g* concentration, matching words with the same sound.

KINESTHETIC/AUDITORY LEARNERS

SMALL GROUP   **Materials:** a hat, two index cards with *c* and *g*

Use the magic hat to make hard letters soft. Hold the *c* card, say "/k/, *carrot*," and place the card in the hat. Pull it out, saying "/s/, *celery*." Have students take turns using the hat to transform *c* and *g*, saying a new example word each time.

Write **H** beside each word in which **g** has a hard sound as in **gain**. Write **S** if the **g** has a soft sound as in **gem**.

> **RULE**
> When **g** is followed by **e, i,** or **y,** the **g** is usually soft. Soft **g** stands for the **j** sound as in **urge**.
> gentle   ginger   gypsy

1. engine	S	2. cage	S	3. rigid	S
4. huge	S	5. orange	S	6. stingy	S
7. magic	S	8. sugar	H	9. giraffe	S
10. stage	S	11. guest	H	12. gas	H
13. game	H	14. badge	S	15. bug	H

Read the following sentences. Underline each word that has a hard **g** sound, and circle each word that has a soft **g** sound. Write the words in the correct columns.

16. The theater group is presenting a (magic) show again this weekend.

17. A (large) (energetic) cast will be on the (stage.)

18. This group has been rehearsing great tricks and grand stunts.

19. Tom, a talented (magician,) will appear in a green and (orange) turban.

20. The audience will never guess how he makes birds appear in an empty (cage!)

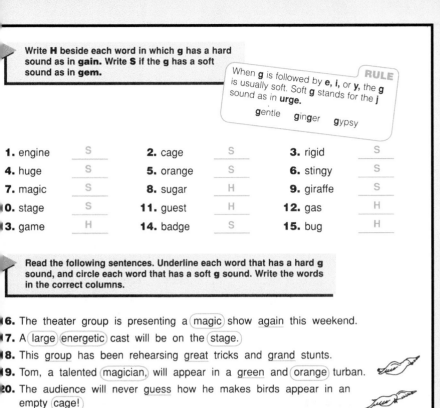

Hard g	Soft g
group	magic
again	large
group	energetic
great	stage
grand	magician
green	orange
guess	cage

SPELLING

Write on the board these phrases and have students take turns adding vowels to complete the spelling words. After each word has been completed, have another student tell whether it has a short or long vowel sound.

1. good l_ck
2. spr_ng
3. r_c_ pudding
4. a g_ntl_ pony
5. a mountain t_p
6. g_ home
7. a h_g_ elephant
8. an army j__p
9. a bl_ck crow
10. a candy c_n_

WRITING

Portfolio Have partners collaborate to write four riddles that can each be answered by a word with a hard or soft *c* or *g* sound: for example, *I am a winter month. I have a soft c sound. Who am I? (December)* Partners should make sure that their clues offer enough information. Have partners exchange riddles with another pair and solve them.

ART

Have interested students find out how to do one or more simple magic tricks. Give students time to practice the tricks and assemble costumes. Plan class time for a magic show.

LANGUAGE ARTS

Have students collect words that have two of the letter-sound correspondences they learned in this lesson. Start them off by giving them these examples: *garage* (hard and soft *g*), *concert* (hard and soft *c*), and *cigar* (soft *c* and hard *g*). Make a Word Wall of the words.

AUDITORY/VISUAL LEARNERS

LARGE GROUP Play "Simon says soft *c*." Write a mix of hard and soft *c* words on the board. Point to each word as you say it. If the word has a hard *c*, students say *Hard* c. If the word has a soft *c*, they must say *Simon says soft* c.

GIFTED LEARNERS

Materials: dictionaries

Have pairs of students use a dictionary to find interesting words that begin with soft *c* and soft *g*, using the phonetic respelling to check each pronunciation. If they are keeping vocabulary notebooks, have students add the words they find to their notebooks.

LEARNERS WHO NEED EXTRA SUPPORT

Materials: tagboard, marker

Have each student make a cue card with words they know that have the hard and soft sounds of *g*. Suggest that they say each word at the top of page 10 and compare its sound of *g* with the sounds of *g* on their cue cards. See Daily Word Study Practice, pages 196–197.

Lesson 4
Pages 11–12

Hard and Soft c and g

* · ◆ · • · * · • · ◆ · ■ · • · ◆ ·

INFORMAL ASSESSMENT OBJECTIVES

Can students

✓ identify words that contain the hard and soft *c* and *g* sounds?

✓ demonstrate reading comprehension by answering questions?

Lesson Focus

REVIEWING THE SKILLS

- Review that the letters *c* and *g* can have both hard and soft sounds.

- Say *traces, category, gold, garage, circle,* and *cool* and have students identify the words in which they hear hard or soft *c* and *g* sounds.

- Ask volunteers to write the words on the board and circle the letters that represent the hard and soft *c* and *g*. Help students notice that the words *circle* and *garage* have both hard and soft sounds.

USING THE PAGES

- Make sure students understand that for the activity on page 11, they should first complete the word-search puzzle and then sort the words.

- For the activity on page 12, they must read the story and answer the questions first and then identify the hard and soft *c* and *g* words in the story.

- **Critical Thinking** When students have completed the pages, have them discuss their responses to the question at the bottom of page 12.

▶ Read the words in the word bank with hard and soft **c** and **g**. Circle the words in the puzzle. Then write them under the correct headings below.

```
C I R C L E G A M E
O H W Y L E G A L C
A U G C I D E R C O
S G O L F C T G E O
T E L E I A J U N L
B R D N C T C E T C
A M U G Y M A S E O
D E C I D E M T R V
G I A N T L E D G E
E R G E N T L E S R
```

		cat
		argue
	legal	ledge
	icy	cool
circle	huge	guest
game	cover	gold
gym	center	engine
cycle	giant	gentle
decide	get	cider
germ	coast	camel
golf	badge	mug

Hard g Words

game	golf
gold	legal
argue	get
mug	guest

Soft g Words

badge	giant
engine	gentle
gym	ledge
huge	germ

Hard c Words

coast	camel
cover	cool
cat	circle
	cycle

Soft c Words

circle	decide
cycle	icy
cider	center

Lesson 4
Hard and soft c and g **11**

FOCUS ON ALL LEARNERS ✳ · ◆ · ●

ENGLISH LANGUAGE LEARNERS/ESL

As background for the story on page 12, have students share what they know or think they know about circuses. You may want to have a fluent English speaker assist each English learner to model pronunciation.

VISUAL LEARNERS

LARGE GROUP

Materials: red chalk

Write soft and hard *c* words on the board in random order, replacing *c* pronounced /k/ with *k* and *c* pronounced /s/ with *s: sirkle, koast, sykle,* and so on. Write the substitute letters in red. Have students rewrite each word with the correct spelling.

KINESTHETIC LEARNERS

SMALL GROUP

Materials: two different colors of markers

Have groups list their first and last names. Then, using one color for *c* and another for *g*, have them circle each soft *c* or *g* and underline each that stands for the hard sound. Some names *(Gracie, Craig, Angelica)* will have more than one mark; some will have none.

Read the story and answer the questions. Then circle each word that has a soft c sound and underline each word that has a soft g sound.

CIRCUS LIFE

Cindy and Gerry are circus children. They and their parents travel with the circus as it goes from city to city. Their home is a car on the circus train.

Cindy and Gerry's father, George, is an animal trainer. He works in a large cage with huge, orange-and-black striped tigers. The tigers sit in a circle on large stools. They growl at George and lunge at him. The tigers act savage and dangerous, but they are gentle with their trainer. The best circus acts are in the center ring.

Celia, Cindy and Gerry's mother, is an acrobat. She dances on a wire high above the ground. She is graceful as she places her feet carefully on the wire. She never loses her balance.

Cindy and Gerry's classroom changes every day, too. A teacher comes with them on the circus train. The children have classes in between shows.

1. Where do Cindy and Gerry's parents work?
They work in the circus.

2. What does their father, George, do?
He works in a cage with huge tigers.

3. Where do George and the tigers perform?
They perform in the center ring.

4. What words describe the tigers? Answers may include _huge,_
orange-and-black striped, savage, dangerous, gentle.

5. What does the children's mother, Celia, do?
She dances on a high wire.

6. Find a word in the story that means "beautiful in movement."
graceful

How is Cindy and Gerry's school different from yours?

Critical Thinking

12 Lesson 4
Hard and soft c and g

See Daily Word Study Practice, pages 196–197.

AUDITORY/VISUAL LEARNERS

LARGE GROUP

Materials: chart paper, markers

Make a chart with the headings _ca, ce, ci, co, cu,_ and _cy._ Have students name words that have these letter combinations and write them under the appropriate headings. Discuss the words in each column to see whether _c_ is usually hard or soft before that vowel letter.

GIFTED LEARNERS

Have students make up their own story about circus life, told from the point of view of one of George's tigers. Challenge them to use as many words with hard and soft _c_ and _g_ sounds as they can.

LEARNERS WHO NEED EXTRA SUPPORT

Suggest that students look for one word at a time when they complete the word-search puzzle. Encourage them to say the words aloud as they sort them.

CURRICULUM CONNECTIONS

SPELLING

Write the spelling words on the board: _cane, luck, spring, rice, gentle, top, go, huge, jeep, black._ Then write these headings and have students take turns writing every word that fits under each one: _Short Vowel (luck, gentle, top, black, spring), Long Vowel (jeep, cane, rice, go, huge), Soft_ g _or_ c _(gentle, jeep, huge, rice), Hard_ g _or_ c _(luck, cane, go, black), Blend with r or l (black, spring)._

WRITING

Portfolio Have students imagine they are Gerry or Cindy and write a diary entry about a day in the circus. They could tell about other circus people, a city they are visiting, or events occuring during a performance. Ask them to circle the words with hard or soft _c_ or _g_ they used.

ART

Materials: posterboard; marker; crayons or paints

Have students think about the most exciting acts in a circus, and then design and illustrate a circus poster. Show examples, if available. Before they begin, help students brainstorm information the posters should contain: the name of the circus, the dates and times when the shows will occur, the location, and the prices of the tickets.

SCIENCE

Training wild animals for circuses and movies involves getting them to behave in ways they wouldn't ordinarily. Have students find out how trainers work with animals to teach them tricks and to work well with people. Invite volunteers to share their findings with the class.

Lesson 5
Pages 13–14

Blends With  r and l

Lesson Focus

INTRODUCING THE SKILLS

Materials: index cards, marker

- Write the following blends on index cards: *br, cr, dr, fr, gr, pr, tr, bl, cl, fl, gl, pl, sl.*

- Pronounce the words *back* and *black.* Ask students to identify the consonant sounds they hear at the beginnings of the words. Help them hear how the letters *bl* blend together in such a way that although the consonants are sounded together, each consonant can be heard. Identify *bl* as an *l* blend.

- Say the word *train.* Have students identify the consonant sound at the beginning of the word. Tell them that *tr* is an *r* blend.

- Display the blend cards. Have students identify the *l* blends and the *r* blends.

USING THE PAGES

Make sure students understand what to do on pages 13 and 14. After they have completed the pages, ask them to share what they learned about *l* and *r* blends.

13

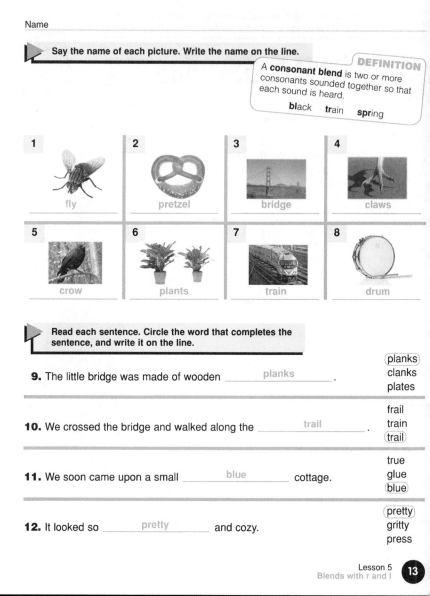

Name

Say the name of each picture. Write the name on the line.

DEFINITION
A **consonant blend** is two or more consonants sounded together so that each sound is heard.
black **tr**ain **spr**ing

| 1 fly | 2 pretzel | 3 bridge | 4 claws |
| 5 crow | 6 plants | 7 train | 8 drum |

Read each sentence. Circle the word that completes the sentence, and write it on the line.

9. The little bridge was made of wooden _____planks_____ .
   (planks)
   clanks
   plates

10. We crossed the bridge and walked along the _____trail_____ .
    frail
    train
    (trail)

11. We soon came upon a small _____blue_____ cottage.
    true
    glue
    (blue)

12. It looked so _____pretty_____ and cozy.
    (pretty)
    gritty
    press

FOCUS ON ALL LEARNERS

ENGLISH LANGUAGE LEARNERS/ESL

As background for the story on page 14, ask students if they have ever been in a club. Invite volunteers to tell what they know about some clubs and what the members do at meetings. Point out the *l* and *r* blend words students use as they talk.

KINESTHETIC LEARNERS

SMALL GROUP

Materials: magazines, scissors, chart paper, glue

Have each group cut out pictures of items whose names begin with *r* and *l* blends and paste the pictures on chart paper. Have the other groups say the picture names and identify the blend in each word.

VISUAL LEARNERS

INDIVIDUAL

Materials: grid paper; markers or pencils

Have students create a word-search puzzle by writing words with *r* and *l* blends across or down and filling in the blank squares with random letters. Have students exchange puzzles for solving.

> Read each word. Complete the word ladders by changing one letter in each line to make a new word. The clue beside each line will help you.

1	flat	fla **p**	(to wave)	2	slip	sl **a** p	(to hit)
		fl **i** p	(to turn over)			sla **m**	(to close)
		fl **o** p	(to fall)			sl **i** m	(thin)

3	brick	**t** rick	(to fool)	4	trade	**g** rade	(a test mark)
		tr **a** ck	(a path)			gra **p** e	(a kind of fruit)
		c rack	(to break)			**d** rape	(a curtain)

5	clank	**p** lank	(a board)	6	trim	tri **p**	(a journey)
		plan **e**	(a jet)			tr **a** p	(to catch)
		pla **c** e	(to put)			tra **m**	(a kind of train)

> Read each sentence. Complete the sentence with a word you wrote above.

7. The girls follow a _____track_____ to their clubhouse.

8. They take a snack of fruit and _____grape_____ juice.

9. It is a long _____trip_____ to the clubhouse.

10. Jo takes along a wooden _____plank_____.

11. The plank is perfect except for one small _____crack_____.

12. Suki will carefully _____place_____ the board in the doorway.

13. The new door looks better than the old cotton _____drape_____.

14. It is too sturdy to _____flap_____ in the breeze.

15. The girls _____flop_____ down in the grass to rest.

14 Lesson 5
    Blends with r and l

SPELLING

The following sentences can be used as a posttest for spelling words with short and long vowels, hard and soft g and c, and blends with r and l.

1. **top**   I want ice cream with a cherry on **top**.
2. **jeep**   Dad drove a **jeep** up the hill.
3. **huge**   I have a **huge** pile of homework!
4. **luck**   Does a four-leaf clover bring **luck**?
5. **cane**   I ate a candy **cane** over the holidays.
6. **black** Hannah's hair is as **black** as ebony.
7. **spring** The river began from a **spring**.
8. **rice**   We all threw **rice** at Mia's wedding.
9. **go**   I **go** to a very friendly school.
10. **gentle** Be **gentle** when you touch the baby.

WRITING

Portfolio Let students have fun making up tongue twisters, using words beginning with two blends from this lesson. For example, *April's pretty plant won a first-place prize*. Students can challenge one another to say the tongue twisters fast, and then vote on the best one.

SOCIAL STUDIES

Have small groups of students imagine that they are the members of a newly formed club. Have them think about the purpose and organization of their club and then work together to write a set of club rules.

ART

Materials: drawing paper; paints and paintbrushes

Have students create a painting of something or someone whose name begins with a blend from this lesson. Tell students to use only colors whose names begin with a blend from this lesson (for example, black, blue, brown, green, gray, crimson). Display their paintings in a group show.

AUDITORY/VISUAL LEARNERS

LARGE GROUP Write these blends and endings on the board: *br, cr, dr, fr, gr, pr, tr, bl, cl, fl, gl, pl, sl; ay, ain, ank, ack, ew, ing, im, ow, own*. Call on volunteers to combine one blend and one ending to make a word. Have everyone say and write each real word created.

GIFTED LEARNERS

Have pairs toss blends: One says a word that begins with an *r* or *l* blend (*print*), the other responds with another word with the same blend (*prune*). They continue until one player can't think of a word. The other player gets a point, and play continues with a new blend.

LEARNERS WHO NEED EXTRA SUPPORT

Before students begin, have them identify each picture on page 13, saying the word and its beginning sounds distinctly: for example, *Fly, I hear /f/ and /l/, fly.* See Daily Word Study Practice, page 197.

Lesson 6
Pages 15–16

Blends With s

Lesson Focus

INTRODUCING THE SKILL

- Say *smile* and *stamp* and have students identify the two consonant sounds they hear at the beginning of each word. Ask which consonant the words have in common.

- Explain that *sm* and *st* are *s* blends. Introduce other *s* blends by having volunteers write the following words on the board as you say them: *skid, slip, spoon, skunk, snug, sway, scat.*

- Point out that *s* blends can also have three letters. Say *spring, stream, splash,* and *screen* slowly and have students identify the consonants they hear that make the initial blend.

- Write *squirt* on the board and have students say it. Explain that in *squ* words, the letter *u* is part of the consonant blend because it stands for the sound of *w.*

USING THE PAGES

Make sure students understand what to do on pages 15 and 16. After they have finished the pages, have them discuss what they learned about *s* blends.

15

Name

▶ Say the name of each picture. Write the name on the line.

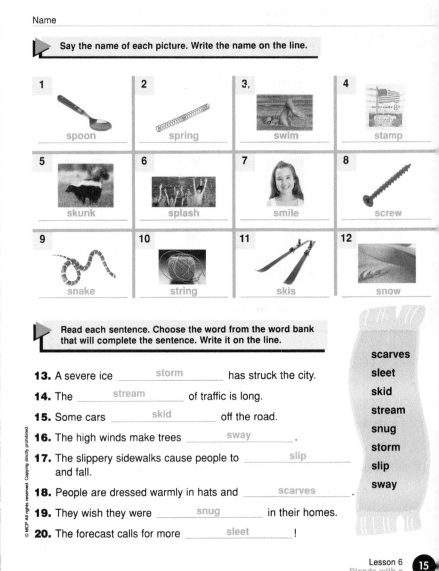

1	2	3,	4
spoon	spring	swim	stamp
5	6	7	8
skunk	splash	smile	screw
9	10	11	12
snake	string	skis	snow

▶ Read each sentence. Choose the word from the word bank that will complete the sentence. Write it on the line.

13. A severe ice _____ storm _____ has struck the city.

14. The _____ stream _____ of traffic is long.

15. Some cars _____ skid _____ off the road.

16. The high winds make trees _____ sway _____.

17. The slippery sidewalks cause people to _____ slip _____ and fall.

18. People are dressed warmly in hats and _____ scarves _____.

19. They wish they were _____ snug _____ in their homes.

20. The forecast calls for more _____ sleet _____!

scarves
sleet
skid
stream
snug
storm
slip
sway

Lesson 6
Blends with s

15

FOCUS ON ALL LEARNERS

ENGLISH LANGUAGE LEARNERS/ESL

If students need help with vocabulary, provide them with a list of words to choose from when identifying the pictures. Have students read the words. Make sure they are pronouncing all the letters in the blend.

VISUAL LEARNERS

SMALL GROUP

Materials: index cards, marker, paper bag

Write *sc, sk, sm, sn, sp, st, sw, scr, spl, spr, squ,* and *str* on cards, place them in a bag, and have each group choose one. Each student in the group writes a sentence with a word that begins with that blend. Groups can exchange papers to identify the blend words.

KINESTHETIC LEARNERS

LARGE GROUP

Make cards for *sc, sk, sm, sn, sp, st, sw, scr, spl, spr, squ,* and *str,* and give each student a card. Say the words below and have students hold up the cards that have the blend heard in that word. Try these words: *sneeze, skip, scoop, scrape, sweet, split, sprinkle, squeak, spark.*

> Say the name of each picture. Listen for the blend. Write the name on the line.

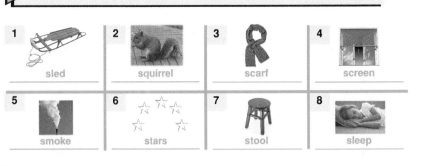

1	2	3	4
sled	squirrel	scarf	screen

5	6	7	8
smoke	stars	stool	sleep

> Read each clue. Find the word in the box that matches the clue. Then write the word in the crossword puzzle.

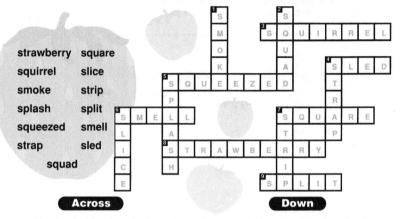

strawberry	square
squirrel	slice
smoke	strip
splash	split
squeezed	smell
strap	sled
squad	

Across

3. a small animal with a long bushy tail
4. used for sliding on the snow
5. pressed or forced together
6. an odor or a scent
7. a flat figure with four equal sides
8. a small, red, juicy fruit
9. to separate into two parts

Down

1. gas and bits of carbon that rise from something burning
2. a small group of football players
4. a narrow strip of leather
5. to make a liquid scatter and fall in drops
6. to cut with a knife
7. a long narrow piece of land or material

16 Lesson 6
Blends with s

SPELLING

The following sentences can be used as a pretest for spelling words that have blends with *s*; final blends; and digraphs *sh*, *th*, *wh*, and *ch*.

1. **string** — I broke a **string** on my banjo.
2. **drink** — Let's get a cool **drink** of water.
3. **wasp** — A **wasp** does not die when it stings.
4. **stamp** — Have you got a **stamp** for my letter?
5. **shoulder** — The parrot sat on her **shoulder**.
6. **thing** — A noun can name a person or a **thing**.
7. **wheel** — A **wheel** fell off my toy car.
8. **chipmunk** — A cute **chipmunk** ate seeds.
9. **chef** — A great restaurant has a great **chef**.
10. **chemist** — The **chemist** mixed two chemicals.

WRITING

Portfolio Invite students to write a short story whose title contains *s*-blend words, such as "The Snake in the Storm." Encourage students to use as many *s*-blend words as they can.

SCIENCE

Assign each small group of students one of the animals pictured on the pages (skunk, snake, squirrel). Have students find out what the animal eats and what kind of home it builds. Invite each group to present a brief oral report to the class.

LANGUAGE ARTS

Materials: grid paper

Review the numbering system for a crossword puzzle. Have students, working alone or in small groups, create their own puzzles using words with *s* blends.

AUDITORY/VISUAL LEARNERS

LARGE GROUP Many familiar sayings include *s*-blend words. Write *__ as a bug in a rug. Where there's __, there's fire.* on the board. Have students supply the missing word and discuss each saying. Then invite students to brainstorm other sayings that have *s*-blend words.

GIFTED LEARNERS

Materials: a dictionary that gives word histories

Many words beginning with *sc*, *scr*, and *sk* are of Old Norse or other Scandinavian origin. Have students browse through the *sc* and *sk* entries and list the words that came from these languages.

LEARNERS WHO NEED EXTRA SUPPORT

Materials: index cards, markers

Have small groups of students make word cards for words from the lesson. Help them cut the words apart just after the *s* blend. (Cut after the *u* if you use *squ*.) Mix up the pieces and have students put the words together. See Daily Word Study Practice, page 197.

Lesson 7

Pages 17–18

Final Blends

✳ · ● · ◆ · · ● · ✳ · ● · ■ · ◆ · ● ·

INFORMAL ASSESSMENT OBJECTIVES

Can students

✓ identify final blends?

✓ recognize words with initial and final blends?

✓ choose correct words to complete sentences?

Lesson Focus

INTRODUCING THE SKILL

● Review with students that in a consonant blend, the sounds of two or more consonants are heard or blended together. Ask students to name some of the r, s, and l blends they know.

● As you say these words, have students listen carefully to the ending sounds: *sink, wasp, hand, lamp, bent, risk.* Explain that the two consonant sounds they hear at the end of each word form a final consonant blend.

● Write or have volunteers write the words on the board. Have them erase the initial consonant in each word and add a blend to make a new word.

USING THE PAGES

● Make sure students understand what to do on pages 17 and 18. When they have completed both pages, ask them to discuss what they learned about the final blends.

● **Critical Thinking** Have students scan the information on page 18 again before answering the question.

17

Name

▶ Circle the word in each pair in which you hear a final blend.

> **HINT**
> Some words end with a consonant blend.
> dent   fast   lamp
> mask   hand
> drink   wasp

1. tin — (tint)
2. (king) — kit
3. cat — (cast)
4. (think) — thin
5. (hunt) — hut
6. (ramp) — ram
7. ten — (tend)
8. (wink) — win
9. (risk) — rise
10. wan — (want)
11. (cramp) — cram
12. (chump) — chum
13. base — (bask)
14. bun — (bunt)
15. mat — (mast)
16. pain — (paint)
17. on — (bond)
18. (bend) — Ben
19. toad — (toast)
20. bad — (band)

▶ Read each definition. Then write the word from the word bank that goes with it. Circle the blends in the words you write.

> **HINT**
> The meaning of a word is its definition.

mask	plank	print	sink	stump
rent	limp	coast	vest	blend

21. a basin in the kitchen that has a drain and water faucets — si(nk)
22. a kind of jacket without sleeves — ve(st)
23. the part of the tree left after it has been cut down — stu(mp)
24. the edge of land facing the sea — coa(st)
25. to walk in a lame way — li(mp)
26. to mix together — ble(nd)
27. the kind of mark often made by a foot or finger — pri(nt)
28. a face covering with openings for the eyes — ma(sk)
29. a long, wide, thick board — pla(nk)
30. money paid for the use of an apartment — re(nt)

Lesson 7
Final blends   **17**

FOCUS ON ALL LEARNERS ✳ · ● · ◆ · ·

ENGLISH LANGUAGE LEARNERS/ESL

Before beginning the activity on page 18, show students some pictures of chimps and other apes, and talk about how their bodies are different from the human body. You might suggest that students try to walk on their feet and their front knuckles, like a chimp.

VISUAL LEARNERS

LARGE GROUP

Write the final blends *nt, st, mp, sk, nd, nk,* and *sp* across the board. Have students take turns thinking of a word with any one of these blends and writing it under the appropriate blend. Challenge the class to think of at least five words for each blend.

KINESTHETIC LEARNERS

INDIVIDUAL   **Materials:** index cards, marker

Make cards for the blends *nt, st, mp, sk, nd, nk,* and *sp.* Have students use the cards to form three words that end with each of the blends.

Read each sentence. Circle the word that correctly completes the sentence. Write it on the line.

1. Each _____kind_____ of animal has its own way of moving.
   mind   (kind)

2. Animals run, crawl, hop, and _____jump_____.
   thump   (jump)

3. Some animals _____spend_____ their days in treetops.
   (spend)   stamp

4. They have strong arms and hands to _____grasp_____ branches.
   (grasp)   wasp

5. They _____must_____ be able to hold on tightly.
   rest   (must)

6. Other animals live on the _____ground_____.
   (ground)   plank

7. Some _____hunt_____ other animals for food.
   point   (hunt)

8. Others are at _____risk_____ of being eaten.
   mask   (risk)

9. Both kinds must be able to move _____fast_____.
   (fast)   vest

10. Most have strong front and _____hind_____ legs.
    band   (hind)

11. People and apes have both feet and _____hands_____.
    sands   (hands)

12. Apes like _____chimps_____ live in trees and on the ground.
    (chimps)   lamps

13. Chimps' spines _____bend_____ at an angle.
    (bend)   send

14. On the ground, chimps walk _____bent_____ over.
    tent   (bent)

15. They walk on their feet and their _____front_____ knuckles.
    (front)   want

16. People's straight spines help them _____stand_____ upright.
    (stand)   tend

17. This leaves our hands free for any _____task_____.
    whisk   (task)

18. Don't you _____think_____ this is a good way to be?
    thank   (think)

Critical Thinking

Why are apes able to climb in trees and walk on the ground?

18 Lesson 7
Final blends

SPELLING

Write the spelling words on the board. *(stamp, chipmunk, wheel, thing, shoulder, chef, wasp, drink, chemist, string)* Write the heading *Nouns* and the subheadings *Person, Animal, _____.* Ask a volunteer to choose and write a spelling word for the third heading. *(Thing)* Call on others to write each spelling word under the correct heading.

WRITING

Portfolio **Materials:** index cards, marker

Make word cards for 20 words with final blends from the lesson. Have each student draw four cards and write the words at the top of a page. Challenge them to write a paragraph that makes sense and includes their four words. Be sure to shuffle the cards well after each student draws.

SCIENCE

Some animals do not move quickly. Have students choose a slow-moving animal (earthworm, koala, panda, sloth, caterpillar, turtle) and find out how it survives (for example, camouflage, bad-tasting, no enemies, poisonous, hard shell, lives in trees, lives underground). Invite students to create a bulletin-board display about these animals.

LANGUAGE ARTS/ART

Materials: drawing paper, markers

Have students consider how humans move. Ask volunteers to walk, crawl, and run across the room while the others observe. Then have pairs of students choose one kind of locomotion and create an illustrated how-to article explaining the movement.

AUDITORY LEARNERS

LARGE GROUP Read the list of words below. Have students identify where a blend exists in each word by saying *beginning* or *end*. If no blend exists in the word, they say *none*. Try these words: *sank, cent, ramp, star, dance, planet, toast, great, wasp, skip, wand, crab, wrap, clown, thank,* and *look.*

GIFTED LEARNERS

Challenge students to think of more final blends (*ld, lk, ct, ft, pt*) and list as many words as they can that end with each. Caution them that combinations with *r* (*rk, rt*) are not blends. Also, point out that when one consonant is silent (*would, walk*), it's not a blend.

LEARNERS WHO NEED EXTRA SUPPORT

Work with students as they begin page 17. Give each a chance to read a word pair aloud while the others listen for the final sounds before they continue independently. See Daily Word Study Practice, page 197.

Lesson 8

Pages 19–20

Reading **W**riting

Reviewing Long and Short Vowels; Hard and Soft c and g; Blends

Lesson Focus

READING

- Write *spend, glad, dump, sleep, wisp, drop,* and *drove* on the board. Have students say the words and identify the vowel sound in each. Then ask them to identify the blend in each word. Ask them for other words they know with blends.

- Write *engine, gold, cigar,* and *cable.* Say each word aloud and have students identify the letters that stand for the hard and soft *c* and *g* sounds.

- Explain that they will read an article about magic tricks and that in the article they will encounter more words with short and long vowels, hard and soft *c* and *g,* and blends.

WRITING

- Before students begin to write, invite them to tell about magic shows they have watched and to recall tricks they have seen.

- Encourage students to use words from the word bank as well as the Helpful Hints in their descriptions.

19

 Reading ▶ Read the article. Then write your answer to the question at the end of the passage.

Magic: Tricks and Treats!

Magic has given pleasure to people all over the world for thousands of years. Records from ancient Egypt describe magicians who made small statues appear to turn into live crocodiles. In India, magicians of the past developed a trick that is still famous today. A young boy climbs up a long rope thrown into the air and seems to disappear at the top.

One of the most spectacular stunts in modern magic is sawing a woman in half. This trick was invented in 1920 by a British magician, P. T. Selbit. His assistant was placed in a wooden box from which only her head protruded. All she had to do was draw her knees up under her chin while he sawed. An American magician, Harry Goldin, improved the trick in 1921. His assistant's head, hands, and feet could be seen clearly as he sawed her in half. What do you think was the secret of this trick? (Turn page upside down.)

Magicians of the present try to improve on tricks created by magicians of the past as well as invent their own illusions. To interest audiences, magicians wear special clothes, wave magic wands, and speak magic words. We do not think that what we are seeing is real. We know we are being fooled, but somehow we still believe it!

Answer: There were two women in the box.

Why do people enjoy seeing magicians perform, even though they know they are being fooled?

_____

_____

_____

_____

FOCUS ON ALL LEARNERS

ENGLISH LANGUAGE LEARNERS/ESL

Before beginning page 19, invite students to tell what they know about magicians and magic tricks. Encourage them to describe any tricks they have seen and guess how they are done.

VISUAL LEARNERS

INDIVIDUAL If possible, have students search the Internet for the subject *magic tricks* and read some of the information they find on Web pages. Encourage them to make lists of words they find that have short and long vowels, hard and soft *c* and *g,* and blends.

KINESTHETIC/VISUAL LEARNERS

LARGE GROUP

Materials: index cards, markers

Write *magic, crocodile, age, Pacific, recipe, garden, center, begin, acorn,* and *genius* on cards. Shuffle the cards and say, *Pick a card, any card.* A student draws a card, says the word, and tells whether it has a hard or soft *c* or *g* sound.

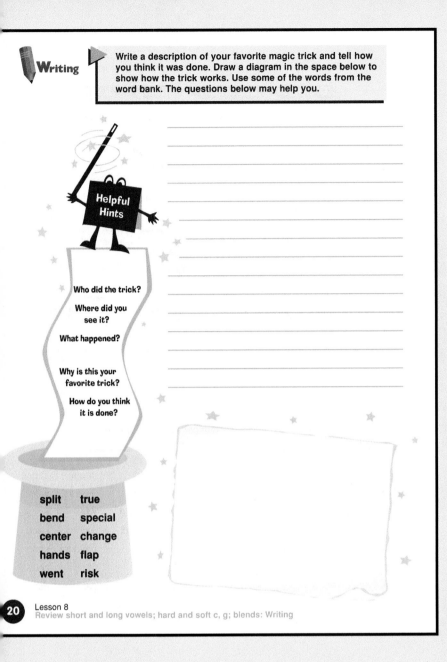

Writing

Write a description of your favorite magic trick and tell how you think it was done. Draw a diagram in the space below to show how the trick works. Use some of the words from the word bank. The questions below may help you.

Helpful Hints

Who did the trick?

Where did you see it?

What happened?

Why is this your favorite trick?

How do you think it is done?

split	true
bend	special
center	change
hands	flap
went	risk

SPELLING

Materials: index cards, markers

Make three identical sets of letter cards: *a, c, d, e, e, f, g, h, i, k, l, m, n, o, p, r, s, t, u, v, w.* Spread them out on three tables. Have students line up in three teams. When you dictate a spelling word *(stamp, thing, chipmunk, string, wasp, shoulder, wheel, chef, drink, chemist),* have the first student in each line run to its table, spell the word with cards, and return to the end of the line. If the word is correct, score one point. The team with the most points after all words have been dictated wins.

LANGUAGE ARTS

Portfolio Point out that while magicians are doing their tricks, they try to distract the audience from what their hands are doing by talking fast and telling silly jokes the whole time. This talk is known as patter. Have students write a paragraph or two of patter that a magician might use to distract the audience.

MATH/SCIENCE

Materials: paper, ruler, pencils, scissors

Here's a disappearing trick your students can do for their families.

1. Using a ruler, draw ten straight, parallel, evenly spaced lines on a piece of paper. The lines should all be the same length.
2. Cut the paper diagonally from the very bottom of the first line to the very top of the last line.
3. Slide the paper down and to the left until there are only nine lines.

Ask students to figure out what happened to the tenth line!

AUDITORY LEARNERS

PARTNER Have students read the description they wrote on page 20 aloud to a partner, slowly and distinctly. When partners hear a word with a blend, they stop the reader, tell what letters form the blend, and say whether it is in the beginning or end of the word.

GIFTED LEARNERS

Challenge students to locate information about a famous magician and then to write about what they found, using as many two- and three-letter blends as possible.

LEARNERS WHO NEED EXTRA SUPPORT

To make sure they have grasped the information, ask students to retell "Magic: Tricks and Treats!" in their own words before they proceed to write their own description of a trick. See Daily Word Study Practice, pages 196-197.

Lesson 9
Pages 21–22

Consonant Digraphs
sh, th, wh, ch

Lesson Focus

INTRODUCING THE SKILL

● Say *shine, chalk, whiskers, thermos,* and *them*. Have volunteers write the words on the board and underline the two consonants that begin each word. Explain that two consonants together, such as *sh* or *ch*, that make one sound is known as a consonant digraph.

● Ask volunteers to write the words *teeth, mother,* and *rich* on the board and read them aloud. Have students identify the position of the digraph in each word. Explain that digraphs can appear at the middle and end as well as at the beginning of words.

USING THE PAGES

● Make sure students understand what to do on pages 21 and 22. After they have finished, ask them what they have learned about consonant digraphs.

● **Critical Thinking** Invite students to discuss and answer the question on page 22.

Name _____

Digraph	Beginning	Middle	Ending
sh	ship	ashes	fish
th	thing	mother	teeth
ch	chicks	exchange	watch
wh	when	awhile	—

▷ Circle two pictures in each row whose names contain the consonant digraph sound you hear in the first word. Write the words on the lines.

DEFINITION
A **consonant digraph** is two or more consonants that together represent one sound.

1 brush — shoulder, elephant, shower

2 thirty — wreath, teeth, shoe

3 wheat — whale, chick, wheel

▷ Read each sentence. Circle the word that correctly completes the sentence and write it on the line.

4. Mr. Batt is the _____coach_____ of the football team. — cough (coach)

5. He wears a shiny _____whistle_____ around his neck. — thistle (whistle)

6. The players _____wheel_____ equipment onto the field. — (wheel) wreath

7. Mr. Batt warns them about a _____patch_____ of mud. — (patch) peach

8. The players wear large _____shoulder_____ pads. — shudder (shoulder)

9. Some players will _____throw_____ the ball. — (throw) chow

10. Other players will _____catch_____ the ball and run. — (catch) rich

Lesson 9
Consonant digraphs sh, th, wh, ch

FOCUS ON ALL LEARNERS

ENGLISH LANGUAGE LEARNERS/ESL

Students learning English often have difficulty pronouncing digraphs. Give them plenty of practice saying words with digraphs and listening to others say them correctly. Help them hear the differences—<u>th</u>in, <u>d</u>in; <u>sh</u>ip, <u>s</u>ip; <u>ch</u>in, <u>sh</u>in.

VISUAL LEARNERS

INDIVIDUAL Write the sentences below on the board. Have students copy them and underline words with the digraphs *th, ch, sh,* and *wh*.

1. They threw a birthday party for their brother.

2. Chad can't reach the branch.

3. Whose wheel is in the wheat field?

KINESTHETIC LEARNERS

SMALL GROUP **Materials:** cardboard, a pushpin, markers

Make a spinner with four areas: *sh, th, wh, ch*. Have students take turns spinning. When the pointer stops, have them say and write a word that contains that digraph.

> Read the article and answer the questions. Then underline each word that has the consonant digraph **th, sh, ch,** or **wh.**

Computers: Machines That Think

In 1822, Charles Babbage asked the British government for funds to build what he called a Difference Engine. He said that this machine could add, subtract, multiply, and divide. Babbage got some money, but the machine was never finished.

Babbage also had thought up a machine—called an Analytical Engine—that could do more complex math. The government refused to give him money for this machine, because they said, "There is no possible use for it." The British government did not know that one day computers would do much more than solve math problems. Today, computers control other machines, guide ships, launch the space shuttle, and play chess. Most important, they can be programmed to think.

Before the microprocessor was introduced in 1971, computers were huge and slow. Their switches were thousands of bulky valves that looked something like lightbulbs. Memories, which were stored on magnetic drums, could fill whole rooms.

The microprocessor, contained in a single chip, changed the computer industry. Though it is as small as a shirt button, the modern microchip can store enormous amounts of information. It is these tiny chips that make laptop computers possible.

How are today's computers different from Charles Babbage's Difference Engine?

Critical Thinking

1. What would Babbage's Difference Engine have done?
   It would have solved math problems.

2. What kinds of things do modern computers do?
   Answers may include controlling other
   machines, guiding ships, launching
   the space shuttle, playing chess.

3. How big were the early computers?
   They could fill whole rooms.

4. What invention made laptop computers possible?
   The microchip made laptop computers possible.

5. How is the size of a microchip described?
   It is as thin as a hair and small as a shirt button.

22 Lesson 9
Consonant digraphs sh, th, wh, ch

SPELLING

Write the spelling words on the board: *wasp, wheel, string, chef, thing, chipmunk, stamp, shoulder, chemist, drink.* Write blanks for the letters in one spelling word. Have a student suggest a letter that might be in the word. If it is, write it in and let the student guess the word. If he or she is correct, proceed to another word. If not, let another student suggest a letter and try to guess the word.

WRITING

Portfolio Have students imagine they are reporters and write a news story about an amazing new invention. Remind them to answer the questions *who, what, when, where,* and *why* in the first paragraph. Then they can go on to give more details about the inventor and the invention.

SCIENCE

Suggest that each student find out about an inventor and make a trading card that shows a picture of the inventor or invention on the front and gives details and statistics on the back. Assemble the class's cards and display them on the bulletin board.

HEALTH

Have small groups of students research current health concerns about using the computer. Suggest that they find out how some problems can be reduced or eliminated by arranging the workspace and lighting and through correct posture, hand positions, and exercise.

AUDITORY LEARNERS

LARGE GROUP Write *sh, ch, th,* and *wh* on the board. Read aloud this list of words and have students name rhyming words that start with the digraphs: *choose, sheet, ship, there, shy, chief, whistle, these.*

GIFTED LEARNERS

Hold a class quiz. Have students write questions whose answers are words that contain digraphs. Remind them to give enough clues in the question. Examples: *What's the opposite of deep? (shallow) What are two close male relatives called? (father, brother)*

LEARNERS WHO NEED EXTRA SUPPORT

Depending on your area's regional pronunciation, you may want to explain that in formal English the digraph *wh* is pronounced /hw/, as if you were blowing out a candle. Point out that many people simply pronounce it /w/. See Daily Word Study Practice, pages 197-198.

Lesson 10

Pages 23–24

Consonant Digraphs

sh, th, wh, ch

Can students

✓ identify words that contain the consonant digraph *ch*?

✓ associate the sounds of *k, ch,* and *sh* with the consonant digraph *ch*?

✓ identify consonant digraphs *ch, sh, th, wh* in initial, medial, and final positions?

Lesson Focus

REVIEWING THE SKILL

● Review with students the consonant digraphs they have been studying: *sh, th, wh, ch.*

● Write *chain, chef,* and *chorus* on the board. Explain that the digraph *ch* usually stands for the sound heard at the beginning of *chain.* Ask students to say *chef* and *chorus.* Help them conclude that *ch* can also stand for the sound of *sh* or the sound of *k.*

● Ask students to name other words that begin with these sounds for *ch.* Write their suggestions on the board.

USING THE PAGES

● Before beginning the pages, you may want to model on the board the two word sorts students are asked to do.

● When students have completed the pages, encourage volunteers to summarize what they learned about the consonant digraphs in the lesson.

23

Name _____

> ▷ Read the sentences and underline each word that contains **ch.** Write the word you underlined under **church** if **ch** stands for its usual sound. Write the word under **chef** if **ch** has the **sh** sound, or under **chord** if **ch** stands for the **k** sound.

RULE

Usually **ch** stands for the sound you hear at the beginning and end of **church.** Sometimes **ch** can stand for the **sh** sound or the **k** sound.

chipmunk   **ch**ef   **ch**emist

1. Mr. Christy took our school choir and orchestra on a field trip.
2. He chauffeured us to a restaurant called the Chic Steakhouse.
3. Pictures of cartoon characters were on the walls.
4. A large, bright chandelier hung from the ceiling.
5. Every table had a vase of fresh chrysanthemums.
6. The chef, Charlene, made delicious chicken.
7. Our waitress, Charlotte, served us with a smile.
8. The chocolate chiffon pie was their specialty.
9. I had grapes and cherries for dessert.
10. At the end of the meal, our teacher paid the check.
11. He left the extra change for our waitress.
12. We, as a chorus, cheered her.

church	chef	chord
chicken	chauffeured	Christy
chocolate	Chic	school
cherries	chandelier	choir
teacher	chef	orchestra
check	Charlene	characters
change	Charlotte	chrysanthemums
cheered	chiffon	chorus

FOCUS ON ALL LEARNERS

ENGLISH LANGUAGE LEARNERS/ESL

To build background for page 23, write the words *restaurant, chef, waitress,* and *check* on the board and ask students what the words have in common. Define the words, and then have students share any experiences they have had at a restaurant.

LARGE GROUP

VISUAL/KINESTHETIC LEARNERS

Materials: index cards, marker

Make cards for *ch, sh, th,* and *wh* and display them. Write a word from page 24 on the board, leaving a blank in place of the digraph (*spina___*). Have a volunteer choose the correct card, hold it over the blank, and say the word.

LARGE GROUP

VISUAL LEARNERS

Have students form four teams and line up at the board. Assign each team a digraph: *ch, sh, th,* or *wh.* Ask a member of each team to write and pronounce a word that contains their digraph. Each correct word earns a point. Continue until everyone has had a turn.

Read each word below and circle its consonant digraph. Then write the word in the correct column according to whether the consonant digraph comes at the beginning, in the middle, or at the end of the word.

architect	spinach	shoulder	cheap
switch	cheese	porch	whale
orchid	mushroom	teeth	dishes
merchant	relish	moth	orchestra
teacher	thin	arch	chemist
shutters	lunchtime	path	crush
ditch	chorus	brother	urchin
think	bunch	mother	whip
leash	wharf	chaperon	pitcher

Beginning	Middle	End
wharf	orchid	switch
shutters	merchant	ditch
think	teacher	leash
cheese	mushroom	spinach
thin	lunchtime	relish
chorus	architect	bunch
shoulder	brother	moth
chaperon	mother	porch
cheap	dishes	teeth
whale	orchestra	arch
chemist	urchin	path
whip	pitcher	crush

24 Lesson 10
Consonant digraphs sh, th, wh, ch

SPELLING

Provide student pairs with a list of the spelling words (*string, drink, wasp, stamp, shoulder, thing, wheel, chipmunk, chef, chemist*) and have them take turns quizzing each other on the spelling of each. Words can be spelled orally or written. Encourage the tester to use each word in a sentence.

WRITING

Portfolio Ask students to turn the sentences on page 23 into a play by deciding on a cast of characters (those seated at one table, for example) and writing dialogue. Encourage them to use words with consonant digraphs when they write. When students have finished writing, have them rehearse the scene and give a performance for the class.

LANGUAGE ARTS

Have small groups choose a poem and prepare it as a choral reading presentation for the rest of the class.

SCIENCE

Suggest that students find out about the history of arches, the different styles of arches, and the role of a keystone in an arch made of stones or blocks. Encourage students to present their findings in an oral report accompanied by illustrations and photographs.

AUDITORY LEARNERS

PARTNER Have pairs make up mnemonic sayings to remember whether a word with /sh/ has the *ch* or *sh* digraph. Examples: for *chef*, say <u>C</u>ats <u>h</u>ave <u>e</u>aten <u>f</u>ish; for *leash*, My <u>sh</u>eep walks on a lea<u>sh</u>. Invite pairs to share the best memory joggers with the class.

GIFTED LEARNERS

Suggest that students collect words that have two consonant digraphs. They can start by finding two words on page 23 that have two: *church* and *chrysanthemums*.

LEARNERS WHO NEED EXTRA SUPPORT

Work with the group to complete page 23 together. Have students take turns reading a sentence aloud and identifying the words that have *ch*. The group can confer to identify the sound the digraph *ch* stands for. See Daily Word Study Practice, pages 197-198.

Lesson 11
Pages 25–26

Syllables

Can students

✔ identify the number of vowels seen in a word?

✔ identify the number of vowel sounds heard in a word?

✔ categorize words as one-, two-, or three-syllable words?

Lesson Focus

INTRODUCING THE SKILL

- Say the word *tan*. Ask students how many vowel sounds they hear. Have a volunteer write the word on the board, say the word, and count the vowels. Explain that if one vowel sound is heard in a word, then the word has one part, or syllable.

- Repeat the procedure with the word *hotel*. Help students conclude that if two vowel sounds are heard in a word, the word has two syllables.

- Repeat again with *something*. Have students note that even though the word has three vowel letters, there are only two vowel sounds and therefore two syllables.

USING THE PAGES

- Encourage students to say the words aloud as they complete pages 25 and 26.

- After they have completed the pages, encourage students to discuss what they have learned about syllables.

25

Name _____

▶ Write the number of vowels you see in each word. Then write the number of vowel sounds you hear.

Vowels	See	Hear		Vowels	See	Hear
1. frame	2	1		**18.** animal	3	3
2. cabin	2	2		**19.** struck	1	1
3. coat	2	1		**20.** butterfly	3	3
4. deep	2	1		**21.** office	3	2
5. cannot	2	2		**22.** children	2	2
6. beat	2	1		**23.** sleeve	3	1
7. hotel	2	2		**24.** sentence	3	2
8. feel	2	1		**25.** Steve	2	1
9. stain	2	1		**26.** music	2	2
10. funny	2	2		**27.** Thanksgiving	3	3
11. visit	2	2		**28.** roasted	3	2
12. rich	1	1		**29.** gently	2	2
13. stand	1	1		**30.** cathedral	3	3
14. read	2	1		**31.** something	3	2
15. basket	2	2		**32.** colt	1	1
16. weed	2	1		**33.** helping	2	2
17. wild	1	1		**34.** travel	2	2

FOCUS ON ALL LEARNERS

ENGLISH LANGUAGE LEARNERS/ESL

In some languages, such as Spanish, almost all words have one syllable per vowel letter. Remind students that in English, two letters often represent one sound, as in *dive, food, friend, due,* and *meet*. Elicit other examples and write them on the board.

VISUAL LEARNERS

PARTNER

Materials: nonfiction books

Have students look through a book to find a one-, a two-, and a three-syllable word. Have partners write each word and exchange papers with a partner, who then circles all the vowels, counts the vowel sounds, and writes each total.

LARGE GROUP

KINESTHETIC/VISUAL LEARNERS

Write *1, 2,* and *3* on sheets of paper. Have the class form teams of four or five. Hold up one numeral and each team thinks of a word containing that many syllables and writes it on the board. Score a point for each correct word.

Read each word in the word bank. Then write the words in the correct columns according to whether they have one, two, or three syllables.

HINT
If you hear one vowel sound in a word, the word has one syllable. If you hear two vowel sounds in a word, the word has two syllables, and so on.

gymnast	garden	gingerbread	happiness	wild
agent	fence	grocery	children	understand
decide	consonant	cage	splashing	celery
including	radio	desk	guest	post
trace	whale	giraffe	pencil	

One Syllable	Two Syllables	Three Syllables
desk	gymnast	happiness
cage	agent	understand
fence	giraffe	radio
whale	garden	celery
wild	pencil	consonant
trace	splashing	gingerbread
guest	decide	grocery
post	children	including

Here are some titles of songs you may know. Circle each two-syllable word and underline each word with three syllables. Write the two-syllable words on the lines.

1. "Old MacDonald Had a Farm"
2. "The (Bluebird) of (Happiness)"
3. "The (Battle) Hymn of the Republic"
4. "America, the Beautiful!"
5. "(Twinkle,) (Twinkle) (Little) Star"
6. "(Yankee) (Doodle) (Dandy)"

Battle	Bluebird
Twinkle	Yankee
Twinkle	Doodle
Little	Dandy

26 Lesson 11
Syllables

AUDITORY/KINESTHETIC LEARNERS

SMALL GROUP

Read words from page 25 aloud, and have students repeat each word, clapping once for each syllable. Next, clap once, twice, or three times, and have students say a word that contains that many syllables.

GIFTED LEARNERS

Materials: chart paper, marker, newspapers, textbooks

Let students hunt for words with more than three syllables, and list them on chart paper under the headings *4 Syllables, 5 Syllables, 6 Syllables, More Than 6 Syllables*.

LEARNERS WHO NEED EXTRA SUPPORT

As students begin to work on pages 25 and 26, suggest that they say each word aloud quietly and listen for the syllables. Visit students as they work and review the items already completed.

See Daily Word Study Practice, page 208.

CURRICULUM CONNECTIONS

SPELLING

Challenge students to write from memory the ten spelling words they have been studying. Write these clues on the board: 1. ch__, 2. ch__, 3. ch__, 4. sh__, 5. th__, 6. wh__, 7. str__, 8. dr__, 9. st__, 10. w__. See if the class can work together to recall the entire list.

WRITING

Portfolio Explain that haiku is a form of Japanese poetry in which the three lines have five, seven, and five syllables, respectively. Read this example aloud, pausing after each line, and have students count the syllables.

Monarch's Flight

Smooth, beautiful, soft
The butterfly soars near me
Flitting to and fro.

Have students write a haiku about a topic from nature, using the correct number of syllables in each line.

MATH

Materials: chart paper, marker

Have students make a human pictograph according to the number of syllables in their given names. Write *1, 2, 3, 4,* and *5 or more* as headings across the paper. Print the title "Syllables in Our Names" above the numerals. Have students identify the number of syllables in their own name, then group themselves under the correct numeral.

ART

Materials: modeling clay

Have students use the clay to create a syllable zoo. Invite students to brainstorm names of animals, then determine how many syllables they hear in each animal name. Suggest that they group animals in display areas by the number of syllables in their names.

Technology

AstroWord Consonant Blends and Digraphs. © 1998 Silver Burdett Ginn Inc. Division of Simon & Schuster.

Lesson 12
Pages 27–28

Reading **W**riting

Reviewing Consonant Digraphs
sh, th, wh, ch; Syllables

INFORMAL ASSESSMENT OBJECTIVES

Can students

✔ read an interview containing words with consonant digraphs *sh, th, wh, ch* and words with varying numbers of syllables?

✔ write safety tips for a poster, using such words?

Lesson Focus

READING

- Write *shower, teacher, much, rather, beneath, awhile,* and *flash* on the board. Ask students to identify the digraph in each word. *(sh, ch, ch, th, th, wh, sh)* Have them explain how they know they are digraphs and not blends.

- Write *flash, molecules,* and *minute* on the board, and ask students to count the vowel letters in each. Then have them count the syllables as a volunteer pronounces each word.

- Tell students that they will come across words with digraphs and words with several syllables as they read an interview with a weather expert.

WRITING

- Explain that on page 28 students will prepare a poster with safety tips for a thunderstorm.

- Encourage students to use the words in the word bank as well as the Helpful Hints as they write their safety tips.

27

 Reading ▶ Read the interview. Then write your answer to the question at the end of the interview.

Shalini Talks With a Weather Expert

For this month's column, I talked with a weather expert about thunder and lightning.

Q: What causes lightning?
A: Think of a storm cloud as an electricity generator. The positive charge is at the top of the cloud, and the negative charge is at its base. A lightning flash is a spark of electricity between the positive and negative charges. This happens within a cloud, from one cloud to another cloud, or from a cloud to the earth.
Q: Why does lightning often strike trees?
A: When lightning flashes from a cloud to the earth, it takes the easiest path. It is drawn to the highest point in an area, which is often a tree.
Q: What causes thunder?

A: When a lightning flash rushes through the air, it heats up the air molecules along its path. The heated molecules expand and smash into each other. Thunder is the sound made by air molecules crashing together.
Q: Why don't we hear thunder at the same time we see the lightning flash?
A: Light waves travel much faster than sound waves. Light whizzes at 186,000 miles a second! Sound chugs along at about 12 miles a minute. We see a lightning flash at almost the same time it happens, but it takes longer for the sound to reach us.

Where is a dangerous place to be in a thunderstorm? Where *should* you go when you hear thunder?
_____
_____
_____
_____
_____

Lesson 12

Review consonant digraphs sh, th, wh, ch; syllables: Reading **27**

FOCUS ON ALL LEARNERS

ENGLISH LANGUAGE LEARNERS/ESL

To familiarize students with vocabulary, invite students to talk about lightning storms before they read page 27. Also, point out the question-and-answer format of the interview.

SMALL GROUP

VISUAL/KINESTHETIC LEARNERS

Materials: gray and yellow construction paper; markers; string

Have students draw and cut out a thundercloud and ten lightning bolts. Have them write *Digraphs* on the cloud and weather words that contain digraphs on the lightning bolts, and assemble the parts into a mobile.

LARGE GROUP

KINESTHETIC LEARNERS

Materials: index cards, markers

Make a card for each digraph: *sh, ch, th, wh*. Read a list of words with digraphs, stressing the digraph. Hold up a card as you say each word. Have students raise their hands if the digraph you hold up is in the word you just read.

Writing Suppose you are working on a safety campaign in your school. Your task is to prepare a poster with thunderstorm safety tips. List as many tips as you can think of. You may want to finish by making the poster. The words in the word bank may help you.

showers choice think bunch
where path should when

List the most important safety tips first. Keep your sentences short. Use lively, interesting words. Print neatly.

Helpful Hints

CURRICULUM CONNECTIONS

SPELLING

The following sentences can be used as a spelling posttest for words that have blends with *s*; final blends; and digraphs *sh, th, wh*, and *ch*.

1. **chef**   My dad is a wonderful pizza **chef**.
2. **string**   Kittens love to play with **string**.
3. **chemist**   I want to be a doctor or a **chemist**.
4. **stamp**   **Stamp** your foot on the floor.
5. **wheel**   To turn, use the steering **wheel**.
6. **shoulder** I drove onto the road's **shoulder**.
7. **thing**   It's too dark; I can't see a **thing**.
8. **drink**   Do you want milk or water to **drink**?
9. **chipmunk** A **chipmunk** is a rodent.
10. **wasp**   Don't go near that big **wasp** nest!

MATH

Sound travels at 12 miles a minute. Have students calculate how many seconds would elapse between a lightning flash and its thunder if the storm were one, three, and eight miles away. *(5, 15, 40 seconds)* They could act out other intervals, flashing the overhead lights for lightning, pausing, then saying *Kaboom!* The class can count the seconds in the pause to figure out how far away the "storm" is.

SOCIAL STUDIES/MATH

Materials: world almanac, chart paper, marker

Encourage students to use a world almanac to find out what cities in the world have the greatest and least average annual precipitation. *(Hong Kong, 95.0 in.; Cairo, Egypt, 1.1 in.)* Have them make a bar graph showing precipitation amounts for ten additional cities and locate these places on a globe.

AUDITORY LEARNERS

PARTNER Have partners read the interview aloud, one playing the interviewer and the other the weather expert. Ask students to listen to the words as they read, and write down three one-syllable, three two-syllable, and three three-syllable words they hear.

GIFTED LEARNERS

Challenge students to write three other interesting questions to ask the weather expert. Then have them research their questions and write the responses the expert would give. Encourage students to use words with digraphs *sh, th, wh*, and *ch*, varying the number of syllables as they write their questions and answers.

LEARNERS WHO NEED EXTRA SUPPORT

Introduce some of the long words in the interview before students begin page 27: *electricity, generator, lightning, positive, negative, molecules, expand.* Read each word slowly and help students determine the number of syllables. See Daily Word Study Practice, pages 197-198, 208.

Lesson 13

Pages 29–30

Unit Checkup

Reviewing Vowels, Hard and Soft *c* and *g*, Blends, Digraphs, and Syllables

INFORMAL ASSESSMENT OBJECTIVES

Can students

✔ identify long and short vowels, hard and soft *c* and *g*, blends, and digraphs in words?

✔ identify the number of syllables in words?

✔ read words that contain long and short vowel sounds, hard and soft *c* and *g*, blends, digraphs, and varying numbers of syllables?

Lesson Focus

PREPARING FOR THE CHECKUP

- On the board, write *Long* and *Short*. Have volunteers write these words under the correct heading as you read them aloud: *fine, stick, pitch, sleeve*.

- Read aloud these words and have students say *soft* or *hard* to identify the sound *c* or *g*: *coat, flag, cereal, genuine, agree*.

- Write the following letter groups on the board. Have students tell you whether each is a blend or a digraph: *sh, dr, sl, ch, spr, sk, nt, wh, th*.

- Read *event, sprain,* and *Saturday* aloud and have students count the number of syllables in each.

USING THE PAGES

Make sure students understand what to do on pages 29 and 30. After they finish, have them discuss what they've learned.

29

Name _____

UNIT 1 CHECKUP

> Read each sentence. Fill in the circle next to the word that correctly completes the sentence. Write the word on the line.

1. Fingerprinting is an important ____police____ tool. ○ grocery ● police

2. Police ____dust____ crime scenes for fingerprints. ● dust ○ post

3. ____Why____ do they do this? ● Why ○ Who

4. Fingers have patterns of ____ridges____. ○ badges ● ridges

5. No two people have the same ____prints____. ● prints ○ agents

6. People leave prints on things they ____touch____. ○ speech ● touch

7. Police can ____check____ prints against prints they have on file. ○ cheer ● check

8. Fingerprint patterns are either ____arches____, loops, or whorls. ● arches ○ inches

9. A plain arch has a wave in the ____center____. ● center ○ cement

10. Loops curve around and ____flow____ out on the same side. ● flow ○ flat

11. A ____whorl____ consists of ridges that go around and around. ○ whistle ● whorl

12. The pattern makes a complete ____circle____. ● circle ○ circus

13. To take prints, you need ____black____ ink. ○ blank ● black

14. You also need a printing ____plate____, a roller, and paper. ● plate ○ please

15. Press a finger onto an ____ink____ pad. ○ kind ● ink

16. Roll each finger onto a ____test____ card. ● test ○ past

Lesson 13 **29**

Review vowels; hard and soft c, g; blends; digraphs; syllables: Checkup

---

FOCUS ON ALL LEARNERS

ENGLISH LANGUAGE LEARNERS/ESL

To build background for the sentences on page 29, engage students in a discussion about fingerprints. Have volunteers tell what they know about fingerprints and how they think the police use them to solve crimes.

VISUAL LEARNERS

INDIVIDUAL List these categories on the board, and have students write an example word for each: *1. short vowel sound 2. long vowel sound 3. soft c sound 4. hard c sound 5. soft g sound 6. hard g sound 7. a blend 8. a digraph 9. a two-syllable word 10. a three-syllable word*.

KINESTHETIC LEARNERS

SMALL GROUP **Materials:** bag, index cards, marker

Make word cards for several words from each blend and digraph lesson in this unit (pages 13–18, 21–24) and place the cards in the bag. Have students take turns drawing out a word, using it in a sentence, and telling whether it has a blend or a digraph or both.

UNIT 1 CHECKUP

▶ Complete each sentence by writing a word from the word bank.

1. Chad and his mom set up the telescope at _____dusk_____.
2. They set it in _____place_____ on the lawn.
3. Then they looked up at the night _____sky_____.
4. The _____stars_____ were just appearing.
5. Chad let out a _____whoop_____ of delight.
6. He _____clapped_____ his hands loudly.
7. "I see _____them_____!" he shouted.
8. "I can see the rings of Saturn!" he _____cried_____.
9. Later, the sky became _____cloudy_____.
10. They _____went_____ back into the house.

Word bank:
sky
place
cried
went
clapped
whoop
cloudy
them
stars
dusk

▶ Read each sentence. Circle the word that correctly completes the sentence. Write it on the line.

11. The _____ice_____ on lakes gets thick in winter.　　(ice)　　ink
12. Then people go ice _____fishing_____.　　washing　(fishing)
13. They _____drill_____ holes in the ice.　　dream　(drill)
14. Some people build _____shacks_____ there.　　(shacks)　shirts
15. Ice fishing is a _____strange_____ sport.　　(strange)　exchange
16. Ice fishers _____sink_____ lines into the water.　　think　(sink)
17. _____Then_____ they wait for fish to bite.　　(Then)　These
18. They _____spend_____ a lot of time waiting.　　stump　(spend)
19. No one knows _____when_____ they will get lucky.　　(when)　while

30 Lesson 13
Review vowels; hard and soft c, g; blends; digraphs; syllables: Checkup

---

AUDITORY/VISUAL LEARNERS

PARTNER Have students write two related words, leaving a blank for the third, which has a blend or a digraph. Ask them to read the words aloud to the partner to complete. The blend or digraph should be given as a clue. Example: *bright, glow, _____ (sh); shine.*

GIFTED LEARNERS

Challenge students to write words that exemplify two or more of the word study elements they have learned in this unit and label them: for example, *garage*, hard *g* and soft *g*; *shone*, digraph *sh* and long *o* sound. Encourage them to try for as many combinations as they can.

LEARNERS WHO NEED EXTRA SUPPORT

Write on the board *gust, champ, sheepish, sprint,* and *age.* Analyze each word with students, pointing out the word study skills they have learned in this unit. See Daily Word Study Practice, pages 196-198, 208.

ASSESSING UNDERSTANDING OF UNIT SKILLS

Student Progress Assessment You may wish to review the observational notes you made as students worked through the activities in this unit. Your notes will help you evaluate the progress students made with short and long vowel sounds, hard and soft *c* and *g*, blends, digraphs, and syllables.

Portfolio Assessment Review the materials students have collected in their portfolios. Talk with students individually to discuss their written work and the progress they have made since the beginning of the unit. As you review students' work, evaluate how well they use the unit word study skills.

Daily Word Study Practice For students who need additional practice with any of the skills in this unit, quick reviews are provided on pages 196–198, 208 in Daily Word Study Practice.

Word Study Posttest To assess students' mastery of skills covered in this unit, use the posttest on pages 3g–3h.

Spelling Cumulative Posttest Review Unit 1 spelling words by using the following words and dictation sentences.

1. **stamp** — May I see your **stamp** collection?
2. **wasp** — The bee and the **wasp** are related.
3. **gentle** — "**Gentle** as a lamb" is a common saying.
4. **jeep** — The general climbed out of the **jeep**.
5. **string** — Grandma gave me a **string** of pearls.
6. **cane** — Blind people often walk with a **cane**.
7. **rice** — Some people like to eat brown **rice**.
8. **thing** — Will you do one **thing** for me?
9. **wheel** — She can spin yarn on a spinning **wheel**.
10. **chipmunk** — A **chipmunk** lives in this tree.
11. **chef** — The **chef** wore an apron.
12. **chemist** — A **chemist** studies chemicals.
13. **huge** — The new sports arena is **huge**.
14. **go** — How fast does your model car **go**?
15. **luck** — I went fishing but I had no **luck**.

Teacher Notes

Words with r-Controlled Vowel Sounds; k, f, s Sounds; Silent Letters; Syllables

Contents

Student Performance Objectives

In Unit 2, students will review *r*-controlled vowel sounds, spelling variations of the consonant /k/, /f/, and /s/, and silent letters. Students will use pictures, words, and words in context to help them associate each element with the sound for which it stands. The following skills will be developed so that students will be able to

♦ Distinguish among the *r*-controlled vowels and the sounds for which they stand

♦ Distinguish among words with *k, f,* and *s* sounds

♦ Recognize words that have silent consonants or silent consonant combinations

♦ Recognize syllables in words with /k/, /f/, or /s/

Assessment Strategy Overview

Throughout Unit 2, assess students' ability to read and write words with *r*-controlled vowel sounds, spelling variations of the consonant sounds *k*, *f*, *s*, and silent letters. There are various ways to assess students' progress. You may also want to encourage students to evaluate their own work and to participate in setting goals for their own learning.

FORMAL ASSESSMENT

The Unit 2 Pretest on pages 31e–31f helps to assess a student's knowledge at the beginning of the unit and to plan instruction.

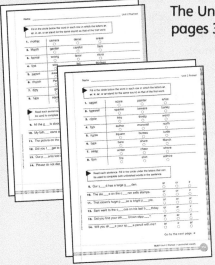

The Unit 2 Posttest on pages 31g–31h helps to assess mastery of unit objectives and to plan for reteaching, if necessary.

PORTFOLIO ASSESSMENT

Portfolio This logo appears throughout the teaching plans. It signals opportunities for collecting students' work for individual portfolios. You may also want to collect the following pages.

❖ Unit 2 Pretest and Posttest, pages 31e–31h

❖ Unit 2 Reading & Writing, pages 41–42, 57–58

❖ Unit 2 Checkup, pages 59–60

INFORMAL ASSESSMENT

The Reading & Writing pages and Unit Checkup in the student book are an effective means of evaluating students' performance.

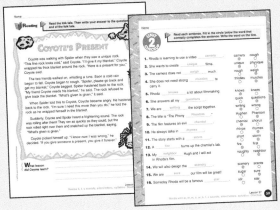

Skill	Reading & Writing Pages	Unit Checkup
r-Controlled Vowels	41–42	59–60
k Sound	57–58	59–60
f Sound	57–58	59–60
s Sound	57–58	59–60
Silent Letters	57–58	59–60
Syllables	57–58	59–60

STUDENT PROGRESS CHECKLIST

Use the checklist on page 31i to record students' progress. You may want to cut the sections apart to place each student's checklist in his or her portfolio.

31c

Administering and Evaluating the
Pretest and Posttest

DIRECTIONS

To help you assess students' progress in learning Unit 2 skills, tests are available on pages 31e–31h. Administer the Pretest before students begin the unit. The results of the Pretest will help you identify each student's strengths and needs in advance, allowing you to structure lesson plans to meet individual needs. Administer the Posttest to assess students' overall mastery of skills taught in the unit and to identify specific areas that will require reteaching.

PERFORMANCE ASSESSMENT PROFILE

The following chart will help you identify specific skills as they appear on the tests and enable you to identify and record specific information about an individual's or the class's performance on the tests.

Depending on the results of the tests, refer to the Reteaching column for lesson-plan pages where you can find activities that will be useful for meeting individual needs or for daily word study practice.

ANSWER KEYS

Unit 2 Pretest, page 31e (BLM 9)

1. artist	6. March	11. ur
2. beware	7. winter	12. ir
3. thirsty	8. shirt	13. er
4. north	9. ar	14. ar
5. turtle	10. or	

Unit 2 Pretest, page 31f (BLM 10)

15. beak	22. unique	28. h
16. fresh	23. quick	29. w
17. pocket	24. graph	30. k
18. tissue	25. music	31. g
19. local	26. rough	32. t
20. school	27. gh	33. c
21. also		

Unit 2 Posttest, page 31g (BLM 11)

1. camera	6. turkey	11. ar
2. garden	7. girl	12. or
3. store	8. square	13. ar
4. thirteen	9. ir	14. ur
5. aware	10. er	

Unit 2 Posttest, page 31h (BLM 12)

15. fish	22. quiet	28. t
16. week	23. trophy	29. k
17. pressure	24. antique	30. g
18. package	25. those	31. w
19. across	26. tough	32. h
20. electric	27. c	33. gh
21. chorus		

PERFORMANCE ASSESSMENT PROFILE

Skill	Pretest Questions	Posttest Questions	Reteaching: Focus on All Learners	Reteaching: Daily Word Study Practice
Vowels with *r: ar*	1, 2, 6, 9, 14	2, 5, 8, 11, 13	33–34, 41–42	198
Vowels with *r: er*	7, 13	1, 10	37–42	198
Vowels with *r: ir*	3, 8, 12	4, 7, 9	37–42	198
Vowels with *r: or*	4, 10	3, 12	35–36, 39-42	198
Vowels with *r: ur*	5, 11	6, 14	37–42	198
/k/: *c, k, ch, ck, que*	15, 17,19, 20, 22	16, 18, 20, 21, 24	43–44, 57–58	198–199
/kw/: *qu*	23	22	45–46, 57–58	198–199
/f/: *f, ph, gh*	16, 24, 26	15, 23, 26	47–48, 57–58	198–199
/s/: *s*; /z/: *s*; /sh/: *s*	18, 21, 25	17, 19, 25	49–50, 57–58	198–199
Silent *gh*	27	33	51–52, 57–58	199–200
Silent letters in *rh, wr*	28, 29	31–32	51–52, 57–58	199–200
Silent letters in *gn, kn, sc, st*	30, 31, 32, 33	27, 28, 29, 30	53–54, 57–58	199–200

▶ Fill in the circle below the word in each row in which the letters **ar**, **er**, **ir**, **or**, or **ur** stand for the same sound as that of the first word.

1. c<u>ar</u>pet	scare ○	painter ○	artist ○
2. f<u>ar</u>ewell	sparkle ○	beware ○	barley ○
3. c<u>ir</u>cle	hire ○	thirsty ○	weird ○
4. f<u>or</u>k	author ○	monorail ○	north ○
5. n<u>ur</u>se	square ○	bureau ○	turtle ○
6. b<u>ar</u>k	bare ○	share ○	March ○
7. sist<u>er</u>	winter ○	cheer ○	where ○
8. f<u>ir</u>m	fire ○	shirt ○	admire ○

▶ Read each sentence. Fill in the circle under the letters that can be used to complete both unfinished words in the sentence.

9. Our y___d has a large g___den.	ar ○	or ○	ir ○
10. The sto___e on the c___ner sells stamps.	er ○	or ○	ir ○
11. That clown's huge p___se is bright p___ple.	ar ○	or ○	ur ○
12. Sam went to the c___cus on his last b___thday.	or ○	ar ○	ir ○
13. Did you find your oth___ brown slipp___?	ar ○	er ○	ir ○
14. Will you sh___e your sp___e pencil with me?	ar ○	ir ○	er ○

Go to the next page. →

BLM 9 Unit 2 Pretest: *r*-controlled vowels

31e

> Fill in the circle beside the word in each
> row with the sound given at the left.

15.	Sound of **k**	○ city	○ sense	○ beak	○ knit
16.	Sound of **f**	○ fresh	○ chin	○ range	○ porch
17.	Sound of **k**	○ knee	○ cement	○ pocket	○ scene
18.	Sound of **sh**	○ vest	○ tissue	○ always	○ dress
19.	Sound of **k**	○ local	○ knight	○ center	○ happy
20.	Sound of **k**	○ cider	○ school	○ knob	○ follow
21.	Sound of **s**	○ cough	○ pose	○ comb	○ also
22.	Sound of **k**	○ know	○ guns	○ tiger	○ unique
23.	Sound of **kw**	○ wise	○ quick	○ knot	○ guard
24.	Sound of **f**	○ graph	○ torch	○ bushes	○ march
25.	Sound of **z**	○ scarf	○ nice	○ music	○ circus
26.	Sound of **f**	○ ghost	○ center	○ glass	○ rough

> Read each word on the left. Fill in the circle beside
> the letter or letters that are silent in the word.

27.	daughter	○ d	○ r	○ gh	○ t
28.	rhinoceros	○ s	○ n	○ r	○ h
29.	wrong	○ w	○ o	○ r	○ n
30.	knotholes	○ n	○ t	○ k	○ s
31.	gnarled	○ r	○ g	○ d	○ n
32.	glistened	○ l	○ s	○ t	○ g
33.	muscles	○ m	○ c	○ u	○ s

Possible score on Unit 2 Pretest is 33. Number correct _____

> Fill in the circle below the word in each row in which the letters **ar**, **er**, **ir**, **or**, or **ur** stand for the same sound as that of the first word.

1. moth**er**	camera ○	derail ○	erase ○
2. M**ar**ch	garden ○	careful ○	flare ○
3. f**or**mal	wrong ○	favor ○	store ○
4. f**ir**st	wire ○	felt ○	thirteen ○
5. p**ar**ent	aware ○	afar ○	parcel ○
6. ch**ur**ch	Peru ○	queer ○	turkey ○
7. d**ir**ty	girl ○	tired ○	variety ○
8. h**are**	square ○	party ○	marimba ○

> Read each sentence. Fill in the circle under the letters that can be used to complete both unfinished words in the sentence.

	er	or	ir
9. All the g___ls stood in a c___cle.	○	○	○

	ar	er	ir
10. My fath___ owns a bak___y.	○	○	○

	ar	or	ur
11. The picture on the c___d is by a famous ___tist.	○	○	○

	or	ar	ir
12. Did you f___get to feed the h___se?	○	○	○

	er	ir	ar
13. Our p___ents told us to be c___eful.	○	○	○

	ar	ur	er
14. Please do not dist___b our pet t___tle.	○	○	○

Go to the next page. →

> Fill in the circle beside the word in each row with the sound given at the left.

15. Sound of **f**	○ cheer	○ fish	○ strange	○ teeth
16. Sound of **k**	○ week	○ signs	○ cement	○ know
17. Sound of **sh**	○ least	○ pressure	○ because	○ season
18. Sound of **k**	○ knot	○ certain	○ package	○ since
19. Sound of **s**	○ easy	○ chief	○ become	○ across
20. Sound of **k**	○ electric	○ knives	○ pencil	○ reach
21. Sound of **k**	○ decide	○ chorus	○ knit	○ chore
22. Sound of **kw**	○ whether	○ quiet	○ knowledge	○ guarantee
23. Sound of **f**	○ trophy	○ page	○ grass	○ inch
24. Sound of **k**	○ guess	○ cheese	○ knew	○ antique
25. Sound of **z**	○ scream	○ release	○ those	○ concert
26. Sound of **f**	○ gypsy	○ tough	○ sugar	○ plastic

> Read each word on the left. Fill in the circle beside the letter or letters that are silent in the word.

27. scented	○ t	○ n	○ c	○ s
28. listen	○ s	○ l	○ n	○ t
29. knickers	○ k	○ r	○ s	○ n
30. gnome	○ n	○ o	○ g	○ m
31. wrist	○ r	○ s	○ w	○ i
32. rhubarb	○ r	○ b	○ u	○ h
33. brought	○ r	○ b	○ gh	○ t

Possible score on Unit 2 Posttest is 33. Number correct _____

BLM 12 Unit 2 Posttest: *k* sounds, *f* sounds, *s* sounds, silent letters

31h

Student Progress Checklist

Make as many copies as needed to use for a class list. For individual portfolio use, cut apart each student's section. As indicated by the code, color in boxes next to skills satisfactorily assessed and mark an X by those requiring reteaching. Marked boxes can later be colored in to indicate mastery.

STUDENT PROGRESS CHECKLIST

Code: ■ Satisfactory   ⊠ Needs Reteaching

Student: _____ _____ Pretest Score: _____ Posttest Score: _____	**Skills** ❏ *r*-Controlled Vowels ❏ *k* Sound ❏ *f* Sound ❏ *s* Sound ❏ Silent Letters	**Comments / Learning Goals**
Student: _____ _____ Pretest Score: _____ Posttest Score: _____	**Skills** ❏ *r*-Controlled Vowels ❏ *k* Sound ❏ *f* Sound ❏ *s* Sound ❏ Silent Letters	**Comments / Learning Goals**
Student: _____ _____ Pretest Score: _____ Posttest Score: _____	**Skills** ❏ *r*-Controlled Vowels ❏ *k* Sound ❏ *f* Sound ❏ *s* Sound ❏ Silent Letters	**Comments / Learning Goals**
Student: _____ _____ Pretest Score: _____ Posttest Score: _____	**Skills** ❏ *r*-Controlled Vowels ❏ *k* Sound ❏ *f* Sound ❏ *s* Sound ❏ Silent Letters	**Comments / Learning Goals**

Spelling Connections

INTRODUCTION

The Unit Word List is a comprehensive list of spelling words drawn from this unit. The words are grouped by phonemic elements studied throughout the unit. To incorporate spelling into your word study program, use the activity in the Curriculum Connections section of each teaching plan. The spelling lessons utilize the following approach for each phonemic element.

1. Administer a pretest of all the words that have not yet been introduced. Dictation sentences are provided.

2. Provide practice.

3. Reassess. Dictation sentences are provided.

A final test is provided at the end of the unit on page 60.

DIRECTIONS

Make a copy of Blackline Master 14 for each student. After administering the pretest for each phonemic element, give students a copy of the appropriate word list.

Students can work with a partner to practice spelling the words orally and identifying the phonemic element in each word. You may want to challenge students to add to the list other words with the phonemic element. Students can also write words of their own on *My Own Word List* (see Blackline Master 14).

Students may store their list words in envelopes or plastic zipper bags in their books or notebooks. You may want to suggest that students keep a spelling notebook, listing words with similar elements. Another idea is to build word walls with students and display them in the classroom. Each section of the wall can focus on words with a single word study element. The walls will become a good resource for spelling when students are engaged in writing.

UNIT WORD LIST

r-Controlled Vowels
ar, or, er, ir, ur

share
corn
serve
birthday
church

Sound of k
kitten
school
technique
quick

Sound of f
dolphin
rough
feature

Sound of s
rose
sure
sudden

Silent Letters gh, rh, wr, gn, kn, sc, st
fought
rhythm
wring
gnaw
knew
scene
listen

Name _____

 **Spelling**   UNIT 2 WORD LIST

r-Controlled Vowels **ar, or, er, ir, ur** share corn serve birthday church	**Sound of k** kitten school technique quick	**Sound of f** dolphin rough feature
Sound of s rose sure sudden	**Silent Letters** **gh, rh, wr, gn,** **kn, sc, st** fought rhythm wring gnaw knew scene listen	**My Own Word List**

Word Study Games, Activities, and Technology

The following collection of ideas offers a variety of opportunities to reinforce word study skills while actively engaging students. The games, activities, and technology suggestions can easily be adapted to meet the needs of your group of learners. They vary in approach so as to consider students' different learning styles.

● WORD PICK-UP

Make word cards for words containing r-controlled vowels *ar, er, ir, or,* and *ur.* Ask students to pick up the card that answers questions such as *I'm thinking of a word that starts with* st *and has the* ar *sound in it. What is it? (star* or *start)* Have students take turns presenting questions and picking up words.

▲ WORD DETECTIVE

Choose a word containing *rh, wr, gn, kn, sc,* or *st.* Write the word on the board, but leave out the silent letter or letter combination. Have volunteers fill in the missing letters. For a more challenging activity, leave out additional letters and give definition clues to the word.

◆ I DOUBT IT!

Divide the class into two teams. Write *ar, er, ir, or,* or *ur* on the chalkboard. Players from opposing teams take turns adding one letter to those on the board. The team's player must have a word in mind, but the added letter must not complete the word. For example, a player with the word *sharp* in mind may add *p* to *ar* to make *arp,* but not *t* to *ar* to make *tar.* If a player adds a letter that completes a word, the opposing team gets a point. If one team adds a letter and the other team doubts that it has a word in mind, that team may shout *"I doubt it!"* If the defending team gives an appropriate word, it gets a point. If not, the doubting team gets the point.

■ COMBO LOTTO

Make a 4-by-4 square game board and 20 small paper markers for each student. On the chalkboard, write a list of words with r-controlled vowel sounds, such as *argue, sister, thirty, corn, church, sparkle, serve, stir, morning, cure, carpet, ever, dirty, cord, purple, person.* Have students write one of the listed words in each square on the game board, leaving out those letters that make the r-controlled sound, for example, *sist__.* On the markers, have them write *ar, er, ir, or,* and *ur* each four times.

To play the game, say one of the words in the list. Students find the marker with the correct letter combination and place it on the blank letter space in the appropriate word on their cards. Follow this procedure until one student has covered a vertical or horizontal line.

Variation: Use words with silent letters or silent-letter combinations.

✳ CONSONANTS IN A ROW

Have students draw four tic-tac-toe grids on a sheet of paper. Direct students to write one of the following letters or letter groups in each square in any order on the first tic-tac-toe game diagram: *ck, ch, que, qu, ph, gh, sh, s.* Read each of the following sounds and words aloud. Then write the word on the board.

1. /sh/—sure	4. /ch/—each	7. /f/—laugh
2. /k/—school	5. /f/—photo	8. /z/—rose
3. /k/—antique	6. /k/—duck	9. /kw/—quick

Have students circle the letter or letters on their papers that stand for the sound indicated. For example, when /z/—*rose* is read, the letter *s* is to be circled. As soon as any student has three circles in a row vertically, horizontally, or diagonally, have him or her stand up. Check answers. Repeat the game by having students write the letters again, in different order, on another diagram. Read the same sounds and words in another order or use other words containing the consonant variants shown.

● SPEED SPELL

Have partners make ten large word cards with words containing *ar, er, ir, or,* or *ur.* Have them cut the cards into individual letters, keeping only the *r*-letter combinations together. Students mix up the cards and then time themselves as they try to put the words back together. Different pairs can also race to put each other's words together.

Variation: Have students cut apart words into separate syllables instead of individual letters.

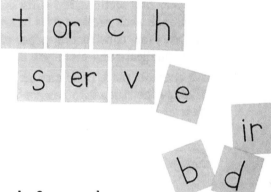

▲ ISOLATING *R*-CONTROLLED VOWEL SOUNDS

Display a set of word cards featuring words with *r*-controlled vowel sounds. Say a word from one of the cards. Ask a volunteer to repeat the word, isolate the medial vowel sound, and find the word card. Continue until each student has had a turn.

◆ SILLY SENTENCES

Have partners brainstorm lists of words from one lesson in Unit 2, such as words with the letter combinations *gh, rh,* or *wr.* Have students take turns making up sentences containing one of the words. However, have them change the word to make a silly sentence — for example, *We need flour to make pizza highways.* The partner must repeat the sentence with the proper word in place: *We need flour to make pizza dough.*

■ MAGIC LETTERS

Tell students that they can make silent letters into magic letters. Show them how to use crayons to write a word such as *gnat* on white paper. Use a dark color crayon to write the *n, a,* and *t* and a white crayon to write the *g* so that it looks as though there is a letter missing. Have students paint lightly over the word with the missing letter —the silent letter will suddenly appear! Have students write words with missing silent letters, exchange the papers, and paint to reveal the silent letters.

✳ MARKETPLACE

Have students look through advertising fliers to find words that contain a certain phonemic element, for example, *f*, *k*, or *s* sounds. Collect the words in a cumulative list. Then have students create marketplace billboards and advertisements using as many words from the list as possible.

● WORD WEBS

Draw a circle on the chalkboard or on a wall chart and write inside it *Vowels with* r. Make a web by drawing five circles off the original circle. Inside each circle, write *ar, er, ir, or, ur*. Draw five more circles off of each of those circles. Have students copy the web on their papers and complete their webs by filling in words with the appropriate vowel sounds.

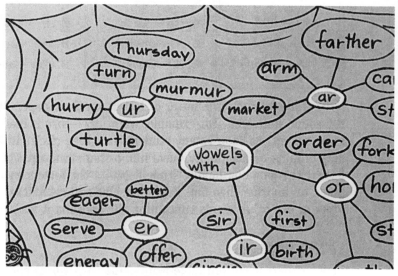

▲ *r*-CONTROLLED VOWEL RACING

Make a spinner by using a brad to fasten an arrow to a circle made of cardboard. Divide the circle into five sections and write one of the following in each section: *ir* as in *girl*, *or* as in *corn*, *ar* as in *farm*, *er* as in *serve*, *ur* as in *fur*. From construction paper of different colors, cut a small race car for each player. Duplicate and distribute Blackline Master 15 to a small group of students.

Have students place their cars on Start. Direct the first student to spin the arrow. Challenge the student to name a word with the same *r*-controlled vowel sound and letters as those indicated by the arrow. If the player can name a word, the car moves forward to the next box containing the indicated letters *ar, er, ir, or,* or *ur*. If he or she cannot name a word, the car remains in place. The first player to reach Finish wins.

Technology

The following software products are designed to enhance students' comprehension and their appreciation of children's literature.

Alien Tales   Classic children's literature is explored through this humorous quiz-show format, with an emphasis on reading comprehension and vocabulary development. Titles include *Charlotte's Web*, *The Wizard of Oz*, and *Matilda*.
** Broderbund Software
   P.O. Box 6125
   Novato, CA 94948-6125
   (800) 521-6263 or (800) 766-4724

Super Solvers: Midnight Rescue!   Children ages 8–10 are challenged to catch the Master of Mischief by using thinking, reading, and reasoning skills during a timed video-game format. The program emphasizes reading for main ideas, recalling key facts, drawing inferences, and building vocabulary.
** The Learning Company
   1 Athenaeum Street
   Cambridge, MA 02142
   (800) 227-5609

Name _____

Home Connection

Home Letter

A letter is available to be sent home at the beginning of Unit 2. This letter informs family members that students will be learning to read and write words that contain the spellings *ar, er, ir, or,* and *ur;* words with the *k, f,* and *s* sounds; words with silent letters; and syllables. The suggested home activity encourages students to draw a picture of a street in their neighborhood, make a list of things included in the drawing, and point out any words on the list with the spellings studied in this unit. This activity promotes interaction between student and family members while supporting students' learning of reading and writing words. A Book Corner feature suggests books family members can look for in a local library and enjoy reading together. A letter is also available in Spanish on page 31q.

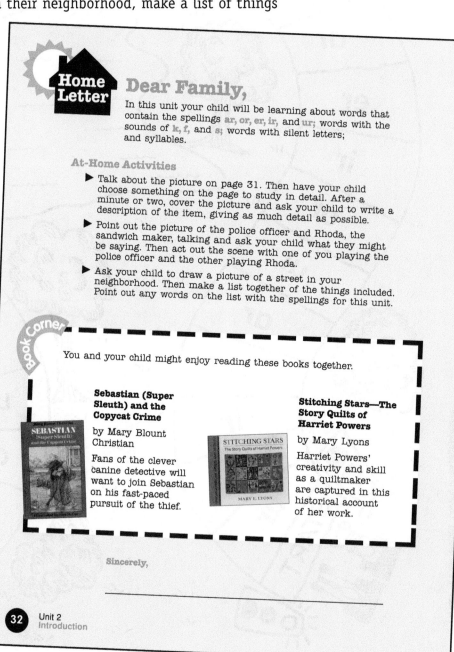

Home Letter

Dear Family,

In this unit your child will be learning about words that contain the spellings ar, or, er, ir, and ur; words with the sounds of k, f, and s; words with silent letters; and syllables.

At-Home Activities

► Talk about the picture on page 31. Then have your child choose something on the page to study in detail. After a minute or two, cover the picture and ask your child to write a description of the item, giving as much detail as possible.

► Point out the picture of the police officer and Rhoda, the sandwich maker, talking and ask your child what they might be saying. Then act out the scene with one of you playing the police officer and the other playing Rhoda.

► Ask your child to draw a picture of a street in your neighborhood. Then make a list together of the things included. Point out any words on the list with the spellings for this unit.

Book Corner

You and your child might enjoy reading these books together.

Sebastian (Super Sleuth) and the Copycat Crime

by Mary Blount Christian

Fans of the clever canine detective will want to join Sebastian on his fast-paced pursuit of the thief.

Stitching Stars—The Story Quilts of Harriet Powers

by Mary Lyons

Harriet Powers' creativity and skill as a quiltmaker are captured in this historical account of her work.

Sincerely,

_____

32 Unit 2
Introduction

Carta para la casa

Estimada familia,

En esta unidad su hijo/a estará aprendiendo palabras en inglés que contienen las letras: **ar, er, ir, or** y **ur**; palabras con los sonidos de **k, f** y **s**; palabras con letras silentes; y sílabas.

Actividades para hacer en casa

▶ Hablen de la ilustración en la página 31. Luego pídanle a su hijo/a que escoja algo en la página para estudiarlo detalladamente. Pasados uno o dos minutos, tapen la ilustración y pídanle a su hijo/a que escriba una descripción del objeto, dando tantos detalles como pueda.

▶ Pídanle a su hijo/a que haga un dibujo de una calle en su barrio. Luego hagan una lista en inglés de las cosas que incluyó. Señalen cualquier palabra en la lista que contenga la ortografía de esta unidad.

▶ Pídanle a su hijo/a que haga un dibujo de una calle de su barrio. Juntos, hagan una lista de las cosas que incluyó en el dibujo. Señalen cualqier palabra de la lista que contenga la ortografía que estamos estudiando en esta unidad.

Rincón del libro

Su hijo/a y ustedes pueden disfrutar juntos de la lectura de estos libros. Búsquenlos en la biblioteca de su localidad.

Sebastian (Super Sleuth) and the Copycat Crime
por Mary Blount Christian

Los fanáticos de este inteligente detective canino querrán unirse a esta desenfrenada persecusión de un ladrón.

Stitching Stars—The Story Quilts of Harriet Powers
por Mary Lyons

La imaginación de Harriet Powers y su habilidad como tejedora de colchas, han sido captadas en este recuento histórico de su trabajo.

Atentamente, _____

Unit 2

Pages 31–32

Words With ar, or, er, ir, ur;
Sounds of k, f, s; **Silent Letters; Syllables**

ASSESSING PRIOR KNOWLEDGE

To assess students' prior knowledge of words with *ar, or, er, ir, ur; k, f,* and *s* sounds; silent letters; and syllables, use the pretest on pages 31e–31f.

Unit Focus

USING THE PAGE

- Talk with students about the importance of being observant in everyday life. Then have them cover the questions at the bottom of page 31 and study the illustration carefully.

- Now have students cover the picture and recall what they saw. Read the questions at the bottom of the page for students to answer.

BUILDING A CONTEXT

- Write on the board *had, hard; cod, cord; gem, germ; bid, bird; bun, burn.* Ask students to say the pairs and notice the vowel sound changes when *r* follows the vowel.

- Write *phone, laugh, face* and *chorus, unique.* Say the words and ask what sound each set has in common. *(/f/, /k/)* Then have students compare the sound of *qu* in *unique* with the *qu* in *quick.* *(/k/ and /kw/)*

- Write *seven, sure,* and *reason* and ask students to compare the sound that *s* stands for in each word. *(/s/, /sh/, /z/)*

- Have students say the name of the sausage vendor in the picture. *(Rhoda)* Write *Rhoda* and ask if they hear the *h* when they say *Rhoda.*

- Write *pointing* on the board. Have students count the vowel letters (3) and vowel sounds (2). Explain that the number of vowel sounds is the number of syllables in a word.

31

UNIT
2

Words with ar, or, er, ir, ur; Sounds of k, f, s; Silent Letters; Syllables

Why is paying attention to details important?

Critical Thinking

> Study this picture carefully. Then answer the questions without looking at the picture.

1. What time was it on the bank clock? 1:30
2. How many sausages did the dog steal? six
3. What were the names of the streets? Birch Road and School Street
4. What was the name on the cart? Rhoda's Sausage Subs
5. Which part of the car with the dog inside it was broken? headlight

UNIT OPENER ACTIVITIES

TRACKING DETAILS

Begin a discussion again about the importance of memory and of keeping track of details. Ask some of the details students must remember each day, such as remembering to do household tasks, feed a pet, or do homework or practice a musical instrument.

EYEWITNESS ACCOUNT

Ask another teacher to dress in a silly disguise and burst unexpectedly into your room, shout something complicated, and erase something from the board before leaving the room. Have each student write down everything they saw and heard. Compare students' accounts and discuss witness reliability.

PICTURE DETAILS

Have students browse through discarded magazines to find a picture in which there is a lot going on. Ask them to make up four questions about details in their picture. Have students exchange pictures for two minutes and then ask their questions. What kind of details are the hardest to remember?

Home Letter

Dear Family,

In this unit your child will be learning about words that contain the spellings ar, or, er, ir, and ur; words with the sounds of k, f, and s; words with silent letters; and syllables.

At-Home Activities

► Talk about the picture on page 31. Then have your child choose something on the page to study in detail. After a minute or two, cover the picture and ask your child to write a description of the item, giving as much detail as possible.

► Point out the picture of the police officer and Rhoda, the sandwich maker, talking and ask your child what they might be saying. Then act out the scene with one of you playing the police officer and the other playing Rhoda.

► Ask your child to draw a picture of a street in your neighborhood. Then make a list together of the things included. Point out any words on the list with the spellings for this unit.

Book Corner

You and your child might enjoy reading these books together.

Sebastian (Super Sleuth) and the Copycat Crime

by Mary Blount Christian

Fans of the clever canine detective will want to join Sebastian on his fast-paced pursuit of the thief.

Stitching Stars—The Story Quilts of Harriet Powers

by Mary Lyons

Harriet Powers' creativity and skill as a quiltmaker are captured in this historical account of her work.

Sincerely,

_____

BULLETIN BOARD

Have volunteers share their earliest happy memory. Then have each student write down and illustrate an early happy memory. Arrange the illustrations on the bulletin board titled "Precious Memories," and discuss how pleasant memories can make people feel good.

HOME CONNECTIONS

● The Home Letter on page 32 is intended to acquaint family members with the word study skills students will be studying in the unit. Suggest that they take the page home and complete the activities on the page with a family member. Encourage them to look for the books listed in the library to share with family members.

● The Home Letter can also be found on page 31q in Spanish.

CURRICULUM CONNECTIONS

WRITING

Portfolio Have students look again at the picture on page 31 and then write a story about Rhoda's predicament and what happens to her next. Is the culprit ever brought to justice? How?

SCIENCE

Making accurate observations and drawing conclusions based on them is central to science. Have each student choose one the following scientists and find out what each scientist observes: paleontologist, ornithologist, embryologist, botanist, herpetologist, geochemist, metallurgist, seismologist, oceanographer, astrophysicist, ichthyologist. Encourage students to share their findings.

LANGUAGE ARTS

Write *GHOTI* on the board. Explain that the writer George Bernard Shaw put together this "word" by using *GH* as in *enough*, *O* as in *women*, and *TI* as in *nation*—it "spells" *fish*. Let students have some fun inventing their own "crazy" spellings based on the different sounds letters can stand for.

Lesson 14

Pages 33–34

Words With ar

Lesson Focus

INTRODUCING THE SKILL

- Say *fat* and *far*. Ask students to identify the sound that stands for the vowel sound they hear in *fat*. *(short a)* Now have them listen to the vowel sound in *far*. Explain that the letters *ar* stand for the vowel sound heard in *far*.

- Ask volunteers to write *far, car,* and *star* on the board. Add a final *e* to each word. Have students read the words aloud. Ask how the vowel sound has changed. *(sounds like* air*)*

- Explain that *ar* can stand for different sounds, as in *car* and *care*. Ask students to apply Long Vowel Rule 1 to *care*.

USING THE PAGES

- Make sure students understand what to do on pages 33 and 34. After they have completed the pages, encourage pairs of students to discuss what they learned about words with *ar*.

- **Critical Thinking** Read the question on page 34 aloud and have students discuss the difference between using money and bartering.

33

Name _____

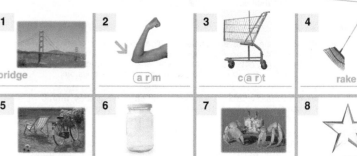

Say the name of each picture. Listen for the **ar** sound as in **farm.** If you hear the sound, write the picture name on the line and circle the **ar** in the word.

RULE
The letters **ar** can stand for the vowel sound you hear in **farm.**

1 bridge	2 a(r)m	3 c a(r) t	4 rake
5 y a(r) d	6 j a(r)	7 crab	8 s t a(r)

Read each sentence. Choose the word from the word bank that correctly completes the sentence and write it on the line.

9. We read a story about Tony, a palace ___guard___ .

10. The best ___part___ of the story described his job.

11. Tony ___marched___ around the palace each day.

12. The brass buttons on his uniform ___sparkled___ .

13. He unrolled the red ___carpet___ for the king.

14. He opened the door of the ___car___ for the king.

15. He investigated if any ___alarms___ rang.

16. He stopped visitors with a wave of his ___arm___ .

17. He even tended the royal flower ___garden___ .

18. Tony never believed his job was ___hard___ .

19. He was proud to keep the king from ___harm___ .

sparkled
alarms
guard
harm
carpet
hard
arm
car
marched
garden
part

FOCUS ON ALL LEARNERS

ENGLISH LANGUAGE LEARNERS/ESL

If Spanish-speaking students are having trouble with the vowel sounds in *car* and *care*, you might mention that *ar* sounds much as it does in Spanish *(andar, guitarra)* and that *are* in *care* sounds much like the *er* in *vaquero*, except that the *r* is not rolled.

VISUAL/AUDITORY LEARNERS

LARGE GROUP
Write these sets of words on the board: *art, charm, aware; glare, yard, farewell; spare, spark, guard; rare, market, prepare; far, scar, stare.* Have students circle the word whose pronunciation does not fit in the set. *(aware, yard, spare, market, stare)*

KINESTHETIC/AUDITORY LEARNERS

SMALL GROUP
Organize students into a *car* group and a *care* group. Say words with *ar*, and have students stand up if the vowel is pronounced like the vowel sound in their word. Try these words: *spark, art, garden, dark, start, barn, arctic, square, bare, March.*

Read the passage and answer the questions. Then underline each **ar** word in the passage.

RULE
The letters **ar** can stand for different vowel sounds. In some words these letters follow Long Vowel Rule 1: If a syllable has two vowels, the first vowel usually stands for the long sound and the second vowel is silent.

c**are**   sh**are**

Markets and Bazaars

Before cars and shopping malls existed, market day was an important weekly event in many parts of the world. Country people carried goods they made or grew to a place in town that was set apart for a market. They bartered their wares for goods they did not have on their farms. One farmer might barter a sackful of carrots for some wool yarn.

Traveling artists came to the market square to entertain the crowds. They often used the bare ground or the back of a cart or wagon for a stage.

Although they are rare in the United States, markets still exist in many other areas. In Asia and North Africa, markets called bazaars can be found in large cities. Along covered streets, shopkeepers and artisans offer food, garments, and all sorts of wares from carpets to glassware. In Arab cities like Baghdad and Cairo, bazaars are permanent markets open every day. Buyers must beware, for the wares sold in a bazaar have no set price. The buyer is expected to bargain with the seller. The smart buyer who can drive a hard bargain gets the best deal!

1. What is the subject of this passage?
　　　　　markets and bazaars

2. What word in the passage means "trade by exchanging one kind of good for another"?
　　　　　barter

3. What did traveling performers use for a stage?
　　bare ground or the back of a cart or wagon

4. What kinds of things are offered for sale in North African bazaars?
　Answers may include food, garments, carpets, glassware.

What is the difference between paying for things with money and bartering?

Critical Thinking

34
Lesson 14
Words with ar

SPELLING

The following sentences can be used as a pretest for spelling words with *r*-controlled vowels *ar, or, er, ir, ur* and the sound of *k*.

1. **corn**　　　Let's have **corn** on the cob for dinner.

2. **share**　　Hannah would not **share** her cookies.

3. **birthday**　I got a great **birthday** present.

4. **serve**　　Shall I **serve** the potatoes now?

5. **kitten**　　Our mother cat had only one **kitten**.

6. **church**　　That **church** has a tall steeple.

7. **school**　　Our class works hard in **school**.

8. **technique**　My violin **technique** needs work.

9. **quick**　　Set the table, and be **quick** about it.

WRITING

Portfolio　Have students reread the sentences on page 33 about Tony. Suggest that they write another story about an unusual job someone has. Ask them to use as many *ar* words as possible.

SOCIAL STUDIES

Hold a bazaar. Have students choose their "wares" (rugs, pots, shoes, food items, camels, clothing, lambs, jewelry), draw on cards pictures of five items to sell, and lay the cards out on a table. They take turns browsing in the "market stalls" to barter, trying to sell what they brought and go home with what they want or need.

MATH/SOCIAL STUDIES

Have students learn about the monetary systems of other countries. Ask each student to choose a country, find out about its currency, and tell what it is worth in U.S. dollars.

Technology

AstroWord *r*-Controlled Vowels.
© 1998 Silver Burdett Ginn Inc.
Division of Simon & Schuster.

● ◆ ● ✳ ● ◆ ● ● ✳ ● ◆ ● ●

LARGE GROUP

AUDITORY LEARNERS

Say these words to students one at a time: *far, star, bar, war, spar, car, scar.* Have them mentally add *e* and pronounce the *ar* sound as in *care. (fare, stare, bare, ware, spare, care, scare)* You may want to have students write the words on the board.

GIFTED LEARNERS

Provide students with word frames and have them add letters to write complete words with the sounds of *ar* in *car.* Examples: __*arm* (charm, harm, alarm); and bar__ (barge, barter, bargain).

LEARNERS WHO NEED EXTRA SUPPORT

Visit with students as they work on these pages to make sure they know what to do and are comfortable following the directions. Together, review the words already completed. **See Daily Word Study Practice, page 198.**

Lesson 15
Pages 35–36

Words With *or*

Lesson Focus

INTRODUCING THE SKILL

- Using the words *car* and *care*, review with students the sounds that the letters *ar* stand for.

- Write *stare* on the board and ask students to identify the vowel sound. Then call on a volunteer to erase the *a* and write the letter *o* in its place. Encourage students to read the new word and identify the vowel sound.

- Help students conclude that the letters *or* can stand for the vowel sound heard in *store, for,* and *corn.* Ask if the letter *e* at the end of *store* changes the sound of *or.*

- Invite students to suggest and write additional words with the vowel sound *or.*

USING THE PAGES

- Point out the word banks on pages 35 and 36 and remind students to choose words from the word bank when doing the second and third activities.

- When students have completed the pages, ask volunteers to summarize what they know about words with *or.*

35

Name _____

▶ Say the name of each picture. Listen for the **or** sound as in **corn.** If you hear the sound, write the picture name on the line and circle the **or** in the word.

> **RULE**
> The letters **or** can stand for the vowel sound you hear in **corn.**

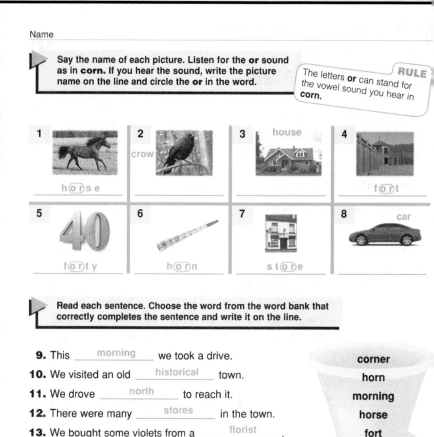

1. h(or)s e
2. crow
3. house
4. f(or)t

5. 40 — f(or)t y
6.
7. s t(or)e
8. car

▶ Read each sentence. Choose the word from the word bank that correctly completes the sentence and write it on the line.

9. This ___morning___ we took a drive.
10. We visited an old ___historical___ town.
11. We drove ___north___ to reach it.
12. There were many ___stores___ in the town.
13. We bought some violets from a ___florist___.
14. A hospital stood on a street ___corner___.
15. My father said he was ___born___ there.
16. We saw an old army ___fort___.
17. A ___torch___ was burning in front of it.
18. We heard a musician playing a ___horn___.
19. He was riding a ___horse___ while he played!

Word Bank
corner
horn
morning
horse
fort
torch
north
historical
born
florist
stores

Lesson 15
Words with *or*

35

FOCUS ON ALL LEARNERS

ENGLISH LANGUAGE LEARNERS/ESL

Work with students in a group to complete the first activity together. Write the names of the pictures in the first activity on the board for students to choose from. Define any unfamiliar words in the other two word banks before students continue independently.

VISUAL LEARNERS

LARGE GROUP Write the following partial words on the board and have students complete each with *ar* or *or*: ___gan, f___tune, m___ket, ch___coal, p___cupine, c___toon, sp___ts, st___ry, ___tist, r___e, c___ner, aff___d, audit___ium, sp___kle.

KINESTHETIC/VISUAL LEARNERS

INDIVIDUAL

Materials: index cards, markers

Make word cards for *car, star, farm, army, bark, hard, fare, stare, dare, rare, beware, mare, or, for, born, story, glory,* and *cork.* Have students shuffle the cards, lay them face down, and play "vowel sound" concentration.

Write the word from the word bank that matches each clue. Then read the letters in the shaded boxes to answer the riddle.

organ	dark	tornado	forget	florist
starve	sparkle	artist	explore	forest
alarm	rare	snort	March	orchid

1. opposite of light — d a r k
2. feel very hungry — s t a r v e
3. month of the year — M a r c h
4. sound a pig makes — s n o r t
5. exotic flower — o r c h i d
6. to shine and glitter — s p a r k l e
7. a place to buy flowers — f l o r i s t
8. musical instrument — o r g a n
9. fail to remember — f o r g e t
10. thick woods — f o r e s t
11. unusual; seldom found — r a r e
12. person who paints or draws — a r t i s t
13. frighten — a l a r m
14. travel to unknown places — e x p l o r e
15. whirling column of air — t o r n a d o

What do you call a flavored ape?

a vanilla gorilla

Riddle

SPELLING

Write the spelling words on the board: *serve, birthday, church, technique, school, quick, share, corn, kitten*. Then have students listen to these rhyming words one at a time: *born, dare, antique, Earth Day, curve, birch, written, rule, brick*. Pause after each word for students to say the spelling word that rhymes with it.

WRITING

Portfolio Have students choose two or three words from the word banks on pages 35 and 36 and use them to write a funny title for a story; for example, *The Organ and the Florist* or *The Artist in the Tornado*. Then have students go on to write the story, using as many *ar* and *or* words as they can.

LANGUAGE ARTS

Materials: drawing paper; markers; crayons

Many of the *ar* and *or* words in this lesson can be found in familiar sayings; for example, *Get off your high horse*, and *I need forty winks*. Have students think of other sayings that contain *ar* and *or* words and illustrate them. You might like to combine the papers to make a class booklet of familiar sayings.

SOCIAL STUDIES

Materials: local reference sources

Help students find out facts about their city or town's beginnings: *When was the town founded? Who first settled there? What were the first public buildings? What was the population a hundred years ago?* Have each student write two questions, find the answers, and give a short oral report to the class.

AstroWord *r*-Controlled Vowels. © 1998 Silver Burdett Ginn Inc. Division of Simon & Schuster.

AUDITORY LEARNERS

PARTNER Have each partner think of a word and offer clues about it that don't mention *ar* or *or*. Example: *It has five letters; it means "frighten"; it rhymes with* rare. *(scare)* After each clue is given, the guessing partner tries to guess the word.

GIFTED LEARNERS

Have students collect as many pairs of words as they can that are spelled the same except for *ar* in one and *or* in the other, such as *park, pork* and *barn, born*.

LEARNERS WHO NEED EXTRA SUPPORT

Remind these students that in *or* words, the vowel sound is the same whether or not there is an *e* after the *r* (*for, fore*). In *ar* words, the vowel sound changes if there is an *e* (*star, stare*). See Daily Word Study Practice, page 198.

Lesson 16
Pages 37–38

Words With *er, ir, ur*

Lesson Focus

INTRODUCING THE SKILL

- Review with students how pairing the vowels *a* or *o* with the letter *r* can influence the vowel sound.

- Write the words *thirst, nurse,* and *fern* on the board and ask volunteers to underline the vowel-with-*r* combination in each. Say each word, then have students repeat them, emphasizing the vowel-plus-*r* sound. Help them conclude that the underlined letters in each word stand for the vowel sound heard in *girl*. Have students identify the letters that spell that sound.

- Invite students to write other words with the vowel sound heard in *girl* on the board. Have them read the words aloud to confirm that they all have the same vowel sound.

USING THE PAGES

- Make sure students understand what to do on pages 37 and 38.

- After students have finished the pages, ask small groups to write a statement that tells what they have learned about *er, ir,* and *ur* words. Invite the groups to share their sentences with the class.

37

▶ Circle the name of each picture. Write the word on the line.

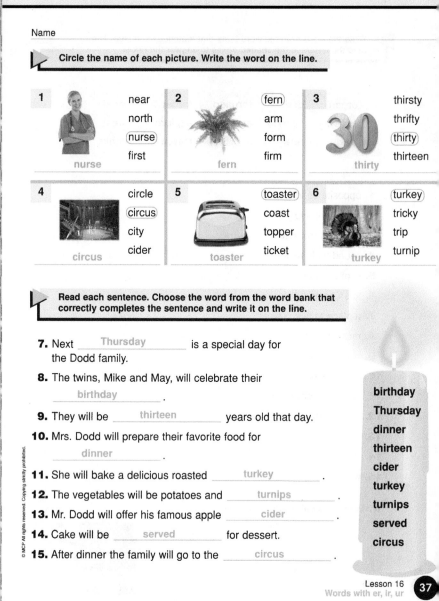

1
near
north
(nurse)
first

nurse

2
(fern)
arm
form
firm

fern

3
thirsty
thrifty
(thirty)
thirteen

thirty

4
circle
(circus)
city
cider

circus

5
(toaster)
coast
topper
ticket

toaster

6
(turkey)
tricky
trip
turnip

turkey

▶ Read each sentence. Choose the word from the word bank that correctly completes the sentence and write it on the line.

7. Next _____Thursday_____ is a special day for the Dodd family.

8. The twins, Mike and May, will celebrate their _____birthday_____.

9. They will be _____thirteen_____ years old that day.

10. Mrs. Dodd will prepare their favorite food for _____dinner_____.

11. She will bake a delicious roasted _____turkey_____.

12. The vegetables will be potatoes and _____turnips_____.

13. Mr. Dodd will offer his famous apple _____cider_____.

14. Cake will be _____served_____ for dessert.

15. After dinner the family will go to the _____circus_____.

Word bank:
birthday
Thursday
dinner
thirteen
cider
turkey
turnips
served
circus

FOCUS ON ALL LEARNERS

ENGLISH LANGUAGE LEARNERS/ESL

To do the first activity, students need to know how to pronounce the four word choices in each box. To play the tic-tac-toe game, they need to identify each picture and pronounce its name correctly. You might have a fluent English speaker work with each English learner.

VISUAL LEARNERS

SMALL GROUP

Materials: dictionaries

Encourage small groups of students to make collections of *er, ir,* and *ur* words. Suggest that students use a dictionary or other reference book to help them.

KINESTHETIC/VISUAL LEARNERS

INDIVIDUAL

Materials: dictionaries

After students have played the tic-tac-toe games, have them write the names of the pictures with the vowel sound in *girl,* circle words with *er,* box words with *ir,* and underline words with *ur.* They can check the spellings in a dictionary.

In each box find the three pictures in a straight or diagonal line whose names have the same vowel sound as **girl**. Draw a line through these pictures.

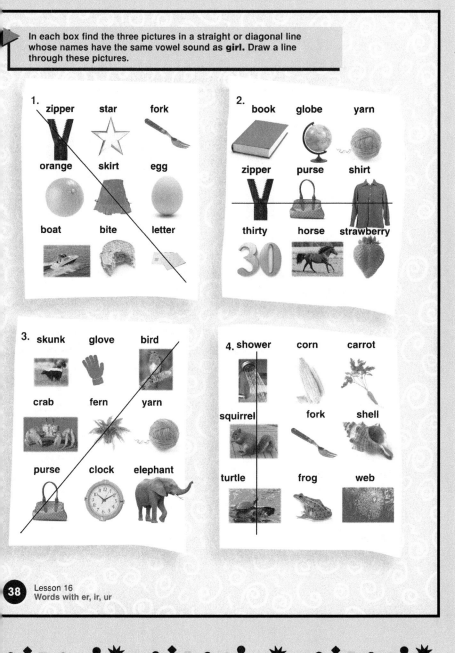

1. zipper star fork
   orange skirt egg
   boat bite letter

2. book globe yarn
   zipper purse shirt
   thirty horse strawberry

3. skunk glove bird
   crab fern yarn
   purse clock elephant

4. shower corn carrot
   squirrel fork shell
   turtle frog web

38 Lesson 16
Words with er, ir, ur

CURRICULUM CONNECTIONS

SPELLING

Write on the board a word shape for each spelling word (*corn, share, birthday, serve, kitten, quick, church, school, technique*). The shape should have a box for each short letter (*c, o, r*), a tall box for each letter with an ascender (*h, b, t, d, k, l*), and a box that extends below the line for each letter with a descender (*y, q*). Then dictate one word at a time. Call on students to come to the board, select the correct shape for the word, and write the word inside the shape.

WRITING

Portfolio Have students imagine that they are Mike or May and that the turkey their mother cooked for their birthday was not good when she bought it at the store. They decide to write a letter of complaint to Mr. Herbert Burger, manager of the turkey processing company. Ask them to use as many *er, ir,* and *ur* words as they can and to underline them.

LANGUAGE ARTS

Write on the board the following sentence:

Oak is to tree as ___ is to sport.

Review that an analogy is two pairs of words that have the same relationship: oak is a kind of tree, so the missing word is a kind of sport. Help students complete the analogy with a word that has the vowel sound in *girl*. (*soccer*) Write several more examples:

Freeze is to cold as ____ is to heat. (burn)

___ is to clean as small is to large. (Dirty)

Then encourage students to create their own analogies for classmates to solve, leaving a blank for a word with the vowel sound in *girl*.

HEALTH

Materials: index cards

Ask students to write a recipe for a nutritious food they know how to prepare. Remind them to include correct amounts of all the necessary ingredients and to write the directions in time order. Combine the recipes into a class cookbook titled "Eating Healthy."

Technology AstroWord *r*-Controlled Vowels. © 1998 Silver Burdett Ginn Inc. Division of Simon & Schuster.

AUDITORY/KINESTHETIC LEARNERS

PARTNER

Materials: index cards, markers

Write a list on the board of words with the vowel sound in *girl*. Partners make three cards each for *ir, er, ur* and shuffle the cards. They then take turns drawing a card, saying a word with that letter combination from the board, and using it in a sentence.

GIFTED LEARNERS

Let students make their own tic-tac-toe games for classmates to solve. Have them draw or cut out pictures of nine items, some with the vowel sound in *girl*. Remind them to make sure that there is only one correct row of items with the target sound.

LEARNERS WHO NEED EXTRA SUPPORT

Make sure students can name all the pictures on these pages before they begin. You may want to complete the first item in the tick-tack-toe game with the group before students tackle the rest on their own. **See Daily Word Study Practice, page 198.**

Lesson 17
Pages 39–40

Words With er, ir, or, ur

Lesson Focus

REVIEWING THE SKILL

- Review with students that different vowels paired with *r* sometimes have the same vowel sound and sometimes have different vowel sounds.

- Say *perfume*, *occur*, and *stirring* and have volunteers write the words on the board. Ask students what they notice about the *r*-controlled vowel sounds. *(They sound the same.)*

- Ask volunteers to write *here*, *core*, *fire*, and *pure* on the board. Encourage them to read the words aloud and then name the letters that stand for the vowel sounds.

- Have students identify which words on the board follow Long Vowel Rule 1: *If a syllable has two vowels, the first usually stands for the long sound and the second is silent.*

USING THE PAGES

- Make sure students know what to do on pages 39 and 40. Point out that to complete the crossword puzzle on page 40, they can choose from the words in the word bank at the top of the page.

- **Critical Thinking** Read aloud the question at the bottom of page 39. Invite students to talk about what people might learn from visiting Williamsburg.

39

Name _____

▷ Read each sentence. Choose the word from the word bank that correctly completes the sentence and write it on the line.

Virginia	printer	stirs
furniture	whirl	churn
cider	preserved	experts
curls	church	purple
Governor's	serve	

1. Williamsburg is a colonial town in ____Virginia____.
2. The town, its streets, and its homes are well ____preserved____.
3. An old ____church____ with a steeple stands as it did in the past.
4. Craftspeople make colonial ____furniture____.
5. A ____printer____ shows how books were made long ago.
6. A woman ____stirs____ hot wax to make candles.
7. The candles are colored red and ____purple____.
8. Other people in colonial costumes make butter in a ____churn____.
9. Restaurants ____serve____ traditional colonial meals.
10. Delicious apple ____cider____ is on every menu.
11. The tour guides are ____experts____ in American history.
12. Street dancers ____whirl____ past the curious crowds.
13. The ____Governor's____ Mansion is a popular attraction.
14. Smoke ____curls____ from its huge brick chimney.

What do people learn from historical places like Williamsburg?

Critical Thinking

FOCUS ON ALL LEARNERS

ENGLISH LANGUAGE LEARNERS/ESL

Materials: history books about colonial life

Before students begin page 39, explain that in Williamsburg, Virginia, visitors can watch demonstrations of how people lived in colonial times. Have available books that contain pictures of colonial life. Invite students to describe what they see.

VISUAL/AUDITORY LEARNERS

LARGE GROUP Write these lists on the board: *more, store, b___, ch___; fire, admire, w___, requ___; firm, worm, t___; worst, burst, fi___; stir, fur, h___*. Students fill in the blanks, give other examples, and conclude that only some vowel-before-*r* words follow a pattern.

KINESTHETIC LEARNERS

SMALL GROUP **Materials:** egg carton, markers, several pebbles

Write *er*, *ir*, *or*, and *ur* at random in the hollows of the egg carton. Have students take turns tossing a pebble into the carton and writing a word with the letter sequence they land on.

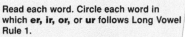

Read each word. Circle each word in which **er, ir, or,** or **ur** follows Long Vowel Rule 1.

RULE In some words, the letters **er, ir, or,** and **ur** follow Long Vowel Rule 1: If a syllable has two vowels, the first vowel usually stands for the long sound and the second is silent.

h**er**e   f**ir**e   c**or**e   p**ur**e

1. (snore)	2. (cures)	3. work	4. firm	5. (floor)
6. thirty	7. burr	8. (core)	9. (hire)	10. worm
11. (severe)	12. (score)	13. (door)	14. purr	15. (retire)
16. (spire)	17. her	18. (more)	19. (tires)	20. very
21. stir	22. (lure)	23. cord	24. fur	25. (store)

Read each clue. Find the word above that matches the clue. Write the word in the crossword puzzle.

Across

1. a thick string
3. these are found on a car or bike
6. greater in number
8. part of a church
9. to attract with bait
10. an opening in a wall
12. to pay someone to do a job
13. a sound made while sleeping
14. the part of a room to walk on

Down

1. the center of an apple
2. to move around
4. teams' points
5. strict or harsh
7. a doctor helps find these
8. a place of business where things are bought and sold
11. to give up a job

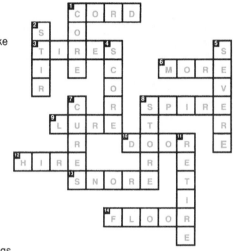

CURRICULUM CONNECTIONS

SPELLING

Write on the board the following misspelled spelling words: *korn, shair, berthday, surve, kittin, kwick, chuch, scool, techneek.* Have students write each word correctly.

WRITING

Portfolio Discuss what it might be like to visit Williamsburg or any other historic town and then have students write a short personal narrative about a day spent there. Encourage students to use as many words with *er, ir, or,* and *ur* as they can.

SOCIAL STUDIES

Many people's surnames are based on their ancestors' occupations. Have students work in small groups to find out what work was once associated with these surnames: Fletcher, Chandler, Miller, Porter, Fuller, Farrier, Turner, Tinker.

ART/SCIENCE

Materials: tempera paints in red, blue, white, black

Purple is made by mixing the primary colors red and blue. Let students experiment with mixing purples by varying the amounts of the primary ingredients and by adding small amounts of black and/or white.

Technology

AstroWord *r*-Controlled Vowels. © 1998 Silver Burdett Ginn Inc. Division of Simon & Schuster.

AUDITORY/VISUAL LEARNERS

SMALL GROUP

Materials: index cards, markers

Make two cards each with the endings __rt, __rve, __rst, __rty, __rr, __rd, __rl, __rm, and four cards with __re. Have students take turns drawing a card, supplying the vowel *e, i, o,* or *u* before the *r,* and adding initial letters as needed to write a word.

GIFTED LEARNERS

The ending of *cider* sounds like the endings of *motor* and *sugar.* Have students make a table with headings *er, or,* and *ar* and collect words with these unstressed endings.

LEARNERS WHO NEED EXTRA SUPPORT

Write the words from the word bank on page 39 on the board in random order. Have students circle *er, ir, or,* and *ur* in the words and then pronounce the words. See Daily Word Study Practice, page 198.

Lesson 18

Pages 41–42

 **Reading** **Writing**

Reviewing Words With

ar, or, er, ir, ur

INFORMAL ASSESSMENT OBJECTIVES

Can students

- read a passage containing words with *ar, or, ir, er,* and *ur*?

- write a journal entry, using words with *ar, or, ir, er,* and *ur*?

Lesson Focus

READING

- Write on the board the pairs *star, share* and *corn, chore*. Have students tell you how the words are alike. *(They all have vowels with* r.*)* Ask them to read each word aloud with you. Ask how the pronunciation of the vowel sound changes when e comes after the *r*.

- Write on the board the pairs *stir, fire*; *he, here*; and *spur, cure*. Follow the same procedure as above.

- Tell students that as they read about the Amish, they will encounter more words with *ar, or, er, ir,* and *ur*.

WRITING

Explain to students that after they read a passage about the Amish, they will write a journal entry about an imaginary day they spend on an Amish farm. For ideas about what details to include in their journal entry, have students refer to the Helpful Hints.

Name _____

 Reading ▸ Read the passage. Then write your answer to the question at the end of the passage.

GROWING UP AMISH

Amish people immigrated here from Switzerland and Germany more than 250 years ago. They were searching for a country where they would be free to follow their religious beliefs. Amish people who follow church rules strictly do not drive cars or use modern farm equipment. They travel by horse-drawn carriage and use horses to pull their plows and carts. They do not have electricity or telephones in their homes.

Amish boys and men wear long black pants, dark shirts, and straw hats. Girls and women wear long solid-color dresses. Starched white caps cover their hair.

In Amish farming communities, young children help plant and weed the vegetable gardens. Older children do chores such as feeding the horses, hogs, and chickens. When crops are planted and harvested, everyone shares the hard work.

Social gatherings in Amish farming communities center on farm activities, such as cornhusking. When a newly married couple needs a barn or a church member's barn has burned down in a fire, the whole community gathers to help build a new barn. Barn raising—in addition to work—is a time for playing, talking, singing, and being together.

What are some of the differences between the Amish way of life and your way of life?

_____
_____
_____
_____
_____

FOCUS ON ALL LEARNERS ✳ • ◆ •

ENGLISH LANGUAGE LEARNERS/ESL

As you review vowel-*r* combinations, give ESL students extra practice seeing and saying such word pairs as *barn, born*; *spare, spire*; *park, pork*; *share, shore*; *fur, fire*; and *torn, turn*. Define each word and use it in a sentence to reinforce their memory.

VISUAL LEARNERS

INDIVIDUAL Write Long Vowel Rule 1 on the board: *If a syllable has two vowels, the first usually stands for the long sound and the second is silent.* Give students a minute to memorize the rule, then cover it and have them each write it from memory, giving examples.

VISUAL/KINESTHETIC LEARNERS

LARGE GROUP

Materials: index cards, markers

Make cards for *ar, er, ir, or,* and *ur*. Write words from this unit on the board, leaving a blank for the vowel-*r* combination (*f__m, h___g_l, c___n, f__niture*). Have students say the word you point to, come to the board, and hold the correct card in the blank.

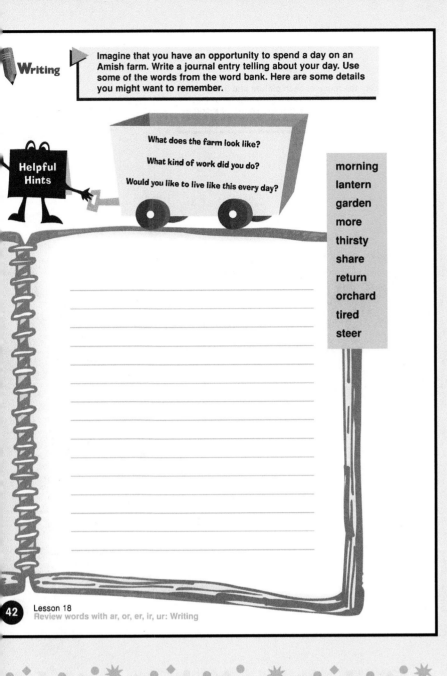

Writing

Imagine that you have an opportunity to spend a day on an Amish farm. Write a journal entry telling about your day. Use some of the words from the word bank. Here are some details you might want to remember.

Helpful Hints

What does the farm look like?

What kind of work did you do?

Would you like to live like this every day?

morning
lantern
garden
more
thirsty
share
return
orchard
tired
steer

SPELLING

Materials: index cards, markers, envelopes

Write *corn, share, birthday, serve, kitten, quick, church, school, technique* on cards. Put each card in an envelope and shuffle the envelopes. One at a time, have students choose an envelope. You open it and dictate the word, and the student writes it on the board. Have the next student correct any incorrect spelling. After going through the pack once, erase the words on the board and repeat until everyone has had a turn.

SOCIAL STUDIES

Have students think about what it might be like to live on an Amish farm. Suggest that they list several things they would miss most from the life they live now, then list things they would might look forward to having as part of their everyday life. Invite students to debate the pros and cons of the Amish life in today's world.

ART

Materials: art books, butcher paper, markers or crayons

Have students look at reproductions of folk art that show many activities taking place at once. Talk about what it would be like to be at a barn raising, a harvest, or a corn-husking party on an Amish farm. Then have students plan a mural that shows a detailed scene from a farming community with many people and animals.

Technology

AstroWord *r*-Controlled Vowels. © 1998 Silver Burdett Ginn Inc. Division of Simon & Schuster.

LARGE GROUP

AUDITORY/KINESTHETIC LEARNERS

Arrange students in five teams: *ar, er, ir, or, ur.* Say *r*-controlled words from the unit. When a team hears a word with its spelling, the first person in line writes the word on the board. Each correctly spelled word gets a point, and the team with the most points wins.

GIFTED LEARNERS

To show that many different spellings stand for vowel sounds with *r*, have students list other spellings for the sounds in this unit. Examples: *ar* as in *farm* sounds like the *ear* in *heart*; *er* as in *herd* sounds like the *or* in *work*; *ir* as in *fire* sounds like the *yr* in *lyre*.

LEARNERS WHO NEED EXTRA SUPPORT

Before students begin to write the journal entry, write on the board the words from the word bank on page 42. Have students say the words aloud and circle *er, ar, ir, or,* or *ur* in each word. See Daily Word Study Practice, page 198.

Lesson 19

Pages 43–44

The k Sound

Lesson Focus

INTRODUCING THE SKILL

- Say the words *color*, *book*, and *pocket*. Ask students what consonant sound the words have in common. *(the sound of k)* Encourage students to tell where in each word they hear the sound of *k*.

- Call on volunteers to write the words on the board and underline the letter or letters that stand for the sound of *k*. Help students conclude that the letters *k* and *ck* stand for the sound of *k*. Explain that if the letter *c* comes before *a, o,* or *u,* it also stands for the sound of *k*.

USING THE PAGES

- Before students begin page 43, help them identify the pictures. After both pages have been completed, encourage pairs to discuss what they learned about the *k* sounds in words.

- **Critical Thinking** Read aloud the question at the bottom of page 44 and invite students to share their ideas with the class.

43

Name

> Say the name of each picture and listen for the **k** sound. Fill in the first, middle, or last circle to show whether the sound of **k** comes at the beginning, middle, or end of the word.

> **DEFINITION**
> The letters **k** and **ck** stand for the sound **k**. If the letter **c** comes before the letters **a, o,** or **u**, it stands for the **k** sound.
>
> **k**itten pi**ck** **c**an

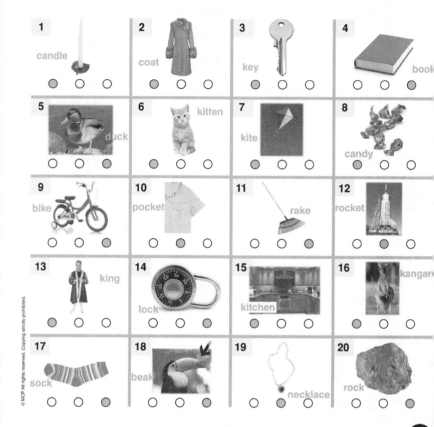

1. candle
2. coat
3. key
4. book
5. duck
6. kitten
7. kite
8. candy
9. bike
10. pocket
11. rake
12. rocket
13. king
14. lock
15. kitchen
16. kangaroo
17. sock
18. beak
19. necklace
20. rock

Lesson 19
Words with the k sound **43**

FOCUS ON ALL LEARNERS

ENGLISH LANGUAGE LEARNERS/ESL

Ask students if they know what a fund-raiser is. Talk about ways school groups raise money, such as selling baked goods or washing cars. You might point out that in Spanish *c* almost always has the *k* sound before *a, o,* or *u* and the *s* sound before *i* or *e*.

VISUAL/AUDITORY LEARNERS

INDIVIDUAL   Have each student write a silly sentence, using several words with the *k* sound. Have them include examples of the *k* sound spelled *c, ck,* and *k*.

KINESTHETIC LEARNERS

SMALL GROUP   **Materials:** small notepads

Have small groups of students walk around the classroom with a pad, listing things whose names have the *k* sound (*chalkboard, desk, book, jacket*). Students could also include names of classmates.

> **Read each sentence. Complete the sentence by writing the word in parentheses that has the k sound. Then circle the letter or letters that stand for the k sound.**

1. The girls' soccer team is _____ ma**k**ing _____ plans for a fund-raiser. (arranging, making)

2. Ms. Garcia, their _____ **c**oach _____, is helping. (coach, sponsor)

3. Jennie, the team _____ **c**aptain _____, is taking notes. (leader, captain)

4. She _____ ta**k**es _____ notes as the girls give suggestions. (takes, writes)

5. Later, Jennie _____ **c**opies _____ her notes. (copies, more)

6. The team uses them to _____ pi**ck** _____ the best idea. (choose, pick)

7. The team votes to hold a _____ ba**k**e _____ sale. (bake, pie)

8. Nicki and Laura will make _____ **c**oo**k**ies _____ to sell. (cheese, cookies)

9. Loni will prepare _____ thi**ck** _____ whipped-cream pies. (rich, thick)

10. Peg will operate the _____ **c**ash _____ register. (cash, change)

11. Ms. Garcia will bring paper _____ sa**ck**s _____ for the customers. (sacks, bags)

12. Everyone will make _____ **c**olored _____ posters to hang. (bright, colored)

13. The sale will be advertised in the _____ lo**c**al _____ papers. (town, local)

14. It will be held in the _____ par**k** _____ near the school. (park, yard)

15. The team will set up a huge _____ **c**anopy _____ there. (canopy, tent)

What is the main idea of this story?

Critical Thinking

44 Lesson 19
Words with the k sound

See Daily Word Study Practice, pages 198–199.

AUDITORY LEARNERS

PARTNER Write this riddle on the board: *What word has the sound of k in the middle and names something people eat on Thanksgiving?* Have a volunteer read and answer the riddle. Then ask partners to make up their own riddles for *k* and share them with the class.

GIFTED LEARNERS

Ask pairs of students to create a simple game, quiz, or other activity that their classmates can use to practice finding /k/ in words. Then have them direct the activity.

LEARNERS WHO NEED EXTRA SUPPORT

Materials: index cards, markers

Make a *c* and a *k* card for each student. On the board write *cat, deck, check, kite, pack, market, camp, second, took,* and *magic.* As you point to and say each word, students hold up the card or cards that show how /k/ is spelled. See Daily Word Study Practice, pages 198–199.

CURRICULUM CONNECTIONS

SPELLING

Write the spelling words *corn, share, birthday, serve, kitten, quick, church, school,* and *technique* on the board and have each student copy the five that are hardest for him or her to spell. Then erase the words and assign partners. Have partners take turns testing each other on their lists of hard words. Encourage them to collaborate on inventing mnemonic devices to help them spell the words.

WRITING

Portfolio Have students write a story about another fund-raiser—a car wash, for instance. When they are finished, have them exchange stories and underline each word with a *k* sound. If a word has two *k* sounds (*cookies*), they underline it twice.

HEALTH/SCIENCE

Materials: posterboard, marker, paints

Encourage students to find out what ingredients in bake-sale treats are more healthful (whole grain flour, nuts, fruit, honey) and which are less healthful (white flour, refined sugar, fats). Ask students to evaluate the ingredients of a few packaged treats and present their findings on a poster.

MATH

Materials: calculator (optional)

Help students draw up a financial plan for the bake sale described on page 44. Let them decide on an amount the team wants to raise, then figure out how many baked goods they need to make, which items are being donated and which they will have to buy, and how much they should charge for each item.

Words With qu and the k Sound

Lesson Focus

INTRODUCING THE SKILLS

- Say *chorus*, and have students identify the beginning consonant sound. Ask a volunteer to write the word on the board and identify the letters that stand for the sound of *k*. Encourage students to name another sound *ch* can stand for. (/ch/ as in children)

- Write and pronounce the words *ache* and *unique*. Ask what consonant sound students hear at the end of each word. Review that *ch* can stand for /k/, and help students discover that *que* also stands for /k/.

- Write and say *quick*. Ask what letters stand for the sound of *k* at the end. Review that *ck* can stand for /k/, and explain that *qu* at the beginning of *quick* stands for /kw/.

USING THE PAGES

- Make sure students understand what to do on pages 45 and 46. After they finish, have them discuss what they learned about words with /k/.

- **Critical Thinking** After students have completed the pages, read and discuss the question at the bottom of page 46.

Name _____

▶ Read each sentence. Underline the words that contain **ch.** Then write the words in the correct columns.

> **RULE**
> The letters **ch** can stand for the **k** sound or the **ch** sound. The letters **que** can also stand for the **k** sound.
> s**ch**ool   **ch**urch   techni**que**

1. Twenty children were chosen to attend a school assembly.
2. Each one sits in a chair in front of a chalkboard.
3. The schedule shows the order of the speakers on a chart.
4. An architect who designs kitchens goes first.
5. An orchestra leader and a choral director speak next.
6. A chemist, a mechanic, and a chemistry teacher speak last.

ch as in **school**		ch as in **church**	
school	choral	children	chalkboard
schedule	chemist	chosen	chart
architect	mechanic	Each	kitchens
orchestra	chemistry	chair	teacher

▶ Read each sentence. Choose the word from the word bank that correctly completes the sentence and write it on the line.

7. We went to an ___antique___ shop that sold interesting, old things.
8. We found many one-of-a-kind, or ___unique___, items.
9. Some were made with ___techniques___ seldom used today.
10. There was not one ___grotesque___ item in the shop!

unique
techniques
grotesque
antique

FOCUS ON ALL LEARNERS

ENGLISH LANGUAGE LEARNERS/ESL

You could remind Spanish and French speakers that, unlike in their languages, *qu* does not usually stand for the *k* sound at the beginning of English words. Before students begin page 46, have them share what they know about the orchestra—musicians and their instruments.

VISUAL LEARNERS

PARTNER   Have each student write five sentences, leaving a blank for a word with /k/ or /kw/. Have them exchange sentences and fill in the blanks. Remind writers to include clues that will help the other student guess the missing words.

KINESTHETIC LEARNERS

SMALL GROUP   **Materials:** construction paper strips, paste, markers

Assign each group one of the following: /k/ spelled *k, que, ch, c,* or *ck*; /kw/ spelled *qu*; /ch/ spelled *ch*. Have groups write words on paper strips that contain their assigned letters and sounds, then make the links into a paper chain. You might combine the individual group chains to make a class chain.

Read each sentence. Choose the word from the word bank that correctly completes the sentence and write it on the line.

RULE
The letters **qu** stand for the **kw** sound.

quote   **qu**ick   **qu**ilt

As you read, think about why an audience applauds at the end of a performance.

Critical Thinking

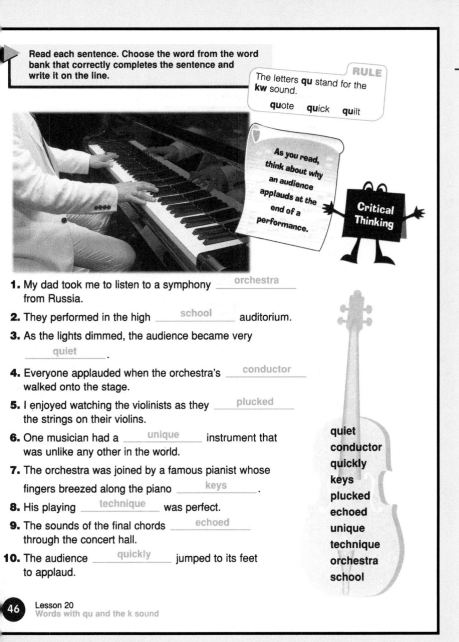

1. My dad took me to listen to a symphony _____orchestra_____ from Russia.

2. They performed in the high _____school_____ auditorium.

3. As the lights dimmed, the audience became very _____quiet_____.

4. Everyone applauded when the orchestra's _____conductor_____ walked onto the stage.

5. I enjoyed watching the violinists as they _____plucked_____ the strings on their violins.

6. One musician had a _____unique_____ instrument that was unlike any other in the world.

7. The orchestra was joined by a famous pianist whose fingers breezed along the piano _____keys_____.

8. His playing _____technique_____ was perfect.

9. The sounds of the final chords _____echoed_____ through the concert hall.

10. The audience _____quickly_____ jumped to its feet to applaud.

quiet
conductor
quickly
keys
plucked
echoed
unique
technique
orchestra
school

46 Lesson 20
Words with qu and the k sound

SPELLING

The following sentences can be used as a spelling posttest for words with r-controlled vowels ar, or, er, ir, ur and the sound of k.

1. **birthday**   Today is Lincoln's **birthday**.
2. **quick**   It's just a **quick** trip to the store.
3. **corn**   Tortillas are made out of **corn**.
4. **school**   Let's study together after **school**.
5. **kitten**   The puppy and **kitten** play nicely.
6. **share**   Why is your **share** bigger than mine?
7. **church**   Paco gets all dressed up for **church**.
8. **serve**   It's your turn to **serve** the tennis ball.
9. **technique**   The surgeon has a fine **technique**.

WRITING

Portfolio Have students think about the kinds of music they like and then write a fan letter to a musical group or individual performer whose music they enjoy, explaining why they like the music. Ask them to identify the words with the /k/ or /kw/ they use. If they plan to send their letters, they could list the words on a separate piece of paper.

SCIENCE

Materials: science books, encyclopedias

Many animals have names with k, kw, or ch sounds. Have students use science books or encyclopedias to find and write one unusual animal name for each of the following sound/letter combinations: /k/ spelled k, que, ch, c, and ck; /kw/ spelled qu, /ch/ spelled ch. (Examples: meerkat, macaque, ichneumon fly, caiman, gecko, quahog, chinchilla)

LANGUAGE ARTS

Host a quiz show. Have students write questions on cards, appoint a quizmaster, and have a trivia quiz. Teams can compete, or it can be a one-on-one, ongoing competition. Questions can be in categories and relate to any subject.

AUDITORY/VISUAL LEARNERS

LARGE GROUP
Write the following words, substituting /k/, /kw/, or /ch/ for the letters that spell these sounds: /kw/iz, e/k/o, /ch/ampion, anti/k/, /kw/een, s/k/edule, /k/orus, e/kw/al, /kw/antity, bir/ch/. Say each word and have students write it with the correct spelling.

GIFTED LEARNERS

Materials: dictionaries

Let students browse through dictionaries and find unusual words that contain qu or que. (arquebus, bisque, quaff, quorum, soliloquy). Have them challenge each other to define the words and use them in sentences of their own.

LEARNERS WHO NEED EXTRA SUPPORT

Materials: colored chalk

On the board write these words: cabbage, chorus, antique, whiskers, stocking, sneakers, terrific, school. Read the words with students. Have a volunteer circle in red the letters that spell /k/. See Daily Word Study Practice, pages 198–199.

Lesson 21

Pages 47–48

The f Sound

* • ◆ • • • ★ • • ● ● ●

INFORMAL ASSESSMENT OBJECTIVES

Can students

✔ identify /f/ in the initial, medial, and final position in words?

✔ identify letters that stand for /f/ in words?

✔ complete sentences with words that contain /f/?

Lesson Focus

INTRODUCING THE SKILL

- Review with students that different letters and combinations of letters can stand for the same sounds.

- Say the following words: *four, orphan,* and *enough.* Invite students to listen for a common consonant sound.

- Then write the words on the board along with the letters *f, ph,* and *gh.* Call on volunteers to underline these letters in the words.

- Help students conclude that the letters *ph* and *gh,* as well as *f,* can stand for /f/.

USING THE PAGES

- Before having students begin page 48, have volunteers read the poem aloud.

- **Critical Thinking** When students have finished the pages, ask a volunteer to read the question on page 48 aloud. Invite students to offer their opinions about whether the story the poem tells could be real or if it is fantasy. Encourage them to support their opinions.

47

Name

Say each word. Underline the letters that stand for the **f** sound. Then write the words under the correct headings.

RULE
The letters **ph** and **gh** can stand for the **f** sound.
dol**ph**in   lau**gh**

feathers	enough	
phones	cough	fine
photo	telegraph	phony
feature	typhoon	digraph
triumph	phonics	fail
orphan	Philip	pamphlet
fingers	graph	tough
telephone	furniture	laugh
rough	finish	nephew
typhoid	sulphur	

ph

phones	triumph	graph
photo	phonics	telephone
telegraph	orphan	nephew
phony	Philip	typhoid
typhoon	pamphlet	sulphur
digraph		

gh

cough	laugh	enough
tough	rough	

f

feathers	fingers	finish
feature	furniture	fine
fail		

© MCP All rights reserved. Copying strictly prohibited.

Lesson 21
Words with the f sound   **47**

FOCUS ON ALL LEARNERS ★ • ● ◆

ENGLISH LANGUAGE LEARNERS/ESL

Students learning English may have difficulty with some of the more difficult words on these two pages—*tycoon, typhoon,* and *phantom.* Take the time to pronounce and define each word, then use it in a context sentence.

VISUAL LEARNERS

INDIVIDUAL   Write on the board the following misspellings: *laufter, teleghone, phingers, triumgh, orfan, nefew, ghurniture, rouph, touf, couph, elefant, paragraf, phrog.* Explain that the f sound in each word is misspelled. Have students write each word correctly.

KINESTHETIC LEARNERS

PARTNER   **Materials:** colored construction paper, scissors, paste

Have partners make three colorful flowers with long stems and write on each blossom *f, ph,* or *gh.* On leaf shapes, have them write words with one spelling of the *f* sound and paste each leaf to the stem of the correct flower.

Read the poem below. Underline each word in the poem that has the sound of **f**. Then read each sentence. Circle the word in parentheses that correctly completes the sentence and write it on the line.

THE FANTASTIC FROG

A frog in a city, it just can't be true.
It must be a phantom or a statue.
A dolphin perhaps, or an elephant maybe.
But how could a frog in a city be happy?
But look! There is Philip, in his suit and tie,
Looking quite smart and not a bit shy.
Reading the papers is one of his crazes.
Finding the meaning from paragraphs and phrases.
He uses the phone like a city tycoon.
And rushes around like a wild typhoon,
Shopping in big stores and riding in autos,
Watching the people and taking some photos.
When asked why he left his home in the pool,
He laughed as he said, "Well, I'm not a fool.
The water was wet and the going was rough.
To tell you quite frankly, I'd had quite enough."
His biography will be read with amazement,
For a frog out of water—that's quite an achievement!

Is this poem fantasy or reality? How can you tell?

Critical Thinking

1. Philip is a _____frog_____ . (elephant, dolphin, (frog))

2. He rushes around like a _____typhoon_____ . (phantom, hyphen, (typhoon))

3. When asked why he left the pool, Philip _____laughed_____ .
   ((laughed,) coughed, phoned)

4. His _____biography_____ will be read with amazement.
   (pamphlet, (biography,) phonograph)

Lesson 21
Words with the f sound

SPELLING

The following sentences can be used as a pretest for spelling words that have the *f* sound, the sounds of *s*, or silent letters in *gh, rh, wr, gn, kn, sc, st*.

1. **dolphin**   A **dolphin** is not a fish.
2. **rose**   Were you up before the sun **rose**?
3. **sure**   I am **sure** we have met before.
4. **fought**   We **fought** hard for our rights.
5. **rhythm**   Hear the **rhythm** of the drums.
6. **wring**   Let's **wring** out the wet towels.
7. **gnaw**   Hamsters **gnaw** with big teeth.
8. **knew**   I **knew** we would be good friends.
9. **scene**   I liked the last **scene** of the movie.
10. **listen**   **Listen** to the birds singing.

WRITING

Portfolio Encourage students to write a story whose title contains words with the *f* sound they learned in this lesson: for example, "The Triumphant Frog Laughed." Suggest that they use as many words that contain the sound of *f* spelled *f, ph,* or *gh* as they can in their stories. Invite volunteers to read their stories aloud, and have the class list the words with /f/ as they listen to each story.

SCIENCE

Encourage students to find out about typhoons and other severe storms, such as monsoons, haboobs (North African dust storms), tornadoes, and hurricanes. *What are the differences between them? Where do they occur?* Set aside time for students to share what they found out about these ferocious weather phenomena.

LANGUAGE ARTS

Materials: dictionaries with word histories

Explain that many words with /f/ spelled *gh* or *ph* have the Greek word parts *graph; phot, photo;* and *phon, phone*. Have students use the dictionary to figure out the meanings of these word parts, then use words with them to build a class word wall. Ask how they think the meaning of *phon* relates to the word *phonics*.

LARGE GROUP

AUDITORY/KINESTHETIC LEARNERS

Materials: index cards, markers

Make three cards for each student with the labels *f, gh,* and *ph*. Read the words at the top of page 47 in random order, and ask students to hold up the card that spells the *f* sound in each word.

GIFTED LEARNERS

Challenge students to write sentences in which all three spellings of /f/ are present: for example, *I've seen enough funny phantoms.*

LEARNERS WHO NEED EXTRA SUPPORT

Stress that there are three ways to spell /f/. Explain that *f* and *ph* almost always have the *f* sound. Have students write example words for the three ways to spell /f/. *(for, phone, tough)* See Daily Word Study Practice, pages 198–199.

Lesson 22

Pages 49–50

The s Sound

Can students

✓ identify words that contain the letter *s*?

✓ identify which sound the letter *s* stands for in words?

Lesson Focus

INTRODUCING THE SKILL

● Review that a consonant can stand for different sounds in words.

● Write *sat, insect, pose, tears, sugar,* and *insure* on the board. Ask students what consonant appears in all six words. Then say or have volunteers say each word aloud. Encourage students to listen carefully and then repeat the different sounds the letter *s* stands for in the words. (/s/, /z/, /sh/)

● Explain to students that the letter *s* can stand for /s/, /z/, or /sh/. Invite students to suggest other words in which the letter *s* stands for these sounds. *(us, music, tissue)*

USING THE PAGES

● Be sure students know what to do on pages 49 and 50. Point out that the first exercise has two steps and the second has three steps.

● When students have finished the pages, have volunteers tell which three sounds the letter *s* can stand for and give examples of each.

Name

▶ Read the sentences below and underline all the words that have the letter **s**. Then write each underlined word in the correct column below.

> **RULE**
> The letter **s** can stand for the **s, z,** or **sh** sounds
> safe   rose   sure

1. A tired <u>sea</u> <u>lion</u> <u>swam</u> <u>surely</u> through the water toward the beach.
2. The powerful <u>waves</u> helped push it onto the land.
3. The <u>sea</u> <u>lion</u> <u>closed</u> its weary <u>eyes</u> and went to sleep.
4. <u>Rosa</u> and her father were walking on the beach when they <u>saw</u> the sea <u>lion</u>.
5. "<u>Does</u> it need help, Dad?" <u>Rosa</u> asked her father.
6. "<u>Is</u> it <u>sick</u>? Do we need to get help for it?"
7. "I'm not <u>sure</u>," her dad <u>said</u>, looking the <u>sea</u> <u>lion</u> over.
8. "We need to <u>observe</u> it for awhile."
9. "That way we can <u>assure</u> <u>ourselves</u> about it."
10. When it heard them, the <u>sea</u> <u>lion</u> <u>raised</u> its head and opened its <u>eyes</u>.
11. That <u>reassured</u> <u>Rosa</u>, who had been very worried.
12. <u>Suddenly</u> the <u>sea</u> <u>lion</u> gave a <u>noisy</u> bark and <u>swam</u> off.

s as in safe	s as in rose	s as in sure
sea lion	waves	surely
swam	closed	sure
its	eyes	assure
sleep	Rosa	reassured
saw	Does	
asked	Is	
sick	observe	
said	ourselves	
ourselves	raised	
Suddenly	noisy	

FOCUS ON ALL LEARNERS

ENGLISH LANGUAGE LEARNERS/ESL

Spanish-speaking students may have difficulty with this lesson. In Spanish, *s* generally has the sound of *s*, not of *z* or *sh*. For example, *Rosa* would have the sound of *s*, not of *z*. Help students practice saying *s* words such as *us, sing, music, days,* and *sure*.

VISUAL/AUDITORY LEARNERS

SMALL GROUP

Materials: index cards, markers

On index cards, write these words: *seven, also, basic, spend, comets, wise, poodles, because, reason, nose, sugar, assure, sure, pressure, issue*. Then shuffle the cards and give them to a small group. Have students say the words, agree on how *s* is pronounced, and sort the cards by sound.

KINESTHETIC/AUDITORY LEARNERS

LARGE GROUP

Read a random list of words in this lesson and other words with *s* pronounced /s/,/z/, and /sh/. After you say each word, ask the class to hiss like a snake (*sssss*), pretend to snore (*zzzzz*), or hush someone (*shhhhh*) to indicate how the *s* in that word is pronounced.

> Read each sentence. Then look at the pictures. In the box under each picture, write the number of the sentence that matches it. Underline each word in which **s** stands for the **z** sound. Circle each word in which **s** stands for the **sh** sound.

1. We rose early on the farm.
2. After rising, we ate breakfast.
3. Andy served oatmeal with (sugar).
4. Then we began our chores.
5. Sam raked the fallen leaves.
6. Cousin Rosie fed the cows.
7. Esther pruned the roses.
8. The morning (surely) flew!

SPELLING

Write the spelling words on the board: *fought, wring, dolphin, rose, scene, gnaw, listen, sure, rhythm, knew*. Then write the following clues and have students supply the spelling word that completes each set.

1. lily, tulip, _____ *(rose)*
2. certain, positive, _____ *(sure)*
3. twist, squeeze, _____ *(wring)*
4. realized, understood, _____ *(knew)*
5. argued, wrangled, _____ *(fought)*
6. tempo, beat, _____ *(rhythm)*
7. whale, porpoise, _____ *(dolphin)*
8. play, act, _____ *(scene)*
9. chew, nibble, _____ *(gnaw)*
10. sniff, look, _____ *(listen)*

WRITING

Portfolio   Invite students to imagine that, like Rosa, they are walking on the beach with a family member and see a seal lying by the water's edge. Have them write a journal entry about what they say and do, and what happens to the animal. Encourage students to include as many *s* words as they can in their journal entry.

LANGUAGE ARTS

Materials: newspapers, chart paper, markers

Have small groups scan newspapers for words with *s* pronounced /s/, /z/, and /sh/. Ask them to make a chart on the chart paper, writing each word in a column by sound to determine which pronunciation of *s* occurs most and least often.

SOCIAL STUDIES

Ask students what they would do if they saw one of the following: a seal lying motionless on the beach, a baby eagle with a broken wing, a hurt squirrel on the lawn, a fox caught in a trap. Have them find out whom to contact for help and then use the information to make a poster titled "Animal Helpline."

AUDITORY/VISUAL LEARNERS

INDIVIDUAL   **Materials:** tape recorder, blank cassette

Ask students to make a tape of words with *s* pronounced /s/, /z/, and /sh/, leaving a pause after each word to give themselves time to write the word when playing it back. Use these words: *Tuesday, tissue, news, raisins, music, sugar, present, pressure, super, us, sure, houses, confuse*.

GIFTED LEARNERS

Suggest students make two lists of plural words: those with a final *s* sound and those with a final *z* sound. Have them make a chart showing which ending sounds in the singular form usually lead to final /s/ in the plural and which lead to final /z/ in the plural.

LEARNERS WHO NEED EXTRA SUPPORT

To make sure that students can discriminate among the three sounds the letter s can stand for, have them read aloud a list of simple words such as *sure, sugar, seven, us, these,* and *dogs*. See Daily Word Study Practice, pages 198–199.

Lesson 23

Pages 51–52

Words With gh, rh, wr

> Read each sentence and draw a picture of it in the box. Then circle the words in the sentence that have a silent **gh**.

HINT
Sometimes the letters **gh** are silent and do not have any sound.

fought

1. Our (neighbor's) (daughter) (brought) us a fish she had (caught).

2. They (sought) the (naughty) cat and found him in the (bough) of a (mighty) tree.

3. The (flight) of the airplane took it (high) over the (mighty) Rocky Mountains.

4. We (weighed) the (dough) and made (eight) pizzas (right) there.

INFORMAL ASSESSMENT OBJECTIVES

Can students

✔ recognize words that contain the letter combinations *gh, rh,* and *wr*?

✔ complete sentences with words that contain the letter combinations *gh, rh,* and *wr*?

Lesson Focus

INTRODUCING THE SKILLS

- Review students' knowledge of the sounds single consonants and consonant combinations can stand for. *(Single consonants can stand for different sounds; different consonant combinations can stand for the same sound.)*

- Write the letters *gh* on a sheet of paper. Write the following on the board: *tau___t, si___, mi___t.*

- Place the *gh* over each line and invite students to read the words. Ask students if they hear a sound represented by *gh.* Help students conclude that the letters *gh* are silent.

- Follow the same procedure with the letter *h* in *rhyme* and the letter *w* in *wrinkle.* Explain that in these words *rh* and *wr* both stand for the sound of *r.* The letters *h* and *w* are silent.

USING THE PAGES

Make sure students understand what to do on pages 51 and 52. After each activity, discuss with them what they have learned about the silent letter or letters.

51

FOCUS ON ALL LEARNERS

ENGLISH LANGUAGE LEARNERS/ESL

Silent letters present special difficulty for students learning to read and write English. Explain that it is especially important to study the words in this lesson.

VISUAL LEARNERS

LARGE GROUP

Write these misspelled words on the board: *dauter, nauty, mity, dou, neibor.* Have volunteers draw a caret (^) and insert the missing silent *gh* in each word. Repeat with silent letters *w* and *h* and misspelled words such as *rinkle* and *rino.*

KINESTHETIC/VISUAL LEARNERS

SMALL GROUP

Materials: small sheet of clear acetate, red marker

On the acetate, make a "no" symbol—a red circle with a line through it. Write these words: *high, though, weigh, taught.* Have students take turns holding the no symbol over each *gh,* pronouncing the words, and writing them.

Read each sentence. Choose the word from the word bank that correctly completes the sentence and write it on the line.

> **RULE**
> The letters **rh** stand for the **r** sound. The **h** is silent.
> **rh**ythm

Rhode Island   rhymes   rhino
rhubarb   rhododendron

1. Tara loves to visit her grandmother in ___Rhode Island___ .

2. She and Tara work outside, tending the flowering ___rhododendron___ bushes.

3. In the cool evenings they make ___rhubarb___ pies.

4. As they work, they make up silly ___rhymes___ .

5. The one about a huge gray ___rhino___ really made them laugh.

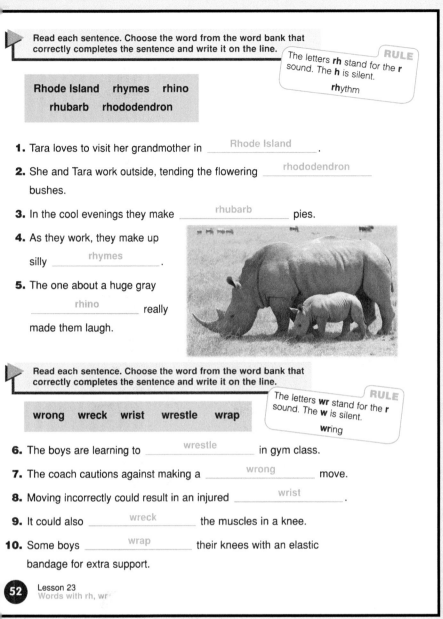

Read each sentence. Choose the word from the word bank that correctly completes the sentence and write it on the line.

> **RULE**
> The letters **wr** stand for the **r** sound. The **w** is silent.
> **wr**ing

wrong   wreck   wrist   wrestle   wrap

6. The boys are learning to ___wrestle___ in gym class.

7. The coach cautions against making a ___wrong___ move.

8. Moving incorrectly could result in an injured ___wrist___ .

9. It could also ___wreck___ the muscles in a knee.

10. Some boys ___wrap___ their knees with an elastic bandage for extra support.

52 Lesson 23
Words with rh, wr

AUDITORY LEARNERS

LARGE GROUP
Read these words aloud and have students raise their hands when a word begins with *rh*: rabbit, report, rhyme, rhino, refrigerator, ready, rhubarb, rowboat, Rhode Island, regular. Have them write the words in two columns, *r* and *rh*, as you read them again.

GIFTED LEARNERS

Have students write sentences using as many words with *wr*, *rh*, and silent *gh* as they can. (Caution them that in some *gh* words, like *laugh* and *tough*, the *gh* is not silent.) See who can write a coherent sentence with the most target words.

LEARNERS WHO NEED EXTRA SUPPORT

Write on the board the words from the two word banks on page 52. Have students say each word aloud, then circle the silent letters. See *Daily Word Study Practice, pages 199–200.*

CURRICULUM CONNECTIONS ✳ ● ◆ ● ●

SPELLING

Write the following paragraph on the board without the underlines. Have students proofread it, identifying the ten misspelled spelling words and writing them correctly.

I had just started to <u>rieng</u> out my swimsuit when I saw the <u>dolfen</u>. It <u>roase</u> out of the water and seemed to <u>lissen</u> to the <u>rithem</u> of our boat's motor. Somehow my dog <u>knoo</u> we had a visitor. He whined and started trying to <u>knaw</u> his way out of the cabin. He <u>shure</u> didn't want to miss this <u>seene</u>! I <u>faugt</u> off the urge to yell at him, and just stood quietly, gazing at the beautiful sea animal.

WRITING

Portfolio Encourage students to write a short story that contains words with *gh*, *rh*, and *wr*. You might provide titles such as "A Rhinoceros Wrestles," "The High Flight," and "Eight Rhubarb Pizzas." Invite students to illustrate their stories and share them with the class.

PHYSICAL EDUCATION

Arm wrestling is gaining in popularity. Have students find out what the rules are for this sport and hold a classroom competition. Your champs might want to challenge another class.

LANGUAGE ARTS/SOCIAL STUDIES

Materials: index cards, marker, a U.S. map, string

Is Rhode Island an island? How did it get its name? Have students find out how this *rh* word became a state name, then go on to find out how all the states got their names. Each students could choose one or two states, writing on cards short captions that explain the names. On a map of the United States, help students connect the cards to their corresponding states with string.

Lesson 24

Pages 53–54

Words With gn, kn, sc, st

INFORMAL ASSESSMENT OBJECTIVES

Can students

✓ recognize words that contain the letter combinations gn, kn, sc, and st?

✓ complete sentences, using such words?

Lesson Focus

INTRODUCING THE SKILLS

● Review with students that some consonants, such as gh, h, and w, can be silent in words. Write these examples on the board: *through, rhyme, wren.*

● Write the word *gnarled* on the board and read it aloud. Ask if any consonant in the word is silent. *(g)*

● Say *knob.* Ask students if there is a silent letter in this word. Call on a volunteer to write the word and underline the silent letter. Explain that gn and kn stand for /n/. The g and k are silent.

● Follow the same procedure for the letters sc and st in the words *scenery* and *listen.* Explain that both sc and st stand for the sound of s in some words, and that the c and t are silent.

USING THE PAGES

● Make sure students understand what to do on pages 53 and 54.

● After students have completed the pages, encourage them to talk about what letter patterns signal that the word may have a silent letter.

53

Name _____

▶ Read each sentence. Choose the word from the word bank that correctly completes the sentence and write it on the line.

RULE
The letters **gn** and **kn** stand for the **n** sound. The **g** and the **k** are silent.
gnaw   **kn**ew

gnarled
know
knotholes
knickers
gnome
knee
knight

1. Sir Lance, a brave ___**knight**___, rides to a forest.
2. The forest is filled with old ___**gnarled**___ trees.
3. Legend says that a tiny ___**gnome**___ lives in one tree.
4. This creature is no taller than your ___**knee**___
5. He dresses in plaid ___**knickers**___ and a red vest.
6. Lance is anxious to get to ___**know**___ this elf
7. Lance searches in the ___**knotholes**___ of every tree

▶ Read each sentence. Choose the word from the word bank that correctly completes the sentence and write it on the line.

RULE
The letters **sc** and **st** will sometimes stand for the **s** sound. The **c** and the **t** are silent.
scene   li**st**en

glistened   hastened   scenic
scent   muscles   whistle

8. The thief escaped into the ___**scenic**___ village.
9. The police ___**hastened**___ to inform the villagers.
10. With a loud ___**whistle**___ the dogs were called.
11. The dogs picked up the ___**scent**___ of the thief.
12. With powerful ___**muscles**___ the dogs chased him.
13. Later, handcuffs ___**glistened**___ on the thief's wrists.

FOCUS ON ALL LEARNERS ✳ ● ◆ ■

ENGLISH LANGUAGE LEARNERS/ESL

Because silent letters are just that—silent!—it's especially difficult for ESL students to recognize words that contain them. Provide extra practice in seeing, saying, and writing these words.

VISUAL LEARNERS

LARGE GROUP

Write the following incomplete words on the board. Ask students to write in the two letters that spell the s sound to complete each word: li___en, cre___ent, ___ientist, whi___le, ha___en, remini__e, ___ent, mu___le, thi___le, ___enery, fa___ener.

KINESTHETIC LEARNERS

INDIVIDUAL **Materials:** four sheets of paper for each student; markers; stapler

Have students each make a "silent letters" booklet by folding four sheets of paper in half, stapling them, and labeling each right-hand page: kn, gn, sc, st, wr, gh, wr. Students can collect silent-letter words on the appropriate pages.

> Circle the two letters that stand for the sounds of **n** or **s**.

1. (kn)ee
2. (gn)ome
3. whi(st)led
4. (kn)oll
5. mu(sc)les
6. (kn)uckles
7. (gn)arled
8. (sc)enery
9. (kn)ew
10. de(sc)ended
11. si(gn)
12. (kn)apsacks
13. (gn)awing
14. (sc)enic
15. gli(st)ened
16. (kn)ow

> Read each sentence and complete it with the correct word from above.

17. There was no ____sign____ of rain when Fern and Carla woke up.

18. They decided to climb a nearby ____knoll____

19. The girls buckled on their ____knapsacks____ .

20. Carla ____whistled____ a tune as they walked.

21. "I ____knew____ this hike was a good idea!" Fern said.

22. At the top of the hill, they admired the ____scenery____ .

23. Sunlight ____glistened____ off a small pond.

24. A beaver was ____gnawing____ on a young tree.

25. "What a ____scenic____ view!" Fern exclaimed.

26. "Yes, but my ____knee____ is hurting," Carla said.

27. "I'm going to rest by this ____gnarled____ old tree."

28. "My ____muscles____ are a little sore, too," said Fern.

29. Fern knocked her ____knuckles____ against the tree.

30. "It's hollow! I wonder if a ____gnome____ lives in it," she said.

31. "I guess we'll never ____know____ ," Carla said.

32. Then the two girls ____descended____ the hill and went home.

54 Lesson 24
Words with gn, kn, sc, st

SPELLING

Review basic alphabetical order with students. Remind them to look at the second letter if two words have the same first letter. Write the spelling words on the board: *fought, wring, dolphin, rose, scene, gnaw, listen, sure, rhythm, knew.* Invite students to race to see who can write the words in alphabetical order the fastest.

WRITING

Portfolio Write this sentence on the board: *The nervous gnu knew that he needed new knickers.* Also write /n/ *gn, kn, n;* /s/ *sc, st, s, c;* /r/ *rh, wr, r.* Then challenge students to write their own sentences that include several words with different spellings of each sound.

ART

Materials: drawing paper, markers or crayons

Invite students to draw a design for a new kind of knapsack or a new kind of whistle. Have them think about the functions and features of their product before they begin. Then give students time to make a diagram of their design, labeling the parts and including a caption that describes it.

PHYSICAL EDUCATION/ART

Materials: fitness reference materials, posterboard, markers, crayons, paints

Ask students to research the fastest and safest way to improve their muscle strength: which exercises they should do, how often, how many repetitions, for how many weeks? Encourage students to make a poster that presents their findings in an attractive, eye-catching format.

AUDITORY LEARNERS

LARGE GROUP Write *kn* and *gn* words on the board. Have students give short definitions, challenging other students to circle the word defined. Use these words: *tiny flying insect (gnat), making a sweater (knitting), from another country (foreign), twisted (gnarled), cutting tool (knife).*

GIFTED LEARNERS

Materials: dictionaries

See how many different silent letters students can list, along with at least one example of each. (*a* in *pharaoh, b* in *debt, d* in *budge*) Provide dictionaries so students can confirm pronunciations.

LEARNERS WHO NEED EXTRA SUPPORT

Before students begin to work, ask them to read the words in the word banks on page 53 and the words in the first activity on page 54. Then help them identify the silent letter in each word. See Daily Word Study Practice, pages 199-200.

Lesson 25

Pages 55–56

Syllables

Lesson Focus

INTRODUCING THE SKILL

● Review with students what a syllable is. *(a word or word part that contains one vowel sound)*

● Say the words *cheese, tomatoes,* and *people.* Ask students how many vowel sounds they hear in each word. *(1, 3, 2)*

● Call on volunteers to write the words on the board. Encourage students to compare the number of vowels seen in each word with the number of vowel sounds heard. Help students understand that a word has as many syllables as it has vowel sounds, regardless of the number of vowel letters in the word.

USING THE PAGES

● Make sure students know what to do on pages 55 and 56. Remind them that the number of vowels they hear is the same as the number of syllables.

● When students have completed the pages, encourage them to discuss what they have learned about syllables. Answer any questions they might have.

55

Name

> Read each word. Write the number of vowels you see in each word. Then write the number of vowel sounds you hear.

Vowels	See	Hear		**Vowels**	See	Hear
1. furniture	4	3		19. wrangler	2	2
2. candle	2	2		20. comical	3	3
3. pose	2	1		21. neighbor	3	2
4. rough	2	1		22. insurance	4	3
5. liquid	3	2		23. antique	4	2
6. kite	2	1		24. boughs	2	1
7. cough	2	1		25. quail	3	1
8. campaign	3	2		26. cyclone	3	2
9. cabbage	3	2		27. ache	2	1
10. scientist	3	3		28. daughter	3	2
11. quote	3	1		29. chorus	2	2
12. gnome	2	1		30. queen	3	1
13. knell	1	1		31. phone	2	1
14. locket	2	2		32. banquet	3	2
15. weigh	2	1		33. knuckle	2	2
16. typhoid	3	2		34. architect	3	3
17. enough	3	2		35. photograph	3	3
18. gnarl	1	1		36. rhinoceros	4	4

FOCUS ON ALL LEARNERS

ENGLISH LANGUAGE LEARNERS/ESL

Before English learners begin, read the words aloud with them to be sure they are pronouncing them correctly. You may wish to pair them with fluent English speakers to count the vowel sounds and syllables.

LARGE GROUP

VISUAL/AUDITORY LEARNERS

Materials: red chalk

List on the board a random selection of words from page 55, writing the vowel letters in red. Then have volunteers say each word and write beside the word how many vowel sounds they hear.

SMALL GROUP

KINESTHETIC/VISUAL LEARNERS

Materials: slips of paper, small box

Have each student print several words from this lesson on slips of paper and put them in a box. Students take turns drawing a word. The first person counts the vowel letters, the second counts the syllables, and the third records the findings.

Write the number of syllables you hear in each word.

1. telephone	3	2. insect	2
3. glisten	2	4. quiz	1
5. magazine	3	6. mechanic	3
7. Philip	2	8. wrist	1
9. campaign	2	10. cough	1
11. locket	2	12. antique	2
13. rhubarb	2	14. tissue	2
15. wise	1	16. candy	2
17. king	1	18. jacket	2
19. kangaroo	3	20. rhythm	2
21. sign	1	22. wrangler	2
23. biography	4	24. whisper	2
25. husband	2	26. science	2
27. basement	2	28. rake	1
29. wrong	1	30. phonograph	3
31. rhinoceros	4	32. cousin	2
33. typhoon	2	34. elephant	3
35. phantom	2	36. positive	3
37. wreck	1	38. knapsack	2
39. photo	2	40. kitchen	2
41. chorus	2	42. equal	2
43. block	1	44. digraph	2
45. answer	2	46. sugar	2
47. fight	1	48. knoll	1
49. treasure	2	50. gnome	1

56 Lesson 25
Syllables in words with k, f, s sounds; silent letters

See Daily Word Study Practice, page 208.

CURRICULUM CONNECTIONS ✳

SPELLING

Write the spelling words on the board: *fought, wring, dolphin, rose, scene, gnaw, listen, sure, rhythm, knew.* Write these headings: *f sound, sounds of s, silent letters.* Have a student choose a spelling word and write it under each heading where it fits. When all words have been categorized, ask other students to circle in column 1 the letter or letters that stand for the *f* sound, in column 2 the letter or letters that stand for a sound of *s,* and in column 3, the silent letter or letters.

WRITING

Portfolio

Materials: paper; markers in red, blue, and green

Have students write a short fairy tale about a gnome. When they are finished, ask them to go through their stories and circle all the one-syllable words in blue, all the two-syllable words in red, and all the words with three or more syllables in green.

SOCIAL STUDIES

Materials: a local map, chart paper

Have students make a chart with the title "Names in Your Town" and the column headings *1, 2, 3, 4, 5.* Students then take turns locating places on the map, reading the names aloud, and writing the names in columns according to the number of syllables.

SCIENCE

Explain that there are only a few species of rhinoceroses left in the world and that all are threatened with extinction. Encourage students to find out about the different kinds of rhinos—where they live, what they eat, and what is being done to try to save them from extinction.

Technology

AstroWord Multisyllabic Words. © 1998 Silver Burdett Ginn Inc. Division of Simon & Schuster.

AUDITORY/VISUAL LEARNERS

LARGE GROUP Write the following categories on the board and have students think of one-, two-, and three-syllable words to fit each category: *Bodies of Water, Birds, Sports, Computer Terms, Weather Words, Foods.*

GIFTED LEARNERS

Challenge students to write a five- or six-word sentence in which each word has a different number of syllables.

LEARNERS WHO NEED EXTRA SUPPORT

Remind students that *y* can be a vowel, as in *typhoid.* To help them focus on the correct task on page 55, have them cover (with a strip of paper) the column they're not working on.

Lesson 26

Pages 57–58

 **R**eading **W**riting

Reviewing Sounds of k, f, s; Silent Letters; Syllables

INFORMAL ASSESSMENT OBJECTIVES

Can students

✓ read a folk tale containing words with *k, f,* and *s* sounds, silent letters, and various numbers of syllables?

✓ write a folk tale, using such words?

Lesson Focus

READING

- Use the words *unique, chorus,* and *quack* to review /k/ and /kw/, and *tough* and *phone* to review /f/ spelled *gh* and *ph*.

- Write *scenery, glisten, sign, knife, through,* and *wrong*. Review the silent letters in these words.

- Review the sounds of *s* with the words *wise, south,* and *tissue*.

- Have students identify the number of syllables in each word on the board.

- Then tell students that as they read a folk tale on page 57, they will encounter more words with the elements reviewed.

WRITING

- Explain that on page 58 students will write their own folk tale about Coyote. As they prepare to write, have students refer to the Helpful Hints.

- After they finish writing, invite volunteers to read their tales aloud and discuss the lessons Coyote learns.

 Reading ▶ **Read the folk tale. Then write your answer to the question at the end of the folk tale.**

COYOTE'S PRESENT

Coyote was walking with Spider when they saw a unique rock. "This fine rock looks cold," said Coyote. "I'll give it my blanket." Coyote wrapped his thick blanket around the rock. "Here is a present for you," Coyote said.

The two friends walked on, whistling a tune. Soon a cold rain began to fall. Coyote began to cough. "Spider, please go back and get my blanket," Coyote begged. Spider hastened back to the rock. "My friend Coyote needs his blanket," he said. The rock refused to give back the blanket. "What's given is given," it said.

When Spider told this to Coyote, Coyote became angry. He hastened back to the rock. "I'm sure I need this more than you do," he told the rock as he wrapped himself in the blanket.

Suddenly, Coyote and Spider heard a frightening sound. The rock was rolling after them! They ran as quickly as they could, but the rock rolled right over them and snatched up the blanket, saying, "What's given is given."

Coyote picked himself up. "I know now I was wrong," he decided. "If you give someone a present, you give it forever."

 What lesson did Coyote learn?

FOCUS ON ALL LEARNERS ✳ • ◆ •

ENGLISH LANGUAGE LEARNERS/ESL

Ask students about folk tales from their native land, and have volunteers tell them to the group. Explain that Coyote is a character in Native American folk tales who always gets into trouble, but then he learns from his mistakes.

VISUAL LEARNERS

INDIVIDUAL Have students hunt through "Coyote's Present" for words with different numbers of syllables, and then list the words they find under these headings on the board: *1 Syllable, 2 Syllables, 3 Syllables*.

KINESTHETIC/VISUAL LEARNERS

 SMALL GROUP

Materials: a beanbag

Write on the board *n sound, silent g; n sound, silent k; s sound, silent t;* and *r sound, silent w*. Have students stand in a circle. Have one student toss the beanbag to a classmate and say one item from the board. The catcher must say a word having that sound and silent letter.

Writing

In Native American folk tales, Coyote is always getting into trouble! Write your own folk tale about a lesson Coyote learns. Use the words in the word bank. Here are some things to think about before you write.

phony	wreck	scene
quickly	tough	gnarled
treasure	muscles	know
	rhythm	

Where does your story take place?
Who are the characters?
What do they do?

Helpful Hints

SPELLING

The following sentences can be used as a posttest for spelling words with the *f* sound, the sounds of *s*, or silent letters in *gh*, *rh*, *wr*, *gn*, *kn*, *sc*, *st*.

1. **gnaw** — My puppy likes to **gnaw** on bones.
2. **scene** — The market was a busy **scene**.
3. **listen** — I told you, but you didn't **listen**.
4. **rose** — Gina grew this pretty pink **rose**.
5. **sure** — Your team is **sure** to win the game.
6. **dolphin** — Out of the water leaped a **dolphin**.
7. **rhythm** — The drums keep the **rhythm**.
8. **wring** — Don't **wring** your hands in worry.
9. **knew** — I **knew** how the story would end.
10. **fought** — Our nation **fought** in the war.

ART

Materials: art supplies, butcher paper

Interested students could turn "Coyote's Present" into a giant comic strip, first dividing the story into scenes. Have each person or pair choose a different scene to illustrate, using voice balloons for the dialogue. Assemble the scenes into a complete story, which students can post on the bulletin board or share with another class.

SCIENCE

Materials: natural history books, field guides

Let interested students find out about the life and habits of the coyote. Suggest that they find out about their size and coloration, what they eat, where they live, and how to identify their tracks. Once students have gathered their information, some might like to speculate how and why coyote came to be known as the trickster. Invite students to share their discoveries and speculations with the class.

AUDITORY LEARNERS

PARTNER Have students take turns reading their folk tales to a partner. When the partner reads a word with a silent letter, have him or her pause after the word and let the partner tell what silent letter the word has.

GIFTED LEARNERS

Challenge students to use all the words in the word bank as well as other *k*, *f*, and *s* words they can think of when writing their folk tale.

LEARNERS WHO NEED EXTRA SUPPORT

Work with students individually to help them outline the plots of their folk tales before they begin writing. Go over the words in the word bank to see which words students might include in their folk tales. See Daily Word Study Practice, pages 198-200, 208.

Lesson 27

Pages 59–60

Unit Checkup

Reviewing Words with *ar*, *or*, *er*, *ir*, *ur*; Sounds of *k*, *f*, *s*; Silent Letters; and Syllables

INFORMAL ASSESSMENT OBJECTIVES

Can students

✔ identify *k* and *f* sounds, the sounds *s* can stand for, and silent letters in words?

✔ identify the number of syllables in words?

✔ use words with *k*, *f*, and *s* sounds, and silent letters in sentences and analogies?

Lesson Focus

PREPARING FOR THE CHECKUP

- Write on the board these headings: *ar, er, ir, or, ur*. Read the following words and have students tell you which spelling of the vowel-before-*r* sound each has: *card, burn, her, torn, bird*.

- Write on the board these headings: *k sound, kw sounds, n sound, f sound, r sound*. Have volunteers write these words under the correct heading as you read them aloud: *ache, gnome, quiet, phone, wrong, unique, laughter, knitted, tough, rhythm, sign*.

- Read these words aloud and have students count the number of syllables in each: *rhubarb, knife, antique, elephant, wrap, wrongfully*.

USING THE PAGES

- Make sure each student understands the directions on pages 59 and 60.

- After students have completed the pages, encourage them to discuss what they've learned about the elements covered in this unit.

59

Name _____

UNIT 2 CHECKUP

> Read each sentence. Fill in the circle below the word that correctly completes the sentence. Write the word on the line.

1. Rhoda is learning to use a video ____camera____ . | camera ● | cough ○
2. She wants to create ____unique____ films. | unique ● | physique ○
3. The camera does not ____weigh____ much. | rough ○ | weigh ●
4. She does not need strong ____muscles____ to carry it. | thistles ○ | muscles ●
5. Rhoda ____knows____ a lot about filmmaking. | knows ● | knees ○
6. She answers all my ____questions____ . | quick ○ | questions ●
7. We are ____writing____ the script together. | writing ● | wrong ○
8. The title is "The Phony ____Phantom____ ." | Hyphen ○ | Phantom ●
9. The film features an evil ____chemist____ . | chemist ● | chorus ○
10. He always talks in ____rhymes____ . | rhinos ○ | rhymes ●
11. The story starts with a ____storm____ . | short ○ | storm ●
12. A ____fire____ burns up the chemist's lab. | fire ● | first ○
13. My ____neighbor____ Hugh and I will act in Rhoda's film. | naughty ○ | neighbor ●
14. We will also design the ____scenery____ . | scenery ● | scents ○
15. We are ____sure____ our film will be great! | sugar ○ | sure ●
16. Someday Rhoda will be a famous ____star____ . | stir ○ | star ●

Lesson 27 **59**

Words with ar, or, er, ir, ur; k, f, s sounds; silent letters; syllables: Checkup

---

FOCUS ON ALL LEARNERS

ENGLISH LANGUAGE LEARNERS/ESL

To build background for the story on page 59, ask students if they have ever used a video camera or watched an amateur video. Have volunteers tell what these experiences were like.

VISUAL LEARNERS

SMALL GROUP

Materials: bag, index cards, markers

Make or have students make 20 cards with various words from the unit and place them in the bag. Students take turns drawing a card, reading the word aloud, and telling what they have studied about words like the word on the card drawn.

KINESTHETIC LEARNERS

PARTNER

Materials: 30-inch strip of adding machine paper, tape

Have partners tape the ends of the strip together, first turning one end over to form an infinity (Mobius) strip. On the strip, they write words with silent letters. Soon they'll find they are writing on the other side of the strip! Encourage them to fill the strip on both sides.

UNIT 2 CHECKUP

Read each sentence. Think about the way the underlined words are related. Then choose one of the words in the word bank to complete the sentence.

rhubarb	wrong	rough	whistle	quack	herd
kitchen	thirsty	gnaw	rose	scent	fur
elephant	knee	antique	ghost	sugar	chorus

1. Nice is to naughty as right is to ___wrong___.

2. Car is to garage as stove is to ___kitchen___.

3. Quill is to porcupine as ___fur___ is to cat.

4. Nose is to person as trunk is to ___elephant___.

5. Elbow is to arm as ___knee___ is to leg.

6. Dolphin is to animal as ___rhubarb___ is to plant.

7. Rare is to unique as old is to ___antique___.

8. Purr is to cat as ___quack___ is to duck.

9. Sour is to lemon as sweet is to ___sugar___.

10. Gnome is to elf as phantom is to ___ghost___.

11. Wreck is to smash as ___gnaw___ is to chew.

12. Hungry is to eat as ___thirsty___ is to drink.

13. Orange is to fruit as ___rose___ is to flower.

14. Forget is to remember as smooth is to ___rough___.

15. Play is to orchestra as sing is to ___chorus___.

16. Sound is to noise as ___scent___ is to odor.

17. Beat is to drum as blow is to ___whistle___.

18. Flock is to birds as ___herd___ is to deer.

60 Lesson 27
Review words with ar, or, er, ir, ur; k, f, s sounds; silent letters; syllables: Checkup

---

AUDITORY LEARNERS

SMALL GROUP

Have students form groups of three. Going clockwise, have one student read aloud a word with the *n* or *s* sound. The next student says "Shhh" if the word has a silent letter, and the third spells the word and tells what the silent letter is, if any. Then students trade roles.

GIFTED LEARNERS

Materials: science or social studies textbooks

Have students choose the topic *words with vowels before* r or *words with silent letters*. Give each student the same chapter of a science or social studies textbook, set a time limit, and have students list words they find in their category. See who can find and write the most words.

LEARNERS WHO NEED EXTRA SUPPORT

To prepare students for the activity on page 60, make sure they understand what an analogy is. Talk about the different kinds of relationships the words in an analogy can have—synonyms, antonyms, part-whole, cause-effect, action-actor, and so on. See *Daily Word Study Practice, pages 198-200, 208.*

ASSESSING UNDERSTANDING OF UNIT SKILLS

Student Progress Assessment You may wish to review the observational notes you made as students worked through the activities in this unit. Your notes will help you evaluate the progress students made with words with *ar, or, er, ir, ur,* sounds of *k, f, s,* silent letters, and syllables.

Portfolio Assessment Review the materials students have collected in their portfolios. You may wish to have interviews with students to discuss their written work and the progress they have made since the beginning of the unit. As you review students' work, evaluate how well they use these word study skills.

Daily Word Study Practice For students who need additional practice with words with *ar, or, er, ir, ur,* sounds of *k, f, s,* silent letters, and syllables, quick reviews are provided on pages 198–200, 208 in Daily Word Study Practice.

Word Study Posttest To assess students' mastery of words with *ar, or, er, ir, ur,* sounds of *k, f, s,* silent letters, and syllables, use the posttest on pages 31g–31h.

Spelling Cumulative Posttest Review Unit 2 spelling words by using the following words and dictation sentences.

1.	**serve**	The waiters **serve** us food.
2.	**scene**	Don't make a **scene** in public.
3.	**listen**	**Listen** to my instructions.
4.	**quick**	He is a **quick** learner.
5.	**birthday**	My **birthday** is July 1.
6.	**sure**	I'm not **sure** if he'll come.
7.	**wring**	**Wring** out the wet clothes.
8.	**corn**	Let's pop **corn** and watch a video.
9.	**fought**	She **fought** with courage.
10.	**dolphin**	Flipper is a famous **dolphin**.
11.	**rhythm**	Clap with a steady **rhythm**.
12.	**church**	Al sings at his **church**.
13.	**rose**	The audience **rose** to its feet.
14.	**technique**	Collage is one art **technique**.
15.	**gnaw**	A mouse can **gnaw** through wood.
16.	**knew**	The dog **knew** that his master was hurt.
17.	**school**	Torey is in my class at **school**.

Teacher Notes

INTRODUCING

Unit 3

Suffixes and Syllables

Contents

Assessment Strategy Overview

Throughout Unit 3, assess students' ability to read and write words with suffixes. There are various ways to assess students' progress. You may also want to encourage students to evaluate their own work and to participate in setting goals for their own learning.

FORMAL ASSESSMENT

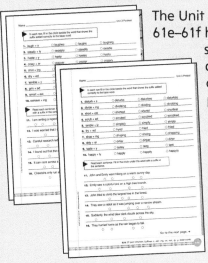

The Unit 3 Pretest on pages 61e–61f helps to assess a student's knowledge at the beginning of the unit and to plan instruction.

The Unit 3 Posttest on pages 61g–61h helps to assess mastery of unit objectives and to plan for reteaching, if necessary.

INFORMAL ASSESSMENT

The Reading & Writing pages and Unit Checkup in the student book are an effective means of evaluating students' performance.

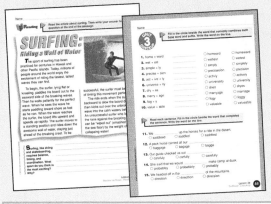

PORTFOLIO ASSESSMENT

This logo appears throughout the teaching plans. It signals opportunities for collecting students' work for individual portfolios. You may also want to collect the following pages.

❖ Unit 3 Pretest and Posttest, pages 61e–61h

❖ Unit 3 Reading & Writing, pages 83–84

❖ Unit 3 Checkup, pages 85–86

STUDENT PROGRESS CHECKLIST

Use the checklist on page 61i to record students' progress. You may want to cut the sections apart to place each student's checklist in his or her portfolio.

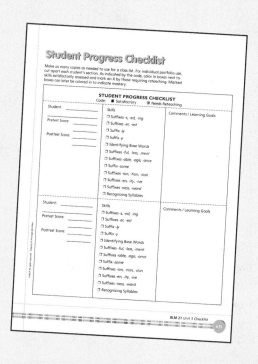

Skill	Reading & Writing Pages	Unit Checkup
Suffixes -s, -ed, -ing	83–84	85–86
Suffixes -er, -est	83–84	85–86
Suffix -ly	83–84	85–86
Suffix -y	83–84	85–86
Identifying Base Words	83–84	85–86
Suffix -able	83–84	85–86
Suffix -ward	83–84	85–86
Suffixes -ion, -tion, -sion	83–84	85–86
Suffixes -en, -ive	83–84	85–86
Suffix -ness	83–84	85–86
Suffix -age	83–84	85–86

Pretest and Posttest

DIRECTIONS

To help you assess student's progress in learning Unit 3 skills, tests are available on pages 61e–61h. Administer the Pretest before students begin the unit. The results of the Pretest will help you identify each student's strengths and needs in advance, allowing you to structure lesson plans to meet individual needs. Administer the Posttest to assess students' overall mastery of skills taught in the unit and to identify specific areas that will require reteaching.

PERFORMANCE ASSESSMENT PROFILE

The following chart will help you identify specific skills as they appear on the tests and enable you to identify and record specific information about an individual's or the class's performance on the tests.

Answers marked with an asterisk (*) indicate words that require a spelling change, such as dropping the final e, doubling the final consonant, or changing y to i.

Depending on the results of the tests, refer to the Reteaching column for lesson-plan pages where you can find activities that will be useful for meeting individual needs or for daily word study practice.

ANSWER KEYS

Unit 3 Pretest, page 61e (BLM 17)

1. disturbs	5. simply	9. tasty
2. dividing	6. fried	10. happily
3. shortest	7. shopping	
4. scrubbed	8. dirtier	

11. sunny	13. largest	15. Suddenly
12. colorful	14. jumping	16. hurried

Unit 3 Pretest, page 61f (BLM 18)

17. homeward	21. sharpen
18. direction	22. package
19. stillness	23. detective
20. breakable	24. division

25. back-ward	29. state-ment
26. thank-ful-ly	30. add-i-tion
27. tire-some	31. in-sur-ance
28. clean-li-ness	32. quick-ened

Unit 3 Posttest, page 61g (BLM 19)

1. laughs	5. shutting	9. smartest
2. steadily	6. dried	10. removing
3. hasty	7. terribly	
4. crazier	8. grinned	

11. writing	13. Careful	15. grassy
12. worried	14. fastest	16. quickly

Unit 3 Posttest, page 61h (BLM 20)

17. backward	21. strengthen
18. discussion	22. baggage
19. happiness	23. education
20. enjoyable	24. collision

25. out-ward	29. move-ment
26. hope-ful-ly	30. am-bi-tion
27. awe-some	31. dis-turb-ance
28. friend-li-ness	32. hur-ried

PERFORMANCE ASSESSMENT PROFILE

Skill	Pretest Questions	Posttest Questions	Reteaching Focus on All Learners	Daily Word Study Practice
Suffixes -s, -ed, -ing	1, 2*, 4*, 6*, 7*, 14, 16*, 32	1, 5*, 6*, 8*, 10*, 11*, 12*, 32*	63–64, 67–70, 83–84	200
Suffixes -er, -est	3, 8*, 13*	4*, 9, 14	65–70, 83–84	200
Suffix -ly	5*, 10*, 15, 26*, 28*	2*, 7*, 16, 26*, 28*	71–74, 83–84	200–201
Suffix -y	9*, 11*	3*, 15, 19*	71–74, 83–84	200–201
Identifying Base Words	1–10	1–10	68–69, 71, 74–76, 79, 83–84	200–202
Suffixes -ful, -ness	12, 19, 26*, 28	13, 19, 26*, 28*	75–76, 83–84	201–202
Suffixes -able, -age	20, 22	20, 22*	75–76, 83–84	201–202
Suffixes -less, -ment, -ance	29, 31*	29, 31	75–76, 83–84	201–202
Suffixes -en, -ity, -ive, -some	21, 23, 27, 32	21, 27	77–78, 83–84	201–202
Suffixes -ion, -tion, -sion	18, 24, 30	18, 23*, 24, 30	77–78, 83–84	201–202
Suffix -ward	17, 25	17, 25	79–80, 83–84	201–202
Syllables	25–32	25–32	81–84	208

> In each row fill in the circle beside the word that shows the suffix added correctly to the base word.

1. disturb + s	○ disturbs	○ disturbes	○ disturbbs
2. divide + ing	○ divideing	○ dividing	○ dividding
3. short + est	○ shortest	○ shortst	○ shorttest
4. scrub + ed	○ scrubed	○ scrubied	○ scrubbed
5. simple + ly	○ simplely	○ simplly	○ simply
6. fry + ed	○ fryed	○ fried	○ friied
7. shop + ing	○ shoping	○ shoing	○ shopping
8. dirty + er	○ dirtier	○ dirtyer	○ dirter
9. taste + y	○ tastey	○ tasty	○ tasti
10. happy + ly	○ happly	○ happily	○ happyly

> Read each sentence. Fill in the circle under the word with a suffix in the sentence.

11. John and Emily went hiking on a warm sunny day.
         ○   ○   ○   ○

12. Emily saw a colorful bird on a high tree branch.
     ○   ○   ○   ○

13. John tried to climb the largest tree in the forest.
      ○   ○ ○   ○

14. They saw a rabbit as it was jumping over a narrow stream.
     ○   ○ ○ ○

15. Suddenly, the wind blew dark clouds across the sky.
  ○   ○   ○   ○

16. They hurried home as the rain began to fall.
   ○   ○   ○   ○

Go to the next page. →

> Read each sentence. Fill in the circle beside the word with the correct suffix to complete the sentence and write it on the line.

17. The twins turned around and headed _____.
  ○ homes   ○ homeward

18. I think we're going in the wrong _____.
  ○ directive   ○ direction

19. We sat outside enjoying the _____ of the night.
  ○ stillness   ○ stiller

20. Be careful, since there are _____ objects in that box.
  ○ breaks   ○ breakable

21. _____ your pencils to do these math problems.
  ○ Sharpen   ○ Sharpness

22. The postage for this _____ is very expensive.
  ○ packer   ○ package

23. The police _____ searched for evidence.
  ○ detecting   ○ detective

24. I like to solve multiplication and _____ problems.
  ○ division   ○ divition

> Fill in the circle beside the answer that shows the word divided into syllables correctly.

25. backward   ○ back-ward   ○ bac-kward _____

26. thankfully   ○ thank-full-y   ○ thank-ful-ly _____

27. tiresome   ○ tire-so-me   ○ tire-some _____

28. cleanliness   ○ clean-liness   ○ clean-li-ness _____

29. statement   ○ state-ment   ○ stat-ement _____

30. addition   ○ add-i-tion   ○ ad-di-tion _____

31. insurance   ○ insur-ance   ○ in-sur-ance _____

32. quickened   ○ quick-ened   ○ quick-en-ed _____

Possible score on Unit 3 Pretest is 32. Number correct _____

BLM 18 Unit 3 Pretest: Suffixes *-able, -ward, -ion, -tion, -sion, -en, -ive, -ness*; syllables

61f

▶ In each row, fill in the circle beside the word that shows the suffix added correctly to the base word.

1. laugh + s   ○ laughes   ○ laughs   ○ laughing

2. steady + ly   ○ steadyly   ○ steadily   ○ steadie

3. haste + y   ○ hasty   ○ hastey   ○ hastiy

4. crazy + er   ○ crazyer   ○ crazier   ○ crazery

5. shut + ing   ○ shutting   ○ shuteing   ○ shuting

6. dry + ed   ○ dried   ○ dryed   ○ drid

7. terrible + y   ○ terribly   ○ terriblley ○ terribley

8. grin + ed   ○ grined   ○ grines   ○ grinned

9. smart + est   ○ smarttest   ○ smartest   ○ smarts

10. remove + ing ○ removeing   ○ removveing ○ removing

▶ Read each sentence. Fill in the circle under the word with a suffix in the sentence.

11. I am writing a report on wild cats.
    ○   ○   ○   ○

12. I was worried that I wouldn't find enough information.
        ○   ○   ○   ○

13. Careful research led me to a great book on cheetahs.
    ○   ○   ○   ○

14. I found out that the cheetah is the fastest runner on earth.
    ○   ○   ○   ○

15. It can race across a grassy plain at 60 miles an hour.
        ○   ○   ○   ○

16. Cheetahs only run short distances because they tire quickly.
        ○   ○   ○   ○

Go to the next page. →

BLM 19 Unit 3 Posttest: Suffixes -s, -ed, -ing, -er, -est, -ly, -y; base words

> ▶ Read each sentence. Fill in the circle beside the word with the
> correct suffix to complete the sentence and write it on the line.

17. The boy jumped _____ off the diving board.
   ○ backed   ○ backward

18. We had a _____ about safety rules.
   ○ discussion   ○ discussen

19. Her smile showed her _____.
   ○ happiness   ○ happyness

20. The picnic would have been _____ if it hadn't rained.
   ○ enjoyment   ○ enjoyable

21. Drinking milk will help _____ your bones.
   ○ strengthing   ○ strengthen

22. We lost our _____ on our trip to Florida.
   ○ baggage   ○ bagless

23. My aunt is continuing her _____ at the local college.
   ○ educating   ○ education

24. An ambulance arrived at the scene of the _____.
   ○ collision   ○ collisen

> ▶ Fill in the circle beside the answer that shows the word divided
> into syllables correctly.

25. outward   ○ out-ward   ○ ou-tward _____

26. hopefully   ○ hope-full-y   ○ hope-ful-ly _____

27. awesome   ○ aw-e-some   ○ awe-some _____

28. friendliness   ○ friend-liness   ○ friend-li-ness _____

29. movement   ○ move-ment   ○ mov-ement _____

30. ambition   ○ am-bit-ion   ○ am-bi-tion _____

31. disturbance   ○ disturb-ance   ○ dis-turb-ance _____

32. hurried   ○ hur-ried   ○ hurr-i-ed _____

Possible score on Unit 3 Posttest is 32. Number correct _____

BLM 20 Unit 3 Posttest: Suffixes *-able, -ward, -ion, -tion, -sion, -en, -ive, -ness*; syllables

Student Progress Checklist

Make as many copies as needed to use for a class list. For individual portfolio use, cut apart each student's section. As indicated by the code, color in boxes next to skills satisfactorily assessed and mark an X by those requiring reteaching. Marked boxes can later be colored in to indicate mastery.

STUDENT PROGRESS CHECKLIST
Code: ■ Satisfactory   ☒ Needs Reteaching

| Student: _____

 _____

 Pretest Score: _____

 _____

 Posttest Score: _____

 _____ | Skills
 ❏ Suffixes -s, -ed, -ing
 ❏ Suffixes -er, -est
 ❏ Suffix -ly
 ❏ Suffix -y
 ❏ Identifying Base Words
 ❏ Suffixes -ful, -less, -ment
 ❏ Suffixes -able, -age, -ance
 ❏ Suffix -some
 ❏ Suffixes -ion, -tion, -sion
 ❏ Suffixes -en, -ity, -ive
 ❏ Suffixes -ness, -ward
 ❏ Recognizing Syllables | Comments / Learning Goals |
| Student: _____

 _____

 Pretest Score: _____

 _____

 Posttest Score: _____

 _____ | Skills
 ❏ Suffixes -s, -ed, -ing
 ❏ Suffixes -er, -est
 ❏ Suffix -ly
 ❏ Suffix -y
 ❏ Identifying Base Words
 ❏ Suffixes -ful, -less, -ment
 ❏ Suffixes -able, -age, -ance
 ❏ Suffix -some
 ❏ Suffixes -ion, -tion, -sion
 ❏ Suffixes -en, -ity, -ive
 ❏ Suffixes -ness, -ward
 ❏ Recognizing Syllables | Comments / Learning Goals |

Spelling Connections

INTRODUCTION

The Unit Word List is a comprehensive list of spelling words drawn from this unit. The words are grouped by suffixes studied throughout the unit. To incorporate spelling into your word study program, use the activity in the Curriculum Connections section of each teaching plan.

The spelling lessons utilize the following approach for each set of words.

1. Administer a pretest of the words that have not yet been introduced. Dictation sentences are provided.

2. Provide practice.

3. Reassess. Dictation sentences are provided.

A final review and test is provided at the end of the unit on page 86.

DIRECTIONS

Make a copy of Blackline Master 22 for each student. After administering the pretest for each suffix, give students a copy of the appropriate word list.

Students can work with a partner to practice spelling the words orally and identifying the suffix in each word. You may want to challenge students to add to the list other words with these suffixes. Students can also write words of their own on *My Own Word List* (see Blackline Master 22).

Students may store their list words in envelopes or plastic zipper bags in the backs of their books or notebooks. Alternatively, you may want to suggest that students keep a spelling notebook, listing words with similar suffixes. Another idea is to build word walls with students and display them in the classroom. Each section of the wall can focus on words with a single word study element or suffix. The walls will become a good resource for spelling when students are writing.

UNIT WORD LIST

Suffixes -s, -ed, -ing, -er, -est, -y, -ly; Suffixes with Words Ending in e or that Double the Final Consonant

learns
cheered
warmer
warmest
saving
slipped
icy
foggy
softly
nimbly

Suffixes -less, -ful, -ment, -ness, -able, -age-, -ance, -en, -ity, -ive, -some, -ion, -tion, -sion, -ward; Suffixes with Words Ending in y

cried
fearless
hopeful
equipment
washable
marriage
golden
humidity
active
creation
backward

 **Spelling**   **UNIT 3 WORD LIST**

Suffixes s, ed, ing, er, est, y, ly; Suffixes with Words Ending in e or that Double the Final Consonant

learns	slipped
cheered	icy
warmer	foggy
warmest	softly
saving	nimbly

Suffixes less, ful, ment, ness, able, age, ance, en, ity, ive, some, ion, tion, sion, ward; Suffixes with Words Ending in y

cried	golden
fearless	humidity
hopeful	active
equipment	creation
washable	backward
marriage	

My Own Word List

Word Study Games, Activities, and Technology

The following collection of ideas offers a variety of opportunities to reinforce word study skills while actively engaging students. The games, activities, and technology suggestions can easily be adapted to meet the needs of your group of learners. They vary in approach so as to consider students' different learning styles.

● TOPIC OF THE DAY

Choose a daily topic for each day of the week. Topics can be related to lessons in this unit or to other curricular areas being studied. (Unit 3 topics include Codes and Mysteries, Surfing in Hawaii, and the American Flag.) Help students brainstorm words that are related to the topic. List the words on the board and have volunteers circle the words that contain suffixes. Add the circled words to a word wall, or have students use them to make word cards for sorting activities.

▲ BUILD A WORD BANK

Have each student choose a different suffix studied in the unit. Have students work in groups to brainstorm a list of words containing those suffixes. Groups then exchange their lists and try to add words to the other group's lists. Groups receive one point for each word they can add.

◆ SUFFIX SORT

Provide a set of word cards featuring words with suffixes. Students can work in pairs to read the words and sort them by suffix, by spelling change, or by number of syllables. Then have the class add the words to an already existing word wall.

■ SUFFIX "MAD LIBS"

Students can create their own version of "Mad Libs," using words with different suffixes. List five suffixes studied in the unit, for example, *-ing, -ly, -est, -ment,* and *-able*. Each student makes a list of words containing each suffix and writes a sentence using each word on his or her list. Partners exchange their word lists but keep their own sentences. They then reread their sentences, replacing the word from their list with a word with the same suffix from their partner's list.

✳ SYLLABLE SCRAMBLE

Have groups of students create sets of cards, each set consisting of separate cards for each syllable in a word. The cards should be large and the syllables printed boldly in marker or cut out of brightly colored paper. One group hands out one set of cards to another group so that each student has one syllable card. The second group must then arrange themselves so that their syllables are in the correct sequence to make a word.

● BREAK THE CODE

Write the code shown in the photograph on the chalkboard and have students copy it. Beneath the code, write the following coded words for students to solve: 2–18–9–7–8–20–30 *(brightest)* and 23–15–18–11–28 *(working)*. When students are familiar with the code, pairs of students can create, exchange, and solve coded words containing suffixes.

Variation: Change the code to include additional or different suffixes for another version of this game.

▲ MAKE-A-WORD CARD GAME

Make three cards for each of the following suffixes: *-ed, -ing, -er, -est*. Make an additional twenty word cards using base words such as *work, learn, plant, large, small*. Place the suffix cards in a pile and pass out five word cards to each player. Players take turns choosing a suffix card. If the suffix makes a word with one of the words in his or her hand, the player spells the new word and lays the pair down on the table. If the suffix does not make a word, the player places the suffix card at the bottom of the pile. The first player out of cards wins

● SUFFIX OPPOSITES

Remind students that the suffix *-ful* means "full of," while the suffix *-less* means "without." Help students brainstorm a list of base words that can be used with both *-ful* and *-less*, for example, *hopeful, hopeless; careful, careless; fearful, fearless*. Have students choose a word from the list to illustrate. Divide sheets of drawing paper in half. On one half, students can illustrate the base word plus *-ful*. On the other half, they illustrate the base word plus *-less*.

◆ WORD EQUATIONS

Challenge partners to make up word equations for words with one or more suffixes. Ask partners to exchange papers and solve each other's equations. Write a sample equation on the chalkboard as a model: *surprise - e + ing + ly = surprisingly*.

■ COMPARISONS IN NATURE

Challenge students to make a series of three posters showing comparisons in nature, such as *The Mississippi is a long river. The Amazon is a <u>longer</u> river. The Nile is the <u>longest</u> river.* Encourage students to use almanacs, books of records, and other resource materials to find information about high mountains, small insects, low temperatures, tall trees, and so on. Have students write a sentence using the base word, an *-er* word, or an *-est* word on each poster and illustrate the comparisons.

✳ SUFFIX WHEEL

Students can use word wheels to practice adding suffixes to words. Use a paper plate for the wheel and attach a small tagboard strip on top with a brad. On the strip, write a suffix, such as *-ness*. On the edges of the wheel, write base words, such as *kind, dark, fair, good, sick, late*. As the strip is moved, students can read the new words that are formed.

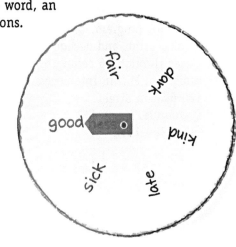

● SUFFIX RUMMY

Have pairs of students make a 24-card deck of word cards. Each deck should contain eight sets of three cards each with words containing the following suffixes: *-age, -ness, -ful, -ive, -ion, -ward, -able,* and *-less.* Students shuffle the decks, pass out eight cards to each other, and place the remaining eight face down on the table. Students try to make sets of three by asking each other for words containing a certain suffix, for example, *Do you have any words with the suffix* -ful? If the other player does not have an appropriate card, the first player draws a card from the pile on the table. The player with the most sets when one player goes out wins.

Variation: Use words containing different suffixes for another version of this game.

▲ SUFFIX BUS

Provide each student with a copy of Blackline Master 23. Have students cut out the square card pattern and then cut out five more cards the same size from a piece of paper. Write the words from List 1 below on the chalkboard. Explain that the goal is to fill the bus with "suffix passengers." Say each word and ask students if that word has a seat on the bus. If it does, they are to write the word on one of their word cards and place the card on the correct seat. Play the game again with the words from List 2.

List 1: *finished, grinning, creation, helps, softly, division, colder, lucky, cheerfully, highest, dirtier, frightening, saving, happily, hiking, finer, kindness, nicest, wrapped, thankful*

List 2: *learned, dripping, equipment, raining, bubbly, impressive, smaller, chilly, wholesome, later, studied, carefully, cutest, merrily, sharpened, paved, hopeless, roughest, slimmer, smiling*

Technology

The following software products are designed to stimulate word play and provide opportunities to "crack the code."

Top Secret Decoder Practice in logical-thinking skills and language is provided for older children through this program, which teaches them how to encode, print, and decode their own written messages through 16 coding tools.
** Houghton Mifflin Interactive
   120 Beacon Street
   Somerville, MA 02143
   (800) 829-7962

Super Solvers: Midnight Rescue! Children ages 8–10 are challenged to catch the Master of Mischief by using thinking, reading, and reasoning skills during a timed video-game format. The program emphasizes reading for main ideas, recalling key facts, drawing inferences, and building vocabulary.
** The Learning Company
   1 Athenaeum Street
   Cambridge, MA 02142
   (800) 227-5609

Name _____

Suffix less, ful, ment, or ness	Base word ending in y	Suffix ive, some, tion, or sion
Double the final consonant of base word	Suffix y or ly	More than one suffix
Suffix s, ed, or ing	Base word ending in e	Suffix compares two or three things

Home Connection

HOME LETTER

A letter is available to be sent home at the beginning of Unit 3. This letter informs family members that students will be learning to read and write words that contain suffixes. The suggested home activities focus on looking for words with suffixes in everyday reading materials, such as newspapers and magazines, and figuring out the meaning of the words. These activities promote interaction between student and family members while supporting students' learning of reading and writing words. A Book Corner feature suggests books that family members can look for in a local library and enjoy reading together. A letter is also available in Spanish on page 61q.

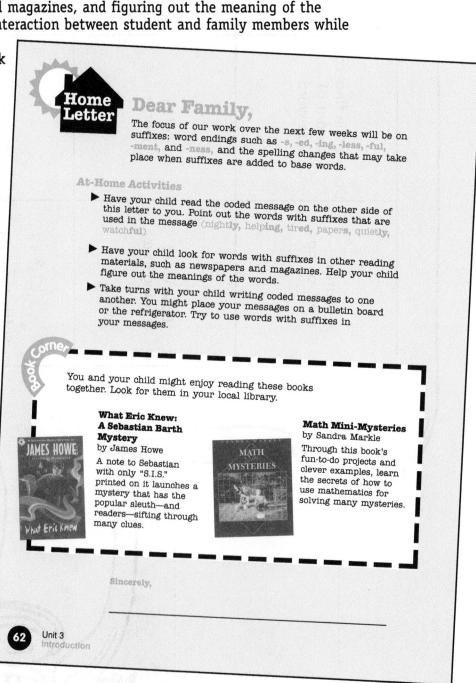

Home Letter

Dear Family,

The focus of our work over the next few weeks will be on suffixes: word endings such as -s, -ed, -ing, -less, -ful, -ment, and -ness, and the spelling changes that may take place when suffixes are added to base words.

At-Home Activities

► Have your child read the coded message on the other side of this letter to you. Point out the words with suffixes that are used in the message (nightly, helping, tired, papers, quietly, watchful)

► Have your child look for words with suffixes in other reading materials, such as newspapers and magazines. Help your child figure out the meanings of the words.

► Take turns with your child writing coded messages to one another. You might place your messages on a bulletin board or the refrigerator. Try to use words with suffixes in your messages.

Book Corner

You and your child might enjoy reading these books together. Look for them in your local library.

What Eric Knew: A Sebastian Barth Mystery
by James Howe

A note to Sebastian with only "S.I.S." printed on it launches a mystery that has the popular sleuth—and readers—sifting through many clues.

Math Mini-Mysteries
by Sandra Markle

Through this book's fun-to-do projects and clever examples, learn the secrets of how to use mathematics for solving many mysteries.

Sincerely,

_____

62 Unit 3
Introduction

Carta para la casa

Estimada familia,

Durante las próximas semanas nos concentraremos en estudiar los sufijos: las terminaciones de palabras en inglés tales como: **-s, -ed, -ing, -less, -ful, -ment** y **-ness** y los cambios ortográficos que pueden ocurrir cuando se agregan sufijos a las palabras base en inglés.

Actividades para hacer en casa

▶ Pídanle a su hijo/a que lea el mensaje en clave en la página 61 de su libro. Señalen las palabras con sufijos usadas en el mensaje: **nightly (cada noche)**; **boatful (barco lleno)**; **helping (ayudando)**; **tired (cansado)**; **papers (papeles)**; **quietly (calladamente)**; **watchful (a la expectativa)**.

▶ Pídanle a su hijo/a que busque palabras con sufijos en otros materiales de lectura tales como periódicos y revistas. Ayuden a su hijo/a a descifrar los significados de las palabras.

▶ Túrnense con su hijo/a en escribirse mutuamente mensajes en clave. Pueden colocar los mensajes en un tablero o en la puerta del refrigerador.

Rincón del libro

Su hijo/a y ustedes pueden disfrutar juntos de la lectura de estos libros. Búsquenlos en la biblioteca de su localidad.

What Eric Knew: A Sebastian Barth Mystery
por James Howe

Una nota hecha para Sebastian sólo con las abreviaturas "S.I.S." escritas en ella, lanza un misterio que tiene al popular investigador—y a los lectores—rebuscando muchas pistas.

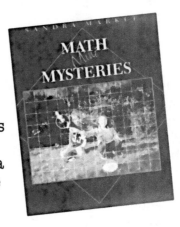

Math Mini-Mysteries
por Sandra Markle

Por medio de los divertidos proyectos de este libro y con sus ingeniosos ejemplos, aprendan los secretos de cómo usar las matemáticas para resolver muchos misterios.

Atentamente, _____

Unit 3

Pages 61–62

Suffixes and Syllables

ASSESSING PRIOR KNOWLEDGE

To assess students' prior knowledge of suffixes and syllables, use the pretest on pages 61e–61f.

Unit Focus

USING THE PAGE

- Explain what a rebus is. Help students say the name of each rebus picture, letter, or number. Then read the message aloud, pausing at each rebus item and having students supply the coded word.

- Invite students to read along with you as you read the message again.

- Ask students what the leaf picture stands for in the last sentence, "Do not 'leaf' footprints." (*the word* leave) Point out that this is a pun, or play on words.

- **Critical Thinking** Read aloud the questions at the bottom of page 61. Encourage students to think of other ways to show the sounds of the words in the message.

BUILDING A CONTEXT

- Write words with suffixes from the coded message on page 61 (*assignment, nightly, boatful, papers, capable, helping, tired, watchful, quietly*) on the board. Tell students that each base word has had a suffix added to it. Have students identify the base words. Remind them that suffixes can change the meaning and use of the base words they're added to.

- Ask students to count the vowel letters in *nightly* and *boatful* and then to count the vowel sounds. Remind them that the number of vowel sounds is the same as the number of syllables. Have students divide the words into syllables.

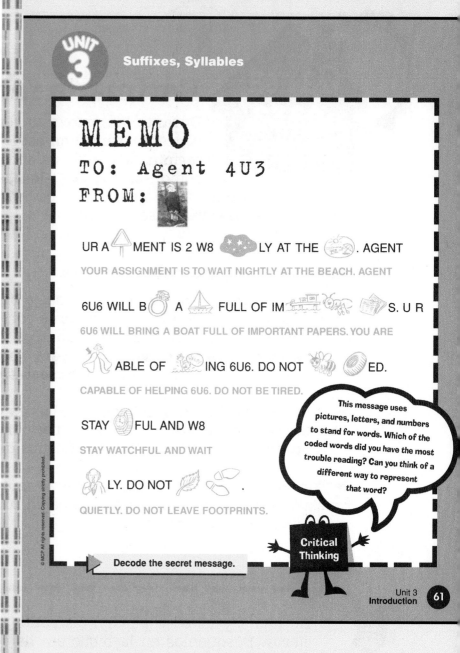

UNIT 3 Suffixes, Syllables

MEMO

TO: Agent 4U3
FROM:

UR A ⊥ MENT IS 2 W8 ⬭⭐ LY AT THE 🏖. AGENT
YOUR ASSIGNMENT IS TO WAIT NIGHTLY AT THE BEACH. AGENT

6U6 WILL B 💍 A ⛵ FULL OF IM 🚢🐜📰 S. U R
6U6 WILL BRING A BOAT FULL OF IMPORTANT PAPERS. YOU ARE

🧤 ABLE OF 🐋ING 6U6. DO NOT 🐝 ⭕ ED.
CAPABLE OF HELPING 6U6. DO NOT BE TIRED.

STAY ⌚ FUL AND W8
STAY WATCHFUL AND WAIT

🤫 LY. DO NOT 🍃 👣 .
QUIETLY. DO NOT LEAVE FOOTPRINTS.

> This message uses pictures, letters, and numbers to stand for words. Which of the coded words did you have the most trouble reading? Can you think of a different way to represent that word?

Critical Thinking

▶ Decode the secret message.

Unit 3 Introduction **61**

UNIT OPENER ACTIVITIES

CODED MESSAGES

Have a volunteer read the decoded message again. Ask students if they know any codes, such as pig Latin, Morse code, or Braille. Then talk about stories they've read that involve a coded message and about the uses of codes such as telegraph messages, smoke signals, and sign language. Discuss which codes are meant to be secret and which are meant to make communication easier.

BREAK THE CODE!

Display the Morse code for each letter and number (A = • –, B = – • • •, and so on). Then write a two- or three-sentence message on the board in Morse code, and challenge students to decipher it.

DO YOU GET THE MESSAGE?

Have students research the semaphore code, a flag code used at sea when radio silence is enforced. Have them make two construction-paper flags (using rulers as handles), make up a short message, and send it to another student who decodes the message and replies.

Home Letter

Dear Family,

The focus of our work over the next few weeks will be on suffixes: word endings such as -s, -ed, -ing, -less, -ful, -ment, and -ness, and the spelling changes that may take place when suffixes are added to base words.

At-Home Activities

▶ Have your child read the coded message on the other side of this letter to you. Point out the words with suffixes that are used in the message (nightly, helping, tired, papers, quietly, watchful)

▶ Have your child look for words with suffixes in other reading materials, such as newspapers and magazines. Help your child figure out the meanings of the words.

▶ Take turns with your child writing coded messages to one another. You might place your messages on a bulletin board or the refrigerator. Try to use words with suffixes in your messages.

 Book Corner

You and your child might enjoy reading these books together. Look for them in your local library.

What Eric Knew: A Sebastian Barth Mystery
by James Howe
A note to Sebastian with only "S.I.S." printed on it launches a mystery that has the popular sleuth—and readers—sifting through many clues.

Math Mini-Mysteries
by Sandra Markle
Through this book's fun-to-do projects and clever examples, learn the secrets of how to use mathematics for solving many mysteries.

Sincerely,

_____

BULLETIN BOARD

Have two teams of students research who developed Braille and who developed American Sign Language. Display their information on a bulletin board entitled "Talking Without Speaking." If possible, include posters of the Braille alphabet and the manual alphabet.

● The Home Letter on page 62 is intended to acquaint family members with the word study skills students will be studying in the unit. Students can tear out page 62 and take it home to share with a family member. Suggest that they also look for the listed books in the library.

● The Home Letter can also be found on page 61q in Spanish.

CURRICULUM CONNECTIONS

 ### WRITING

Portfolio Ask students to imagine they found the message on page 61. Where was it? Who sent the message? What information is in the important papers? Why does Agent 6U6 need help? Have them write a story that answers these questions.

SCIENCE

Materials: potatoes, paper, knife, toothpicks, lamp

Students can make invisible ink and write messages. First cut a potato and scoop out the center, scraping the potato juice into the hole. Then use a toothpick to write a message with the juice. Help students hold the message over a light. As the paper is heated, the message will appear.

MATH

Materials: two identical copies of a book

In one number code, the sender and receiver use identical copies of a book. The sender writes the message of words found in the book, writing numbers to indicate the page, line, and word number of each word. (For example, "15-8-4" would mean page 15, line 8, word 4.) Only a person with the same book could read the code. Suggest that student pairs try it.

Lesson 28

Pages 63–64

Suffixes -s, -ed, -ing

INFORMAL ASSESSMENT OBJECTIVES

Can students

✓ add suffixes -s, -ed, -ing to base words?

✓ associate the suffix -ed with /ed/, /d/, or /t/?

Lesson Focus

INTRODUCING THE SKILL

- Say the word *find* and then say *finds*. Ask students to tell what word part was added. Explain that *find* is a base word and *-s* is a suffix that can be added to the end.

- Write the word *pull* on the board and ask a volunteer to add the suffix *-s*. Then say *pulling* and *pulled*. Encourage volunteers to name the suffixes and write the new words below *pulls*.

- Next write the suffix *-ed*. Explain that when this suffix is added to certain words, it stands for different sounds. Say the words *cheered, jumped,* and *planted* while volunteers write them. Ask students what sound the suffix *-ed* stands for in each word. (/d/, /t/, /ed/) Help students conclude that when *-ed* is added to a base word ending in *d* or *t*, it stands for /ed/; at other times it stands for /d/ or /t/.

USING THE PAGES

Make sure students understand what to do on pages 63 and 64. After completing the pages, have volunteers explain what they learned about adding -s, -ed, and -ing to base words.

63

Name _____

Form new words by adding the suffixes **s, ed,** and **ing** to the base words. Write the new words on the lines.

DEFINITION
The word to which a suffix is added is called the **base word**.

	s	ed	ing
1. cook	cooks	cooked	cooking
2. learn	learns	learned	learning
3. work	works	worked	working
4. clean	cleans	cleaned	cleaning
5. pick	picks	picked	picking
6. help	helps	helped	helping
7. shiver	shivers	shivered	shivering
8. disturb	disturbs	disturbed	disturbing

Write the base word for each word.

9. walks	walk	10. covered	cover
11. guessed	guess	12. frightens	fright
13. talking	talk	14. lifts	lift
15. hitched	hitch	16. cleaned	clean
17. buys	buy	18. raining	rain
19. rolling	roll	20. loves	love
21. packed	pack	22. burned	burn
23. spelling	spell	24. picking	pick

Lesson 28
Suffixes -s, -ed, -ing
63

FOCUS ON ALL LEARNERS

ENGLISH LANGUAGE LEARNERS/ESL

Write *burn, walk, wait,* and *guard* on the board in white chalk. Say each word, then add *-ed* to each word, using red chalk for *wait* and *guard*. Say the words and help students see that *-ed* added to a base word ending in *t* or *d* forms another syllable.

VISUAL LEARNERS

INDIVIDUAL Provide students with the following words: *work, learn, help, wash, call, succeed, cook.* Have students write each word with *-ing, -ed,* and *-s* in these sentence frames: *We are _____ now. I have _____. She _____ every day.*

AUDITORY LEARNERS

SMALL GROUP **Materials:** index cards, small bags

Label the bags /d/, /t/, and /ed/. Have students print the words in items 1–18 on page 64 on index cards and shuffle them, then take turns drawing a card, saying the word, and placing the word card in the bag with the appropriate ending sound.

> Say each word and listen for the sound **ed** stands for. If **ed** has the same sound as in **planted**, write **ed** on the line. If **ed** has a **d** or **t** sound, write **d** or **t** on the line.

RULE

When **ed** is added to a base word ending in **d** or **t**, it stands for the **ed** sound. Other times **ed** will stand for the sound of **d** or **t**.

They plant**ed** a tree.

He cheer**ed** for the team.

She jump**ed** over the rope.

1. learned _d_
2. heaped _t_
3. squirted _ed_
4. walked _t_
5. shirked _t_
6. fixed _t_
7. served _d_
8. scalded _ed_

9. called _d_
10. rushed _t_
11. carted _ed_
12. asked _t_
13. planted _ed_
14. finished _t_
15. turned _d_
16. searched _t_

17. hunted _ed_
18. handed _ed_

> Read each sentence. Circle the word that correctly completes the sentence and write it on the line.

9. Last summer we _____traveled_____ to California.
- tripped
- climbed
- (traveled)

0. We _____departed_____ on a warm, sunny morning.
- (departed)
- fixed
- asked

1. My brother was _____seated_____ next to me.
- (seated)
- moaned
- risked

2. I _____asked_____ him if I could sit by the window.
- planted
- blinked
- (asked)

3. The airplane _____lifted_____ off smoothly.
- loaned
- (lifted)
- hatched

SPELLING

The following sentences can be used as a spelling pretest for words with suffixes *-s, -ed, -ing, -er, -est, -y, -ly*, including words whose base words end in *e* and that require doubling the final consonant.

1. **learns** I hope he **learns** from his mistake.
2. **cheered** We **cheered** as Laura cut the cake.
3. **warmer** I like soup a bit **warmer** than this.
4. **warmest** This is the **warmest** day of the week.
5. **saving** What are you **saving** money to buy?
6. **slipped** Susan **slipped** on the steps and fell.
7. **icy** It was dark and the steps were **icy**.
8. **foggy** Ted hates to drive when it is **foggy**.
9. **softly** People listen when you speak **softly**.
10. **nimbly** A cat ran **nimbly** along the fence.

WRITING

Portfolio Invite students to write a fantasy story about two skunks who take a trip to California. Encourage students to use the verbs *visit, travel, climb, walk, enjoy, bask, sail,* and *stroll* with *-ed* and *-ing* endings in their stories.

SOCIAL STUDIES

When gold was discovered in California, thousands of people rushed to the state, hoping to get rich quick. Have students read about the gold rush and write a short news article about who discovered gold and what happened afterwards. Ask them to circle any *-s, -ed,* or *-ing* endings they use in their articles.

AstroWord Suffixes. © 1998 Silver Burdett Ginn Inc. Division of Simon & Schuster.

AUDITORY/KINESTHETIC LEARNERS

LARGE GROUP

Divide the class into three groups. Assign each team one ending sound: /d/ as in *feared,* /t/ as in *soaked,* /ed/ as in *landed.* Say each base word on pages 63 and 64, using an *-ed* ending. Have students raise their hands when they hear their group's ending sound.

GIFTED LEARNERS

Have students list rhyming words with *-ed* endings that have different spelling patterns, such as *jerked, worked; dressed, test; kissed, mist; turned, earned; called, hauled.* Then suggest they use some of the words to write a rhyming poem.

LEARNERS WHO NEED EXTRA SUPPORT

You may want to pair these students with more proficient partners to complete these pages. See Daily Word Study Practice, page 200.

Lesson 29

Pages 65–66

Comparative Forms -er, -est

✳ · ● · ◆ · ● · ✳ · ● · ◆ · ●

INFORMAL ASSESSMENT OBJECTIVES

Can students

✔ recognize that many words ending in -er are used to compare two things?

✔ recognize that words ending in -est are used to compare more than two things?

✔ add suffixes -er and -est to base words?

✔ write sentences that use the correct comparative form?

Lesson Focus

INTRODUCING THE SKILL

Materials: three pencils of different lengths

● Display the short pencil and ask students for a word that describes its length. (*short*) Place the medium pencil next to the first one. Ask students to compare the pencils. (*shorter* or *longer*) Call on a volunteer to write the comparative word on the board and identify the suffix.

● Display the long pencil. Ask students to describe its length, relative to the other two pencils. (*longest*) Explain that -er is used to compare two things and -est is used to compare more than two things.

USING THE PAGES

Make sure students understand what to do on pages 65 and 66. After completing the pages, have them discuss what they have learned about adding -er and -est to words.

Name

Read each sentence. Underline each word that is used to compare two things. Circle each word that is used to compare more than two things.

RULE

The suffix **er** is added to words to compare two things. The suffix **est** is added to words to compare more than two things.

My jacket is **warm**.
My coat is **warmer**.
My winter parka is the **warmest** of all.

1. This winter went <u>faster</u> than last winter.
2. It is because the weather was <u>nicer</u>.
3. We had the (warmest) winter in ten years.
4. Temperatures were much <u>higher</u> than usual.
5. Some days were <u>warmer</u> than others.
6. Precipitation was <u>lighter</u> than usual.
7. Last year the winter wind was <u>stronger</u>.
8. That wind was the (wildest) I have ever seen.
9. It brought the (lowest) temperatures ever.

Add the suffixes **er** and **est** to form new words.

	er	**est**
10. clear	clearer	clearest
11. dark	darker	darkest
12. low	lower	lowest
13. young	younger	youngest
14. short	shorter	shortest
15. bright	brighter	brightest
16. narrow	narrower	narrowest
17. smooth	smoother	smoothest
18. dull	duller	dullest
19. rough	rougher	roughest

Lesson 29
Comparative forms -er, -est **65**

FOCUS ON ALL LEARNERS ✳ · ● · ◆ · ●

ENGLISH LANGUAGE LEARNERS/ESL

In Spanish and French, comparatives always precede the adjective. (Spanish: *más grande, el más grande*; French: *plus grand, le plus grand*) The suffixes -er and -est may confuse speakers of these languages, so offer extra support.

VISUAL LEARNERS

INDIVIDUAL **Materials:** drawing paper, crayons or markers

Write on the board *tall, sweet, bright, fast, deep, green, small, rich, dark*. Have students choose two words and illustrate each comparative form (for example, *tall, taller, tallest*). Let students share their pictures and talk about them.

KINESTHETIC/VISUAL LEARNERS

PARTNER

Materials: small objects of different sizes and shapes, a bag

Place a dozen items in a bag. Invite partners to take turns pulling out an item and comparing it to the preceding one (for example, *smaller, brighter, straighter, newer*). Then have them choose items that can be described with the comparative form -est.

> Read each sentence. Add **er** or **est** to the words in parentheses to complete the sentence with the correct comparative form. Write the new word on the line.

1. We have the _____greatest_____ class of all! (great)
2. Joe is the _____fastest_____ runner in the class. (fast)
3. He is even _____faster_____ than Rodney. (fast)
4. Pamela gets the _____highest_____ grades of all. (high)
5. She has the _____neatest_____ writing in the class. (neat)
6. I am the _____tallest_____ student in the school. (tall)
7. Even Mr. Stevens is _____shorter_____ than I am! (short)
8. Mr. Stevens is _____funnier_____ than your teacher. (funny)
9. He tells the _____funniest_____ jokes I've ever heard. (funny)
10. I always laugh the _____loudest_____ of all. (loud)

> Write a sentence that tells about each idea listed below. Use a comparative form in each sentence. The first sentence is done for you.

11. the age of two people
Sam is older than Gretchen.

12. the height of three trees
Possible response: This is the tallest tree of the three.

13. the size of two boxes
Possible response: This box is larger than that one.

14. the length of three baseball bats
Possible response: Please hand me the longest baseball bat.

66 Lesson 29
Comparative forms -er, -est

SPELLING

Write on the board the spelling words *learns, cheered, warmer, warmest, saving, slipped, icy, foggy, softly, nimbly*. For each word, call on a student to spell the base word aloud. Then have another student tell what suffix was added to the base word. Have a third student tell what spelling change to the base word, if any, was needed before the suffix was added.

WRITING

Portfolio Invite students to imagine that they are TV meteorologists who write a weather or news report about a day of very exciting weather—unusual changes in temperature, high winds, record rainfall or snowfall. Encourage them to use as many comparative forms as they can.

LANGUAGE ARTS

Read aloud to the class a tall tale that contains many comparatives—stories about Paul Bunyan or Pecos Bill, for instance. Then have pairs collaborate to write their own humorous tall tale. Have volunteers share their tale with the class. As they listen, have the class make a list of words that contain the *-er* or *-est* ending.

MATH

Materials: classroom objects, rulers, scale

Have students measure classroom objects that are similar in weight, length, height, and depth, and use the measurements to make comparisons. Make sure that the comparisons contain the correct comparative forms.

Technology **AstroWord** Suffixes. © 1998 Silver Burdett Ginn Inc. Division of Simon & Schuster.

AUDITORY LEARNERS

SMALL GROUP Have four students sit in a circle. The first says, "I have an old bike"; the second, "My bike is older than yours"; the third, "My bike is the oldest of all." The fourth begins with another noun and adjective (for instance, *plump pig, cold nose*).

GIFTED LEARNERS

Point out that there are many adjectives whose comparatives are not formed by adding *-er* and *-est*, such as *important, dangerous,* and *likely.* Have students list such words and discover how comparisons with these words are made.

LEARNERS WHO NEED EXTRA SUPPORT

Write these words on the board: *brighter, shorter, smarter, neatest, loudest, newest.* Ask students whether each word compares two or more than two things and have a volunteer use it in a sentence that demonstrates that usage. See Daily Word Study Practice, page 200.

Lesson 30

Pages 67–68

Suffixes With Words Ending in Final _e_

INFORMAL ASSESSMENT OBJECTIVES

Can students

✔ apply spelling rules when adding suffixes to base words that end in final _e_?

✔ identify base words in words containing the suffix _-s_, _-ed_, _-ing_, _-er_, or _-est_?

Lesson Focus

INTRODUCING THE SKILL

- Invite volunteers to write _like_, _write_, _safe_, and _wise_ in a column on the board. Ask what these base words have in common. (_All have long vowels; all end with silent_ e.)

- Add the following after the words: _-ed_, _-ing_, _-er_, and _-est_. Ask students how the suffixes are alike. (_All begin with a vowel._) Then ask them what words are formed when the suffixes are added. (_liked_, _writing_, _safer_, and _wisest_)

- Help students conclude that if a word ends with a silent _e_, the _e_ is dropped before adding a suffix that begins with a vowel.

USING THE PAGES

Provide guidance as needed while students complete pages 67 and 68. After students have finished the pages, call on volunteers to summarize for the class the rule for adding suffixes to words ending in silent _e_.

Name

Form new words by adding the correct suffixes. Write the new words on the lines.

> **RULE**
> When a word ends in silent **e**, drop the **e** before adding a suffix that begins with a vowel.
> save + **s** = saves   save + **ed** = saved
> save + **ing** = saving   nice + **er** = nicer
> nice = **est** = nicest

	s	**ed**	**ing**
1. pave	paves	paved	paving
2. tease	teases	teased	teasing
3. blame	blames	blamed	blaming
4. describe	describes	described	describing
5. divide	divides	divided	dividing
6. wave	waves	waved	waving

	er	**est**
7. late	later	latest
8. grave	graver	gravest
9. fine	finer	finest
10. cute	cuter	cutest
11. polite	politer	politest
12. crude	cruder	crudest

Write the base word for each word.

13. skating	skate	14. glides	glide
15. traced	trace	16. hugest	huge
17. grazing	graze	18. later	late

Lesson 30
Suffixes with words ending in final _e_   **67**

FOCUS ON ALL LEARNERS

ENGLISH LANGUAGE LEARNERS/ESL

To build background for the story on page 68, invite students to share their experiences with home video cameras. Talk about the special events that families might want to videotape.

VISUAL LEARNERS

LARGE GROUP

Materials: index cards, markers

Prepare cards with _-s_, _-ed_, and _-ing_. Write _dance_, _smile_, _hike_, _prepare_, _name_, and _rule_ on the board. As a volunteer holds the _-s_ card after each final _e_, the rest of the group writes the words formed. Follow the same procedure with _-ed_ and _-ing_.

KINESTHETIC/VISUAL LEARNERS

SMALL GROUP

Materials: index cards of two colors

Prepare one set of cards with _r_, _u_, _l_, _e_, the other with _-s_, _-ed_, _-ing_. Make duplicates of each set so that there are enough cards for the groups. Shuffle the cards. In turn, players draw one card each round to form _rule_, _ruled_, or _ruling_. If _e_ must be dropped and the player forms the word correctly, he or she gets a point.

Form a new word by putting each base word and suffix together. Write the new word on the line.

> **RULE**
> If a word ends in silent **e**, drop the e before adding a suffix that begins with a vowel.
>
> ride + **ing** = riding

1. dive + ing   diving
2. wave + ing   waving
3. late + est   latest
4. smile + ing   smiling
5. wade + ed   waded
6. leave + ing   leaving
7. come + ing   coming
8. loose + er   looser

9. love + ed   loved
10. wise + er   wiser
11. grade + ed   graded
12. nice + er   nicer
13. cute + est   cutest
14. face + ing   facing

Complete each sentence with one of the new words you formed above.

15. Let's watch the videotape of our _____latest_____ day at the beach.
16. Here we are _____coming_____ up the walkway.
17. Everyone is smiling and _____waving_____ their hands at the camera.
18. Joe is the one not _____facing_____ the camera.
19. Beth really has the _____cutest_____ smile of all of us!
20. Is this part of the _____diving_____ contest?
21. This is when Mom _____waded_____ with Beth in the shallow water.
22. Here we are getting into the car and _____leaving_____ for home.
23. We all certainly _____loved_____ that day at the beach!
24. It was _____nicer_____ than the last time we went.

SPELLING

Materials: number cube

List on the board the numbers 1–6 and draw a smiley face beside the 6. Make yourself a numbered list of these spelling words: 1. *nimbly* 2. *foggy* 3. *slipped* 4. *warmest* 5. *cheered*. Have students take turns rolling a number cube. Dictate the word that matches the number they roll and have them write it on the board. Erase each word after it is written correctly. If they roll the smiley face, they don't have to write a word. Play again with the rest of the words: 1. *learns* 2. *warmer* 3. *saving* 4. *icy* 5. *softly*.

WRITING

Portfolio Have students imagine they are sports commentators. Ask them to write a one–paragraph narrative of part of a sports event, using the present tense to explain what the players are doing. (An example is "*Rico scores a goal!*") Then have them rewrite their narrative in the past tense. Have them circle the *-s, -ed, -ing, -er*, and *-est* endings they used.

PHYSICAL EDUCATION

Materials: markers, crayons or paints, poster paper

Have students find out about different kinds of exercise, then create a poster promoting physical fitness. Encourage them to feature a slogan and facts about the physical benefits gained from exercise. When they are finished, have students make a list of all the words that contain the suffixes they learned so far.

LANGUAGE ARTS

Have students form teams to build words. Prepare a sheet of paper for each team, each with the same five base words from the lesson. Ask the teams to create new words by adding *-s, -ed, -ing, -er*, or *-est* to the base words. Have students begin at the same time, working for perhaps two minutes. The team with the most correctly–spelled words wins.

Technology AstroWord Suffixes. © 1998 Silver Burdett Ginn Inc. Division of Simon & Schuster.

AUDITORY/KINESTHETIC LEARNERS

LARGE GROUP

Have students stand. Read base words from the lesson along with the ending to add; for example, "*Cute*—add *-er*." Have students chorus "Drop the *e*!" each time e should be dropped. Anyone shouting "Drop the *e*!" when you've asked for *-s* must sit down.

GIFTED LEARNERS

Challenge students to prepare an activity like the one at the bottom of page 68 for classmates to complete. The sentences should form a coherent story, and the answer words should be provided in a word bank in random order.

LEARNERS WHO NEED EXTRA SUPPORT

Work with students as they begin page 68. Be sure each student has successfully completed several items before continuing independently.
See Daily Word Study Practice, page 200.

Lesson 31
Pages 69–70

Words That Double the Final Consonant to Add a Suffix

INFORMAL ASSESSMENT OBJECTIVES

Can students

✔ apply the spelling rule to double the final consonant before adding the suffix?

✔ add the suffixes -ed, -ing, -er, and -est to base words?

Lesson Focus

INTRODUCING THE SKILL

● Write the words *sad* and *sadder* on the board. Ask students to name the suffix. Encourage students to describe how the base word was changed when the suffix was added. (*The final consonant was doubled.*)

● Explain that when a one-syllable, short-vowel word ends in a single consonant, the consonant is doubled before a suffix that begins with a vowel is added.

● Have volunteers add the suffixes -ed and -ing to *wrap* and *slip*, and -est to the word *hot*. Encourage them to use the rule about doubling the final consonant, and to explain what they did.

USING THE PAGES

● Make sure that students understand how to complete pages 69 and 70 before they begin to work.

● When students have completed the pages, call on volunteers to explain how to add suffixes to one-syllable, short-vowel words.

69

Name _____

▷ Circle each word that ends in a single consonant. Then add the suffixes to make new words.

> **RULE**
> When a one-syllable short-vowel word ends in a single consonant, double the consonant before adding a suffix that begins with a vowel.
> slip   slipped   slipping

	ed	**ing**
1. (fit)	fitted	fitting
2. act	acted	acting
3. (wrap)	wrapped	wrapping
4. rest	rested	resting
5. (blot)	blotted	blotting
6. (knit)	knitted	knitting

	er	**est**
7. (fat)	fatter	fattest
8. fond	fonder	fondest
9. (mad)	madder	maddest
10. (hot)	hotter	hottest
11. cold	colder	coldest
12. (sad)	sadder	saddest

▷ Circle each word with a suffix and write its base word on the line.

13. Our cat, Alex, (washed) his fur.   wash
14. Then he (wrapped) himself into a ball.   wrap
15. Alex lay on the windowsill and (napped.)   nap
16. He will be (resting) until bedtime!   rest

Lesson 31
Words that double the final consonant to add a suffix
69

FOCUS ON ALL LEARNERS ※ • ◆ ● ●

ENGLISH LANGUAGE LEARNERS/ESL

Pronounce lesson words with students to be sure they are saying the base words correctly. Provide extra practice in doubling the final consonant before adding suffixes by demonstrating with these words: *big, fat, thin, red, cut, win, drum.*

VISUAL LEARNERS

LARGE GROUP

Write a base word on the board. Have students call out "Double it!" if the final consonant should be doubled when a suffix is added. Invite a volunteer to add a suffix and write the new word. Use these words: *flat, swim, nap, dark, tall, fast, warm, drip, grin, rest, slip.*

KINESTHETIC/VISUAL LEARNERS

SMALL GROUP

Materials: index cards, marker, scissors

Have each student make five word cards using words that have a doubled consonant in front of the suffix -er, -est, -ed, or -ing. Then have students cut the words apart between the doubled consonants. Have the group pool their word parts, mix them up, and reassemble them together.

Form a new word by putting each base word and suffix together. Write the new word on the line.

> **RULE**
> When a one syllable short-vowel word ends in a single consonant, double the consonant before adding a suffix that begins with a vowel.
>
> ma**d** ma**dder** ma**ddest**

1. slim + er — slimmer
2. flat + er — flatter
3. bold + est — boldest
4. run + ing — running
5. grin + ed — grinned
6. scrub + ed — scrubbed
7. drip + ing — dripping
8. plot + ed — plotted
9. swim + ing — swimming
10. hot + est — hottest
11. set + ing — setting
12. hug + ed — hugged

Complete each sentence with one of the new words you formed above. Then circle the base word in the word you wrote.

13. Diane, an explorer, was __(set)ting__ out on an exciting trip.
14. On the __(hot)test__ day of the summer, she departed.
15. She had __(plot)ted__ her course on a map.
16. Diane would be __(run)ning__ along trails part of the time.
17. She would move easily over the __(flat)ter__ terrain.
18. When she reached the river, she would do some __(swim)ming__.
19. The sun would quickly dry her wet and __(drip)ping__ clothes.
20. Diane __(hug)ged__ her parents before leaving.
21. She __(grin)ned__ happily as she waved goodbye.

AUDITORY/VISUAL LEARNERS

LARGE GROUP Write *hope, hoped,* and *hoping* on the board and say the words aloud. Write *hop* and have students say *-ed* and *-ing* forms of the word. Write, "The rabbit hoped/hopped across the lawn" and have a volunteer circle the correct word and read the sentence aloud.

GIFTED LEARNERS

Suggest that the group write a progressive story. In turn, each student writes a sentence containing a different word whose final consonant has been doubled before adding a suffix. Have students continue until they have completed a coherent story.

LEARNERS WHO NEED EXTRA SUPPORT

Write *later* and *batter*. Say the words with students. Then write *fat*. Ask students *How would you write the comparative form of fat, like later or batter?* (*batter*) Write *taping* and *napping*, and ask how they would write the *-ing* form of *wrap*. See Daily Word Study Practice, page 200.

CURRICULUM CONNECTIONS

SPELLING

Write on the board the base words *save, learn, ice, warm, nimble, soft, cheer, slip, fog.* Write these sets of words and ask students to identify base words that could have the same ending added in the same way.

1. drummed/hugged/stopped (*slip, fog*)
2. hardly/sickly/costly (*soft, warm*)
3. soared/opened/feared (*cheer, learn, warm*)
4. sunny/muddy/baggy (*fog*)
5. longest/smallest/quickest (*warm, soft*)
6. simply/bristly/crumbly (*nimble*)
7. poky/shiny/fleecy (*ice*)
8. hoping/caring/loving (*save, ice*)
9. comes/eats/burns (*learn, save, warm, cheer, slip*)
10. sweeter/older/calmer (*warm, soft*)

WRITING

Portfolio Encourage students to reread the story on page 70 about Diane's trip. Then have them add a few sentences telling about her continuing adventure. What will be on the other side of the river? How will she respond to the encounter? Will she be excited? surprised? fearful?

MATH

Suggest that students collect words that have doubled consonants before suffixes and make a table to sort the words according to the doubled consonant. Which consonants are doubled most? least?

PHYSICAL EDUCATION

Have students line up across one end of the room or gym. When they hear you say an action word, they perform the action only if the word has a doubled consonant. If the word does not have a doubled consonant, anyone who moves is out. Use these words: *hopping, jogging, jumping, strutting, running, dancing, stepping, twirling, spinning, skipping, waltzing.*

Technology **AstroWord** Base Words and Endings. © 1998 Silver Burdett Ginn Inc. Division of Simon & Schuster.

Lesson 32

Pages 71–72

Suffixes -y, -ly; Words Ending in le

INFORMAL ASSESSMENT OBJECTIVES

Can students

✓ apply the spelling rules when adding -y and -ly to base words?

✓ apply the spelling rule when adding -ly to base words that end in le?

Lesson Focus

INTRODUCING THE SKILLS

● Have a volunteer write the word *ice* on the board. Write + *y* next to the word. Ask how the base word should be changed to add the suffix. Have the student write *icy.* Explain that when a word ends in silent e, the e is dropped before adding -*y*.

● Ask how -*y* can be added to *fog.* Help students conclude that in a word ending in a single consonant preceded by a short vowel sound, the final consonant is doubled before adding -*y*.

● Introduce the suffix -*ly.* Write *quietly* on the board and explain that the suffix -*ly* forms words that tell how.

● Point out that when -*ly* is added to a word ending in *le,* the *le* is dropped. Call on a volunteer to write *nimble* and apply the rule for adding -*ly*.

USING THE PAGES

Go over the directions and rules on pages 71 and 72. When students have completed the pages, have one volunteer who understands the concepts review them for the class.

71

Name _____

> Form new words by adding the suffix **y** to the base words. Write the new words on the lines.

> **RULE**
> When a word ends in silent **e**, drop the **e** before adding **y**. When a word ends in a single consonant preceded by a short-vowel sound, double the consonant before adding **y**.
> ice + y = icy   fog + y = foggy

1. crab _____ crabby
2. luck _____ lucky
3. spice _____ spicy
4. edge _____ edgy
5. haste _____ hasty
6. chill _____ chilly
7. flop _____ floppy

8. rose _____ rosy
9. noise _____ noisy
10. smog _____ smoggy

> Read each sentence. Complete the sentence by adding **ly** to the correct word in the word bank. Write the new word on the line.

> **RULE**
> The suffix **ly** can be added to many words to form a word that tells how.
> soft + ly = softly

11. Dana and Tad's baby-sitting business is _____ slowly _____ becoming a success.
12. They take their job _____ seriously _____.
13. They look forward _____ gladly _____ to the children's arrival.
14. When the baby naps, Tad asks the others not to play _____ loudly _____.
15. Dana also tells the children to talk _____ quietly _____.
16. Before they go home, the children must put away their toys _____ neatly _____.

glad
loud
slow
quiet
serious
neat

FOCUS ON ALL LEARNERS

ENGLISH LANGUAGE LEARNERS/ESL

Students learning English may have trouble—particularly out of context—with the idiomatic uses of some of these words with -y or -ly added. Define such words as *crabby, edgy,* and *pebbly* before students begin the pages.

VISUAL LEARNERS

PARTNER   **Materials:** index cards, markers, a small box

On index cards have pairs write six base words that take -y and six that take -ly from page 71. Have students put the cards in the box and take turns drawing a card, writing the word with -y or -ly, and saying it.

KINESTHETIC LEARNERS

SMALL GROUP   Read the sentences below. Have students demonstrate each, then write the word or words that end in -y. *1. I feel all limp and floppy. 2. I'm quite nervous and edgy today. 3. I feel grumpy and crabby. 4. It's chilly with the window open.*

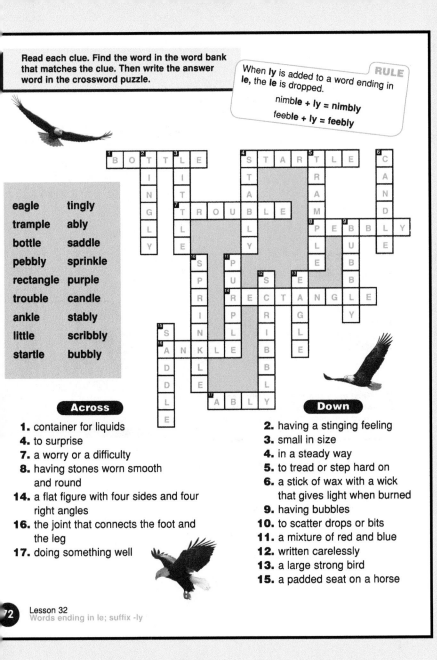

Read each clue. Find the word in the word bank that matches the clue. Then write the answer word in the crossword puzzle.

RULE

When **ly** is added to a word ending in **le**, the **le** is dropped.

nim**ble** + ly = nimbly
fee**ble** + ly = feebly

Word Bank

eagle	tingly
trample	ably
bottle	saddle
pebbly	sprinkle
rectangle	purple
trouble	candle
ankle	stably
little	scribbly
startle	bubbly

Across

1. container for liquids
4. to surprise
7. a worry or a difficulty
8. having stones worn smooth and round
14. a flat figure with four sides and four right angles
16. the joint that connects the foot and the leg
17. doing something well

Down

2. having a stinging feeling
3. small in size
4. in a steady way
5. to tread or step hard on
6. a stick of wax with a wick that gives light when burned
9. having bubbles
10. to scatter drops or bits
11. a mixture of red and blue
12. written carelessly
13. a large strong bird
15. a padded seat on a horse

Lesson 32
Words ending in le; suffix -ly

SPELLING

The following sentences can be used as a spelling posttest for words with suffixes -s, -ed, -ing, -er, -est, -y, -ly, including words whose base words end in e and that require doubling the final consonant.

1. **foggy** — London is known for **foggy** days.
2. **slipped** — Dad **slipped** a dollar into my hand.
3. **cheered** — Seeing my friends **cheered** me up.
4. **softly** — The dove cooed **softly** in its nest.
5. **warmer** — Your hands are **warmer** than mine.
6. **nimbly** — Lee climbed **nimbly** up the cliff.
7. **warmest** — He gave us his **warmest** smile.
8. **icy** — I was glad he didn't give us an **icy** glare!
9. **learns** — The student who listens **learns**.
10. **saving** — Dawn's hobby is **saving** stamps.

WRITING

Portfolio Have students write a TV commercial. Suggest that they begin by deciding on their product, then brainstorm words to describe it and the feelings of someone using or eating it. Besides a written script, students might like to make storyboards to show how scenes from the commercial might look. Encourage them to use words ending with -y and -ly.

ART

Have each student make a crayon drawing that represents a word from the lesson. Pictures can be literal (a saddle, an eagle) or figurative (noisy or bubbly). Display the pictures and let students guess what words are illustrated.

Technology

AstroWord Suffixes. © 1998 Silver Burdett Ginn Inc. Division of Simon & Schuster.

AUDITORY/VISUAL LEARNERS

LARGE GROUP On the board, write these words: *little, sparkle, double, rifle, sensible, noble, beagle, cradle, ukulele, wriggle, snuggle, single, bicycle, possible, drizzle, gamble, riddle*. Have students try to add -ly orally to each word and use it in a sentence. Which are real words when -ly is added? Have students use each word in a sentence of their own.

GIFTED LEARNERS

Discuss nouns that become describing words when -y is added (for example, *dirt, dirty; juice, juicy*) and adjectives that become adverbs when -ly is added (*neat, neatly; gentle, gently*). Have students brainstorm other examples of word pairs in which addition of -y or -ly changes the function of the first word.

LEARNERS WHO NEED EXTRA SUPPORT

On index cards write these words: *health, speed, sad, quick, spice, drizzle*. Put the cards in the box. Then write -y and -ly on the board, and call on students to pick a card and hold it in front of the appropriate suffix. Then have them write the words on the board.

See Daily Word Study Practice, pages 200-201.

Lesson 33

Pages 73–74

Suffixes With Words Ending in y

Lesson Focus

INTRODUCING THE SKILL

● Tell students that there are other words besides those that end in a silent *e* that must be changed before adding a suffix.

● Have a volunteer write *cry* on the board. Ask students how they might add the *-es*. Explain that when a word ends in *y* preceded by a consonant, the *y* is changed to *i* before adding the suffix. Write *happy*. Have a student apply the rule to make *happily*.

● Tell students that there are exceptions to the *y* to *i* rule. Write the words crying, dryly, and enjoys. Help them conclude that *y* is not changed to *i* when adding *-ing*, as in crying, when adding *-ly* to a one-syllable word ending in *y* preceded by a consonant, as in dryly, or when adding a suffix to a word that ends in *y* preceded by a vowel, as in enjoys.

USING THE PAGES

● Make sure students understand what to do on pages 73 and 74.

● After students have finished, ask a volunteer to explain how to add suffixes to words ending in *y*.

73

Name

▶ Form a new word by combining each base word and suffix. Write the new word on the line.

1. fly + es	flies
2. employ + s	employs
3. dirty + er	dirtier
4. coy + ly	coyly
5. fly + ing	flying
6. clumsy + ly	clumsily
7. study + ed	studied
8. sly + ly	slyly
9. curl + er	curlier
10. reply + ed	replied

> **RULE**
>
> If a word ends in **y** preceded by a consonant, change the **y** to **i** and add **es**, **ed**, or **ly**. Do not change the **y** to **i** when adding the suffix **ing** or when adding **ly** to a one-syllable word that ends in **y** preceded by a consonant. If a word ends in **y** preceded by a vowel, just add the suffix.
>
> cry + **es** = **cries**
> cry + **ed** = **cried**
> happy + **ly** = **happily**
> cry + **ing** = **crying**
> dry + **ly** = **dryly**
> enjoy + **s** = **enjoys**

▶ Read each sentence. Underline each word with a suffix added to a base word that ends in **y**. Then write the base word on the line.

11. We were all <u>studying</u> together at the library.	study
12. Helen <u>multiplied</u> numbers on her calculator.	multiply
13. Tomás <u>copied</u> his rough draft.	copy
14. I <u>shyly</u> asked a librarian for help.	shy
15. The librarian said she <u>enjoyed</u> helping me.	enjoy
16. <u>Luckily</u> she found the book I needed.	lucky

Lesson 33
Suffixes with words ending in y
73

FOCUS ON ALL LEARNERS

ENGLISH LANGUAGE LEARNERS/ESL

Use sentence frames to show students how suffixes change the use of a word. For example: *I cry, She <u>cries</u>, Yesterday I <u>cried</u>, Now I am <u>crying</u>;* and *I am <u>clumsy</u>, You are <u>clumsier</u> than I, He is <u>clumsiest</u> of all, He did it <u>clumsily</u>.*

VISUAL LEARNERS

LARGE GROUP Write the following words on the board: *crying, hurries, spies, messier, shyly, silliest, healthier, annoying.* Have students write the base words and explain how the suffixes were added.

KINESTHETIC LEARNERS

SMALL GROUP **Materials:** a tagboard spinner with three sections, markers

Label the spinner sections *-s, -es, -ed, -ing.* Fasten a spinner to the center. Write on the board these words: *stay, study, spy, cry, hurry,* and *rely.* Have students choose a base word, spin, and write the word with the indicated suffix added. Repeat the procedure with the suffixes *-er, -est,* and *-ly,* using these words: *pretty, heavy, muddy, shy, ugly, spooky.*

Form new words by adding suffixes to base words. Write the words on the lines.

		s/es	**ed**	**ing**
cry	1.	cries	cried	crying
enjoy	2.	enjoys	enjoyed	enjoying
reply	3.	replies	replied	replying
carry	4.	carries	carried	carrying
play	5.	plays	played	playing
study	6.	studies	studied	studying

		er	**est**	**ly**
clumsy	7.	clumsier	clumsiest	clumsily
easy	8.	easier	easiest	easily
lucky	9.	luckier	luckiest	luckily
sly	10.	slyer	slyest	slyly
scary	11.	scarier	scariest	scarily
heavy	12.	heavier	heaviest	heavily

Read the passage. Underline words with y that have had suffixes added.

In the 1700s, ladies often wore straw bonnets. These were imported from other countries because they could not be made easily at home. Then a woman named Betsey Metcalf invented an easier way of braiding the straw. She taught her method to many women employed in bonnet making. Because she never applied for a patent, however, she couldn't profit from her discovery.

SPELLING

The following sentences can be used as a spelling pretest for words with suffixes added to base words that end in *y* and for those with the suffixes *-less, -ful, -ment, -ness, -able, -age, -ance, -en, -ity, -ive, -some, -ion, -tion, -sion,* and *-ward.*

1.	**cried**	Kelly rocked the baby when it **cried**.
2.	**fearless**	I'm timid, but my sister is **fearless**.
3.	**hopeful**	Are you **hopeful** about the future?
4.	**equipment**	I'll carry the soccer **equipment**.
5.	**washable**	My new sweater is not **washable**.
6.	**marriage**	He took her hand in **marriage**.
7.	**golden**	The queen wore a **golden** crown.
8.	**humidity**	**Humidity** makes my hair curl.
9.	**active**	**Active** sports are good exercise.
10.	**creation**	My costume is my own **creation**.
11.	**backward**	Can you run **backward**?

WRITING

Portfolio Have students choose one of the following sayings and write a paragraph about the meaning and whether they agree with it:

No use crying over spilled milk.
Many a good tune is played on an old fiddle.
Don't jump out of the frying pan into the fire.

After students finish writing, have them underline each word in which a suffix has been added to the base word.

SOCIAL STUDIES

Help students understand that helping people is an important part of a librarian's job. Ask a librarian to visit the classroom and talk about the work and the kinds of questions people ask.

AstroWord Suffixes. © 1998 Silver Burdett Ginn Inc. Division of Simon & Schuster.

AUDITORY LEARNERS

LARGE GROUP Read a list of base words ending in *y* and have students listen to each word, think of a suffix that can be added to it, and say the new word. Try these words: *lucky, deny, angry, merry, spy, heavy, stay, enjoy, satisfy.*

GIFTED LEARNERS

Have students list words ending in *y* that are nouns and tell whether the same *y* to *i* rules are used to make them plural. *(toy, fly, party, pony, joy, day, lady, baby, Friday, ferry, trolley)*

LEARNERS WHO NEED EXTRA SUPPORT

As students complete these pages, stop by each student's desk to answer questions and review together work already finished. See *Daily Word Study Practice, pages 200–201.*

Suffixes -less, -ful, -ment, -ness, -able, -age, -ance

✳ ◦ ◦ ◦ ◦ ✳ ◦ ◦ ◦ ◦ ◦ ●

INFORMAL ASSESSMENT OBJECTIVE

Can students

✓ add the suffixes -less, -ful, -ment, -ness, -able, -age, and -ance to base words?

Lesson Focus

INTRODUCING THE SKILL

● Introduce the lesson suffixes by writing the following words on the board: *statement, darkness, hopeful, fearless, baggage, enjoyable, reliance.* Invite volunteers to circle the base words and name the suffixes that are left.

● Discuss any spelling changes made in the base words. (*consonant doubled in* bag; y *changed to* i *in* rely)

● Explain that some suffixes have meanings and that their meanings can change a base word's meaning slightly. Provide the following definitions: *-less* = "without"; *-ful* = "full of"; *-ment* = "the act of"; *-ness* = "being"; *-able* = "can be"; *-age* = "the result of"; *-ance* = "the state of being".

● Have volunteers apply the meanings to the words on the board and use the words in sentences.

USING THE PAGES

● Be sure students understand how to complete pages 75 and 76.

● When they have finished, have them exchange papers for correcting. Call on volunteers to summarize what they learned about the suffixes.

75

Name _____

▶ **Circle the suffix in each word.**

1. pay(ment)
2. need(less)
3. glad(ness)
4. state(ment)
5. hope(ful)
6. fear(less)
7. thank(ful)
8. great(ness)
9. mind(ful)
10. good(ness)
11. dark(ness)
12. govern(ment)
13. rest(ful)
14. fair(ness)
15. ship(ment)
16. develop(ment)

▶ **Form a new word by putting each base word and suffix together. Write the new word on the line. Then use the words you wrote to complete the sentences below.**

17. equip + ment _____equipment_____
18. help + ful _____helpful_____
19. color + ful _____colorful_____
20. spot + less _____spotless_____
21. cold + ness _____coldness_____
22. assign + ment _____assignment_____
23. cheer + ful _____cheerful_____
24. hope + less _____hopeless_____
25. fear + less _____fearless_____
26. kind + ness _____kindness_____
27. bright + ness _____brightness_____
28. enjoy + ment _____enjoyment_____

29. The newly fallen snow raised my spirits and made me _____cheerful_____.

30. The _____brightness_____ of the sunlight on the snow hurt my eyes.

31. The _____coldness_____ of the air nipped my nose.

32. I had my ski _____equipment_____ with me.

33. The ski instructor gave me some _____helpful_____ tips.

34. I was _____fearless_____ as I skied down the hill.

35. When I got to the bottom, my _____assignment_____ was complete.

FOCUS ON ALL LEARNERS ✳ ◦ ◦ ◦ ◦

ENGLISH LANGUAGE LEARNERS/ESL

To build background for the items 29–35 on page 75, encourage students to talk about their experiences on the ski slope. Discuss the weather conditions good for skiing and the equipment and clothing needed for the sport.

VISUAL LEARNERS

LARGE GROUP Write the following vertical lists side by side on the board and have volunteers draw a line from the base word to the suffix that forms a word. Use the base words *spot, cool, post, avail, content, health, allow;* and the suffixes *-age, -able, -ment, -ness, -ance, -less, -ful.*

KINESTHETIC LEARNERS

PARTNER Have partners clap slowly in time. One starts by saying *-less, -ful, -ness,* or *-ment;* the other thinks of a word with that suffix and then supplies the next suffix. Have students try to keep the rhythm. (An example is *"Less!"* clap, *clap, clap, "Helpless!" clap, clap, clap.*)

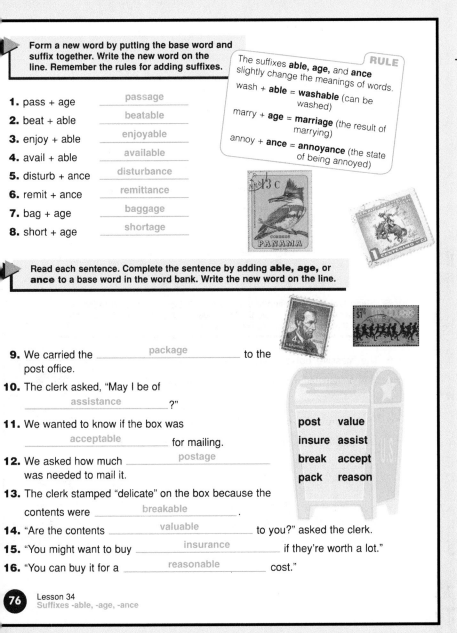

Form a new word by putting the base word and suffix together. Write the new word on the line. Remember the rules for adding suffixes.

RULE

The suffixes **able**, **age**, and **ance** slightly change the meanings of words.

wash + **able** = **washable** (can be washed)

marry + **age** = **marriage** (the result of marrying)

annoy + **ance** = **annoyance** (the state of being annoyed)

1. pass + age   passage
2. beat + able   beatable
3. enjoy + able   enjoyable
4. avail + able   available
5. disturb + ance   disturbance
6. remit + ance   remittance
7. bag + age   baggage
8. short + age   shortage

Read each sentence. Complete the sentence by adding **able**, **age**, or **ance** to a base word in the word bank. Write the new word on the line.

9. We carried the _____ package _____ to the post office.

10. The clerk asked, "May I be of _____ assistance _____?"

11. We wanted to know if the box was _____ acceptable _____ for mailing.

12. We asked how much _____ postage _____ was needed to mail it.

13. The clerk stamped "delicate" on the box because the contents were _____ breakable _____.

14. "Are the contents _____ valuable _____ to you?" asked the clerk.

15. "You might want to buy _____ insurance _____ if they're worth a lot."

16. "You can buy it for a _____ reasonable _____ cost."

post	value
insure	assist
break	accept
pack	reason

76   Lesson 34
Suffixes -able, -age, -ance

SPELLING

Materials: index cards, markers

Write on the board *backward, creation, active, humidity, golden, marriage, washable, hopeful, equipment, cried, fearless*. Make a base word card and suffix card for each word, duplicating as needed so that each student gets a card. Shuffle and distribute the cards. Have students find a partner with the other half of their spelling word. Then ask the pair to write their word.

WRITING

Portfolio

Materials: books on winter sports, travel brochures

Let students read about winter sports and examine some travel brochures. Then have them work in pairs to write and illustrate a brochure for a ski resort. Suggest that they use as many words with suffixes as possible in describing the features of their ski area.

MATH

Have students find out how much it costs to send first-class mail in the United States for up to one ounce and for each additional full or partial ounce, then make up math problems for others to solve. For example: If a letter weighs two-and-a-half ounces, how much will it cost to mail? (*at 33 cents for the first ounce and 22 cents for each additional ounce, 77 cents*)

SCIENCE

Coldness—what is considered *cold* in your climate? Have students find out about average lows for your locale for this month and how the average compares to the record low. Students can also compare their local temperatures with those of other areas. Encourage them to organize the information they have gathered in a chart form.

Technology

AstroWord Suffixes. © 1998 Silver Burdett Ginn Inc. Division of Simon & Schuster.

AUDITORY LEARNERS

SMALL GROUP

Have each student, in turn, choose a word with a suffix from this lesson and say a context sentence for the word, leaving the word out. Group members try to guess what the word is.

GIFTED LEARNERS

Materials: dictionaries

Have students list base words that can take more than one lesson suffix and the resulting words: for example, *help, helpful, helpless; govern, government, governable, governance*. Have them use a dictionary to confirm that the words they build are real words.

LEARNERS WHO NEED EXTRA SUPPORT

Because there are so many suffixes to think about in this lesson, you may want to have some students work on only one or two of the activities. Explain that other suffixes are added in the same way.
See Daily Word Study Practice, pages 201–202.

Suffixes -en, -ity, -ive, -some, -ion, -tion, -sion

INFORMAL ASSESSMENT OBJECTIVES

Can students

✔ apply spelling rules when adding suffixes -en, -ity, -ive, -some, -ion, -tion, and -sion to base words?

✔ complete sentences, using the correct words?

Lesson Focus

INTRODUCING THE SKILL

● Ask students to listen for the suffixes -en, -ity, -ive, -some, -ion, -tion, and -sion as you read aloud these words: *earthen, humidity, attractive, worrisome, rotation, creation, collision.*

● Have volunteers write the words on the board and circle the suffixes. Discuss any spelling changes in the base words.

● Provide meanings for the suffixes: *-en* = "to make or become like"; *-ity* = "the quality of being"; *-ive* = "full of"; *-some* = "having or like"; *-ion, -tion,* and *-sion* = "act, condition, or result of". Then have students use the meanings to define the words on the board.

USING THE PAGES

● Make sure students know what to do on pages 77 and 78. After they have completed the pages, have them form small groups to review what they have learned about adding suffixes.

● **Critical Thinking** Have a volunteer read the questions on page 78 aloud. Have students compare the activities in their school to those at Oak Park School.

Name _____

▶ Form a new word by putting the base word and suffix together. Write the new word on the line.

RULE
The suffixes **en, ity, ive,** and **some** change the way a base word is used.
gold + **en** = **golden** (to make or become like gold)
humid + **ity** = **humidity** (the quality of being humid)
act + **ive** = **active** (full of action)
lone + **some** = **lonesome** (having a lonely feeling)

1. detect + ive ____ detective
2. whole + some ____ wholesome
3. sad + en ____ sadden
4. disrupt + ive ____ disruptive
5. tire + some ____ tiresome
6. sharp + en ____ sharpen
7. national + ity ____ nationality
8. universe + ity ____ university

▶ Read each sentence and find the picture that goes with it. Write the number of the sentence on the line under the picture. Then circle each word that contains **ity, en, ive,** or **some.**

9. The (massive) hot-air balloon was (awesome.)
10. The (broken) lamp suggested the (possibility) of foul play.
11. The speaker was (impressive) and not (tiresome.)
12. The (quarrelsome) cat jumped on the (wooden) box.
13. The (creative) artist painted an (impressive) (golden) sun.

10

13

9

11

12

FOCUS ON ALL LEARNERS

ENGLISH LANGUAGE LEARNERS/ESL

Make sure students understand the meanings of the base words and suffixes in this lesson. Ask Spanish speakers how they would say and write the same ideas in Spanish. Be aware that many *-tion* words in Spanish are spelled with *c* (*donación, educación,* for example).

VISUAL LEARNERS

LARGE GROUP

Have students copy this story from the board and circle words with suffixes: *Kyle watched a news show on television. An impressive discussion on pollution featured a well-known authority who gave some worrisome facts. She said the situation could only worsen.*

KINESTHETIC LEARNERS

LARGE GROUP

Materials: index cards, marker

Write the suffixes for this lesson across the board (with *-ion, -tion,* and *-sion* in a group). Make a base-word card for each student. On a signal, have students walk to a suffix that works with their base word. Have each student say the complete word aloud. Shuffle the cards and play again.

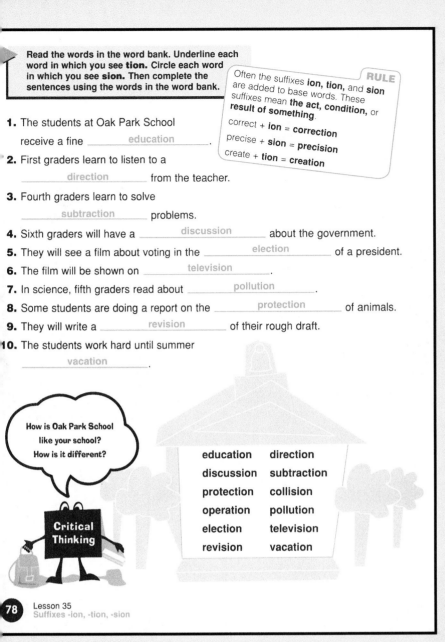

Read the words in the word bank. Underline each word in which you see **tion**. Circle each word in which you see **sion**. Then complete the sentences using the words in the word bank.

RULE

Often the suffixes **ion, tion,** and **sion** are added to base words. These suffixes mean **the act, condition,** or **result of something.**

correct + **ion** = **correction**

precise + **sion** = **precision**

create + **tion** = **creation**

1. The students at Oak Park School receive a fine _____education_____.

2. First graders learn to listen to a _____direction_____ from the teacher.

3. Fourth graders learn to solve _____subtraction_____ problems.

4. Sixth graders will have a _____discussion_____ about the government.

5. They will see a film about voting in the _____election_____ of a president.

6. The film will be shown on _____television_____.

7. In science, fifth graders read about _____pollution_____.

8. Some students are doing a report on the _____protection_____ of animals.

9. They will write a _____revision_____ of their rough draft.

10. The students work hard until summer _____vacation_____.

How is Oak Park School like your school? How is it different?

Critical Thinking

education	direction
discussion	subtraction
protection	collision
operation	pollution
election	television
revision	vacation

SPELLING

Materials: index cards, marker

Make a card for each student with a spelling word on each. (*fearless, equipment, washable, golden, active, creation, humidity, marriage, hopeful, cried*) On some cards, spell the words correctly; on others, spell them incorrectly. Shuffle the cards and give one to each student. On your signal, have students go to two areas—*Correct Spelling* and *Incorrect Spelling*. Check the cards in each group. Anyone in the wrong group is out of the game. Play again.

WRITING/MUSIC

Portfolio Have students list words that end with *-ion*, *-tion*, and *-sion* and then write a rap song using their words. Let volunteers practice their raps and perform them for the class.

SOCIAL STUDIES/LANGUAGE ARTS

What's going on at your school today? Have students find out what other classes (all grade levels) are doing today and write a bulletin entitled "On This Day at [your school name]." The bulletin can be duplicated so that each class can have a copy.

SOCIAL STUDIES

Materials: state map

Display a large map of your state. Write a numbered list of ten names of other cities, towns, and physical features in your state on the board for students to locate. Have students locate the places and write the direction each place is from your school. Before beginning, you might want to review how to use a compass rose and how to write directions.

AstroWord Suffixes. © 1998 Silver Burdett Ginn Inc. Division of Simon & Schuster.

AUDITORY LEARNERS

INDIVIDUAL **Materials:** tape recorder, blank tapes

Have students read words ending with *-ion*, *-tion*, and *-sion* into the recorder, leaving about ten seconds between the words. Then have them play back their tape and write each word. You may want to have students exchange tapes.

GIFTED LEARNERS

Have pairs list words ending in *-sion* and *-tion* (not *ition*). Ask them to examine the words and draw conclusions about what base-word spellings usually take each ending. Here are some words to get them started: *pretension, intrusion, admission, attention, promotion, permission, adoption.*

LEARNERS WHO NEED EXTRA SUPPORT

Have students work with one suffix at a time. For example, write these words and have students add *-en* to each to form a new word: *wool, silk, gold, thick, dark, tough, glad.* Discuss the meaning of the *-en* suffix. **See Daily Word Study Practice, page 201–202.**

Lesson 36
Pages 79–80

Suffix -ward; Words With More Than One Suffix

INFORMAL ASSESSMENT OBJECTIVES

Can students

✔ identify the meaning of words with the suffix -*ward*?

✔ identify suffixes in words with multiple suffixes?

Lesson Focus

INTRODUCING THE SKILLS

Materials: colored chalk

- Invite students to name some of the suffixes they have been studying. Add to their list the suffix -*ward*.

- Write -*ward* on the board, explaining that this suffix means "in the direction of" or "toward." Ask students to suggest a word with this suffix that means "in the direction of home." (*homeward*)

- Tell students that some words may have more than one suffix. Call on volunteers to write the words *saddened, surprisingly, enjoyably,* and *frightening* on the board.

- Have students identify the base word and then underline the suffixes in each word with different colors of chalk. Discuss spelling changes when suffixes are added.

USING THE PAGES

Make sure students understand what to do on pages 79 and 80. When they have completed the pages, review the lesson together.

Name _____

Read the sentence in each box. Draw a picture to show what the sentence means. Then circle the words in the sentence that have the suffix **ward**.

> **RULE**
> The suffix **ward** means **in the direction of** or **toward**.
> back + ward = backward (toward the back)
> home + ward = homeward (in the direction of home)

1. Kurt looked (upward) and saw a colorful balloon drifting (toward) him.

2. Mother stopped the car from rolling (backward) down the hill.

3. The hikers carefully climbed (downward) from the top of the mountain.

4. The band marched (forward, toward) the center of town.

Lesson 36
Suffix -ward **79**

FOCUS ON ALL LEARNERS

ENGLISH LANGUAGE LEARNERS/ESL

To familiarize students with vocabulary for page 80, make a word web with *museum* in the center. Invite students to talk about museums they have visited and what they saw at each. Add such words as *skeleton, dinosaur, mammoth, exhibits,* and *guide* to the web.

VISUAL LEARNERS

LARGE GROUP On the board, list base words (*care, thought, help, fear, defense, attract, act, straight, dark, soft, sharp*) and suffixes (*-ful, -ly, -ing, -ness, -some, -en, -ing, -ive, -ed, -ity, -able*). Have students choose one base word, add two suffixes that fit, and write the word they have made.

KINESTHETIC LEARNERS

SMALL GROUP Have students follow these commands: *Tiptoe forward soundlessly. Point skyward excitedly. Go toward the windows with great cheerfulness. Cringe backward fearfully. Gesture outward expressively.* Each time have students name the suffixes you used.

You will often read words that have more than one suffix. Each word below has two suffixes. In each word, underline the first suffix and circle the second suffix.

1. careful**ly**
2. sharpen**ed**
3. seeming**ly**
4. surprising**ly**
5. alarming**ly**
6. frighten**ing**
7. cheerful**ness**
8. hearten**ed**
9. sadden**ed**
10. handsome**ly**
11. active**ly**
12. flatten**ed**
13. acceptan**ces**
14. defensive**ly**
15. enjoya**bly**

Read each sentence. Underline the word with more than one suffix. Then write the base word on the line.

16. Our trip to the museum went surprisingly quickly.

surprise

17. We appreciated the thoughtfulness of our guide.

thought

18. The guide told us to study the exhibits carefully.

care

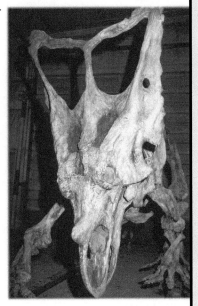

19. The dinosaur exhibit was attractively displayed.

attract

20. Some of the skeletons were alarmingly huge.

alarm

21. A live mammoth would have been frightening.

fright

22. The guide involved us actively in discussions.

act

23. He cheerfully answered all our questions.

cheer

24. We were saddened when it was time to leave.

sad

SPELLING

Make two identical lists of the spelling words, scrambled and numbered. (Words: *golden, backward, humidity, fearless, cried, equipment, marriage, creation, active, washable, hopeful*) Divide students into two teams lined up at the board. Give the first person in each team the scrambled list. That student unscrambles the first word, writes it on the board, and passes the list to the second student, and so on. The team to unscramble all the words first wins.

WRITING

 Portfolio Have students list directional words that contain the suffix *-ward*, then write a story about a stone that rolls from place to place, using the words they listed to tell where the stone rolls and what it sees and does. Encourage students to share their stories with the class.

SCIENCE

Assign each student a prehistoric animal, such as the mammoth, mastodon, or pterodactyl. Have students research their animals, make a class time line to show when each animal lived, and present brief oral reports to the class.

LANGUAGE ARTS

Explain that a palindrome is a word, phrase or sentence that reads the same way forward and backward. Write some of these on the board and ask students to add others: *rotor, gag, kayak, tot, radar, pep, did, eye, nun, level, noon, peep, toot, sees, deed, eve, pop, dud.* Then write these sentences and encourage students to figure out how the sentences were made: *Madam, I'm Adam. Step on no pets. A man, a plan, a canal—Panama! Name no one man.* Invite students to create their own sentences that are palindromes.

 AstroWord Suffixes. © 1998 Silver Burdett Ginn Inc. Division of Simon & Schuster.

AUDITORY LEARNERS

LARGE GROUP Read aloud a random list of words with one or two suffixes that students have been studying. Before saying each word, call on a different student to listen carefully and identify how many suffixes the word has.

GIFTED LEARNERS

Have students list the suffixes they know, then list words that have more than two suffixes (*respectfully, deniably, frighteningly*, for example).

LEARNERS WHO NEED EXTRA SUPPORT

To reinforce meaning before doing the activity on page 79, have students act out these words with you: *upward, downward, backward, forward, toward.* See Daily Word Study Practice, pages 201–202.

Lesson 37
Pages 81–82

Syllables

INFORMAL ASSESSMENT OBJECTIVES

Can students

✔ identify the number of syllables in a word?

✔ apply spelling rules to syllabicate compound words, words with suffixes, and words ending in *le*?

Lesson Focus

INTRODUCING THE SKILL

● Have students name the number of syllables in these words: *storage, readiness,* and *respectful.* Ask how they decided on the number of syllables. (*listened for the vowel sounds*)

● Write these words on the board: *good, sunset, sewing, cable,* and *tackle.* Ask students to draw lines between the syllables as you explain these rules:

1. Never divide a one-syllable word.

2. Divide a compound word between the two smaller words.

3. Divide a word with a suffix between the base word and the suffix.

4. Divide a word ending in a consonant and *le* before the consonant; however, if the word ends in *ckle,* divide it between *ck* and *le.*

USING THE PAGES

Make sure students understand what to do on pages 81 and 82. After completing both pages, have students exchange papers and check each other's work.

Name _____

For each word, write the number of vowels you see, the number of vowel sounds you hear, and the number of syllables.

	Vowels You See	Vowel Sounds You Hear	Syllables		Vowels You See	Vowel Sounds You Hear	Syllables
cloudy	3	2	2	curly	2	2	2
carrier	3	3	3	happiness	3	3	3
cheer	2	1	1	sleepier	4	3	3
fanciest	3	3	3	heavily	4	3	3
pities	3	2	2	handsome	3	2	2
available	5	4	4	paying	3	2	2
storage	3	2	2	nationality	6	5	5
carrying	3	3	3	equipment	4	3	3
employment	4	3	3	insurance	4	3	3
disruptive	4	3	3	fog	1	1	1
dust	1	1	1	destroying	4	3	3
readiness	4	3	3	collision	4	3	3
sharpen	2	2	2	rectangle	3	3	3
humidity	4	4	4	longingly	3	3	3
northward	2	2	2	defensive	4	3	3
buckle	2	2	2	lucky	2	2	2
hedge	2	1	1	laughter	3	2	2
rehearse	4	2	2	spaghetti	3	3	3
shoulder	3	2	2	sailor	3	2	2
mosquito	4	3	3	conscious	4	2	2

FOCUS ON ALL LEARNERS

ENGLISH LANGUAGE LEARNERS/ESL

Students learning English will need to be able to pronounce the words accurately before completing these pages. Work with them, or pair them with fluent English speakers.

VISUAL/KINESTHETIC LEARNERS
LARGE GROUP

Write a list of simple compound words on the board and have students pronounce and define them. Ask volunteers to divide each word by drawing a line between the two smaller words. Let students suggest other compound words for division.

KINESTHETIC LEARNERS

SMALL GROUP

Materials: index cards, markers, scissors

Have each student print five words from page 82 in fairly large letters on cards and cut each word apart into its two syllables, following the rules. Have the entire group mix up their syllables and work together to reassemble the words.

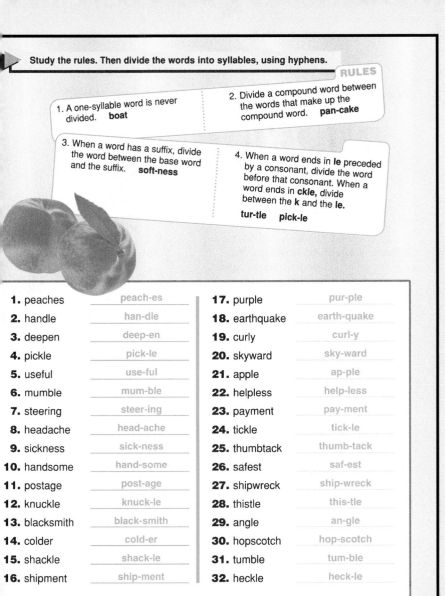

Study the rules. Then divide the words into syllables, using hyphens.

RULES

1. A one-syllable word is never divided. **boat**

2. Divide a compound word between the words that make up the compound word. **pan-cake**

3. When a word has a suffix, divide the word between the base word and the suffix. **soft-ness**

4. When a word ends in **le** preceded by a consonant, divide the word before that consonant. When a word ends in **ckle**, divide between the **k** and the **le**.
   tur-tle   **pick-le**

1. peaches	peach-es		17. purple	pur-ple
2. handle	han-dle		18. earthquake	earth-quake
3. deepen	deep-en		19. curly	curl-y
4. pickle	pick-le		20. skyward	sky-ward
5. useful	use-ful		21. apple	ap-ple
6. mumble	mum-ble		22. helpless	help-less
7. steering	steer-ing		23. payment	pay-ment
8. headache	head-ache		24. tickle	tick-le
9. sickness	sick-ness		25. thumbtack	thumb-tack
10. handsome	hand-some		26. safest	saf-est
11. postage	post-age		27. shipwreck	ship-wreck
12. knuckle	knuck-le		28. thistle	this-tle
13. blacksmith	black-smith		29. angle	an-gle
14. colder	cold-er		30. hopscotch	hop-scotch
15. shackle	shack-le		31. tumble	tum-ble
16. shipment	ship-ment		32. heckle	heck-le

AUDITORY LEARNERS

SMALL GROUP Read to the group a random list of one– and two–syllable words. Have them call out "No!" after the one–syllable words and "Yes–yes!" after the two–syllable words.

GIFTED LEARNERS

Materials: dictionaries

Write *mul-ti-cul-tur-al* and *un-be-liev-a-bil-i-ty* on the board, divided into syllables. Challenge students to write other multisyllablic words and try dividing them according to the examples and the rules on page 82. Encourage them to check their syllabication in a dictionary.

LEARNERS WHO NEED EXTRA SUPPORT

Check on students' progress as they complete these pages to make sure they are comfortable following the directions and writing in the appropriate columns. See Daily Word Study Practice, page 208.

CURRICULUM CONNECTIONS

SPELLING

Write all the spelling words on the board (*golden, backward, humidity, fearless, cried, equipment, marriage, creation, active, washable, hopeful*), but leave a blank for every other letter. (Example for *humidity*: h_m_d_t_.) Call on students to come to the board and complete any word.

WRITING

 Portfolio Have students try writing a paragraph using only words of one syllable. Then have them try to write another paragraph, using only words of two syllables. Let students compete, if they want to, receiving a point for each word with the correct number of syllables. The student with the most points wins.

LANGUAGE ARTS

Challenge students to collect words that have more vowels than consonants. Some examples are *receive, earache, tuition, goalie.*

ART

Materials: paints, crayons, markers, poster paper

Have each student make an eye–catching poster, presenting one of the rules for dividing words on page 82. Choose one poster for each rule and display all four together on the bulletin board.

Technology

AstroWord Multisyllabic Words. © 1998 Silver Burdett Ginn Inc. Division of Simon & Schuster.

Lesson 38

Pages 83–84

Reading **W**riting

Reviewing Suffixes

INFORMAL ASSESSMENT OBJECTIVES

Can students

✔ read a magazine article containing words with suffixes?

✔ write a magazine article, using words with suffixes?

Lesson Focus

READING

- Write *waits, staying, excited, patiently, excitement, successful, calmer,* and *finest* on the board. Have volunteers read the words and underline the suffixes. Remind students how the suffix changes the meaning of each base word.

- Write *Juan shouted. He was excited.* Then write *Juan shouted _____.* Ask students to add a second suffix to *excited* to make it describe how Juan shouted. (*excitedly*)

- Explain to students that when they read the magazine article about surfing on page 83, they will be reading many more words with suffixes.

WRITING

Tell students to imagine that they are reporters at a surfing competition and write a children's magazine article about it on page 84. For ideas about what details to include, remind students to refer to the Helpful Hints.

83

 Reading ▶ Read the article about surfing. Then write your answer to the question at the end of the passage.

SURFING:
Riding a Wall of Water

*T*he sport of surfing has been practiced for centuries in Hawaii and other Pacific islands. Today, millions of people around the world enjoy the excitement of riding the fastest, tallest waves they can find.

To begin, the surfer, lying flat or kneeling, paddles his board out to the seaward side of the breaking waves. Then he waits patiently for the perfect wave. When he sees the wave he starts paddling toward shore as fast as he can. When the wave reaches the surfer, the board lifts upward and speeds up rapidly. The surfer moves to a standing position and rides down the awesome wall of water, staying just ahead of the breaking crest. To be successful, the surfer must be capable of timing this movement perfectly.

The ride ends when the surfer leans backward to slow the board down and then kicks out over the unbroken wave into the calm waters behind it. An unsuccessful surfer who loses the race against the breaking wave can be "wiped out" (smashed onto the sea floor) by the weight of the collapsing water!

*S*urfing, like skiing and skateboarding, requires balance, timing, and coordination. What sport do you think is the most exciting? Why?

_____
_____
_____
_____
_____
_____

FOCUS ON ALL LEARNERS ✳ • ◆

ENGLISH LANGUAGE LEARNERS/ESL

To build background, ask if anyone has ever gone surfing or body-surfing in the ocean. Encourage students to talk about any surfing they may have watched in person or on television.

VISUAL LEARNERS

LARGE GROUP

Write these base words on the board: *care, enjoy, act, lone, soft, connect, polite, thick, complete, love, argue, happy, post, home,* and *equal.* Write one suffix from this unit at a time at the top of the board and have students tell you which base words can take that suffix. Have students say the complete words, then write them.

KINESTHETIC/AUDITORY LEARNERS

SMALL GROUP

Materials: butcher paper, markers, scissors

Have students make a paper surfboard. Then let them take turns standing on it and pantomiming surfing. Say a word and have the surfer tell you how many syllables it has. If correct, the surfer goes again. If not, he or she "wipes out" and pantomimes falling!

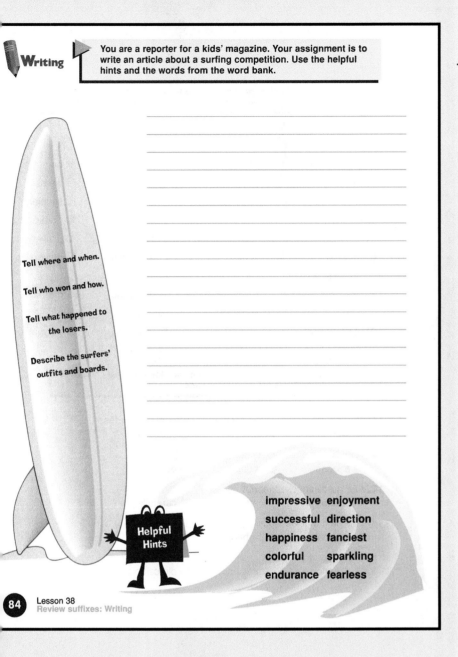

Writing

You are a reporter for a kids' magazine. Your assignment is to write an article about a surfing competition. Use the helpful hints and the words from the word bank.

Tell where and when.

Tell who won and how.

Tell what happened to the losers.

Describe the surfers' outfits and boards.

Helpful Hints

impressive	enjoyment
successful	direction
happiness	fanciest
colorful	sparkling
endurance	fearless

CURRICULUM CONNECTIONS ✳ • ◆ • •

SPELLING

The following sentences can be used as a spelling posttest for words with suffixes added to base words that end in *y* and for those with the suffixes *-less, -ful, -ment, -ness, -able, -age, -ance, -en, -ity, -ive, -some, -ion, -tion, -sion,* and *-ward.*

1. **golden** — I walked in **golden** fields of wheat.
2. **hopeful** — The game contestant was **hopeful.**
3. **backward** — Walk **backward** and forward.
4. **washable** — Is it dry-cleanable, or **washable**?
5. **humidity** — **Humidity** is the air's moisture.
6. **active** — Marla is **active** in the chess club.
7. **fearless** — The **fearless** hero saved two boys.
8. **creation** — The baker's **creation** was a cake.
9. **cried** — When Chris cut his hand, he **cried.**
10. **marriage** — Love and **marriage** go together.
11. **equipment** — This is my fishing **equipment.**

ART

Have students design a fancy surfboard and surfing outfit and then draw a picture of a surfer standing on the beach with the board. Have them add a voice balloon for their surfer, in which the surfer says a sentence that tells how he or she feels about the equipment.

PHYSICAL EDUCATION

Have students work in groups to create a small brochure about swimming safety tips. Students can research topics, such as how to keep from getting too cold, how to prevent sunburn, and how to avoid drowning.

 Technology **AstroWord** Suffixes. © 1998 Silver Burdett Ginn Inc. Division of Simon & Schuster.

 LARGE GROUP

AUDITORY/KINESTHETIC LEARNERS

Materials: index cards in two colors, markers

Have students make *yes* cards from one color, *no* cards with the other. Read aloud the words below. Have students raise *yes* if the *y* changes to *i* before adding a suffix, *no* if it doesn't. Use these words: *hurry, reply, enjoy, ugly, sly, merry, play, fancy, say, copy.*

GIFTED LEARNERS

Materials: children's sports magazines

Have students read a sports magazine and collect more sports words that have the suffixes they learned about in this unit.

LEARNERS WHO NEED EXTRA SUPPORT

As a prewriting activity, have students plan what happens in their surfing competition. Have them limit the contest to three surfers, name the surfers, decide the order they surf in, and decide who wins before they start writing. See Daily Word Study Practice, pages 200–202.

Lesson 39

Pages 85–86

Unit Checkup

Reviewing Suffixes

Can students

✔ identify and write correct spellings of words with suffixes?

✔ read text that includes words with suffixes?

✔ read a passage and then answer comprehension questions about the passage?

Lesson Focus

PREPARING FOR THE CHECKUP

- Write on the board the following words and ask students what they have in common: *properly, facing, raised, upward, helpless, thicken, happiness, creation.* (*They all have suffixes.*) Have students identify each suffix, then name other suffixes they have studied in this unit.

- Write these words and ask what they have in common: *friendlier, hopelessly, forgetfulness, longingly, darkening.* (*They each have two suffixes.*) Have students identify the base words.

USING THE PAGES

- Make sure students understand the directions on page 85.

- Before students read the passage on page 86, ask them to say the Pledge of Allegiance and think about what the words mean. Remind students to write the answers in complete sentences.

85

Name _____

UNIT 3 CHECKUP

▶ Fill in the circle beside the word that correctly combines each base word and suffix. Write the word on the line.

1. home + ward	*homeward*	○ homward	● homeward
2. wet + est	*wettest*	● wettest	○ wetest
3. simple + ly	*simply*	● simply	○ simplely
4. precise + sion	*precision*	○ precisesion	● precision
5. act + ive + ly	*actively*	○ activly	● actively
6. universe + ity	*university*	○ universsity	● university
7. dry + es	*dries*	● dries	○ dryes
8. marry + age	*marriage*	○ marryage	● marriage
9. fog + y	*foggy*	○ fogy	● foggy
10. value + able	*valuable*	● valuable	○ valueable

▶ Read each sentence. Fill in the circle beside the word that completes the sentence. Write the word on the line.

11. We ___*saddled*___ up the horses for a ride in the desert.
○ saddleed   ● saddled   ○ saddlied

12. A pack horse carried all our ___*baggage*___ .
● baggage   ○ bagage   ○ bagge

13. Our guide checked us out ___*carefully*___ .
○ carefuly   ○ carfully   ● carefully

14. She said that we would ___*probably*___ make camp at dusk.
○ probabley   ○ probablely   ● probably

15. We headed off in the ___*direction*___ of the mountains.
● direction   ○ directtion   ○ direcsion

FOCUS ON ALL LEARNERS

ENGLISH LANGUAGE LEARNERS/ESL

Take students outside and show them the flag flying outside the school. Ask if they know what the stars and stripes stand for. Encourage students to talk about other flags they know.

VISUAL/KINESTHETIC LEARNERS

LARGE GROUP

On the board write a number of multisyllablic words such as *organization, weightlifter, competition, calendar, yesterday, measurement, million.* With colored chalk, divide each word into syllables, marking some words correctly and others incorrectly. Ask volunteers to come to the board and correct the words you have divided incorrectly.

KINESTHETIC LEARNERS

PARTNER   **Materials:** index cards, markers

Make cards for base words and suffixes that go together and + and = signs. One student chooses a base word and a suffix and writes an equation for a partner to solve. (An example is *smile + ing = _____.*) The partner writes the complete word on a card and places it after the equal sign. Have partners switch roles.

▶ **Read the passage. Then answer the questions at the end of the passage.**

THE AMERICAN FLAG

The sight of the U.S. flag can be awesome. It is a powerful symbol of our country's greatness. As our country's symbol, the flag must be treated respectfully, never carelessly. Congress has written laws and guidelines for the flag's care and handling.

The flag should always be displayed near the main administration building of every public institution. That includes every school, college, and university. It must be flown at government buildings. The flag should never be displayed lower than other flags. It should be in the center—at the highest point—in a fan-shaped group of flags. When carried, the flag should be held aloft and free.

The flag should never appear on anything temporary or disposable, such as paper napkins, paper plates, or boxes. Its image should not appear on easily soiled items. It should never be used for advertising.

When the flag is raised, lowered, or presented, people in uniform, like soldiers and police officers, should stand at attention and salute. Others should stand facing forward, with their right hands over their hearts.

1. What is the flag a symbol of?

   The flag is a symbol of our country's greatness.

2. How should the U.S. flag be treated?

   It should be treated respectfully.

3. Where should the U.S. flag be displayed?

   It should be displayed at all public institutions.

4. On what items should the flag's image never appear?

   The flag should never appear on temporary or disposable items.

5. What should people do when the flag is raised or lowered?

   They should stand at attention.

86 Lesson 39
Suffixes: Checkup

AUDITORY LEARNERS

Have students close their eyes, listen as you read a list of multisyllablic words, and tell you how many syllables there are in each word. Use these words: *prefer, foundation, secret, sensation, hypnotize, disaster, encourage,* and *tournament.*

GIFTED LEARNERS

Materials: dictionaries

Challenge students to write a word with each number of syllables up to eight, such as *egg, parlor, services, additional, university, misinterpretation, indivisibility,* and *institutionalization.* Then have them divide each word they wrote by syllable. Encourage them to check their syllabication in a dictionary.

LEARNERS WHO NEED EXTRA SUPPORT

Before having students work independently, you might wish to model the first item in each activity on page 85. See Daily Word Study Practice, pages 200–202.

ASSESSING UNDERSTANDING OF UNIT SKILLS

Student Progress Assessment Review the observational notes you made as students worked through the activities in this unit to help you evaluate the progress they made with words that have suffixes and varying numbers of syllables.

Portfolio Assessment Review the students' portfolios with them, and discuss their written work and the progress they have made since the beginning of the unit. As you review students' work, evaluate their mastery of various suffixes and syllabication.

Daily Word Study Practice If students need additional practice with suffixes and syllabication, use the quick reviews on pages 200–202 in Daily Word Study Practice.

Word Study Posttest To assess students' mastery of words with suffixes and multisyllabic words, use the posttest on pages 61g–61h.

Spelling Cumulative Posttest Review Unit 3 spelling words by using the following words and dictation sentences.

1.	**saving**	I'm **saving** money by shopping here.
2.	**icy**	An **icy** glass of lemonade sounds good.
3.	**humidity**	The **humidity** makes the heat unbearable.
4.	**cried**	"Come back!" **cried** Tom.
5.	**backward**	Look **backward** into history.
6.	**equipment**	My mom sells office **equipment**.
7.	**nimbly**	Her fingers **nimbly** tied the yarn.
8.	**foggy**	My glasses are too **foggy** to see.
9.	**warmest**	I send my **warmest** wishes to your family.
10.	**active**	Opossums are most **active** at night.
11.	**marriage**	Laura and Ty exchanged **marriage** vows.
12.	**slipped**	The afternoon has **slipped** away.
13.	**creation**	Artists love the joy of **creation**.
14.	**golden**	Her skin had a **golden** glow.

Teacher Notes

Contents

Student Performance Objectives

In Unit 4, students will review and extend their understanding of vowel pairs, vowel digraphs, diphthongs, and syllables. As these skills are developed, students will be able to

♦ Associate vowel pairs with their sounds

♦ Associate vowel digraphs with their sounds

♦ Associate diphthongs with their sounds

♦ Recognize the number of syllables in words that contain vowel pairs, vowel digraphs, and diphthongs

Assessment Strategy Overview

Throughout Unit 4, assess students' ability to read and write words containing vowel pairs, vowel digraphs, and diphthongs and to recognize syllables in words with vowel pairs. There are various ways to assess students' progress. You may also want to encourage students to evaluate their own work and to participate in setting goals for their own learning.

FORMAL ASSESSMENT

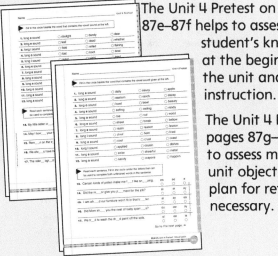

The Unit 4 Pretest on pages 87e–87f helps to assess a student's knowledge at the beginning of the unit and to plan instruction.

The Unit 4 Posttest on pages 87g–87h helps to assess mastery of unit objectives and to plan for reteaching, if necessary.

INFORMAL ASSESSMENT

The Reading & Writing pages and Unit Checkup in the student book are an effective means of evaluating students' performance.

Skill	Reading & Writing Pages	Unit Checkup
Vowel Pairs *ai, ay*	105–106	119–120
Vowel Pair *ow*	105–106	119–120
Vowel Pairs *ei, ee, ea*	105–106	119–120
Vowel Pairs *oe, oa*	105–106	119–120
Vowel Pair *ie*	105–106	119–120
Vowel Digraph *ea*	105–106	119–120
Vowel Digraphs *aw, au*	105–106	119–120
Vowel Digraph *oo*	117–118	119–120
Diphthongs *ou, ow*	117–118	119–120
Diphthongs *oi, oy*	117–118	119–120
Diphthong *ew*	117–118	119–120
Syllables	117–118	119–120

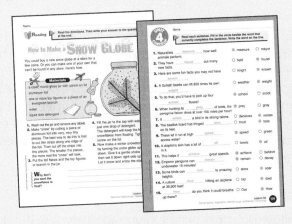

PORTFOLIO ASSESSMENT

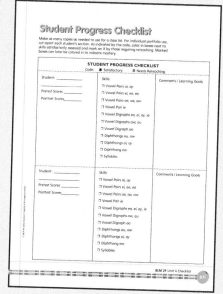

Portfolio This logo appears throughout the teaching plans. It signals opportunities for collecting students' work for individual portfolios. You may also want to collect the following pages.

❖ Unit 4 Pretest and Posttest, pages 87e–87h

❖ Unit 4 Reading & Writing, pages 105–106, 117–118

❖ Unit 4 Checkup, pages 119–120

STUDENT PROGRESS CHECKLIST

Use the checklist on page 87i to record students' progress. You may want to cut the sections apart to place each student's checklist in his or her portfolio.

Administering and Evaluating the
Pretest and Posttest

DIRECTIONS

To help you assess students' progress in learning Unit 4 skills, tests are available on pages 87e–87h. Administer the Pretest before students begin the unit. The results of the Pretest will help you identify each student's strengths and needs in advance, allowing you to structure lesson plans to meet individual needs. Administer the Posttest to assess students' overall mastery of skills taught in the unit and to identify specific areas that will require reteaching.

PERFORMANCE ASSESSMENT PROFILE

The following chart will help you identify specific skills as they appear on the tests and enable you to identify and record specific information about an individual's or the class's performance on the tests.

Depending on the results of the tests, refer to the Reteaching column for lesson-plan pages where you can find activities that will be useful for meeting individual needs or for daily word study practice.

ANSWER KEYS

Unit 4 Pretest, page 87e (BLM 25)

1. daily 2. decay 3. bowl 4. ceiling 5. toe 6. street 7. reason 8. fried 9. coast 10. applied 11. seize 12. crayons

13. ee 14. ay 15. ai 16. ow 17. ie

Unit 4 Pretest, page 87f (BLM 26)

18. dreadful 19. autumn 20. chowder 21. driftwood 22. voyage 23. chewing 24. gloomy 25. squawk 26. poison 27. clown 28. blew

29. 3 30. 2 31. 2 32. 2 33. 2 34. 2 35. 1 36. 2 37. 2 38. 3

Unit 4 Posttest, page 87g (BLM 27)

1. daylight 2. leaf 3. relied 4. boat 5. tried 6. season 7. wheel 8. doe 9. seizure 10. pillow 11. delay 12. explain

13. ie 14. ow 15. ai 16. ay 17. ee

Unit 4 Posttest, page 87h (BLM 28)

18. pleasure 19. author 20. allowed 21. understood 22. royal 23. fewer 24. smooth 25. draw 26. poison 27. flower 28. newest

29. 3 30. 2 31. 2 32. 2 33. 2 34. 2 35. 1 36. 2 37. 2 38. 3

PERFORMANCE ASSESSMENT PROFILE

Skill	Pretest Questions	Posttest Questions	Reteaching: Focus on All Learners	Reteaching: Daily Word Study Practice
Vowel Pairs *ai, ay*	1, 2, 12, 14, 15	1, 11, 12, 15, 16	89–90, 105–106	202
Vowel Pairs *ei, ee, ea*	4, 6, 7, 11, 13	2, 6, 7, 9, 17	91–92, 105–106	202
Vowel Pair *ie*	8, 10, 17	3, 5, 13	91–92, 105–106	202
Vowel Pair *ow*	3, 16	10, 14	93–94, 105–106	202
Vowel Pairs *oe, oa*	5, 9	4, 8	93–94, 105–106	202
Vowel Digraphs *ea, ei, ey*	18, 30	18, 30	95–96, 105–106	202–203
Vowel Digraph *ie*	32, 35	32, 35	97–98	202–203
Vowel Digraph *oo*	21, 24, 31, 37	21, 24, 31, 37	99–102, 105–106	202–203
Vowel Digraphs *aw, au*	19, 25, 33, 38	19, 25, 33, 38	103–106	202–203
Diphthongs *oi, oy*	22, 26, 29	22, 26, 29	107–110, 113–114, 117–118	203–204
Diphthong *ew*	23, 28, 34	23, 28, 34	109–110, 113–114, 117–118	203–204
Diphthongs *ou, ow*	20, 27, 36	20, 27, 36	111–114, 117–118	203–204
Syllables	29–38	29–38	115–118	208

> Fill in the circle beside the word that contains the vowel sound given at the left.

1. long **a** sound	○ daily	○ saucy	○ apple
2. long **a** sound	○ eastern	○ ranch	○ decay
3. long **o** sound	○ bawl	○ bowl	○ beauty
4. long **e** sound	○ selling	○ ceiling	○ ready
5. long **o** sound	○ toe	○ out	○ wood
6. long **e** sound	○ street	○ break	○ bellow
7. long **e** sound	○ raisin	○ reason	○ lesson
8. long **i** sound	○ chief	○ field	○ fried
9. long **o** sound	○ cost	○ crust	○ coast
10. long **i** sound	○ applied	○ cousin	○ dishes
11. long **e** sound	○ seize	○ cheerful	○ metal
12. long **a** sound	○ sandy	○ crayons	○ happen

> Read each sentence. Fill in the circle under the letters that can be used to complete both unfinished words in the sentence.

13. Certain kinds of pollen make me f___l like sn___zing.

ea	ee	e
○	○	○

14. Did the m___or give you p___ment for the job?

ai	ei	ay
○	○	○

15. I am afr___d our furniture won't fit in that tr___ler.

ai	ay	ea
○	○	○

16. Did Mom sh___ you the nest of baby sparr___s?

ou	ow	oy
○	○	○

17. We tr__d to wash the dr__d paint off the sofa.

ei	ee	ie
○	○	○

Go to the next page. →

> Fill in the circle beside the word that contains the same vowel sound as the pair of vowels underlined in the first word.

18. w<u>ea</u>ther	○ creature	○ dreadful	○ reason
19. <u>aw</u>kward	○ angry	○ staying	○ autumn
20. m<u>ou</u>ntain	○ chowder	○ cargo	○ snow
21. f<u>oo</u>tball	○ driftwood	○ cartoon	○ throat
22. turqu<u>oi</u>se	○ hopeful	○ oboe	○ voyage
23. j<u>e</u>wel	○ thawed	○ chewing	○ leisure
24. classr<u>oo</u>m	○ barefoot	○ gloomy	○ pillow
25. l<u>au</u>nch	○ vanish	○ painted	○ squawk
26. l<u>oy</u>al	○ poison	○ blooming	○ boast
27. <u>ou</u>tskirts	○ coins	○ clown	○ bowl
28. cr<u>ew</u>s	○ weigh	○ ceiling	○ blew

> Say each word. Fill in the circle next to the number of syllables you hear.

29. annoyance	○ 1	○ 2	○ 3
30. threadbare	○ 1	○ 2	○ 3
31. gloomy	○ 1	○ 2	○ 3
32. relieved	○ 1	○ 2	○ 3
33. because	○ 1	○ 2	○ 3
34. nephew	○ 1	○ 2	○ 3
35. shriek	○ 1	○ 2	○ 3
36. thousand	○ 1	○ 2	○ 3
37. woolen	○ 1	○ 2	○ 3
38. somersault	○ 1	○ 2	○ 3

Possible score on Unit 4 Pretest is 38. Number correct _____

BLM 26 Unit 4 Pretest: Vowel digraphs, diphthongs, syllables

▶ Fill in the circle beside the word that contains the vowel sound at the left.

1. long **a** sound	○ daylight	○ dandy	○ dear
2. long **e** sound	○ leaf	○ dead	○ whether
3. long **i** sound	○ field	○ relied	○ fishing
4. long **o** sound	○ lost	○ boot	○ boat
5. long **i** sound	○ relief	○ yield	○ tried
6. long **e** sound	○ praising	○ season	○ melon
7. long **e** sound	○ wheel	○ weather	○ welcome
8. long **o** sound	○ doe	○ doubt	○ doll
9. long **e** sound	○ shells	○ seizure	○ sweater
10. long **o** sound	○ paw	○ pillow	○ pool
11. long **a** sound	○ least	○ ladder	○ delay
12. long **a** sound	○ explain	○ exhaust	○ exact

▶ Read each sentence. Fill in the circle under the letters that can be used to complete both unfinished words in the sentence.

	ie	ee	ea
13. My little sister cr___d when our fish d___d.	○	○	○

	ou	oy	ow
14. May I borr___ your yell___ sweater?	○	○	○

	ay	ai	ea
15. Rem___n on the tr___n until the last stop.	○	○	○

	ei	ay	ai
16. We alw___s have homework on Tuesd__s.	○	○	○

	ee	ei	ea
17. The refer__ agr__d that the ball was out of bounds.	○	○	○

Go to the next page. →

▶ Fill in the circle beside the word that contains the same vowel sound as that of the pair of vowels underlined in the first word.

18. r<u>ea</u>dy	○ peanut	○ pleasure	○ cleaner
19. <u>aw</u>ful	○ aim	○ author	○ after
20. f<u>ou</u>ntain	○ allowed	○ owner	○ foam
21. w<u>oo</u>den	○ understood	○ kangaroo	○ wound
22. v<u>oi</u>ce	○ piano	○ problem	○ royal
23. fl<u>ew</u>	○ yawn	○ fewer	○ feel
24. shamp<u>oo</u>	○ notebook	○ smooth	○ choice
25. d<u>au</u>ghter	○ dampen	○ drain	○ draw
26. destr<u>oy</u>	○ poison	○ down	○ coach
27. <u>ou</u>ch	○ odd	○ flower	○ own
28. thr<u>ew</u>	○ west	○ flow	○ newest

▶ Say each word. Fill in the circle next to the number of syllables you hear.

29. corduroy	○ 1	○ 2	○ 3
30. widespread	○ 1	○ 2	○ 3
31. wooden	○ 1	○ 2	○ 3
32. believed	○ 1	○ 2	○ 3
33. faucet	○ 1	○ 2	○ 3
34. renew	○ 1	○ 2	○ 3
35. brief	○ 1	○ 2	○ 3
36. mountain	○ 1	○ 2	○ 3
37. hooded	○ 1	○ 2	○ 3
38. autograph	○ 1	○ 2	○ 3

Possible score on Unit 4 Posttest is 38. Number correct _____

BLM 28 Unit 4 Posttest: Vowel digraphs, diphthongs, syllables

Student Progress Checklist

Make as many copies as needed to use for a class list. For individual portfolio use, cut apart each student's section. As indicated by the code, color in boxes next to skills satisfactorily assessed and mark an X by those requiring reteaching. Marked boxes can later be colored in to indicate mastery.

STUDENT PROGRESS CHECKLIST

Code: ■ Satisfactory ☒ Needs Reteaching

| Student: _____

 _____

 Pretest Scores _____

 Posttest Scores_____ | **Skills**
 ❒ Vowel Pairs *ai, ay*
 ❒ Vowel Pairs *ei, ee, ea*
 ❒ Vowel Pairs *oe, oa, ow*
 ❒ Vowel Pair *ie*
 ❒ Vowel Digraphs *ea, ei, ey, ie*
 ❒ Vowel Digraphs *aw, au*
 ❒ Vowel Digraph *oo*
 ❒ Diphthongs *ou, ow*
 ❒ Diphthongs *oi, oy*
 ❒ Diphthong *ew*
 ❒ Syllables | **Comments / Learning Goals** |
| Student: _____

 _____

 Pretest Scores _____

 Posttest Scores_____ | **Skills**
 ❒ Vowel Pairs *ai, ay*
 ❒ Vowel Pairs *ei, ee, ea*
 ❒ Vowel Pairs *oe, oa, ow*
 ❒ Vowel Pair *ie*
 ❒ Vowel Digraphs *ea, ei, ey, ie*
 ❒ Vowel Digraphs *aw, au*
 ❒ Vowel Digraph *oo*
 ❒ Diphthongs *ou, ow*
 ❒ Diphthongs *oi, oy*
 ❒ Diphthong *ew*
 ❒ Syllables | **Comments / Learning Goals** |

Spelling Connections

INTRODUCTION

The Unit Word List is a comprehensive list of spelling words drawn from this unit. The words are grouped by the phonemic elements studied throughout the unit. To incorporate spelling into your word study program, use the activity in the Curriculum Connections section of each teaching plan.

The spelling lessons utilize the following approach for each set of words.

1. Administer a pretest of the words that have not yet been introduced. Dictation sentences are provided.

2. Provide practice.

3. Reassess. Dictation sentences are provided.

A final test is provided at the end of the unit on page 120.

DIRECTIONS

Make a copy of Blackline Master 30 for each student. After administering the pretest for each phonemic element, give students a copy of the appropriate word list.

Students can work with a partner to practice spelling the words orally and identifying the phonemic element in each word. You may want to challenge students to add to the list other words with the same phonemic element. Students can also write words of their own on *My Own Word List* (see Blackline Master 30).

Students may store their list words in envelopes or plastic zipper bags in the backs of their books or notebooks. Alternatively, you may want to suggest that students keep a spelling notebook, listing words with similar phonemic elements. Another idea is to build word walls with students and display them in the classroom. Each section of the wall can focus on words with a single word study element. The walls will become a good resource for spelling when students are writing.

UNIT WORD LIST

Vowel Pairs *ai, ay, ee, ea, ei, ie, oa, oe, ow*

paint

gray

sneeze

peach

ceiling

supplies

road

toe

pillow

Vowel Digraphs *ea, ei, ey*

steady

weigh

obey

Vowel Digraphs *ie, oo, au, aw*

piece

proof

shook

stood

autumn

draw

Diphthongs *oi, oy*

coin

royalty

Diphthongs *ew, ou, ow*

threw

cloud

flowers

snow

brown

shout

Name _____

 Spelling

UNIT 4 WORD LIST

Vowel Pairs ai, ay, ee, ea, ei, ie, oa, oe, ow

paint
gray
sneeze
peach
ceiling
supplies
road
toe
pillow

Vowel Digraphs ea, ei, ey

steady
weigh
obey

Vowel Digraphs ie, oo, au, aw

piece
proof
shook
stood
autumn
draw

Diphthongs oi, oy

coin
royalty

Diphthongs ew, ou, ow

threw
cloud
flowers
snow
brown
shout

My Own Word List

Word Study Games, Activities, and Technology

The following collection of ideas offers a variety of opportunities to reinforce word study skills while actively engaging students. The games, activities, and technology suggestions can easily be adapted to meet the needs of your group of learners. They vary in approach so as to consider students' different learning styles.

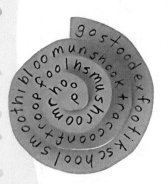 

✳ WORD SPIRALS

Draw a spiral on the chalkboard. Use words with the digraph *oo* or other spellings studied in this unit to create a word spiral as shown. Have volunteers find and circle the words in the spiral. Then have students create their own word spirals for others to solve, using words with vowel pairs, digraphs, and diphthongs studied in this unit.

● VOWEL-PAIR CONCENTRATION

Have students make word cards for the following words: *pillow, bowl, feather, thread, soil, moist, ceiling, receive, cries, pie, brown, flower, thousand, cloud, broom, spoon, piece, field, nail,* and *rain.* Students mix the cards and place them face down on the table. They take turns turning two cards up at a time to find matching pairs that have both the same vowel sound and the same vowel spelling.

▲ CHANGE-A-LETTER

Provide students with letter cards to build and read words containing a vowel combination studied in this unit, such as *drain.* Then have them replace the vowels to create a new word, such as *drawn* or *drown.* Partners can take turns building words and replacing vowels to create new words. Challenge students to keep lists to find out which beginning and ending sounds make the most words.

◆ NO! NO!

Help students brainstorm words with common phonograms containing vowel pairs, digraphs, or diphthongs studied in this unit, such as *ain, ay, own, eep, ead,* or *oom.* Begin by giving a word and then a definition for a rhyming word rather than the word itself, such as *Chain, something that falls from the sky.* Model how to continue, by giving the word defined and yet another definition for another rhyming word: *No! No! I mean rain, something that moves along railroad tracks.* Encourage students to keep the chain of rhyming, misdefined words growing.

■ HINK PINKS

Write the following rhyming pairs, or hink pinks, on the chalkboard: *neat seat; round hound; pleasant pheasant.* Challenge students with these riddles: *What do you call a tidy chair? a fat dog? a cheerful game bird?* Help students brainstorm other rhyming word pairs containing vowel sounds studied in this unit. Encourage students to draw pictures of their hink pinks and label their pictures with the rhyming word pairs.

round hound

✳ VOWEL-PAIR MASTERMIND

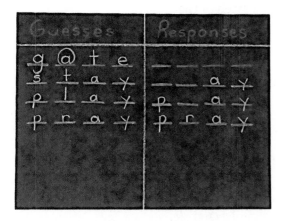

Draw a diagram on the chalkboard like the sample in the photograph. Choose a three- or four-letter word from the unit and tell students the number of letters in the word and the vowel sound, but not the vowel spelling, for example, *My word has four letters and the long* a *sound.* To begin a round, ask a volunteer to guess the word and write the guess in the "guess" space on the diagram. In the "response" column, record the correct letters and leave the incorrect spaces blank. (If a letter is correct but in the wrong position, circle it in the guess column.) Ask another volunteer to study the responses and write another guess in the guess column. Count the number of guesses taken before the correct word is guessed. Begin again with a new word, and have the class try to beat its score.

Variation: After students are familiar with the pattern of guessing and responding, partners can take turns guessing and responding to each other's words.

⬤ TOSS THE CUBE

Place pieces of masking tape on the sides of a large number cube. On each side, write the letters *ei, ee, ea, oe, oa, ie.* Make word cards for the words *ceiling, street, reason, toe, roast,* and *tried.* Students roll the cube and find the card with the word whose vowel sound matches the spelling shown on the face-up side of the cube.

Variation: You can encourage students to make their own versions of the game by using vowel digraphs and diphthongs. For a more challenging version, do not use word cards, but rather have students say and spell a word with the vowel spelling shown on the cube.

▲ QUESTIONS

Encourage partners to choose a vowel sound such as the sound of the diphthong *ew.* One partner writes down a word containing that sound and covers the word so that the other partner can't see it. The second partner asks questions about the word. The questions can be about the spelling *(Does it begin with a vowel?)* or about the meaning *(Is it an animal?),* but they must be able to be answered with either *yes* or *no.* Partners take turns and keep track of the number of questions asked. The partner who guesses the word with the fewest questions wins the round.

Variation: For an easier version of this game, help students make up a list of words with the vowel sound. Students must use a word from the list in their game.

◆ VOWEL-PAIR PASSWORD

Help students brainstorm a list of words containing one or two vowel combinations studied in this unit, for example, *ow* and *ou.* Make word cards for each of the words. Divide the class into two teams and have the teams divide into partners. The first player on the first team draws a card, reads the word, and gives his or her partner a one-word clue for the word. The partner has one minute to guess the word. The first player may continue to give one-word clues throughout the minute. Teams receive one point for each correctly guessed word.

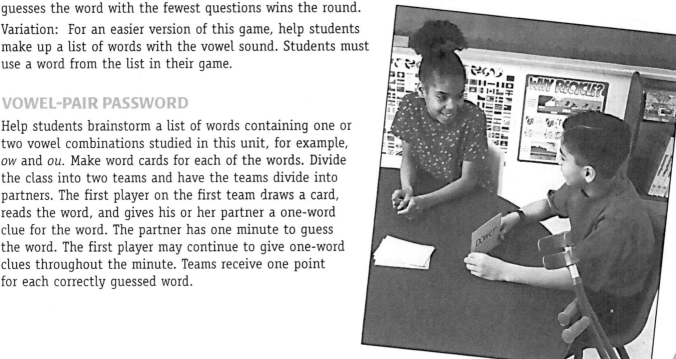

■ HOT POTATO DIPHTHONGS

Use a beanbag or other soft object as a hot potato. Write the diphthongs *oi* and *oy* on the chalkboard and have students sit or stand in a circle. Students must pass the beanbag around the circle as quickly as possible. Each time a student receives the beanbag, he or she must say a word containing the diphthong *oi* or *oy*. You may wish to time how long it takes for the beanbag to pass around the complete circle and then challenge students to beat the record.

Variation: Repeat the game with other vowel sounds studied in this and other units.

✳ CASTLE TOWERS

Choose a vowel pair or vowel digraph from this unit, for example, *oo,* and have students use bright markers to print the letters in a column down the center of a sheet of grid paper. Beginning at the bottom of the page, students can build towers of words by adding letters to either side, as shown.

Variation: You can build a large class tower by pasting construction-paper squares in a column on butcher paper. Use one color of paper for the chosen vowel pair and another color for the other letters.

● BATTER UP!

Give pairs of students a copy of Blackline Master 31, a dictionary, and three paper clips, coins, or other objects to use as game pieces. Have students cut out the squares at the bottom of the page. Students place the squares face down and decide who will be batter and pitcher. The pitcher holds up a square. The batter must say a word that contains the vowel spelling shown and spell the word correctly. The pitcher checks the word. If it is spelled correctly, the batter moves a game piece to first base, and the pitcher holds up another square. If not, the batter gets an out. After three outs, the other student becomes the batter. The player with the most runs after three innings wins the game.

Technology

The following software products are designed to reinforce students' knowledge of grammar.

Grammar Games An introductory quiz assesses grammar skills and then places students into various activities accordingly. Four games offer practice in: fragmented vs. complete sentences, use of correct noun and verb forms, and punctuation.
** Davidson & Associates, Inc.
    19840 Pioneer Avenue
    Torrance, CA 90503
    (800) 545-7677

I. M. Meen Students practice spelling, grammar, and pronunciation as they find and proofread 150 scrolls while navigating through a spooky mazelike dungeon and fighting off evil pirates. (There are 36 levels of text included.)
** Simon & Schuster Interactive
    P.O. Box 2002
    Aurora, CO 80040-2002
    (800) 910-0099

Name _____

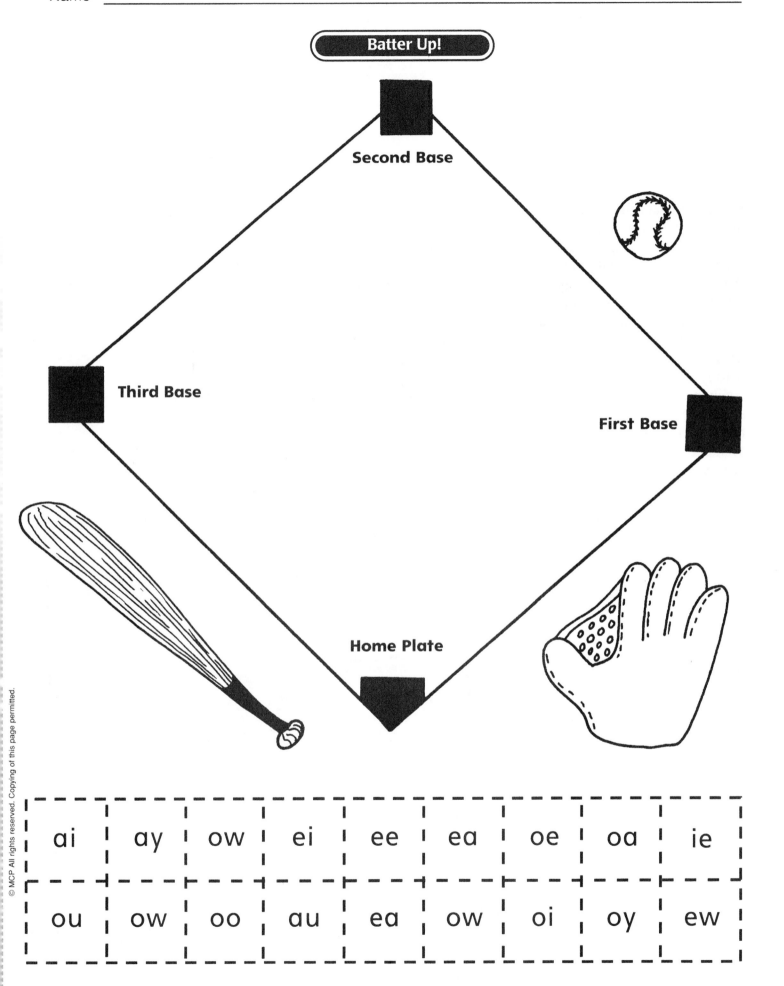

Batter Up!

Second Base

Third Base

First Base

Home Plate

ai	ay	ow	ei	ee	ea	oe	oa	ie
ou	ow	oo	au	ea	ow	oi	oy	ew

BLM 31 Unit 4 Activity

87o

Home Connection

A letter is available to be sent home at the beginning of Unit 4. This letter informs family members that students will be learning to read and write words with vowel combinations that can represent a variety of vowel sounds. The suggested home activity encourages parents to ask their children to list words that have vowel pairs, digraphs, and diphthongs. This activity promotes interaction between student and family members while supporting students' learning of reading and writing words. A Book Corner feature suggests books that family members can look for in a local library and enjoy reading together. A letter is also available in Spanish on page 87q.

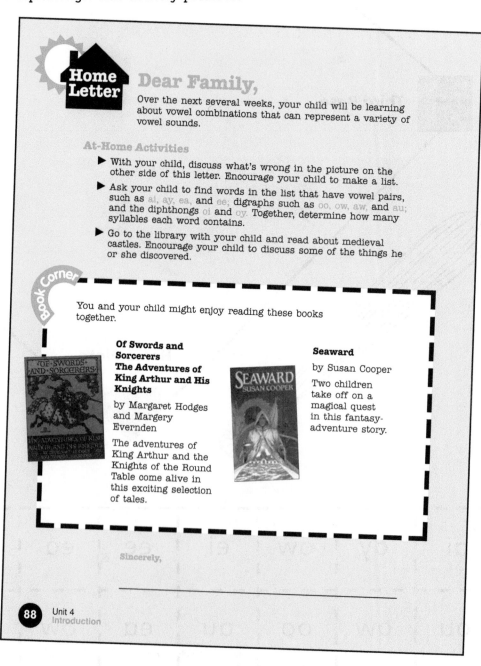

Home Letter

Dear Family,

Over the next several weeks, your child will be learning about vowel combinations that can represent a variety of vowel sounds.

At-Home Activities

▶ With your child, discuss what's wrong in the picture on the other side of this letter. Encourage your child to make a list.

▶ Ask your child to find words in the list that have vowel pairs, such as ai, ay, ea, and ee; digraphs such as oo, ow, aw, and au; and the diphthongs oi and oy. Together, determine how many syllables each word contains.

▶ Go to the library with your child and read about medieval castles. Encourage your child to discuss some of the things he or she discovered.

Book Corner

You and your child might enjoy reading these books together.

Of Swords and Sorcerers
The Adventures of King Arthur and His Knights

by Margaret Hodges and Margery Evernden

The adventures of King Arthur and the Knights of the Round Table come alive in this exciting selection of tales.

Seaward

by Susan Cooper

Two children take off on a magical quest in this fantasy-adventure story.

Sincerely,

88 Unit 4
Introduction

Carta para la casa

Estimada familia,

Durante las próximas semanas su hijo/a estudiará las combinaciones de vocales que pueden representar una variedad de sonidos de vocal en inglés.

Actividades para hacer en casa

▶ Con su hijo/a, comenten qué tiene de mal la lámina de la página 87 de su libro. Anímenlo a hacer una lista.

▶ Pídanle a su hijo/a que busque palabras en la lista que tienen pares de vocales, tales como **ai, ay, ea** y **ee**; digramas o vocales dobles como **oo, ow, aw** y **au;** y diptongos como **oi** y **oy**. Juntos, determinen cuántas sílabas contiene cada palabra.

▶ Vayan a la biblioteca con su hijo/a y lean acerca de los castillos medievales. Animen a su hijo/a a hablar de algunas cosas que ha descubierto.

Rincón del libro

Su hijo/a y ustedes pueden disfrutar juntos de la lectura de estos libros. Búsquenlos en la biblioteca de su localidad.

Of Swords and Sorcerers: The Adventures of King Arthur and His Knights
por Margaret Hodges y Margery Evernden

Las aventuras del rey Arturo y los caballeros de la mesa redonda cobran vida en esta emocionante selección de cuentos.

Seaward
por Susan Cooper

Dos niños parten en una búsqueda mágica en esta aventura de fantasía.

Atentamente, _____

Unit 4

Pages 87–88

Vowel Pairs, Digraphs, Diphthongs, Syllables

ASSESSING PRIOR KNOWLEDGE

To assess students' prior knowledge of vowel pairs, digraphs, diphthongs, and syllabication, use the pretest on pages 87e–87f.

Unit Focus

USING THE PAGE

- With students, examine the picture. Ask what kind of hat the boy is wearing. (*It's a loaf of bread, not a hat.*) Have students work in pairs to find and list everything else that is wrong or unusual about the picture.

- Have volunteers read their lists as other students check off on their own lists each item named.

- **Critical Thinking** Read aloud the question at the bottom of page 87. Invite students to share and discuss their responses.

BUILDING A CONTEXT

- Write these groups of words on the board: *gain, play; mean, sleep, seize; lie; boat, show, toe.* Have the words read aloud and ask what kinds of vowel sounds they have. (*long*) Explain that they are vowel pairs; they have the long sound of the first letter in the pair.

- Now write *reins, they; niece, pool, bread,* and *cause, fawn* on the board. Explain that these words do not have the long vowel sound of the first vowel. These words contain vowel digraphs—two vowels together that can make a long or short sound.

- Say these words slowly: *boy, few, now.* Write the words, underline the digraphs, and explain that these glided sounds are called diphthongs.

Boo-hoo! Who eight one of my pies?

What do you think it would be like to live here?

Critical Thinking

There are some very unusual things happening in this picture. See how many you can find.

UNIT OPENER ACTIVITIES

VOWEL SOUND HUNT

Have students search the picture for items whose names contain the vowel sounds spelled with two letters. (*oo: boots, balloon, boo-hoo, blooming, moon, brook, hook; ou, ow: cloud, flowers, crown, upside-down, shower, crow*) Invite volunteers to read their lists.

HIDE IN PLAIN SIGHT

Show students a small object such as a wooden match or a short piece of ribbon. Then, while students cover their eyes, hide it "in plain sight," making sure it's visible. Ask them to silently search for it, write down where it is, and sit down. Let students take turns hiding it.

FUNNY PUNNY SENTENCES

Write on the board the queen's question, *Who eight one of my pies?* Invite students to list homophone pairs and then write their own funny sentences that replace a word with its homophone; for example, *The knight was dark. The king is raining. Get out of my weigh!*

Home Letter

Dear Family,

Over the next several weeks, your child will be learning about vowel combinations that can represent a variety of vowel sounds.

At-Home Activities

▶ With your child, discuss what's wrong in the picture on the other side of this letter. Encourage your child to make a list.

▶ Ask your child to find words in the list that have vowel pairs, such as ai, ay, ea, and ee; digraphs such as oo, ow, aw, and au; and the diphthongs oi and oy. Together, determine how many syllables each word contains.

▶ Go to the library with your child and read about medieval castles. Encourage your child to discuss some of the things he or she discovered.

Book Corner

You and your child might enjoy reading these books together.

Of Swords and Sorcerers
The Adventures of King Arthur and His Knights

by Margaret Hodges and Margery Evernden

The adventures of King Arthur and the Knights of the Round Table come alive in this exciting selection of tales.

Seaward

by Susan Cooper

Two children take off on a magical quest in this fantasy-adventure story.

Sincerely,

_____

● The Home Letter on page 88 is intended to acquaint family members with the word study skills students will be studying in the unit. Students can tear out page 88 and take it home. You may want to suggest that they complete the activities on the page with a family member. Encourage students to look for the books pictured on page 88 in the library and read them with family members.

● The Home Letter can also be found on page 87q in Spanish.

CURRICULUM CONNECTIONS

WRITING

Ask pairs of students to collaborate on writing a funny detective story about a detective who isn't good at his or her job and gets into big trouble because of it. They might use the title "The Defective Detective."

SCIENCE

Invite students to talk about interesting weather and physical phenomena they have experienced or read about: simultaneous rain and sunshine (as in the picture on page 87); a double rainbow; lightning striking nearby; an eclipse; northern lights; sunspots; a hailstorm; and so on. Then have students choose a phenomenon and do some research to find out why it occurs and where it occurs. Invite volunteers to share their findings with the class by giving a brief oral report.

LANGUAGE ARTS

Portfolio Tell students that there are many folk rhymes about the weather. Write these examples on the board and have volunteers read them aloud.

A sunshiny shower won't last half an hour.

April showers bring May flowers.

No weather's ill if the wind be still.

Red sky in the morning, sailors take warning.

Invite students to discuss the meaning of each folk rhyme and then create rhymes of their own about the weather.

BULLETIN BOARD

Invite each student to draw part of the scene on page 87 and label it with a sentence such as There are _flowers_ on the _clouds_. Have students underline each word that has a vowel sound spelled with two letters. Display the pictures on a bulletin board "What's Wrong Here?"

Lesson 40
Pages 89–90

Vowel Pairs ai, ay

▶ Look at each picture. Find its name in the word bank and write it on the line.

RULE

In a **vowel pair,** two vowels come together to make one long sound. The first vowel in the pair usually stands for its long sound, and the second is silent.

da**i**sy

road	train	hay	beads
creature	nails	crow	tie
queen	sheep	toes	cheese

1 toes **2** beads **3** nails **4** road

5 queen **6** hay **7** crow **8** cheese

▶ Read each sentence. Complete the sentence with a word from the word bank at the top of the page.

9. Our class rode a _____train_____ to visit a farm.

10. At the farm we saw brown cows and white _____sheep_____.

11. We saw a farm worker making _____cheese_____ in a churn.

12. The farmer made a strange _____creature_____ to put in the field.

13. The scarecrow wore a _____tie_____ around its neck.

14. Every single _____crow_____ flew out of the field because it was scared.

Lesson 40
Vowel pairs
89

INFORMAL ASSESSMENT OBJECTIVE

Can students

✔ associate vowel pairs with their sounds?

Lesson Focus

INTRODUCING THE SKILL

- Have students name the vowels. (*a, e, i, o, u*) Ask what kinds of sounds vowels can stand for in words. (*long, short*)

- Invite volunteers to write the following words on the board: *clean, foam, seem, weird, glue, sail, ray*. Have students read the words aloud and name the long vowel sound they hear in each one. Ask students which vowel they do not hear in each word. (*the second one*)

- Explain that in a vowel pair, two vowels come together to make one long sound. The first vowel in the pair usually stands for its long sound, and the second vowel is silent.

- Encourage students to name additional words with vowel pairs and write them on the board. Have students underline the vowel pair in each word.

USING THE PAGES

- Read the directions on pages 89 and 90 aloud with students before they begin working. Make sure they understand that for the second activity, they are to use the words in the word bank at the top of page 89.

- When students have finished both pages, have a volunteer explain what he or she has learned about vowel pairs.

89

FOCUS ON ALL LEARNERS

ENGLISH LANGUAGE LEARNERS/ESL

Before assigning students these pages, make sure they can name the pictures and pronounce words in the word bank correctly.

VISUAL LEARNERS

SMALL GROUP

Materials: chart paper, markers

Have students write these three headings on chart paper: *Names, Places, Things*. Then have them work together to write a list of words with vowel pairs for each category. Provide these words to get them started: *Jean, Spain, tray*. Encourage them to use their words to write a story.

KINESTHETIC LEARNERS

LARGE GROUP

Materials: index cards, markers

Make a card for each of these vowel pairs: *oe, ea, ai, oa, ow, ee, ay*. (Save these, and add to them as you proceed through the unit.) Write words with missing vowel pairs; for example, *b__t, tr__*, on the board and have students come up, hold an appropriate card over the blank, and say the word.

> **Read the sentences. Underline each word in which you hear the long a sound of the vowel pairs ai and ay. Circle the number of the sentence that describes the picture.**

1. Jay wanted to go straight home.
2. He had to wait in line to get a ticket.
3. Jay failed to get on the train.

4. A gray donkey strayed into the daylight.
5. It went straight to the hay.
6. The donkey brayed as it raided the hay.

> **Read each sentence. Complete the sentence with a word from the word bank.**

7. Fay _____complained_____ that her room was dreary.

8. The brown walls were too _____plain_____ .

9. Fay decided to _____paint_____ her room.

10. She wanted light _____gray_____ walls.

11. She used one _____pail_____ of paint.

12. She did one wall a different _____way_____ .

13. She put up wallpaper with _____daisies_____ .

14. It _____rained_____ outside while Fay painted.

15. She _____waited_____ for the paint to dry.

16. She didn't like the _____delay_____ .

17. Then she hung the pictures on _____nails_____ .

18. She put yellow curtains on her large _____bay_____ window.

bay	gray
rained	waited
plain	delay
paint	way
pail	nails
daisies	
complained	

90
Lesson 40
Vowel pairs ai, ay

CURRICULUM CONNECTIONS ✳ • ◆ • •

SPELLING

The following sentences can be used as a spelling pretest for words with vowel pairs *ai*, *ay*, *ee*, *ea*, *ei*, *ie*, *oa*, *oe*, and *ow* and with vowel digraphs *ea*, *ei*, and *ey*.

1. **gray** — Battleships are **gray** in color.
2. **paint** — Let's **paint** with watercolors.
3. **sneeze** — Please cover your mouth when you **sneeze**.
4. **peach** — A **peach** is covered with fuzz.
5. **ceiling** — The balloon rose up to the **ceiling**.
6. **supplies** — Campers carry food **supplies**.
7. **road** — This **road** will lead to the park.
8. **pillow** — Do you sleep using a **pillow**?
9. **steady** — It takes a **steady** hand to sew.
10. **weigh** — The cement blocks **weigh** 100 kilograms.
11. **obey** — You have to **obey** the rules when using a public pool.
12. **toe** — This shoe hurts my big **toe**.

WRITING

Portfolio Ask students to read two or three animal fables, such as those of Aesop, and then write their own fable starring one of the animals mentioned in this lesson— a crow, a sheep, or a donkey. Have them plan their fable so that it ends with a moral. Invite students to share their fables with the class.

MUSIC

Write the names of these rounds on the board, omitting the underlines: "Three Blind Mice"; "Row, Row, Row Your Boat"; "Are You Sleeping, Brother John?" Have volunteers underline the words with vowel pairs. Then divide the class into two groups and teach them to sing one of the rounds. Have the second group begin singing at the beginning eight bars after the first group begins.

SCIENCE

Invite interested students to research how cheese and butter are made from milk and then give a brief oral report to the class.

AUDITORY LEARNERS

LARGE GROUP Write on the board these sentences, omitting the underlines: *Joe will _____ the garden. I need to pull every _____ . The toad hopped across the _____ .* Read the sentences aloud and encourage students to complete each with a word that rhymes with the underlined word.

GIFTED LEARNERS

Have students collect as many spellings of the long *a* sound as they can, provide an example of each spelling, and then combine lists; for example, *ai (rain), a (acre), ay (say), ei (rein), eigh (weigh), aigh (straight), a-consonant-e (take), ai-consonant-e (aide).*

LEARNERS WHO NEED EXTRA SUPPORT

On the board, write the words from the word bank on page 90. Have students in turn come to the board and circle the vowel pairs in each word and pronounce the word. See Daily Word Study Practice, page 202.

Lesson 41

Pages 91–92

Vowel Pairs ee, ea, ei, ie

Lesson Focus

INTRODUCING THE SKILL

- Review that when two vowels come together in a vowel pair, the first vowel usually stands for its long sound and the second vowel is silent.

- Say the words *neat*, *seize*, and *green*. Ask students what vowel sound they hear. Have volunteers write the words on the board. Ask what students notice about the spelling of the long e sound.

- Have students apply Long Vowel Rule 1 to the words on the board and identify the silent vowels.

- Write *pies* and have students pronounce it. Have them identify the vowel sound and apply Long Vowel Rule 1.

USING THE PAGES

- Go over the directions for page 91, pointing out that each activity has two steps: *circle* and *write*.

- After students have completed both pages, discuss what *ee*, *ea*, and *ei* have in common. (*They can all spell the long e sound.*) Ask what sound the vowel pair *ie* often stands for. (*long i*)

- **Critical Thinking** Invite students to share their responses to the question at the bottom of page 92.

91

Name _____

▷ Say each word in the word bank. Circle the vowel pair in each word that stands for the long e sound. Then write each word in the correct column.

sneeze	meek	leisure	heed	keen	reach
seizure	neat	ceiling	peach	seize	reason

see	**leaf**	**Neil**
sneeze	reach	leisure
meek	neat	seizure
heed	peach	ceiling
keen	reason	seize

▷ Read each sentence. Circle the word that correctly completes the sentence and write it on the line.

1. Peaches are _____cheap_____ at this time of year.

    beaded / reach / (cheap)

2. Unripened peaches are _____green_____ and hard.

    meat / (green) / keen

3. People sometimes _____peel_____ off the fuzzy skin.

    flee / lee / (peel)

4. Eat a juicy peach slowly and at your _____leisure_____.

    (leisure) / seizure / ceiling

FOCUS ON ALL LEARNERS

ENGLISH LANGUAGE LEARNERS/ESL

In Spanish, vowel letters almost always occur singly. Remind students whose first language is Spanish that, in English, a vowel sound is often represented by two letters, and that several different two-letter combinations can stand for the same sound.

VISUAL LEARNERS

INDIVIDUAL Have students use their books for word ideas and write sentences (serious or silly) in which several words have the long e sound spelled *ee*, *ea*, *ei*, or the long i sound spelled *ie*; for example, *Jean eats peaches for a reason*. Let volunteers share their sentences with the class.

KINESTHETIC/AUDITORY LEARNERS

SMALL GROUP **Materials:** index cards, markers

Make three cards for each student: *ee*, *ea*, *ei*. Read this list of words and have students hold up the card that spells the long e sound in each word: *tree, leaf, seed, weird, read, ceiling, steam, sleep, conceited, peach, bleed, seizing, mean, feet, beach, neither*.

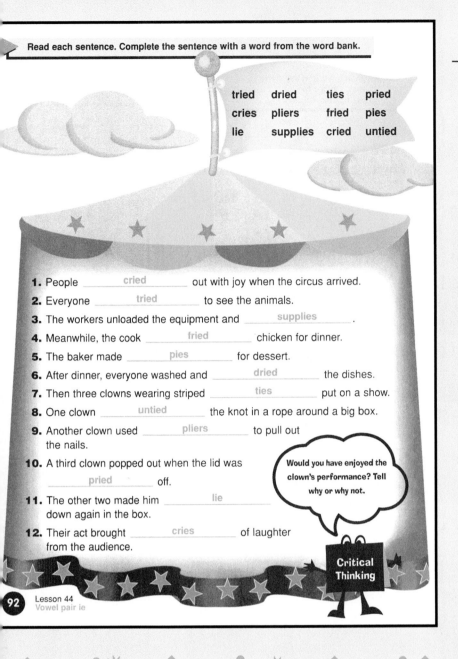

Read each sentence. Complete the sentence with a word from the word bank.

tried	dried	ties	pried
cries	pliers	fried	pies
lie	supplies	cried	untied

1. People _____cried_____ out with joy when the circus arrived.

2. Everyone _____tried_____ to see the animals.

3. The workers unloaded the equipment and _____supplies_____.

4. Meanwhile, the cook _____fried_____ chicken for dinner.

5. The baker made _____pies_____ for dessert.

6. After dinner, everyone washed and _____dried_____ the dishes.

7. Then three clowns wearing striped _____ties_____ put on a show.

8. One clown _____untied_____ the knot in a rope around a big box.

9. Another clown used _____pliers_____ to pull out the nails.

10. A third clown popped out when the lid was _____pried_____ off.

11. The other two made him _____lie_____ down again in the box.

12. Their act brought _____cries_____ of laughter from the audience.

> Would you have enjoyed the clown's performance? Tell why or why not.
>
> **Critical Thinking**

AUDITORY LEARNERS

SMALL GROUP Write on the board this word list: *seek, each, leisure, dream, either, feel.* Have students take turns reading a word aloud and spelling its long *e* sound.

GIFTED LEARNERS

Challenge students to create four lists of words: (1) *ei* stands for long *e*, as in *ceiling, seize,* and *weird*; (2) *ei* does *not* stand for long *e*, as in *stein, veil,* and *heir*; (3) *ie* stands for long *i*, as in *pie, lie,* and *tie*; and (4) *ie* does *not* stand for long *i, as in fierce, friend,* and *niece.*

LEARNERS WHO NEED EXTRA SUPPORT

Write two headings, *ei* and *ie*. In another area on the board, write *seize, tie, receive, fries, cried,* and *ceiling* and have students tell which heading to write each word under. Then have them pronounce all the words in each column. See Daily Word Study Practice, page 202.

CURRICULUM CONNECTIONS

SPELLING

Write the spelling words on the board (*steady, supplies, sneeze, pillow, paint, gray, obey, weigh, ceiling, road, peach, toe*), leaving two blanks for each vowel pair or digraph. Call out a brief clue to each word's meaning. (Example for *steady:* st_ _dy—*not shaky*) Invite student volunteers to name the appropriate vowel pair or digraph and then come up to fill in the two vowel letters to complete each spelling word.

WRITING

Portfolio Point out that many words with the long *e* sound spelled *ee, ea,* and *ei* have homophones, words that sound exactly the same but are spelled differently. Give these examples: *peek, peak; ceiling, sealing.* Have students think of more homophone pairs with the vowel spellings *ee, ea,* and *ei* and make a list of the words. Then invite them to write a description of a circus act they have seen in real life or on television. Encourage them to use some of the homophones they listed.

MATH

How high is your classroom's ceiling? Have teams of students think of creative ways to make a close estimate without climbing up to measure. (Sample methods: *1. If your walls are concrete block, measure one block and multiply by the number of blocks. 2. Attach a small weight to a helium balloon so that it rises slowly. Time how long it takes to rise one foot. Let the balloon rise to the ceiling, calculate the number of feet, and add the length of the balloon and string.*) When each team has agreed on one idea, have teams make their estimates. Declare a winner for creativity as well as for accuracy.

HEALTH

Materials: posterboard, markers or crayons

When someone sneezes, the germs the sneeze carries with it can travel 12 feet at 100 mph! Have students use this information to make a poster urging people to cover their mouths when they sneeze.

Lesson 42
Pages 93–94

Vowel Pairs oa, oe, ow

Lesson Focus

INTRODUCING THE SKILL

- Review with students that vowel pairs in words often stand for the long sound of the first vowel.

- Say the following sentence: *Joe rows the boat.* Ask students to identify the vowel sound they hear in almost every word in the sentence. *(long o)*

- Call on a volunteer to write the sentence on the board. Encourage students to note the vowel pairs that stand for the long o sound. Explain that these vowel pairs commonly have the long o sound. Ask students to suggest other words with these vowel pairs.

- Finally, have students apply Long Vowel Rule 1 to the words and identify the silent letters.

USING THE PAGES

- Provide guidance as necessary as students complete pages 93 and 94.

- After students have completed the pages, discuss what they have learned about words with *oa*, *oe*, and *ow*.

- **Critical Thinking** Have a volunteer read aloud the question at the bottom of page 94. Then have students work with a partner to make a list of three gardening rules, which they can compare with the other pairs.

93

Name _____

▶ Say each word in the word bank. Circle the vowel pair that stands for the long **o** sound. Then write the word in the correct column.

> **RULE**
> The vowel pairs **oa, oe, ow** usually have the long **o** sound.
> road   toe   blow

hoe	snow	float	pillow	toe	bowl	poach	foe
boast	doe	row	throat	soap	woe	bow	

coat	**Joe**	**crow**
float	hoe	snow
poach	toe	pillow
boast	foe	bowl
throat	doe	row
soap	woe	bow

▶ Read each definition. Choose a word from the word bank at the top of the page that matches the definition and write it on the line.

1. one way to move a boat — row
2. something soft for your head — pillow
3. a garden tool — hoe
4. a hair ribbon — bow
5. one way to cook eggs — poach
6. sadness — woe
7. used when you swallow — throat
8. what you eat cereal from — bowl
9. something to wash with — soap

Lesson 42
Vowel pairs oa, oe, ow   **93**

FOCUS ON ALL LEARNERS

ENGLISH LANGUAGE LEARNERS/ESL

To build background for the story on page 94, ask students if anyone has ever planted a garden or worked in one. Encourage students to talk about the kinds of plants that grow in gardens and what plants need to grow.

VISUAL LEARNERS

PARTNER   Have each partner write several words from the word bank on page 93, leaving out the vowel pair. Ask the other partner to complete the words.

KINESTHETIC/VISUAL LEARNERS

SMALL GROUP

Materials: index cards, markers

Print these words on the index cards: *boat, snow, soap, toast, show, throat, oak, slow, yellow.* Distribute the cards to students and have them sort the words by vowel pairs. Encourage them to add their own words to each group of words.

Read each sentence. Complete the sentence with a word from the word bank.

Word bank:
- tomorrow
- pleased
- speak
- seeds
- main
- due
- row
- straight
- eat
- goat
- peek
- hoe
- boasting
- keep
- continue
- narrow
- receive
- need

1. A gardener will _____speak_____ to the class.
2. Then _____tomorrow_____ we will plant vegetables.
3. He will _____continue_____ to give us help when we need it.
4. A report about gardening will be _____due_____ next week.
5. It will _____need_____ to include the following rules.
6. First buy _____seeds_____ to plant in the garden.
7. Use a _____hoe_____ to dig up the dirt.
8. Complete one _____row_____ before starting another.
9. The rows should be _____narrow_____, not wide.
10. The rows should also be _____straight_____, not crooked.
11. The _____main_____ thing is to water the seeds.
12. Seeds will grow if they _____receive_____ water and get sun.
13. Soon, little plants will _____peek_____ out of the soil.
14. You will be _____boasting_____ to everyone about your garden.
15. Do not let a _____goat_____ get into the garden.
16. It will _____eat_____ all your plants.
17. You will not be _____pleased_____ if that happens.
18. Build a fence to _____keep_____ animals out.

What do you think are the three most important rules for planting and caring for a garden?

Critical Thinking

Seeds

CURRICULUM CONNECTIONS

SPELLING

On the board, create a word search puzzle using the spelling words (*ceiling, gray, pillow, supplies, steady, sneeze, paint, obey, weigh, road, peach, toe*). When students are out of the room, draw a grid of 10 squares by 10 squares. Then fill in words horizontally, vertically, and diagonally. Fill in the extra spaces with random letters, making sure they don't spell words. Then have students take turns coming to the board and circling spelling words. Have them say each word they find, name the vowel pair or digraph, and spell the entire word aloud.

WRITING

Portfolio

Materials: newspapers, magazines

Distribute random paragraphs from newspaper or magazine articles. Ask students to look for words with the vowel pairs *oa, oe,* and *ow*. Encourage them to take these words and create a new paragraph on a related or different topic.

ART/LANGUAGE ARTS

Materials: tagboard, markers, crayons, string, scissors

Have students each make a mask of one of these animals: goat, doe, crow. On the back of the mask, have them write the name of the animal and underline the vowel pair. Then have them pass the masks around the class until you say *Stop*. Each student puts on a mask and, in turn, says a word with the same vowel pair found in the name of his or her animal.

HEALTH/MATH

Materials: various cereal boxes, chart paper, markers, heart stickers

Have students examine the nutritional information on different cereal boxes. Explain that fiber is good for one's health and that sugar and fat are not. Then have them make a table showing what grain or grains and how much fiber, sugar, and fat are in one bowl of each cereal. Let students place a heart sticker on the cereals that are highest in fiber, lowest in fat, and lowest in sugar and then agree on the most healthful one to eat.

AUDITORY LEARNERS

LARGE GROUP

Write words such as the following on the board: *boat, toast, foe, slow*. Invite volunteers to add rhyming words that have the same vowel pairs; for example, *float, coat, goat; coast, boast, roast; toe, floe, woe; show, grow, below*. Encourage students to write couplets using the words.

GIFTED LEARNERS

Invite students to make up sentences for other students to complete, leaving a blank for words with the long *o* sound spelled *oa, oe,* and *ow*. Remind them to include enough clues. Here is an example: *Look both ways before you cross the busy _____. (road)*

LEARNERS WHO NEED EXTRA SUPPORT

Model the pronunciation of all the words in the word bank for students before they begin page 93. See Daily Word Study Practice, page 202.

Lesson 43

Pages 95–96

Vowel Digraphs ea, ei, ey

✳ • • • • • ✳ • • • • • •

INFORMAL ASSESSMENT OBJECTIVE

Can students

✓ associate vowel digraphs *ea*, *ei*, and *ey* with their sounds?

Lesson Focus

INTRODUCING THE SKILL

● Review Long Vowel Rule 1 with students.

● Say the words *sweater* and *bread*. Have students identify the vowel sound. (*short e*) Write the words on the board. Point out that the letters *ea* can stand for the short *e* sound. Ask students if *ea* can also stand for the long *e* sound.

● Tell students that *ea* is a vowel digraph. Explain that in a vowel digraph, two vowels together, can make a long or short sound (as in *meat* or *bread*), or can have a special sound all their own (as in *break*).

● Have volunteers write the words *reins* and *they*. Have students pronounce the words and identify the vowel sound. Explain that the vowel digraphs *ei* and *ey* can stand for the long *a* sound.

USING THE PAGES

● The first and last activities on these pages have different formats from those used so far, so go over the directions carefully with students.

● After the pages have been completed, have pairs of students discuss what they have learned about vowel digraphs *ea*, *ei*, *ey*.

▶ Say the name of each picture. Circle the picture if you hear the short sound of **e** in its name.

> **RULE**
> In a **vowel digraph**, two vowels together can make a long or short sound, or have a special sound all their own. The vowel digraph **ea** can stand for the short **e** sound
>
> st**ea**dy

1 bread	2 peach	3 thread	4 wheat
5 meal	6 head	7 leaf	8 beak
9 feather	10 seal	11 sweater	12 steak

▶ Read each sentence. Complete the sentence with a word from the word bank.

13. The _____weather_____ was windy and cool.
14. Beth got _____ready_____ to go outside.
15. A walk would make her feel _____healthy_____ .
16. Beth put a hat on her _____head_____ .
17. She took out her _____leather_____ gloves.
18. Her favorite _____sweater_____ had a hole in it.
19. Beth needed _____thread_____ to mend it.
20. She used the needle with a _____steady_____ hand.

sweater	ready
weather	healthy
thread	head
steady	leather

FOCUS ON ALL LEARNERS ✳ • • ◆ •

ENGLISH LANGUAGE LEARNERS/ESL

Have students say the name of each picture in the first exercise. Make sure everyone is pronouncing the words correctly before beginning to work.

VISUAL/AUDITORY LEARNERS

INDIVIDUAL Have students make up shopping lists for real people or fictional characters. Each list must include at least one word from the lesson. Here are two examples: *Santa Claus: reindeer food, sleigh paint, beard shampoo. Betsy Ross: thread, red cloth, white cloth, blue cloth.*

KINESTHETIC LEARNERS

SMALL GROUP **Materials:** number cube, tape, paper, marker

Tape one of the following to each face of a number cube: *oa, oe, ow, ea, ei, ey*. Have students take turns rolling the cube and saying and writing a word with the vowel pair or vowel digraph that comes up.

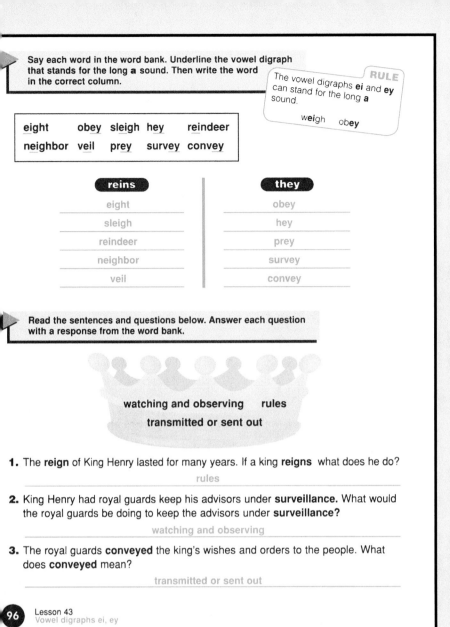

Say each word in the word bank. Underline the vowel digraph that stands for the long **a** sound. Then write the word in the correct column.

RULE

The vowel digraphs **ei** and **ey** can stand for the long **a** sound.

w**ei**gh   ob**ey**

| eight | obey | sleigh | hey | reindeer |
| neighbor | veil | prey | survey | convey |

reins	**they**
eight	obey
sleigh	hey
reindeer	prey
neighbor	survey
veil	convey

Read the sentences and questions below. Answer each question with a response from the word bank.

watching and observing   rules

transmitted or sent out

1. The **reign** of King Henry lasted for many years. If a king **reigns** what does he do?

rules

2. King Henry had royal guards keep his advisors under **surveillance.** What would the royal guards be doing to keep the advisors under **surveillance?**

watching and observing

3. The royal guards **conveyed** the king's wishes and orders to the people. What does **conveyed** mean?

transmitted or sent out

SPELLING

The following sentences can be used as a spelling posttest for words with vowel pairs *ai, ay, ee, ea, ei, ie, oa, oe,* and *ow* and with vowel digraphs *ea, ei,* and *ey.*

1. **peach**   Do you prefer apple to **peach** pie?
2. **road**   Don't cross the **road** without looking.
3. **ceiling**   Paint the **ceiling** and then the walls.
4. **weigh**   Let's **weigh** ourselves on the scale.
5. **obey**   **Obey** the rules and you won't get into trouble.
6. **gray**   Grandfather's hair is silvery **gray**.
7. **paint**   The house needs a coat of **paint**.
8. **pillow**   Here are your blanket and **pillow**.
9. **sneeze**   Pepper can make you **sneeze**.
10. **supplies**   I need to buy some art **supplies**.
11. **steady**   The **steady** rain did not let up.
12. **toe**   There is a hole in the **toe** of my sock.

WRITING

Portfolio Have students make up couplets that have rhyming words from this lesson with the vowel digraph *ea*. Encourage them to read their couplets aloud for the class.

SOCIAL STUDIES

Suggest that students find out about the career of surveying. What is surveying, and why is it necessary? How and where does a surveyor work? What kinds of tools are used? What education is required?

SCIENCE

Ask students if they can guess what one feature describes a bird. *(feathers)* Have students look through old magazines and cut out pictures of birds or draw their own pictures. Then have them make a bulletin-board display titled "Feathered Friends." Encourage them to include examples of very different birds, such as the ostrich, pelican, hummingbird, puffin, heron, and toucan.

AUDITORY LEARNERS

SMALL GROUP Have students take turns making up and asking riddles whose answers are the names of the pictures on page 95 or words from the word banks; for example, *What is something woolly to wear when it's cold? (sweater)* Have other group members answer the riddles.

GIFTED LEARNERS

Invite students to write analogies using words from this lesson; for example, *Hair is to mammal as _____ is to bird. (feather) Sick is to _____ as rough is to smooth. (healthy)* Remind students that in an analogy the relationship of the words in each pair has to be the same.

LEARNERS WHO NEED EXTRA SUPPORT

You may wish to model the pronunciation of all the words in the word bank at the top of page 96 before students begin. See Daily Word Study Practice, pages 202–203.

Lesson 44

Pages 97–98

Vowel Digraph *ie*

Lesson Focus

INTRODUCING THE SKILL

- Review that vowel digraphs can stand for long or short sounds or have special sounds all their own.

- Write the letters *ie* on the board. Ask students what vowel sound these letters usually stand for in words. (*long i*) Have volunteers write examples, such as *ties* and *dried*.

- Then say *grief* and *piece*. Ask students what vowel sound they hear in each word. (long e) Write the words and have students name the letters that stand for the long e sound. (*ie*)

- Explain that the vowel digraph *ie* can stand for the long e sound heard in *grief* as well as the long i sound heard in *dried*.

- Encourage students to suggest additional words in which the vowel digraph *ie* stands for the long e sound. (*brief, chief, believe, achieve*)

USING THE PAGES

- Make sure everyone understands that each activity on pages 97 and 98 has more than one step.

- After both pages have been completed, have students discuss what they have learned about the vowel digraph *ie*.

97

Name _____

▶ Read each pair of sentences. Then underline each word in which **ie** stands for the long **e** sound. Circle the number of the sentence that describes the picture.

> **RULE**
> The vowel digraph **ie** can stand for the long **e** sound.
> *piece*

1. The army marched across the field.
2. The castle was under siege by an army.

3. The chief lifted up his shield.
4. The battle stopped for a brief moment.

5. Everyone believed that the castle was lost.
6. A piece of stone fell off the wall.

▶ Read each sentence. Circle the word that correctly completes the sentence and write it on the line.

7. "Please hand me that _____piece_____ of blue cloth," said Aunt Betsy.
   achieve   siege   (piece)

8. Her _____niece_____, Lucy, gave her the cloth.
   piece   (niece)   wield

9. "The flag will have thirteen stars on a _____field_____ of blue," Betsy told Lucy
   yield   (field)   shield

10. "It will be the _____chief_____ symbol of our new nation," she said.
    (chief)   grief   thief

Lesson 44
Vowel digraph ie **97**

FOCUS ON ALL LEARNERS

ENGLISH LANGUAGE LEARNERS/ESL

Explain that the story at the bottom of page 97 is about Betsy Ross, who is said to have sewn the first U.S. flag with stars and stripes. Show a picture of the flag and, if available, one of Betsy Ross. Tell students that there were 13 stars because at that time there were only 13 states.

VISUAL LEARNERS

LARGE GROUP

Write on the board several correct and several misspelled words from this lesson. Have volunteers proofread. They should circle an incorrect word, write it correctly, and pronounce it correctly. You may also want to have them tell what the word means.

KINESTHETIC LEARNERS

SMALL GROUP

Materials: index cards, markers

Make word cards for the following *ie* or *ei* words: *achieve, believe, shield, field, chief, thief, niece, piece, either, seize, leisure, receive, reindeer, veil, reign,* and *deceit*. Shuffle the cards and have students take turns drawing one, saying the word, and sorting it into a long e pile or a long a pile.

> Read each definition. Write the word from the word bank that matches the definition. Put a check (✓) beside the answer if the letters **ie** stand for the long **e** sound.

grief	chief	field	mantelpiece
relieved	fielder	piece	shield
shriek	dried	die	belief
fried	brief	pierce	thief

1. a place where corn and wheat grow — field ✓
2. another word for **faith** — belief ✓
3. a portion of something can also be called this — piece ✓
4. a loud, shrill sound — shriek ✓
5. eggs can be cooked this way — fried
6. the way you feel when news is good — relieved ✓
7. head person in the fire department — chief ✓
8. what flowers do without water — die
9. no longer wet or damp — dried
10. shelf on a fireplace — mantelpiece ✓
11. a word that describes something short — brief ✓
12. person on a baseball team — fielder ✓
13. deep sorrow — grief ✓
14. a police officer's badge — shield ✓
15. to make a hole through something — pierce ✓
16. a person who steals — thief ✓

98
Lesson 44
Vowel digraph ie

SPELLING

The following sentences can be used as a spelling pretest for words with vowel digraphs *ie, oo, au,* and *aw* and vowel diphthongs *oi* and *oy*.

1. **piece** — Which **piece** of pizza do you want?
2. **proof** — I have **proof** that you were there.
3. **shook** — My dog **shook** water all over us.
4. **stood** — Kim **stood** nervously by the door.
5. **draw** — Let's **draw** pictures of each other.
6. **autumn** — The leaves fall in **autumn**.
7. **coin** — The dime is our smallest **coin**.
8. **royalty** — The king and queen are **royalty**.

WRITING

Portfolio

Materials: drawing paper, marker

Invite students to draw a cartoon showing a scene from a medieval battle. They could show a knight battling another knight or a fierce dragon. Have them write a caption using several words with digraph *ie* from this lesson.

SOCIAL STUDIES

Materials: reference books on chivalry or medieval warfare in Europe

Ask students to find out more about warfare in the Middle Ages and give a brief oral report on one of these topics: the feudal system, armor, weaponry, or castle construction.

ART/SOCIAL STUDIES

Materials: red, white, and blue cloth; needles, thread, scissors, white glue

Have students research Betsy Ross and locate a picture of her flag. Provide sewing materials and encourage small groups to work together to make a copy of the flag. Have them sew or glue the blue field and red stripes onto a white rectangle, and then cut out and glue on 13 stars. Finally, have them write a paragraph telling the story of when, where, and for whom Betsy Ross made the flag. They might display the flag and their paragraph on a bulletin board in a school common area.

AUDITORY LEARNERS

LARGE GROUP

Write these words and have students list rhyming words with the same digraph for each one: *achieve (believe, relieve, retrieve); shield (field, yield, wield); thief (chief, relief, brief); apiece (niece, piece, masterpiece).* Have them make up couplets using the words.

GIFTED LEARNERS

Have students collect two lists of *ie* words: those with the long *i* sound and those with the long *e* sound. Challenge them to make a generalization about words with each sound. (*Long* i *words have* y *changed to* i, *or end in* ie, *with or without a suffix; long* e *words have* ie *in the middle.*)

LEARNERS WHO NEED EXTRA SUPPORT

Remind students of the mnemonic device "*i* before *e* except after *c*." Point out that there are a few exceptions (*either* is one), but that this rule will help them spell all the words in this lesson. See Daily Word Study Practice, pages 202–203.

Lesson 45

Pages 99–100

Vowel Digraph oo

Can students

✔ associate the vowel digraph *oo* with its sounds?

Lesson Focus

INTRODUCING THE SKILL

Materials: index cards, markers

- Make word cards for *too, good, moon,* and *look.* Recall with students that vowel digraphs can have long or short vowel sounds as well as their own special sounds.

- Then invite four volunteers to hold up the word cards. Ask the class what they notice about the vowels in the words.

- Call on students to read the words aloud. Have them listen carefully for the two different vowel sounds represented by *oo.*

- Explain that the vowel digraph *oo* can stand for the vowel sound heard in *moon* or that heard in *good.*

USING THE PAGES

- Have a volunteer read the directions aloud before students begin each activity.

- After the last activity has been completed, encourage pairs to discuss what they have learned about the digraph *oo* and share their ideas with the class.

Name _____

Say the name of each picture. Circle the picture if its name has the same vowel sound you hear in **too** and **moon**.

RULE

One sound the vowel digraph **oo** can stand for is the vowel sound you hear in **too** and **moon**.

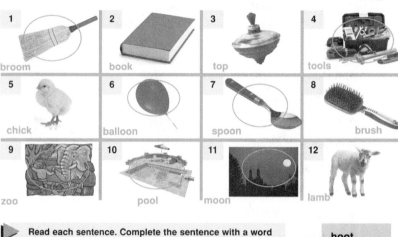

1 broom	2 book	3 top	4 tools
5 chick	6 balloon	7 spoon	8 brush
9 zoo	10 pool	11 moon	12 lamb

Read each sentence. Complete the sentence with a word from the word bank.

13. An owl sat silently in the _____ moonlight _____.
14. A _____ pool _____ of light fell on a small rabbit.
15. Suddenly, the owl _____ swooped _____ off the branch.
16. Her flight was _____ smooth _____ and silent.
17. She made a quick _____ loop _____ and dove down.
18. The owl let out a soft _____ hoot _____ of pride.
19. She would not let her catch get _____ loose _____.
20. She carried the _____ food _____ to her waiting owlets.

Word bank:
hoot
zoom
loop
loose
smooth
pool
moonlight
food
proof
swooped

Lesson 45
Vowel digraph oo **99**

FOCUS ON ALL LEARNERS

ENGLISH LANGUAGE LEARNERS/ESL

In a small group, discuss the pictures at the top of page 99. Make sure everyone can pronounce the name of each picture before beginning to work. Explain that owlets are baby owls and define any other difficult words on these pages.

VISUAL/AUDITORY LEARNERS

LARGE GROUP

Have students write sentences. In each sentence they should use one word with *oo* as in *book* and one word with *oo* as in *pool.* Let students read their sentences aloud to the class. After each sentence is read, have a volunteer go to the board and write both *oo* words.

KINESTHETIC LEARNERS

SMALL GROUP

Materials: index cards, paste, marker, scissors

Photocopy page 99, cut out the 12 pictures, and paste each on a card. Make additional cards if you wish. Deal one card to each student. If the name of the picture has a vowel sound as in *cool,* he or she says the word. Shuffle and deal again.

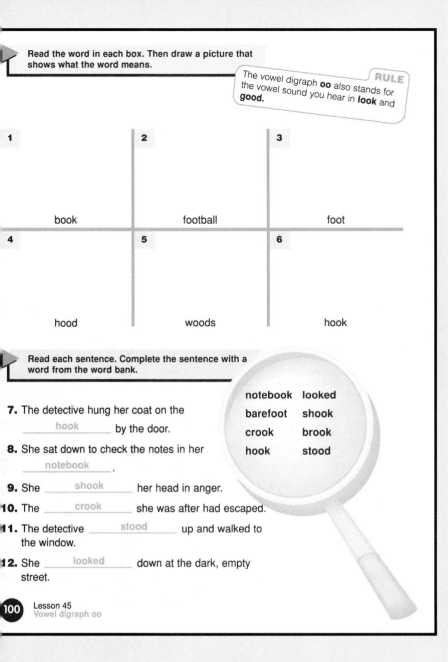

Read the word in each box. Then draw a picture that shows what the word means.

> **RULE**
> The vowel digraph **oo** also stands for the vowel sound you hear in **look** and **good**.

1	2	3
book	football	foot
4	5	6
hood	woods	hook

Read each sentence. Complete the sentence with a word from the word bank.

notebook	looked
barefoot	shook
crook	brook
hook	stood

7. The detective hung her coat on the _____hook_____ by the door.

8. She sat down to check the notes in her _____notebook_____.

9. She _____shook_____ her head in anger.

10. The _____crook_____ she was after had escaped.

11. The detective _____stood_____ up and walked to the window.

12. She _____looked_____ down at the dark, empty street.

100 Lesson 45
Vowel digraph oo

SPELLING

Explain that you will read aloud some sentences that contain a spelling word plus a spelling clue word. Read these sentences aloud and call on students to spell the spelling word they hear you say, using the clue word to help them. Emphasize the pronunciation of the spelling word and the clue word.

1. My dog <u>took</u> a bath and then **shook**.
2. I **stood** still like a piece of <u>wood</u>.
3. The fingerprints on the <u>roof</u> are **proof**.
4. The <u>author</u> was born in **autumn**.
5. I'd like to give a **piece** of this cake to my <u>niece</u>.
6. I wrapped the **coin** in <u>foil</u>.
7. The <u>boy</u> is a member of **royalty**.
8. First I <u>saw</u> it; now I'll **draw** it.

WRITING

Portfolio Have students reread the story on page 99 and then write a paragraph that tells what happened from the perspective of one of the animals: the owl, the rabbit, or the owlet. Remind students to use the pronoun *I* to refer to the animal.

LANGUAGE ARTS

Over the centuries, many animals have come to symbolize human traits. Write on the board the simile *as wise as an owl*. Have students think of an "as ____ as a ____" expression for each of these animals: fox (*sly*), lion (*brave*), lamb (*gentle*), mule (*stubborn*), swan (*graceful*), bear (*hungry*), ox (*strong*), bunny (*quick*).

ART/SCIENCE

Materials: drawing paper, markers, crayons

Animal sounds are often represented by words with vowel digraphs: *squeak, peep, shriek, hee-haw, growl, neigh, howl, roar, hoot, meow, scream, woof, moo, squawk*. Have students work in small groups to draw a woodland, jungle, or barnyard scene with many animals, writing appropriate animal sounds in voice balloons. Then have them write in thought balloons what the animals are trying to say.

AUDITORY LEARNERS

INDIVIDUAL **Materials:** cassette recorder, blank cassettes

Write a list of *oo* words on the board, mixing words like *book* and words like *cool*. Have each student make an audiotape, pausing between words so that there is time to write the word. A few days later, have students listen to the tape and write the words.

GIFTED LEARNERS

Ask students to write couplets for other students to complete, using rhyming words with *oo* as in *book* or as in *cool*. Have students draw a small illustration to provide clues. Here is an example: *I went to the ____ / In a hot-air ____.* (Picture: girl in balloon near the moon)

LEARNERS WHO NEED EXTRA SUPPORT

On the board, write *Moon* and *Look* as headings as you say them aloud. Then say the following words one at a time: *foot, fool, shook, stool, crook, hood, pool, broom.* Have students tell under which heading to write each word. Then have students pronounce all the words in each column. See Daily Word Study Practice, pages 202–203.

Lesson 46

Pages 101–102

Vowel Digraph oo

Lesson Focus

INTRODUCING THE SKILL

- Write the digraph *oo* on the board. Ask for examples of words that illustrate the sounds this digraph can stand for. (*moon, wood, good, cool*)

- Invite students to suggest how they would know which vowel sound to use for *oo* in words they might not recognize. (*Try both sounds to see which one makes sense.*)

- Say the sentence *The flowers are in bloom.* Ask students to identify the word with the digraph *oo*. Suggest that students say *bloom* with both sounds the digraph can stand for. Point out that often seeing a word in context can help students identify it.

USING THE PAGES

- Make sure students understand what to do on pages 101 and 102. After both pages have been completed, discuss what students have learned about the digraph *oo*.

- **Critical Thinking** Have students read the direction at the top right corner of page 102. Invite them to share the clues they find in the story.

101

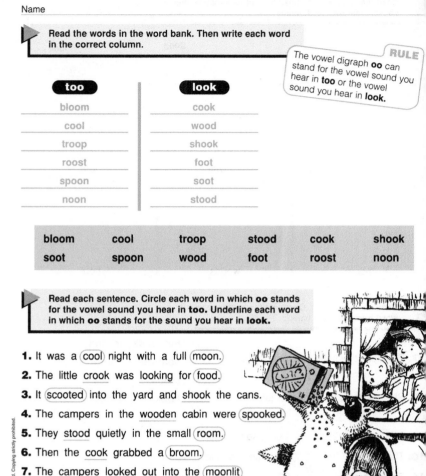

Name _____

▶ Read the words in the word bank. Then write each word in the correct column.

RULE
The vowel digraph **oo** can stand for the vowel sound you hear in **too** or the vowel sound you hear in **look**.

too	**look**
bloom	cook
cool	wood
troop	shook
roost	foot
spoon	soot
noon	stood

bloom	cool	troop	stood	cook	shook
soot	spoon	wood	foot	roost	noon

▶ Read each sentence. Circle each word in which **oo** stands for the vowel sound you hear in **too**. Underline each word in which **oo** stands for the sound you hear in **look**.

1. It was a (cool) night with a full (moon.)
2. The little crook was looking for (food.)
3. It (scooted) into the yard and shook the cans.
4. The campers in the wooden cabin were (spooked.)
5. They stood quietly in the small (room.)
6. Then the cook grabbed a (broom.)
7. The campers looked out into the (moonlit) night.
8. They felt like (fools) when they took in the sight.
9. Their crook was a (raccoon.)

Lesson 46
Vowel digraph oo
101

FOCUS ON ALL LEARNERS

ENGLISH LANGUAGE LEARNERS/ESL

Write several word pairs on the board (*took, tooth; good, goof*) and use them in sentences that illustrate their meaning. Have students say the words after you and underline the letters that stand for the vowel sound.

VISUAL LEARNERS

INDIVIDUAL Read aloud nouns with *oo*, pausing after each word to let students draw a small picture to represent it. Use these words: *school, moon, book, roof, boots, foot, pool, hook, noon, tooth, root.* After the entire list is read, have students go back and label each picture with its name. Have them underline the digraph in each word.

KINESTHETIC LEARNERS

SMALL GROUP **Materials:** number cube, tagboard, markers, game pieces

Make a game board with a path from Start to Goal. In each square, write an *oo* word. Players roll a number cube to advance their pieces. They must say the word they land on and use it in a sentence. The first to reach the goal wins.

> Read the story and answer the questions. Then circle each word in which **oo** stands for the vowel sound you hear in **too**. Underline each word in which **oo** stands for the sound you hear in **look**.

A Walk in the Woods

Leslie and Carrie Underwood put on their boots and took moonlit walk after the heavy rainfall. The blooming owers in the yard drooped from the rain. The kids set ut down the footpath and into the woods. Along the ath, the moonlight shined on mushrooms and toadstools. raccoon snooped around the dogwood trees. Leslie and Carrie crossed a brook and passed the house of a woodcutter. They ame out of the woods on the other side of a grove of cottonwood trees.

Soon the kids came to the smooth sandy shore of a lagoon. Many little reatures lived there in nooks and holes. Nearby they took a look at an nsect emerging from its cocoon. A coot or a loon, they were not sure vhich, swooped down on the deck of a sloop anchored in the lagoon.

It began to grow cool, so Leslie and Carrie trooped back home. 'uddenly Carrie let out a whoop. Something wet and furry had cooted past her. They guessed it was a woodchuck who had een looking for food. After a good snack, Leslie and Carrie oon called it a day.

As you read look for clues that tell you what time of year the story takes place.

Critical Thinking

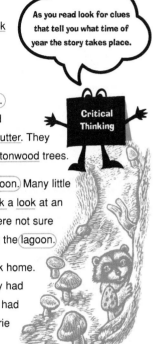

1. What word tells you it was nighttime? _____ moonlight

2. What snooped around the dogwoods? _____ raccoon

3. What body of water did the girls come upon? _____ lagoon

4. What kind of boat was anchored there? _____ sloop

5. Name two birds you read about. _____ coot, loon

02 Lesson 46
Vowel digraph oo

SPELLING

Write the spelling words on the board for reference: *proof, autumn, piece, draw, shook, royalty, stood, coin*. Then start writing the first numbered set slowly, telling students to speak up when they can guess which spelling word fits in with the set. Have the student who volunteers come up and point to the spelling word, point out how the word is similar to the other words in the set, and spell the word aloud. Continue with the remaining sets of words.

1. toys, enjoying, annoyed, _____ *(royalty)*
2. fawn, awkward, brawny, _____ *(draw)*
3. moon, troops, groom, _____ *(proof)*
4. spoil, hoisted, tinfoil, _____ *(coin)*
5. brook, wool, _____, _____ *(shook, stood)*
6. brownies, field, chiefly, _____ *(piece)*
7. taut, fault, author, _____ *(autumn)*

WRITING

Portfolio Folk tales often feature animals behaving like humans. A Japanese folk tale tells about a rabbit who keeps the moon swept clean with a broom. An English fairy tale tells about the adventures of Puss in Boots. Have each student write his or her own short folk tale whose main character is an animal doing something human. Ask students to use several words with *oo* as in *book* and as in *moon*.

MUSIC

Invite students to write a poem or song using rhyming words such as *moon, soon* or *room, gloom*. They can use a melody they know or create their own. Invite students to perform their songs for the class.

SOCIAL STUDIES

Materials: drawing paper, crayons or colored pencils, markers

Talk about Alex Haley's search for his family history and why this history might be called *Roots*. Encourage students to ask family members about their grandparents and other ancestors. Then show students how to create a family tree with their own name on the trunk, their parents' names on two main roots, and their grandparents' and great-grandparents' names on smaller and smaller roots.

AUDITORY/VISUAL LEARNERS

PARTNER Fill a page with *oo* words pronounced like *book* and *cool*. Organize students in pairs and give each student a photocopy of the page. Have one partner circle all the words with one sound and the other circle all those with the other sound. Have them trade papers and check each other's work.

GIFTED LEARNERS

Challenge students to make lists of words with *oo* as in *book* and *oo* as in *moon* that are *not* in this lesson; for example, *hoof, brook, whoosh, soot, childhood, baboon, spook, moose, cocoon*. See who can collect the most words.

LEARNERS WHO NEED EXTRA SUPPORT

Materials: index cards, markers

For each student, make two word cards for *moon* and *book*, underlining the digraph in each word. Say the words in the word bank on page 101 one at a time and have students hold up the card with the word that has the digraph with the same sound. See Daily Word Study Practice, pages 202–203.

Lesson 47

Pages 103–104

Vowel Digraphs au, aw

INFORMAL ASSESSMENT OBJECTIVES

Can students

✓ associate the vowel digraphs *au* and *aw* with their sounds?

✓ complete sentences using words with /aw/?

Lesson Focus

INTRODUCING THE SKILL

● Review that one vowel digraph can stand for different sounds, such as *oo* in *cook* and *loop*. Explain that different digraphs can have the same sound.

● Say the words *draw* and *pause*. Ask students to repeat the vowel sound they hear in the words.

● Then have volunteers write the words on the board and underline the letters that stand for the vowel sound. Encourage students to read the words aloud.

● Explain that the vowel digraphs *aw* and *au* both stand for the vowel sound heard in *draw* and *pause*.

USING THE PAGES

● Make sure students know what to do on pages 103 and 104. Point out that in the sentences on page 104, they need to circle two or three words in each sentence before numbering the pictures.

● After students have finished the pages, have a volunteer write on the board two ways that /aw/ can be spelled.

Name _____

▶ Say the name of each picture. Then circle its name.

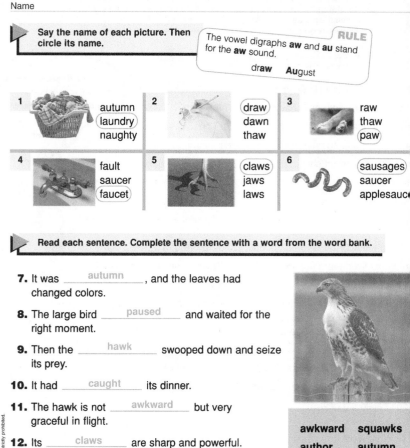

| 1 | autumn / (laundry) / naughty | 2 | (draw) / dawn / thaw | 3 | raw / thaw / (paw) |
| 4 | fault / saucer / (faucet) | 5 | (claws) / jaws / laws | 6 | (sausages) / saucer / applesauce |

▶ Read each sentence. Complete the sentence with a word from the word bank.

7. It was ___autumn___, and the leaves had changed colors.

8. The large bird ___paused___ and waited for the right moment.

9. Then the ___hawk___ swooped down and seize its prey.

10. It had ___caught___ its dinner.

11. The hawk is not ___awkward___ but very graceful in flight.

12. Its ___claws___ are sharp and powerful.

13. It is a patient and ___cautious___ hunter.

14. The hawk ___hauled___ the food back to its nest.

15. The baby hawks greeted it with ___squawks___.

awkward	squawks
author	autumn
claws	hawk
hauled	caught
cautious	paused

Lesson 47
Vowel digraphs au, aw   **103**

FOCUS ON ALL LEARNERS

ENGLISH LANGUAGE LEARNERS/ESL

The /aw/ is especially difficult for students learning English because it can be spelled in many ways. Have students focus on one or two spelling patterns at a time.

VISUAL LEARNERS

LARGE GROUP Write on the board incomplete words such as these: *str__, s__cer, l__yer, j__s, c__tion, __thor, __ful, y__n, __ditorium.* Have students fill in the missing digraph that stands for /aw/, say the word, and then copy it under *raw* or *sauce*, depending on how /aw/ is spelled.

KINESTHETIC LEARNERS

SMALL GROUP Write /aw/ words on the board and have students take turns acting them out. Have the others guess the word, say it, and write it. Use these words: *faucet, draw, applause, jaws, awkward, caught, hauled, hawk, gnaw, haunted, haughty, jaunty, bawled.*

Read each sentence and find the picture that goes with it. Write the number of the sentence on the line under the picture. Then circle the words in the sentence that have the aw sound.

1. A (jaunty) (dinosaur) (draws) a picture.
2. The (saucy) (leprechaun) does a (somersault.)
3. The (haunted) house looks (gaudy.)
4. A (haughty) (fawn) is (sprawled) on the ice.
5. The (scrawny) cat slept in a (drawer.)
6. The (paunchy) clown sat on the (lawn) and (bawled.)
7. A (straw) was (caught) in the (faucet.)
8. The (cautious) puppy (gnawed) a bone.

8

5

3

4

1

6

2

7

AUDITORY/KINESTHETIC LEARNERS

LARGE GROUP

Read aloud a list of words such as this: *keep, caught, book, laws, pool, brief, home, sauce, bread, raw, obey, boast, dawn, snow, autumn, soap.* When you come to a word with /aw/, have students raise their hands. Call on volunteers to tell whether /aw/ is spelled *au* or *aw*.

GIFTED LEARNERS

Invite students to write a silly story, using as many words as possible with /aw/ spelled *au* or *aw*; for example, *One autumn day, Shawn did his laundry on the lawn. . . .*

LEARNERS WHO NEED EXTRA SUPPORT

For the first exercise on page 103, encourage students to say the three word choices aloud. You may also want to have them read the sentences on page 104 aloud, listening for the words with /aw/.

See Daily Word Study Practice, pages 202–203.

CURRICULUM CONNECTIONS

SPELLING

Materials: beanbag

Have students stand in a circle and pass the beanbag. When you say *Stop*, the person with the beanbag must spell the word you say. (Words: *draw, coin, stood, autumn, piece, shook, proof, royalty*) As soon as you say the word, the beanbag starts around the circle again. The speller must spell the word correctly before it returns to him or her.

WRITING

Portfolio Have students think of an author whose book they have enjoyed reading recently. Have them think of a question or two that they would like to ask the author about the book's topic or characters. Then encourage them to write a letter to the author, asking their questions. Review the letter form if necessary.

LANGUAGE ARTS

Materials: dictionaries

Many of the words in this lesson are unusual adjectives: *paunchy, scrawny, gaudy, jaunty, saucy, cautious, awkward.* Have students look each one up in the dictionary to find out its exact meaning. Then have them think of one or more synonyms or antonyms for each one.

SCIENCE

The hawk is a raptor. Have students research what distinguishes raptors from other birds and research one kind of raptor (hawks, falcons, eagles, condors, ospreys, owls, vultures). Have them take notes and then write an encyclopedia-type article about their bird, telling such facts as where it lives, what it eats, how big it is, how many eggs it lays, and whether it is endangered. Encourage students to illustrate their subjects with drawings or photographs.

Lesson 48

Pages 105–106

Reading **W**riting

Reviewing Vowel Pairs and Digraphs

INFORMAL ASSESSMENT OBJECTIVES

Can students

✔ read a passage containing words with vowel pairs and vowel digraphs?

✔ write a description using words with vowel pairs and vowel digraphs?

Lesson Focus

READING

- Write on the board the words *pay* and *rain*. Ask a volunteer to read the words aloud and explain how they are alike. (*They both have the long a sound spelled with a vowel pair.*)

- Write *head*, *veil*, and *prey* and have a volunteer read them aloud. Have another student tell what vowel sound each word has and what digraph spells the sound. (*short e, ea; long a, ei; long a, ey*)

- Repeat the procedure with *cookie* and *shriek*, *shook* and *stool*, *autumn* and *awful*.

- Tell students that the passage they will read on dinosaurs contains many more words with these letter patterns.

WRITING

- Have volunteers recall information from the passage on page 105. Explain that students will "journey back in time," observe some seismosaurs, and write a description of what they saw.

- Before students begin writing, suggest that they refer to the Helpful Hints.

105

Name

 Reading ▶ Read the passage. Then write your answer to the question at the end of the passage.

THE GREAT AND SMALL OF DINOSAURS

If you believe that all dinosaurs were huge, meat-eating creatures, you are wrong. The smallest dinosaur yet found, Compsognathus, was the size of a large chicken. It measured two feet in length and weighed about 6.6 pounds. Its name means "pretty jaw"! Compsognathus walked on two legs and caught its food—bugs and lizards—with its small, clawed front paws.

Another small dinosaur, the three-foot-long *Lesothosaurus*, lived on plants. *Lesothosaurus* had flat, leaf-shaped teeth and a hooked beak.

The largest dinosaurs—nicknamed "supersaurs" by the scientists who discovered them—were plant eaters, too. They had very small brains and moved slowly. Scientists estimate that they measured 50 feet in height. That's tall enough to look into the windows of a five-story building!

However, even this giant was dwarfed by a dinosaur whose remains have been found in New Mexico. The earth probably shook when the awesome *Seismosaurus* roamed the land. The *Seismosaurus* surveyed the land from a height of more than 130 feet. If you ever saw *Seismosaurus*, you would know why scientists named it "earth shaker"!

Which of the dinosaurs mentioned in the passage would you like to learn more about? Why?

Lesson 48
Review vowel pairs, digraphs: Reading **105**

FOCUS ON ALL LEARNERS ✳ • ◆ •

ENGLISH LANGUAGE LEARNERS/ESL

Review that in English many vowel digraphs can stand for the long sound of the first vowel in the pair, such as long *a* (*ai, ay*), long *e* (*ee, ea, ei*), and long *o* (*oa, oe, ow*). Caution students that many do not, such as *ey* as in *they*, *ea* as in *bread*, *oo* as in *book* or *moon*, *au* and *aw*, and so on.

VISUAL LEARNERS

LARGE GROUP Write on the board *ai, ay, ee, ea, ei, ie, oa, oe, ow, ey, oo, au, aw* and the following incomplete words: *s__ze, w__fully, st__k, p__nful, __tograph, n__ce, pill__, fl__ce, suppl__s*. Have volunteers add a vowel pair or digraph to write a correct word and then say it.

KINESTHETIC LEARNERS

PARTNER **Materials:** envelopes, index cards, markers

Choose several words from "The Great and Small of Dinosaurs" that contain vowel pairs or digraphs. For each word, make a card for each letter and put the letters in an envelope. Distribute two envelopes to each pair of students and have the partners work together to reassemble the words.

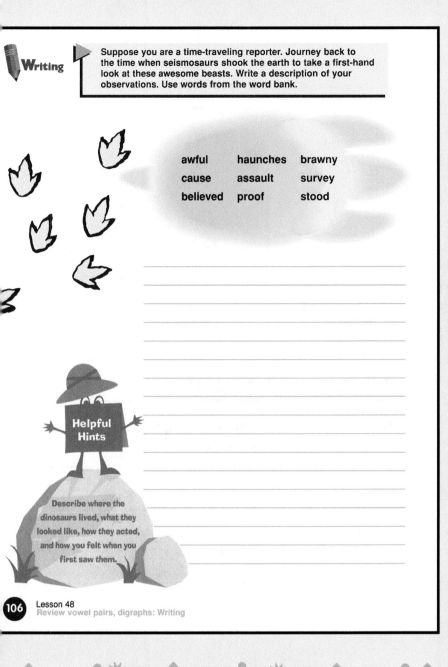

Suppose you are a time-traveling reporter. Journey back to the time when seismosaurs shook the earth to take a first-hand look at these awesome beasts. Write a description of your observations. Use words from the word bank.

awful	haunches	brawny
cause	assault	survey
believed	proof	stood

Helpful Hints

Describe where the dinosaurs lived, what they looked like, how they acted, and how you felt when you first saw them.

CURRICULUM CONNECTIONS

SPELLING

Materials: large index cards, markers

Make large letter cards for each spelling word. (*autumn, proof, shook, piece, draw, stood, royalty, coin*) Shuffle the letters for each word and put them face down in separate stacks. Have six students come to the front of the room, and distribute to them in random order the letters for the first word (*m, u, a, t, n, u*). Have them hold up the letter cards in front of them and quickly rearrange themselves to spell a spelling word so that the other students can read it left to right. (*autumn*) Repeat with the other words, calling on the appropriate number of students for each one.

MATH/SCIENCE

Encourage students to research the lengths, heights, and weights of several other dinosaurs and then write sentences stating the differences in their sizes; for example, *The 3-foot lesothosaur was 1.5 times longer than the 2-foot compsognathus. The supersaur was less than half as tall as the seismosaur.*

SCIENCE/ART/MATH

Materials: butcher paper, art supplies

Have students make a mural of scale drawings of several different dinosaurs so that their relative sizes can be easily seen. Suggest a scale of 1 inch to 1 yard. (They may have to add extra paper for the 130-foot seismosaur!) Also suggest that they include a six-foot human for comparison.

AstroWord Vowel Digraphs & Diphthongs. ©1998 Silver Burdett Ginn Inc. Division of Simon & Schuster.

AUDITORY LEARNERS

SMALL GROUP

Materials: index cards, markers

Make word cards for the following words and have small groups of students sort them into piles of words with the same vowel sound: *rain, spied, stay, lean, steep, seize, head, tries, veil, float, foes, sweat, slow, prey, fault, straw, threat, lie, yawn, steak, east.* (long *a: rain, stay, prey, veil, steak;* long *e: lean, steep, seize, east;* long *o: float, foes, slow;* long *i: tries, lie, spied;* /aw/: *fault, straw, yawn;* short *e: threat, head, sweat*)

GIFTED LEARNERS

Have students review the rules in the unit so far and write a short explanation of the difference between a vowel pair and a vowel digraph, giving examples of each.

LEARNERS WHO NEED EXTRA SUPPORT

Students may need additional practice with vowel digraphs that have more than one pronunciation, such as *cookie, lies; heat, breath; veil, seize; slow, how; booth, stood.* Encourage students to give additional examples of words with digraphs that have more than one pronunciation. See Daily Word Study Practice, pages 202–203.

Lesson 49

Pages 107–108

Diphthongs oi, oy

Lesson Focus

INTRODUCING THE SKILL

- Remind students that two vowels together in a word can form a vowel pair or a vowel digraph. Tell students that vowels that come together can form another type of sound.

- Say the words *boy* and *coin*. Ask students what letters they think represent the vowel sound they hear in each word.

- Call on volunteers to write the words on the boards and underline the letters *oy* and *oi*. Explain that *oy* and *oi* are diphthongs, or two vowels that glide together as a single sound.

USING THE PAGES

- The second activity on page 107 has an unusual format. Remind students to write the letter of each definition.

- **Critical Thinking** After students complete page 108, read aloud the question at the bottom of the page. Encourage students to share their ideas and opinions.

Name

▶ Look at each picture. Find its name in the word bank and write it on the line.

DEFINITION

A **diphthong** is made up of two vowels sounded so that both vowels blend together as one sound. The diphthongs **oi** and **oy** stand for the same sound.

coin   boy

boil	noise	coins	royalty
soil	boy	cowboy	

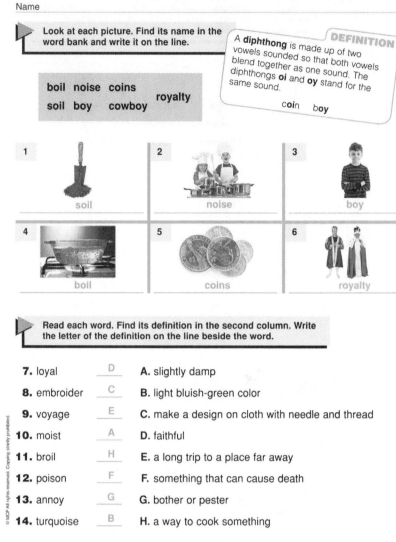

1. soil
2. noise
3. boy
4. boil
5. coins
6. royalty

▶ Read each word. Find its definition in the second column. Write the letter of the definition on the line beside the word.

7. loyal   D   **A.** slightly damp

8. embroider   C   **B.** light bluish-green color

9. voyage   E   **C.** make a design on cloth with needle and thread

10. moist   A   **D.** faithful

11. broil   H   **E.** a long trip to a place far away

12. poison   F   **F.** something that can cause death

13. annoy   G   **G.** bother or pester

14. turquoise   B   **H.** a way to cook something

FOCUS ON ALL LEARNERS

ENGLISH LANGUAGE LEARNERS/ESL

To build background for the passage on page 108, ask students if they have ever made popcorn, and if so, how (for example, microwave, stovetop, hot-air popper, popper over campfire). Have volunteers explain how to make popcorn and tell what it's like to eat it or how it tastes.

VISUAL LEARNERS

LARGE GROUP

Write the following scrambled words on the board: *oinpt (point), oyjen (enjoy), oilsp (spoil), oiyns (noisy)*. Ask volunteers to unscramble the letters to spell words with *oi* and *oy*. Then have volunteers create their own scrambled words for the class to unscramble.

KINESTHETIC LEARNERS

SMALL GROUP

Materials: popcorn, string, needles, paste, posterboard, markers

Have partners string popcorn and use the strings to make a large *oy* and *oi*, cutting as necessary. Have them paste the popcorn diphthongs to posterboard and write *oy* words around *oy* and *oi* words around *oi*.

Read the passage and answer the questions. Then underline each word in which you hear the diphthong oi or oy.

Oil sizzles in the pan. Pour in corn kernels. Put the lid on tightly to <u>avoid</u> being hit by flying kernels. Then listen for the first <u>noise</u>. Pop! After that first <u>joyful</u> pop, all the kernels seem <u>poised</u> to explode at once. The <u>noisy</u> pops come rapidly. When the <u>noise</u> stops, it's safe to remove the lid. Then <u>enjoy</u> your first taste of popcorn. You'll never be <u>disappointed</u>. Yum!

What makes popcorn pop? It's the <u>moisture</u> inside the hard kernel. When popcorn is heated, the <u>moisture</u> in it <u>boils</u> and forms steam. The steam makes the kernel explode and pop.

You can <u>boil</u> corn in water. You can <u>broil</u> it on a grill. But every <u>boy</u> and girl's favorite <u>choice</u> is popping it. Did you know that scientists found popcorn more than 5,000 years old in a cave? (Do you think it was too <u>spoiled</u> to eat?) Some Native Americans used popcorn, instead of <u>coins</u>, for money. Others <u>enjoyed</u> wearing it as jewelry. At the first Thanksgiving, in 1621, Native Americans brought popcorn to the feast for the Pilgrims' <u>enjoyment</u>!

1. Which word tells how popping corn sounds?
   noisy

2. Why should you cover the pan tightly?
   You should cover it tightly to avoid being hit by flying kernels.

3. Name three ways popcorn can be cooked.
   You can boil it, broil it, or pop it.

4. What causes popcorn to pop?
   The moisture in the kernel causes it to explode.

What fact about popcorn did you find the most interesting?

Critical Thinking

108 Lesson 49
Diphthongs oi, oy

CURRICULUM CONNECTIONS

SPELLING

The following sentences can be used as a spelling posttest for words with vowel digraphs *ie, oo, au,* and *aw* and vowel diphthongs *oi* and *oy*.

1. **coin**   Let's flip a **coin** to see who goes first.
2. **royalty**   The United States has no **royalty**.
3. **stood**   I've **stood** it for as long as I can.
4. **draw**   The juggler started to **draw** a crowd.
5. **piece**   Write it on a **piece** of notebook paper.
6. **shook**   Dad **shook** hands with my teacher.
7. **proof**   He showed **proof** of his identity.
8. **autumn**   Fall is another name for **autumn**.

WRITING

Portfolio Have students imagine that they are the early cave-dwelling humans who have just discovered popcorn. Have them write a diary entry telling about the discovery. *How did they discover popcorn? What was it like to eat it for the first time? What did they call it?*

MATH

Materials: unpopped popcorn, hot-air popper, measuring cup

Show students half a cup of unpopped popcorn and ask them to estimate how many cups of popped popcorn it will make. Pop the corn (making sure that nearly all the kernels pop) and see whose estimate was closest. Have students figure out the volume of the popped corn compared with the unpopped corn. Then enjoy the popcorn!

HEALTH/ART

Materials: poster paper, crayons, markers

Have the class brainstorm a list of snacks. Discuss the nutritional value of each. On the board, have them sort the foods into two categories: *Foods to Enjoy* and *Foods to Avoid*. Then have students choose three healthful snacks, make a poster titled "Good for You!" and illustrate it with a picture of themselves eating the healthful snacks.

108

Lesson 50

Pages 109–110

Diphthongs ew, oi, oy

INFORMAL ASSESSMENT OBJECTIVES

Can students

✔ associate the diphthong *ew* with its sound?

✔ distinguish among the diphthongs *oi, oy*, and *ew*?

Lesson Focus

INTRODUCING THE SKILL

- Review the definition of a diphthong. *(two vowels sounded so that both vowels blend together as one sound)*

- Introduce the diphthong *ew* by saying *flew* and *jewel*. Encourage students to repeat the sound of *ew*. Then call on volunteers to write the words on the board. Have students identify the diphthong while those at the board underline *ew* in each word.

- Explain that the diphthong *ew* stands for the vowel sound heard in *new*. Ask students what digraph sound this is similar to. *(oo as in moon)*

- Say *toy* and *coin* and call on volunteers to write the words on the board and underline the diphthongs. *(oy, oi)*

USING THE PAGES

- Make sure students know what to do on pages 109 and 110. In the second activity on page 110, have them identify the relationship between the first two boldfaced words in each sentence.

- After students have completed the pages, ask a volunteer to share what he or she has learned about words with diphthongs *ew, oi, oy.*

Name _____

> Read each pair of sentences. Then underline each word in which **ew** stands for the sound you hear in **new**. Circle the number of the sentence that describes the picture.

> **RULE**
> The diphthong **ew** stands for the vowel sound you hear in **new**. This is almost the same sound you hear in **moon**.

1. The spaceship <u>flew</u> through space on its long journey.
2. The stars were like <u>jewels</u> in the dark of space.

3. The crew exercised a few hours every day.
4. Earth <u>grew</u> smaller in the <u>view</u> screen.

5. They <u>knew</u> their story would be in all the <u>newspapers.</u>
6. The <u>crew</u> set foot on <u>new</u> ground.

> Read each sentence. Complete the sentence with a word from the word bank.

7. The _____ shrewd _____ pitcher eyed the batter closely.

8. He _____ knew _____ he had to strike out the batter to win the game.

9. The pitcher _____ drew _____ back his arm and let the ball fly.

10. Crack! The runner _____ flew _____ around the bases.

11. The outfielder _____ threw _____ the ball to home too late.

12. The final score would be on the late _____ news _____.

> drew   blew
> news   strewn
> threw   knew
> shrewd
> flew

FOCUS ON ALL LEARNERS ＊ ● ◆ ●

ENGLISH LANGUAGE LEARNERS/ESL

To build background for the first story on page 109, ask students if they have ever read a science-fiction story about space travel. Have volunteers tell about the characters, setting, and events in the story they read.

VISUAL LEARNERS

LARGE GROUP

Write on the board the following sets of words and misspellings: *fliu, flew, floo; knoo, knew, knue; crewe, croo, crew; nephew, nephyou, nephyew; shrood, shrewed, shrewd; juwels, jewels, joowels.* Have volunteers circle the correct spelling in each set and say the word.

VISUAL/KINESTHETIC LEARNERS

PARTNER

Materials: encyclopedia, drawing paper, crayons, markers

Have pairs of students find a picture of the solar system in an encyclopedia and then draw it. Ask them to write *ew* on the sun and an *ew* word from the lesson on each planet.

Say each word and circle the diphthong.

1. l(oy)al
2. J(oy)ce
3. j(ew)el
4. n(oi)sy
5. ann(oy)
6. ch(ew)
7. sp(oi)led
8. s(oi)l
9. neph(ew)
10. p(oi)son
11. empl(oy)
12. thr(ew)
13. destr(oy)
14. c(oi)n
15. st(ew)
16. p(oi)nt
17. (oi)l
18. r(oy)al
19. d(ew)
20. m(oi)st
21. n(ew)spaper
22. scr(ew)s
23. av(oi)d
24. fl(ew)

Read each sentence. Think about the way the first two words in boldface are related. Then choose one of the words from above to complete the analogy.

> **DEFINITION**
> An **analogy** compares different things. Analogies show how pairs of things are alike.
> A **car** is to a **road** as a **boat** is to **water**.

25. **Hammer** is to **nails** as **screwdriver** is to  _screws_ .

26. **Vegetables** are to **salad** as **meat** is to ___ stew ___ .

27. **Desert** is to **dry** as **swamp** is to ___ moist ___ .

28. **Niece** is to **girl** as ___ nephew ___ is to **boy**.

29. **Dollar** is to **bill** as **quarter** is to ___ coin ___ .

30. **Milk** is to **sip** as **apple** is to ___ chew ___ .

31. **Dismiss** is to **fire** as **hire** is to ___ employ ___ .

32. **Radio** is to **listen** as ___ newspaper ___ is to **read**.

33. **Hay** is to **horse** as ___ oil ___ is to **machine**.

34. **Fresh** is to **food** as ___ spoiled ___ is to **garbage**.

35. **Whisper** is to **quiet** as **shout** is to ___ noisy ___ .

36. **Run** is to **ran** as **throw** is to ___ threw ___ .

37. **Build** is to **create** as **demolish** is to ___ destroy ___ .

38. **Tip** is to **brush** as ___ point ___ is to **pencil**.

39. **See** is to **saw** as **fly** is to ___ flew ___ .

40. **Ice** is to **frost** as **water** is to ___ dew ___ .

10 Lesson 50
Diphthong oi, oy, ew

LARGE GROUP

AUDITORY LEARNERS

Materials: pink and white index cards, markers

Make each student a pink /oo/ card and a white /oy/ card. Read aloud a mixed list of *ew*, *oi*, and *oy* words. After each word, have students hold up its vowel sound. If it is /oy/, ask whether the word is spelled with *oi* or *oy*.

GIFTED LEARNERS

Have students list as many different spellings for the long *u* sound as they can and collect several words with each spelling: *ue* (blue), *oo* (room), *ew* (drew) *u*-consonant-*e* (rude); *u* (super); *ui* (suit), *eu* (rheumatism), *ou* (soup), and so on. You may wish to combine their lists into a class table.

LEARNERS WHO NEED EXTRA SUPPORT

Tell students that many words they use every day—past-tense verbs—end with the *oo* sound spelled *ew*, such as *know, knew; blow, blew; grow, grew; draw, drew; throw, threw; fly, flew*. Have students give additional examples of past-tense verbs with *ew*. See Daily Word Study Practice, pages 203–204.

SPELLING

The following sentences can be used as a spelling pretest for words with vowel diphthongs *ew*, *ou*, and *ow*.

1. **threw**   I **threw** your letter away by mistake.
2. **cloud**   A thunder **cloud** has a unique shape.
3. **flowers**   Dad sent Mom a bunch of **flowers**.
4. **snow**   You can't ski unless there is **snow**.
5. **brown**   One kind of bear is the **brown** bear.
6. **shout**   At a ball game, we yell and **shout**.

WRITING

Portfolio The *ew* words in the baseball story on page 109 could appear in almost any sports story! Invite students to write a short news article reporting on a game in a different sport. Challenge them to use at least four of the words from the word bank on page 109.

LANGUAGE ARTS

Challenge students to write their own analogies. Remind them that the words in each pair of an analogy must have the same relationship. Have students leave a blank for an *ew* word in each analogy and ask a classmate to complete them.

LANGUAGE ARTS

Materials: index cards, marker

Help students learn to tell how /oy/ is spelled in a word. Together with students, make word cards for *soil, hoist, appoint, oil, join, toy, loyal, loin, poison, coin, moist, voyage, foil, ointment, boisterous, poise, spoil, boil, annoy, destroy, coil, joint, royal, noise*. Have students sort the words into two piles: *oi* and *oy*. Then have them sort the *oi* words by the letter after *oy*. (oy: *toy, annoy, destroy, loyal, voyage, royal*; oil: *soil, oil, foil, spoil, boil, coil*; ois/oist: *poison, poise, noise, hoist, moist, boisterous*; oin/oint: *join, loin, coin, appoint, ointment, joint*) Ask students to make a generalization about each pile. (*Possible answer: oy comes at the end of a word or before a; oi comes before l, before s, or before n.*)

Lesson 51

Pages 111–112

Diphthongs ou, ow

INFORMAL ASSESSMENT OBJECTIVE

Can students

✔ associate the diphthongs *ou* and *ow* with their sounds?

Lesson Focus

INTRODUCING THE SKILL

- Review the diphthongs *oi*, *oy*, and *ew* by encouraging students to explain how they know that these vowel combinations are diphthongs. (*The vowels blend together as one sound in a word.*)

- Have students listen for another diphthong as you say the word *crowd*. Ask students to identify the vowel sound and suggest what letters stand for that sound. (*ow*) Have a volunteer write the word on the board and underline *ow*.

- Then write the word *cloud* and have students say it aloud. Ask what they notice about the vowel sound. (*It is the same as in* crowd.)

- Explain that the diphthongs *ou* and *ow* stand for the vowel sound heard in *crowd* and *cloud*. Ask students to name another diphthong pair they know that stands for one vowel sound. (*oy, oi*)

USING THE PAGES

Make sure everyone knows what to do on pages 111 and 112. After students have completed the pages, have a volunteer summarize what he or she learned about the diphthongs *ou* and *ow*.

111

Name _____

▶ **Say the name of each picture. Then circle its name.**

> **RULE**
> The diphthongs **ou** and **ow** often stand for the vowel sound you hear in **loud** and **down**.

1. claw (clown)
2. bless (blouse)
3. (thousand) thaw
4. (shower) shout
5. floors (flowers)
6. (cloud) clog

▶ **Read the sentences and questions below. Answer each question with a response from the word bank. Write it on the line.**

7. The crew on the boat was **rowdy** and had to be quieted down. What does **rowdy** mean?
   disorderly and rough

8. The crew was on a **scow** that was hauling garbage down the river. What is a **scow**?
   a boat used to haul cargo

9. The crew was **doused** when a sudden rainstorm came up. What does **doused** mean?
   drenched

10. The captain **scowled** at the bad behavior of the crew. What did the captain do if he **scowled**?
    looked angry

a boat used to haul cargo
drenched
disorderly and rough
looked angry

FOCUS ON ALL LEARNERS

ENGLISH LANGUAGE LEARNERS/ESL

Before students begin working on page 111, have them pronounce the words under each picture at the top of the page. Explain that the words in the second exercise are difficult and that almost everyone in the class will have to figure out their meanings from context.

VISUAL LEARNERS

PARTNER Have students write antonyms for words with /ow/ spelled *ou* or *ow* and ask their partner to supply the word; for example, *north (south); valley (mountain); weak (powerful); up (down); quiet (loud).* Encourage them to use /ow/ words not in the lesson.

KINESTHETIC/AUDITORY LEARNERS

LARGE GROUP Write *Turn around* and *Sit down* on the board. Have students stand up. Read one /ow/ word at a time and have students turn around if the word has *ou* and sit down if it has *ow*. Use these words: *town, sound, brown, loud, cloud, cow, flower, house, towel.*

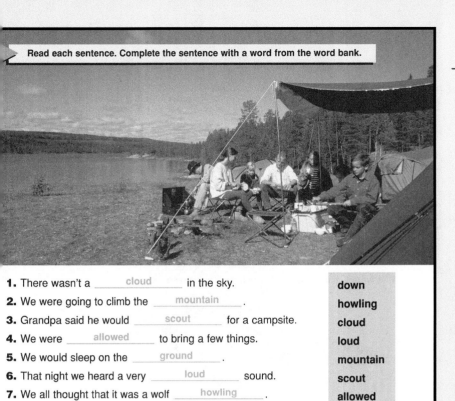

1. There wasn't a ____cloud____ in the sky.
2. We were going to climb the ____mountain____ .
3. Grandpa said he would ____scout____ for a campsite.
4. We were ____allowed____ to bring a few things.
5. We would sleep on the ____ground____ .
6. That night we heard a very ____loud____ sound.
7. We all thought that it was a wolf ____howling____ .
8. The next morning we went ____down____ the mountain.

down
howling
cloud
loud
mountain
scout
allowed
ground

9. There was a celebration in the ____town____ .
10. A large ____crowd____ of people gathered.
11. They were ____rowdy____ and noisy.
12. The town ____council____ was dedicating the fountain.
13. The mayor ____counted____ , "one, two, three!"
14. Water spurted from the ____fountain____ .
15. The crowd ____shouted____ loudly and clapped.
16. The people were ____proud____ of their town.

fountain
proud
council
town
counted
shouted
crowd
rowdy

112 Lesson 51
Diphthongs ou, ow

CURRICULUM CONNECTIONS

SPELLING

Display the spelling words (*brown, cloud, flowers, snow, shout, threw*). Invite students to secretly think of and write down three questions, each of whose answers is one of the spelling words. (Example: *What's white and cold and falls in winter?*) Then erase the spelling words. Have individuals ask their questions and others take turns answering by spelling the word that fits. (Example: *s-n-o-w*) A student giving a correct answer asks the next question.

WRITING

 Portfolio **Materials:** poster paper, markers, crayons

Have students collect words in their environment that have /ow/ spelled *ou* or *ow*. They should look on billboards, food packages, buses, storefronts, signs on buildings, and so on. After several days of collecting, let them work in groups to make a poster listing their words, titled "Words About Town." Encourage students to use some of the words in a short description of their town or city.

SCIENCE/ART

Materials: books about weather, art materials

Display pictures of clouds and discuss the different types. Have students look up facts about kinds of clouds, including cumulonimbus, cirrus, altocumulus, altostratus, stratocumulus, and stratus. Have students draw their own cloud pictures and label them.

GEOGRAPHY/MATH

Materials: world atlas, chart paper, marker

Remind students that on charts and graphs, large numbers are often rounded to the nearest thousand. Have students look up some of the world's highest mountains and make a bar graph showing their heights, rounded to the nearest thousand feet. Have students find out which country each mountain is in and locate it on a map or globe.

 SMALL GROUP

AUDITORY/KINESTHETIC LEARNERS

Materials: index cards, markers

Make five word cards for each of these diphthongs: *oi, oy, ow, ou*. Shuffle the cards and then have students work together to sort the words into two stacks according to the pronunciation of the diphthong, /oy/ or /ow/.

GIFTED LEARNERS

Invite students to write a short essay about something that makes them feel proud. Ask them to use as many words with /ow/ spelled *ou* or *ow* as possible.

LEARNERS WHO NEED EXTRA SUPPORT

Help students create mnemonic devices to aid them in recalling the spellings of troublesome /ow/ words. Here are two examples: *Ow! The clown hit me! I found a thousand dollars.* See Daily Word Study Practice, pages 203–204.

Lesson 52

Pages 113–114

Diphthongs  ou, ow, oi, oy, ew

INFORMAL ASSESSMENT OBJECTIVES

Can students

✔ associate the diphthong *ow* with its sound?

✔ distinguish among the diphthongs *oi, oy, ew, ou,* and *ow?*

Lesson Focus

INTRODUCING THE SKILL

- Review the sound the diphthongs *ou* and *ow* can stand for. (*the sound heard in* loud *and* crowd)

- Tell students that the diphthong *ow* can stand for another sound.

- Write the words *show* and *pillow* on the board. Have students pronounce the words. Ask what sound the letters *ow* stand for in these words.

- Explain that *ow* can stand for the vowel sound heard in *snow* as well as for the vowel sound heard in *cow.*

USING THE PAGES

- Read aloud with students the directions for each page before students begin it. Make sure all students understand each step they are to do.

- After page 113 has been finished, have students tell what they know about the diphthong *ow* pronounced as in *cow* and as in *snow.*

- After students finish page 114, encourage them to share and discuss their work.

113

 Name

> Read each sentence. Circle each word in which **ow** stands for the vowel sound you hear in **cow.** Underline each word in which **ow** stands for the vowel sound you hear in **snow.** Then write each **ow** word in the correct column.

1. Do you <u>know</u> that tomorrow is the party?
2. No one will be (allowed) in without a costume.
3. I will be a (clown) wearing a big bow.
4. Ted is going to show up as a (flower) in a bowl.
5. Kim is going to be a (brown)(owl.)
6. She will borrow a pillow to stuff in her costume.
7. Dad said we should be mellow, not (rowdy.)
8. (Anyhow,) the band will (drown) out our noise.

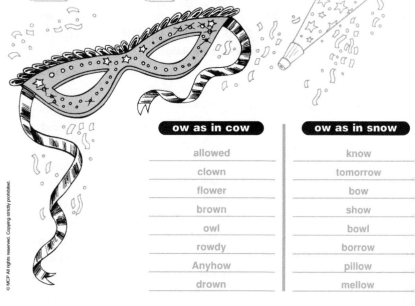

ow as in cow	ow as in snow
allowed	know
clown	tomorrow
flower	bow
brown	show
owl	bowl
rowdy	borrow
Anyhow	pillow
drown	mellow

Lesson 52
Diphthong ow
113

FOCUS ON ALL LEARNERS

ENGLISH LANGUAGE LEARNERS/ESL

To build background for the story on page 113, ask students if they have ever dressed up in a costume to go to a party, to be in a play, or to march in a parade. Encourage students to describe the costumes they wore.

VISUAL LEARNERS

 INDIVIDUAL

Materials: large index cards, markers

Make large word cards for several words with *ow* as in *now* and several with *ow* as in *slow.* Have students write two headings on their paper: *Now* and *Slow.* Silently hold up the words one at a time and have students write each word in the correct column.

VISUAL/KINESTHETIC LEARNERS

LARGE GROUP

Materials: pink and white index cards, markers

Make a white *slow* card and a pink *now* card for each student. Read the *ow* words from page 113 and have students hold up the card that has the same vowel sound as each word you read.

Read the sentence in each box and then draw a picture to show what the sentence means. Circle the words with diphthongs in each sentence.

1. The (frowning) (clown) was (employed) to make the (crowd) of (thousands) (howl) with (joy).

2. The (shrewd) (cowboy) (pounced) on the steer while (avoiding) the (points) of his long horns.

3. The (noisy) (nephew) (annoyed) his aunt when he (pointed) and (shouted) at the (flower) show.

4. The (powerful) family (threw) (coins) from a (tower) into a (fountain).

AUDITORY/VISUAL LEARNERS

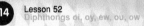

PARTNER   Have students each write three sentences that include at least one *ow* word pronounced /ow/ and one pronounced long *o*. Then ask them to switch papers and read their partner's sentences aloud. Examples include *A clown sat on a yellow pillow. I know I am not allowed to be rowdy.*

GIFTED LEARNERS

Write five headings on the board: *oi, oy, ew, ow, ou*. Have students look through books or magazines to find examples of each diphthong and write them in the correct columns, avoiding duplication.

LEARNERS WHO NEED EXTRA SUPPORT

Before students work on page 114, write on the board the five different diphthongs they will be looking for: *oi, oy, ew, ow*, and *ou*.
See Daily Word Study Practice, pages 203–204.

CURRICULUM CONNECTIONS ✳ • ◆ • ◆

SPELLING

Materials: index cards, markers (optional)

Write the spelling words *brown, cloud, flowers, shouted, threw, snow* on the board. Let students have fun seeing how many different smaller words they can make using the letters in one spelling word. Example for *brown:* bow, born, brow, no, nor, now, own, on, or, row, rob, won, worn. You may want to have students make letter cards so that they can physically rearrange the letters.

WRITING

Portfolio   Have students think of something they know how to do well, such as grow flowers, throw a pitch, or make stew. Then have them write a short how-to article explaining how to do it. Remind them to begin with a list of ingredients or supplies and then list the steps in time order.

ART

Materials: drawing paper, crayons or markers, face-painting supplies (optional), pictures of clown faces (optional)

Show students several examples of happy and sad clown faces. Then have students imagine that your class is going to run a face-painting booth at a school fair, painting clown faces on visiting children. Ask each student to draw and color a happy clown face and a sad clown face that could be used in this project. If you have the supplies, you may want to let students paint each other's faces following their designs.

SOCIAL STUDIES

In the Old West, being a cowboy wasn't as romantic as the movies would have us think! Have interested students research what the life of a cowboy was really like and give a brief oral report to the class.

Syllables in Words With Two Vowels

Can students

✓ recognize the number of syllables in words containing vowel pairs, vowel digraphs, or diphthongs?

Lesson Focus

INTRODUCING THE SKILL

- Ask students how they know how many syllables a word has. *(They listen for the number of vowel sounds.)*

- Write the words *painting* and *because*. Ask students to read them and compare the number of vowels with the number of vowel sounds heard. Have volunteers divide the words into syllables.

- Remind students that vowel pairs, digraphs, and diphthongs make one sound, and therefore would not be divided between the two vowels. Point out that in contrast, a word like *duet* would be divided between the *u* and *e* because the two vowels are sounded separately.

USING THE PAGES

- Remind students to write the pair of vowels in the first column on page 115. Before they begin working on page 116, you may want to review the rules students have learned so far about dividing words into syllables.

- After completing both pages, have volunteers demonstrate how to divide several words with vowel pairs, digraphs, and diphthongs.

115

Name

Say each word. Write its pair of vowels on the first line. Then write the number of syllables you hear in the word on the second line.

RULE

When you listen for the number of syllables in a word, remember that a vowel pair or a diphthong stands for **one** vowel sound.

g**oa**t   **oi**ntment

	Pair of Vowels	Number of Syllables		Pair of Vowels	Number of Syllables
1. spoonful	oo	2	19. loyal	oy	2
2. noisy	oi	2	20. double	ou	2
3. repeat	ea	2	21. moisten	oi	2
4. thought	ou	1	22. appear	ea	2
5. haunted	au	2	23. breakfast	ea	2
6. wealthy	ea	2	24. piece	ie	1
7. instead	ea	2	25. ounce	ou	1
8. receive	ei	2	26. because	au	2
9. jewelry	ew	3	27. straight	ai	1
10. awkward	aw	2	28. pillow	ow	2
11. lied	ie	1	29. soup	ou	1
12. chief	ie	1	30. eighty	ei	2
13. moonlight	oo	2	31. touch	ou	1
14. house	ou	1	32. soul	ou	1
15. avenue	ue	3	33. laundry	au	2
16. withdraw	aw	2	34. annoy	oy	2
17. flow	ow	1	35. true	ue	1
18. dainty	ai	2	36. blooming	oo	2

Lesson 53
Syllables in words containing vowel pairs   **115**

FOCUS ON ALL LEARNERS

ENGLISH LANGUAGE LEARNERS/ESL

Because these pages can't be completed without knowing how to pronounce the words, you may wish to appoint a fluent English speaker as a pronunciation resource for these students. Allow them to consult him or her as needed while working.

VISUAL LEARNERS

PARTNER   Have students find five two-syllable words that contain a vowel pair, digraph, or diphthong. Have them write all the first syllables down the left side of a page and all the second syllables in mixed-up order down the right side. Have students exchange papers and draw lines to match the syllables.

KINESTHETIC LEARNERS

SMALL GROUP   **Materials:** index cards, markers, dictionary

Write these word pairs on cards: *reach, react; raccoon, cooperate; diet, shriek; people, rodeo; casual, guard; carriage, piano; aorta, pharaoh; nucleus, feud*. Have students take turns drawing a card and reading both words aloud. Ask the group to agree on the pronunciations. Have students verify them by consulting the dictionary.

Underline the pair of vowels in the words. If the two vowels stand for one sound, write **1** on the first line. If the two vowels are sounded separately, write **2** on the first line. Then divide the words into syllables using hyphens, and write them on the second line.

RULES

When two vowels stand for one vowel sound, do not divide the word between the two vowels.

por-tr**ai**t   r**ea**-son

When two vowels are sounded separately, divide the word between the two vowels.

ra-d**i-o**   cr**u-e**l

	Vowel Sounds	Syllables		Vowel Sounds	Syllables
poison	1	poi-son	dialect	2	di-a-lect
diagnose	2	di-ag-nose	couch	1	couch
dinosaur	1	di-no-saur	create	2	cre-ate
area	2	ar-e-a	quiet	2	qui-et
saucer	1	sau-cer	tower	1	tow-er
diary	2	di-a-ry	thousand	1	thou-sand
casual	2	cas-u-al	ideas	2	i-de-as
season	1	sea-son	screw	1	screw
raccoons	1	rac-coons	loudest	1	loud-est
riot	2	ri-ot	defiant	2	de-fi-ant
survey	1	sur-vey	royalty	1	roy-al-ty
situate	2	sit-u-ate	realize	2	re-al-ize
pheasant	1	phea-sant	shriek	1	shriek
cereal	2	cer-e-al	headline	1	head-line
really	2	re-al-ly	diesel	1	die-sel

SPELLING

Write the spelling words across the board as headings: *threw, shout, snow, flowers, cloud, brown.* Invite students to list under each heading as many rhyming words as they can. Have them underline any diphthong that is the same as the diphthong in the spelling word. (Example for *threw: fl<u>ew</u>, bl<u>ue</u>, cr<u>ew</u>, do, shoe, who, ch<u>ew</u>, too, two*)

WRITING

 Portfolio Write the following on the board: *I am a ro-bot Cre-a-ting me was a good i-de-a You no-tice that I have cleared the a-re-a of a-li-ens I al-so play pi-an-o and vi-o-lin* Read what you've written in a mechanical monotone with no inflection and no pauses. Then have students write a short speech as spoken by a robot, correctly hyphenating all the words to show syllables and omitting periods. Encourage them to use words with two vowels together that are sounded separately, like *giant* and *cereal.* Let students read their finished speeches aloud in a robot monotone.

MATH

Materials: calculators

If you double and redouble an amount, it adds up fast! If you put a penny in the bank one day, put two pennies in the bank the next day, and so on, doubling the amount every day, how long will it take to save a million dollars? *(about a month; the amount after Day 28's deposit is $1,342,177.28)*

SCIENCE

Many science words (including the word *science*) have two vowels that are sounded separately. Have each student look up one of these words and tell the class what it means: *sodium, biomass, uranium, bionic, nutrient, helium, aorta, meteor, amphibian, neon, nucleus.* Students can use their research to create a class dictionary of scientific terms.

 Technology

AstroWord Multisyllabic Words. © 1998 Silver Burdett Ginn Inc. Division of Simon & Schuster.

 LARGE GROUP

AUDITORY/VISUAL LEARNERS

Write a mixed list of words from this lesson on the board. Invite students to choose a word and divide it into syllables—incorrectly if they wish! The class must then decide whether the word is divided correctly. Any challenges must be explained and verified by consulting a dictionary.

GIFTED LEARNERS

Challenge students to find and list words with every possible combination of vowel letters. Give them *bazaar* as an example for *aa*. Suggest that they begin systematically, with *aa, ae, ai, ao, au, aw, ay,* then proceeding to the *e's,* and so on.

LEARNERS WHO NEED EXTRA SUPPORT

Explain to students that for items 1–36 on page 115, they should look for the two vowels that come together and write them in the first column. When they are finished with the page, suggest that they sort the words by vowel pairs and list them in categories. See *Daily Word Study Practice, page 208.*

116

Lesson 54

Pages 117–118

 **R**eading **W**riting

Reviewing Diphthongs

INFORMAL ASSESSMENT OBJECTIVES

Can students

✓ read a passage containing words with diphthongs?

✓ write a set of directions using words with diphthongs?

Lesson Focus

READING

- Read this sentence aloud: *That boy is noisy*. Have a volunteer write it on the board and underline the letters that spell /oy/. Repeat with *I knew he was on the crew* and /oo/, and with *We live down south* and /ow/. Ask what kind of sound all of the underlined digraphs represent. (*diphthong*)

- Now ask what other vowel sound *ow* can make. (long *o*) Have someone write and read aloud *This plant grows slowly* and underline *ow*. Have a student tell what a diphthong is and how it differs from a long vowel sound.

- Tell students that they'll find more words with diphthongs when they read the directions for making a snow globe.

WRITING

- Review the information in the set of directions on page 117. Point out the title, the statement of what is being made, the list of materials, and the step-by-step directions. Then have students write the answer to the question.

- As students prepare to write a set of directions, have them refer to the Helpful Hints at the bottom of page 118.

117

 Reading ▶ **Read the directions. Then write your answer to the question at the end.**

How to Make a SNOW GLOBE

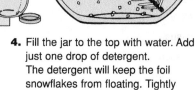

You could buy a new snow globe at a store for a few coins. Or you can make one of your own that can't be found in any store. Here's how.

Materials

a clear, round glass jar with screw-on lid

aluminum foil

one or more toy figures or a piece of an evergreen branch

water

liquid dish detergent

1. Wash out the jar and remove any labels.
2. Make "snow" by cutting a piece of aluminum foil into very, very tiny pieces. The best way to do this is first to cut thin strips along one edge of the foil. Then cut off the strips into tiny pieces. The smaller the pieces, the more real the "snow" will look.
3. Put the foil flakes and the toy figures or branch in the jar.

4. Fill the jar to the top with water. Add just one drop of detergent. The detergent will keep the foil snowflakes from floating. Tightly screw on the lid.
5. Now make a winter snowstorm by turning the snow globe upside down. Give it a gentle shake and then set it down right-side up. Let it snow and enjoy the storm!

Why don't you want the snowflakes to float?

FOCUS ON ALL LEARNERS

ENGLISH LANGUAGE LEARNERS/ESL

Ask if anyone has ever been in a snowstorm and encourage volunteers to report or imagine what it is like. Show students a commercial snow globe, if possible.

VISUAL LEARNERS

 PARTNER   **Materials:** discarded magazines, paste, scissors

Have students cut out or draw small pictures whose names include diphthongs and paste them onto a sheet of paper. Then have them exchange papers and label each other's pictures.

KINESTHETIC LEARNERS

SMALL GROUP   **Materials:** dark construction paper, ruler, marker, white paper, scissors

Have four students use the ruler and marker to divide a sheet of dark paper into four areas. Write one student's name in each. Cut white paper into tiny squares; write a diphthong on each square. Sprinkle this "snow" onto the paper. Each student collects the "snow" from his or her area and says a word for each diphthong.

Writing ▶ Could you teach someone how to do an art project, play a game, or make a toy? Write a set of directions for how to make or do something. Use words from the word bank.

around
moisten
newspaper
down
employ
screw
found
few
join
powerful

List materials at the
   beginning.
Think about each step you do.
Write the steps in order.
Use numbers or words such
   as first, then, and next.

Helpful Hints

118 Lesson 54
Review dipthongs: Writing

SPELLING

The following sentences can be used as a spelling posttest for words with vowel diphthongs *ew*, *ou*, and *ow*.

1. **brown**   Overripe bananas turn **brown**.
2. **cloud**   Look at the white **cloud** in the sky.
3. **flowers**   Our apple tree **flowers** in May.
4. **shout**   I **shout**, but no one hears me.
5. **threw**   He **threw** down the bat and ran.
6. **snow**   Let's shovel the **snow** on the sidewalk.

MATH/SCIENCE

Materials: calculators (optional)

The water content of snow is much less than that of rain. Six inches (15 cm) of wet snow or 30 inches (76 cm) of dry, fluffy snow contains the water of one inch (2.5 cm) of rain. Invite students to make up word problems about these numbers, such as *How many inches of rain does the water in 10 inches of wet snow equal? (1 2/3 inches) How many inches of dry snow equals the water in 1 cm of rain? (12 inches)*

ART

Materials: those listed in the set of directions on page 117, glue, scissors

Ask students to bring in small round glass jars and small plastic toy figures or evergreen twigs. Have students follow the directions on page 117 to make a snow globe. If supplies are limited, you may want to have students work in pairs or small groups.

AUDITORY LEARNERS

LARGE GROUP

Write these word pairs. Have students say the pairs, underline each vowel digraph, and say *yes* if the words rhyme and *no* if they don't: *boys, noise; wounded, rounded; moo, stew; chowder, louder; dew, sew; crowd, proud; shower, grower; frowned, found; yellow, allow.*

GIFTED LEARNERS

Ask students to write a poem about snow. It doesn't need to rhyme, but suggest that they use as many words with the vowel spellings they learned in this unit as possible.

LEARNERS WHO NEED EXTRA SUPPORT

Have each student choose a word from this unit that they have trouble with, learn to spell it, and teach it to a classmate. See Daily Word Study Practice, pages 203–204.

Lesson 55

Pages 119–120

Unit Checkup

Reviewing Vowel Pairs, Digraphs, Diphthongs, and Syllables

INFORMAL ASSESSMENT OBJECTIVES

Can students

✔ identify and write correct spellings of words that include vowel pairs, digraphs, diphthongs, and more than one syllable?

✔ read text that includes these words and then answer comprehension questions?

Lesson Focus

PREPARING FOR THE CHECKUP

- Write the words *gray, paint, toe, blow, oats, leaf, speed, seize,* and *tie* on the board. Ask students to circle the letters that spell each vowel sound.

- Write *health, vein, they, died, brook,* and *goof* and have a volunteer circle the letters that spell the vowel sound, say the words, and name the vowel combinations. (*digraphs*)

- Ask someone to write *clown, joy, mouth, noise,* and *few.* Have a volunteer circle the letters that spell the vowel sound, say the words, and name these vowel combinations. (*diphthongs*)

- Write *diet, usual, create, poem, seizure, healthfully,* and *Vietnam* on the board. Have students pronounce each word and divide it into syllables.

USING THE PAGES

Make sure students understand what to do on pages 119 and 120. When they have completed the pages, encourage them to discuss what they have learned in this unit.

119

Name _____

Read each sentence. Fill in the circle beside the word that correctly completes the sentence. Write the word on the line.

1. Naturalists ____measure____ how well animals perform.
   - ● measure ○ mayor

2. They have ____found____ out many new facts.
   - ○ field ● found

3. Here are some fun facts you may not have ____known____.
   - ○ knight ● known

4. A Goliath beetle can lift 850 times its own ____weight____.
   - ○ weather ● weight

5. To do that, you'd have to pick up four ____school____ buses!
   - ● school ○ scoot

6. When hunting its ____prey____ of birds, the peregrine falcon dives at over 100 miles per hour!
   - ● prey ○ gray

7. It ____seizes____ a bird in its strong talons.
   - ○ deceives ● seizes

8. The basilisk lizard has fringed ____toes____ on its feet.
   - ○ trout ● toes

9. These let it run at high ____speed____ across water!
   - ● speed ○ green

10. A dolphin's skin has a lot of ____oil____ in it.
    - ○ bowls ● oil

11. This helps it ____achieve____ great speeds.
    - ● achieve ○ believe

12. Emperor penguins can ____remain____ underwater 18 minutes!
    - ● remain ○ decay

13. Some birds can ____soar____ to amazing heights.
    - ○ store ● soar

14. A vulture ____died____ hitting an airplane at 36,900 feet!
    - ○ hid ● died

15. ____How____ do you think it could breathe up there?
    - ○ Out ● How

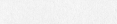

Lesson 55

Vowel pairs, digraphs, diphthongs, syllables: Checkup

119

FOCUS ON ALL LEARNERS

ENGLISH LANGUAGE LEARNERS/ESL

Ask students if they've ever visited a war memorial and if so, how they felt. Ask what a memorial is for. Then ask if anyone ever got a creative idea that seemed to come suddenly.

VISUAL LEARNERS

LARGE GROUP Remind students that a vowel pair has the long sound of the first vowel, and a digraph does not. Write on the board a mixed list of words with vowel pairs and digraphs. Call on students one by one to say the next word and tell whether it has a vowel pair or a digraph.

KINESTHETIC LEARNERS

PARTNER **Materials:** paper clips, box

Have students link paper clips into five chains each of three clips, two clips, and single clips, and place them in a box. Have students reach in and draw out one item and write a word with that many syllables. Ask the partner to say the word and divide it, using hyphens.

Read the story and answer the questions.

MAYA LIN, MEMORIAL MAKER

When the Vietnam Veterans Memorial in Washington, D.C., was first built, it caused a lot of talk. It was a new idea for a memorial—just two walls cut into the earth, with the names of those who died in the war. Angry crowds tried to keep the memorial from being built. But the government went ahead, and it was dedicated on Veterans Day 1982.

People were awed by the "Wall." Many cried as they stood before it reading the soldiers' names. Everyone agreed that the memorial had power to cause deep feelings. Now thousands of visitors are drawn to it each year.

Architect Maya Lin was just 21 years old and a Yale University student when she drew up plans for the memorial. Her design beat out those of 1,420 people who entered the contest to design the memorial. Because her work is so good, Lin keeps very busy. She enjoys what she does and is always ready to begin a new project.

1. Why did the Vietnam Veterans Memorial cause a lot of talk?

It was a new idea for a memorial.

2. How did people react to the completed memorial?

They were awed by it, and many cried.

3. What did people agree about the Wall?

It had the power to cause deep feelings.

4. What did Maya Lin have to do to win the contest to design the memorial?

She had to beat out the designs of 1,420 people.

5. How does Lin feel about her work?

She enjoys it and is always ready to start a new project.

LARGE GROUP

AUDITORY/VISUAL LEARNERS

Write on the board a mixed list of words with the vowel spellings taught in this unit. Underline each vowel pair, digraph, or diphthong. Point to a word and have students shout the vowel sound represented by the underlined vowel combinations. Examples include *enjoy*—"Oy!" *chain*—"Ay!" *spool*—"Ooh!"

GIFTED LEARNERS

Challenge students to collect words with two vowel sounds sounded separately, like *neon* and *client*. Have them try to list three words with *a* as the first letter in the pair, three with *e*, three with *i*, three with *o*, three with *u*, and three with *y*.

LEARNERS WHO NEED EXTRA SUPPORT

Show students one-syllable words from this unit, one word at a time. Have them copy the word, say it, and circle the letters that spell the vowel sound. See Daily Word Study Practice, pages 202–204, 208.

ASSESSING UNDERSTANDING OF UNIT SKILLS ✳ • ◆ • • •

Student Progress Assessment You may wish to review the observational notes you made as students worked through the activities in this unit. Your notes will help you evaluate the progress students made with vowel pairs, digraphs, diphthongs, and syllables.

Portfolio Assessment Review the materials students have collected in their portfolios. You may wish to have interviews with students to discuss their written work and the progress they have made since the beginning of the unit. As you review students' work, evaluate how well they use their knowledge of vowel pairs, digraphs, diphthongs, and syllables.

Daily Word Study Practice For students who need additional practice with vowel pairs, digraphs, diphthongs, and syllables, quick reviews are provided on pages 202–204, 208 in Daily Word Study Practice.

Word Study Posttest To assess students' mastery of vowel pairs, digraphs, diphthongs, and syllables, use the posttest on pages 87g–87h.

Spelling Cumulative Posttest Review Unit 4 spelling words by using the following words and dictation sentences.

1.	**draw**	After I shuffle, you **draw** a card.
2.	**obey**	Drivers have to **obey** traffic rules.
3.	**royalty**	Granny treats us like **royalty**.
4.	**gray**	It's a chilly, **gray**, drizzly day.
5.	**supplies**	This stove **supplies** heat.
6.	**flowers**	April showers bring May **flowers**.
7.	**autumn**	Halloween comes in **autumn**.
8.	**stood**	The soldier **stood** at attention.
9.	**proof**	A receipt is **proof** that you paid.
10.	**threw**	We **threw** a party for Ed's birthday.
11.	**ceiling**	Turn on the **ceiling** light.
12.	**piece**	Would you like a **piece** of pizza?
13.	**cloud**	There's not a **cloud** in the sky.
14.	**paint**	The walls need a coat of **paint**.
15.	**coin**	To play the jukebox, put in a **coin**.
16.	**weigh**	The vet had to **weigh** the cat.
17.	**road**	We walked along the sandy **road**.
18.	**pillow**	My dog sleeps on a soft **pillow**.
19.	**steady**	Slow and **steady** wins the race.
20.	**toe**	He stepped on my **toe**.

Teacher Notes

Unit 5

Plurals, Possessives, Contractions, Syllables

Student Performance Objectives

In Unit 5, students will review and extend their understanding of forming regular and irregular plurals and contractions. Students will be introduced to the use of the apostrophe in forming singular and plural possessive nouns. As these skills are introduced and developed, students will be able to

◆ Recognize and form the plural of words ending in *ss, z, x, sh, ch, y, f, fe,* and *o*

◆ Recognize and form the singular and plural possessives of nouns

◆ Recognize contractions

◆ Recognize and practice the use of the apostrophe in possessive nouns and contractions

◆ Recognize the number of syllables in words

Contents

Assessment Strategy Overview

Throughout Unit 5, assess students' ability to read and write regular and irregular plurals, contractions, and possessives. There are various ways to assess students' progress. You may also want to encourage students to evaluate their own work and to participate in setting goals for their own learning.

FORMAL ASSESSMENT

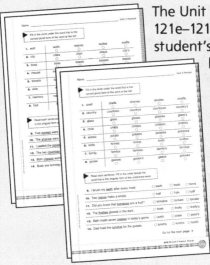

The Unit 5 Pretest on pages 121e–121f helps to assess a student's knowledge at the beginning of the unit and to plan instruction.

The Unit 5 Posttest on pages 121g–121h helps to assess mastery of unit objectives and to plan for reteaching, if necessary.

INFORMAL ASSESSMENT

The Reading & Writing pages and Unit Checkup in the student book are an effective means of evaluating students' performance.

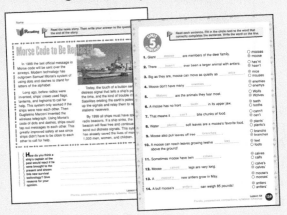

Skill	Reading & Writing Pages	Unit Checkup
Plurals Ending in *f, fe*	137–138	139–140
Plurals Ending in *y*	137–138	139–140
Plurals Ending in *ss, ch*	137–138	139–140
Plurals Ending in *o*	137–138	139–140
Plurals that Become Different Words	137–138	139–140
Contractions with *will*	137–138	139–140
Contractions with *not*	137–138	139–140
Contractions with *have*	137–138	139–140
Contractions with *are*	137–138	139–140
Contractions with *is*	137–138	139–140
Contractions with *am*	137–138	139–140

PORTFOLIO ASSESSMENT

This logo appears throughout the teaching plans. It signals opportunities for collecting students' work for individual portfolios. You may also want to collect the following pages.

❖ Unit 5 Pretest and Posttest, pages 121e–121h

❖ Unit 5 Reading & Writing, pages 137–138

❖ Unit 5 Checkup, pages 139–140

STUDENT PROGRESS CHECKLIST

Use the checklist on page 121i to record students' progress. You may want to cut the sections apart to place each student's checklist in his or her portfolio.

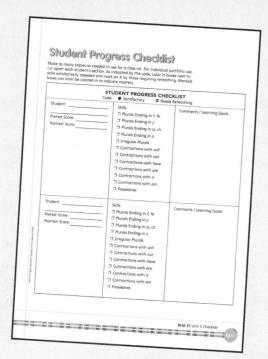

Administering and Evaluating the

Pretest and Posttest

DIRECTIONS

To help you assess students' progress in learning Unit 5 skills, tests are available on pages 121e–121h. Administer the Pretest before students begin the unit. The results of the Pretest will help you identify each student's strengths and needs in advance, allowing you to structure lesson plans to meet individual needs. Administer the Posttest to assess students' overall mastery of skills taught in the unit and to identify specific areas that will require reteaching.

PERFORMANCE ASSESSMENT PROFILE

The following chart will help you identify specific skills as they appear on the tests and enable you to identify and record specific information about an individual's or the class's performance on the tests.

Depending on the results of the tests, refer to the Reteaching column for lesson-plan pages where you can find activities that will be useful for meeting individual needs or for daily word study practice.

ANSWER KEYS

Unit 5 Pretest, page 121e (BLM 33)

1. shelves
2. countries
3. glasses
4. children
5. potatoes
6. knives
7. families
8. geese

9. tooth
10. half
11. tomato
12. firefly
13. pass
14. lunch

Unit 5 Pretest, page 121f (BLM 34)

15. can not
16. have not
17. would not
18. I have
19. you will
20. they are
21. she is
22. do not
23. I am

24. contraction
25. possessive
26. contraction
27. contraction
28. possessive
29. plural
30. possessive

Unit 5 Posttest, page 121g (BLM 35)

1. wolves
2. cities
3. bosses
4. mice
5. tomatoes
6. wives
7. memories
8. feet

9. woman
10. shelf
11. potato
12. country
13. class
14. branch

Unit 5 Posttest, page 121h (BLM 36)

15. will not
16. did not
17. could not
18. you have
19. they will
20. we are
21. it is
22. are not
23. let us

24. contraction
25. possessive
26. contraction
27. contraction
28. possessive
29. plural
30. possessive

PERFORMANCE ASSESSMENT PROFILE

Skill	Pretest Questions	Posttest Questions	Reteaching: Focus on All Learners	Reteaching: Daily Word Study Practice
Plurals ending in *f, fe*	1, 6, 10	1, 6, 10	125–126, 128, 137	204
Plurals ending in *y*	2, 7, 12	2, 7, 12	124, 137	204
Plurals ending in *ss, ch*	3, 13, 14	3, 13, 14	124, 137	204
Plurals ending in *o*	5, 11	5, 11	125–126, 137	204
Irregular Plurals	4, 8, 9, 29	4, 8, 9, 29	127–128, 137	204
Contractions with *will*	19, 26, 27	15, 19, 24, 26, 27	133–134, 137	204–205
Contractions with *not*	15, 16, 17, 22, 24	15, 16, 17, 22, 24	133–134, 137	204–205
Contractions with *have*	16, 18	18	133–134, 137	204–205
Contractions with *are, is*	20, 21	20, 21	133–134, 137	204–205
Contractions with *am, us*	23	23	133–134, 137	204–205
Possessives	25, 28, 30	25, 28, 30	129–132, 137–138	204–205

▶ Fill in the circle under the word that is the correct plural form of the word at the left.

1. shelf	shelfs ○	shelves ○	shelfes ○	shelffs ○
2. country	countries ○	countrys ○	countryes ○	country's ○
3. glass	glass ○	glases ○	glasses ○	glass's ○
4. child	childs ○	childes ○	children ○	childies ○
5. potato	potato ○	potatos ○	potaties ○	potatoes ○
6. knife	knives ○	knifes ○	knifs ○	kniffes ○
7. family	familys ○	families ○	family's ○	famillys ○
8. goose	geeses ○	goose's ○	geese ○	goosies ○

▶ Read each sentence. Fill in the circle beside the word that is the singular form of the underlined word.

9. I brush my <u>teeth</u> after every meal.   ○ teeth   ○ tooth   ○ toovs

10. Two <u>halves</u> make a whole.   ○ half   ○ halv   ○ halff

11. Did you know that <u>tomatoes</u> are a fruit?   ○ tomatoe   ○ tomate   ○ tomato

12. The <u>fireflies</u> glowed in the dark.   ○ firefli   ○ firefly   ○ firefly's

13. Beth made seven <u>passes</u> in today's game.   ○ pass   ○ pase   ○ pass's

14. Dad fixed the <u>lunches</u> for the guests.   ○ lunchs   ○ lunchs'   ○ lunch

Go to the next page. →

▶ Fill in the circle beside the two words that stand for each contraction.

15. can't	○ could not	○ can not	○ can be
16. haven't	○ has not	○ have to	○ have not
17. wouldn't	○ would not	○ will not	○ would have
18. I've	○ I would	○ I can	○ I have
19. you'll	○ you will	○ you are	○ I will
20. they're	○ they have	○ we are	○ they are
21. she's	○ she will	○ she is	○ he will
22. don't	○ do not	○ does not	○ do you
23. I'm	○ I will	○ I have	○ I am

▶ Read each sentence. Fill in the circle beside the word that tells if the underlined word is a contraction, a possessive, or a plural.

24. I <u>don't</u> think Sandra will be late.	○ possessive	○ contraction	○ plural
25. The <u>dentist's</u> office is on the fifth floor.	○ possessive	○ contraction	○ plural
26. <u>You'll</u> like the actors in that new play.	○ possessive	○ contraction	○ plural
27. The Morgans say <u>they'll</u> visit us soon.	○ possessive	○ contraction	○ plural
28. <u>Someone's</u> boots are on the couch.	○ possessive	○ contraction	○ plural
29. The <u>children</u> raced down the hill.	○ possessive	○ contraction	○ plural
30. <u>Danny's</u> parents are both teachers.	○ possessive	○ contraction	○ plural

Possible score on Unit 5 Pretest is 30. Number correct _____

▶ Fill in the circle under the word that is the correct plural form of the word at the left.

1. wolf	wolfs ○	wolves ○	wolfes ○	wolffs ○
2. city	cities ○	citys ○	citeys ○	city's ○
3. boss	boss ○	boses ○	bosses ○	bosse ○
4. mouse	mouses ○	meese ○	mice ○	mices ○
5. tomato	tomato ○	tomatos ○	tomatoos ○	tomatoes ○
6. wife	wives ○	wifes ○	wifs ○	wiffes ○
7. memory	memorys ○	memories ○	memores ○	memorries ○
8. foot	feets ○	foot's ○	feet ○	footses ○

▶ Read each sentence. Fill in the circle beside the word that is the singular form of the underlined word in the sentence.

9. Two women were jogging in the park. ○ women ○ woman ○ wommen

10. The shelves were filled with new books. ○ shelf ○ shelv ○ shelve

11. I peeled the potatoes for dinner. ○ potatoe ○ potate ○ potato

12. The two countries were at war. ○ countri ○ countrie ○ country

13. Both classes went on a field trip. ○ class ○ clase ○ class's

14. Buds are forming on the tree branches. ○ branchs ○ branche ○ branch

Go to the next page. →

> Fill in the circle beside the two words that stand for each contraction.

15. won't   ○ would not   ○ will not   ○ will have

16. didn't   ○ did to   ○ do not   ○ did not

17. couldn't   ○ could not   ○ can not   ○ could have

18. you've   ○ you would   ○ you can   ○ you have

19. they'll   ○ they will   ○ they are   ○ they have

20. we're   ○ we have   ○ you are   ○ we are

21. it's   ○ it will   ○ it is   ○ is not

22. aren't   ○ are not   ○ is not   ○ are you

23. let's   ○ let me   ○ let it   ○ let us

> Read each sentence. Fill in the circle beside the word that tells if the underlined word is a contraction, a possessive, or a plural.

24. I <u>won't</u> make you wait much longer.   ○ possessive   ○ contraction   ○ plural

25. The <u>player's</u> uniform was muddy.   ○ possessive   ○ contraction   ○ plural

26. <u>We'll</u> go early to get good seats.   ○ possessive   ○ contraction   ○ plural

27. Dad says <u>he'll</u> help with the party.   ○ possessive   ○ contraction   ○ plural

28. We put <u>everyone's</u> coat in the closet.   ○ possessive   ○ contraction   ○ plural

29. It took six <u>oxen</u> to pull the wagon.   ○ possessive   ○ contraction   ○ plural

30. I found <u>Angela's</u> glove on the bus.   ○ possessive   ○ contraction   ○ plural

Possible score on Unit 5 Posttest is 30. Number correct _____

Student Progress Checklist

Make as many copies as needed to use for a class list. For individual portfolio use, cut apart each student's section. As indicated by the code, color in boxes next to skills satisfactorily assessed and mark an X by those requiring reteaching. Marked boxes can later be colored in to indicate mastery.

STUDENT PROGRESS CHECKLIST
Code: ■ Satisfactory ☒ Needs Reteaching

Student: _____	Skills	Comments / Learning Goals
_____	❏ Plurals Ending in *f, fe*	
Pretest Score: _____	❏ Plurals Ending in *y*	
Posttest Score: _____	❏ Plurals Ending in *ss, ch*	
	❏ Plurals Ending in *o*	
	❏ Irregular Plurals	
	❏ Contractions with *will*	
	❏ Contractions with *not*	
	❏ Contractions with *have*	
	❏ Contractions with *are*	
	❏ Contractions with *is*	
	❏ Contractions with *am*	
	❏ Possessives	

Student: _____	Skills	Comments / Learning Goals
_____	❏ Plurals Ending in *f, fe*	
Pretest Score: _____	❏ Plurals Ending in *y*	
Posttest Score: _____	❏ Plurals Ending in *ss, ch*	
	❏ Plurals Ending in *o*	
	❏ Irregular Plurals	
	❏ Contractions with *will*	
	❏ Contractions with *not*	
	❏ Contractions with *have*	
	❏ Contractions with *are*	
	❏ Contractions with *is*	
	❏ Contractions with *am*	
	❏ Possessives	

Spelling Connections

INTRODUCTION

The Unit Word List is a list of spelling words drawn from this unit. The words are grouped by plurals and contractions studied throughout the unit. To incorporate spelling into your word study program, use the activity in the Curriculum Connections section of each teaching plan.

The spelling lessons utilize the following approach for each set of words.

1. Administer a pretest of the words that have not yet been introduced. Dictation sentences are provided.

2. Provide practice.

3. Reassess. Dictation sentences are provided.

A final test is provided at the end of the unit in Lesson 64, on page 140.

DIRECTIONS

Make a copy of Blackline Master 38 for each student. After administering the pretest for each word, give students a copy of the appropriate word list.

Students can work with a partner to practice spelling the words orally and identifying whether the word is a plural or a contraction. You may want to challenge students to add to the list other plurals and contractions. Students can also write words of their own on *My Own Word List* (see Blackline Master 38).

Students may store their list words in an envelope in the back of their books or notebooks. You may want to suggest that students keep a spelling notebook, listing similar plurals and contractions. Another idea is to build word walls with students and display them in the classroom. Each section of the wall can focus on a type of word. The walls will become a good spelling resource when students are writing.

UNIT WORD LIST

Plurals of Words with Endings *ss, z, x, sh, ch, y, f, o*

messes

waltzes

boxes

dishes

batches

activities

wolves

potatoes

Irregular Plurals

geese

sheep

Contractions

it's

can't

Name _____

 Spelling   **UNIT 5 WORD LIST**

**Plurals of Words with Endings
ss, z, x, sh, ch, y, f, o**

messes
waltzes
boxes
dishes
batches
activities
wolves
potatoes

Irregular Plurals

geese
sheep

Contractions
it's
can't

My Own Word List

Word Study Games, Activities, and Technology

The following collection of ideas offers a variety of opportunities to reinforce word study skills while actively engaging students. The games, activities, and technology suggestions can easily be adapted to meet the needs of your group of learners. They vary in approach so as to consider students' different learning styles.

● MIXED-UP PARAGRAPHS

Have students look through newspapers and magazines and cut out paragraphs that contain plurals, possessives, and contractions. Give each student an envelope. Ask students to cut the paragraphs into separate sentences and number the sentences on the back according to paragraph order. Have them place the sentences in their envelope. Students may exchange envelopes, put the sentences in the correct order, and circle the plurals, possessives, and contractions they find in the sentences.

▲ CONTRACTION JIGSAW PUZZLES

Students can use index cards to make contraction puzzles. On one side of the card, they write a contraction, such as *wouldn't*. On the other side of the card, they write the two words that make up the contraction. Then they cut the card in a jagged line between the two words. Partners can make a number of puzzles, mix up the pieces, and time each other to see how quickly they can put all the puzzles together.

◆ NAME THAT RULE

Divide the class into seven groups. Assign each group one of the following rules for making plurals.

> 1. Regular nouns: Add *s*.
> 2. Nouns ending in *s*, *ch*, *sh*, or *x*: Add *es*.
> 3. Nouns ending in *y* preceded by a consonant: Change the *y* to *ies*.
> 4. Nouns ending in *y* preceded by a vowel: Add *s*.
> 5. Nouns ending in *f* or *fe*: Change to *ves*.
> 6. Some nouns become different words.
> 7. Some nouns do not change.

Ask each group to make a poster illustrating its rule. Then ask each to make five word cards for words that follow the rule. Have each group write the singular form of the word on one side of the card and the plural form on the other. Display the posters along the ledge of the chalkboard and mix up the word cards. Hold up one card at a time so that only the singular form of the word shows. Ask volunteers to place the card next to the rule that governs it, spell the plural form, and turn the card over to check the spelling.

■ CONTRACTION SEAT SWITCH

Write contractions on index cards for half of the students in the group. On other index cards, write the two words that make up each contraction. Pass out the cards and choose a student to be "it." Call out one of the contractions. The two students who have the corresponding cards must switch seats with one another. As they do, "it" tries to take one of their seats. The student left standing becomes the next "it."

✳ PLURAL RELAY

Divide the class into two to five teams. Each team chooses a rule for making plurals, such as adding -es to nouns ending in -s, -ch, -sh, or -x, and makes word cards for words that follow the rule. There should be one card for each team member. Collect the cards from each team, mix them, and place them along the chalkboard ledge. Have teams line up relay-style at the other end of the room. At the starting signal, the first member of each team runs to the chalkboard, finds a word card for his or her team's rule, and returns to the line. The first team to collect all its cards wins.

● WANDERING APOSTROPHE

Make a set of large letter cards, including double cards for each of the vowels and the letters s, t, and r. Make another card with a large apostrophe on it. Choose a possessive or contraction and hand out the letters, one per student, including the apostrophe. Call out the word and use it in a sentence. Students must arrange themselves to spell the word, placing the apostrophe in the appropriate position.

Variation: For a quieter version of this game, allow students to make their own letter cards. Students spell the chosen word with their cards at their own desks.

▲ PLURAL JUMBLE

On the board, write a set of four plural nouns connected to a topic of study, for example, pennies, nickels, dimes, quarters. Have students copy the words onto their papers and then combine the letters in the words to make as many new plural words as possible. At the end of a set time—for example, ten minutes—have students exchange papers and check that each new word is made up of letters in the original set and is spelled correctly. To encourage more difficult spellings, assign one point to each word that is formed by adding s and two points for irregular spellings.

◆ ADD-A-SENTENCE STORY

Write a variety of plural words on the board, such as scarves, tornadoes, dresses, men, queens, crutches, knives, women, cherries, pickles, boxes, children, churches, bushes, heroes, mice. Begin a story with a sentence that contains one or more words from the list on the board, such as It was true: Tornadoes were heading straight for our town! Ask a volunteer to continue the story by adding another sentence containing one of the words on the board. Continue until all the words have been used. You may wish to record the story for students to illustrate later.

Variations: Listing words with other elements such as possessives or contractions.

■ ANIMALS GALORE

Help students brainstorm a list of animals whose names each begin with a different letter of the alphabet. Write the singular form of each animal name on the board. Then ask volunteers to write the plural form of each name. Encourage students to sort the names by how their plurals are formed. For example, you might underline all plurals formed by adding *-es*. You may wish to have students make word cards for the words to place in their personal word banks or to use in open sorts.

✴ CONTRACTION CONCENTRATION

Have student partners make ten pairs of word cards. One card in each pair will be a contraction and its match will be the two words it stands for. Have students use the cards to play a game of concentration. Ask students to turn all cards face down. Then ask one student to turn up two cards. If the cards match, the player keeps the cards and turns up two more cards. If they do not match, another player then takes a turn turning up two cards.

Variation: Another version of concentration may be played by using cards for words and their matching plurals.

● GRAB BAG

Make word cards for the following words: *I, am, you, are, do, not, we, have, they, will, would, could, he, she, it, is.* Place the words in a paper bag. Students reach into the bag, pick two words, decide if the words can be combined to make a contraction, and spell the contraction.

▲ ZANY ZOO GAME

Give pairs of students copies of Blackline Master 39, a number cube, and two paper clips or game pieces. Have students cut out the cards at the bottom of the page and place them in a pile face down. The first player rolls the number cube and draws a card. He or she reads the sentence aloud and chooses the word that belongs in the blank. If the word is correct, the player may move the number of spaces shown. If not, the turn passes to the next player. The first player to reach the zany zoo wins.

Technology

The following software products are designed to provide practice in spelling.

Word Attack 3   A "vocabulary builder" for students ages 10 and up, this product uses crossword puzzles and arcade games to encourage students to master definitions, spellings, and pronunciations. Thousands of words are categorized by subject and level of difficulty.
** Davidson & Associates, Inc.
    19840 Pioneer Avenue
    Torrance, CA 90503
    (800) 545-7677

Spider Hunt Spelling   Students in grades 1–8 go "spider hunting" by standing with a bag underneath words, each of which has a spider dangling from it. As students spell each word correctly, a spider falls into the bag, and the player earns points. A variety of levels are available and can be customized by teachers.
** GAMCO Educational Materials/Siboney
    Learning Group
    P.O. Box 1911
    Big Spring, TX 79721
    (800) 351-1404

Name _____

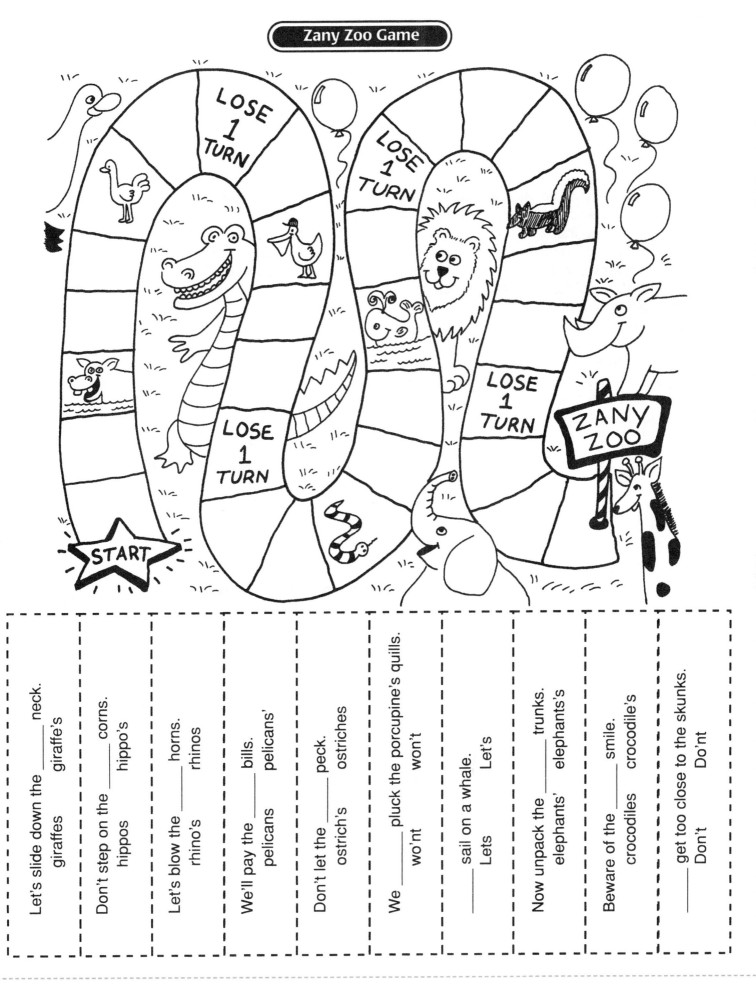

Zany Zoo Game

LOSE 1 TURN

LOSE 1 TURN

LOSE 1 TURN

LOSE 1 TURN

ZANY ZOO

START

Let's slide down the _____ neck.
giraffe's
giraffes

Don't step on the _____ corns.
hippo's
hippos

Let's blow the _____ horns.
rhino's
rhinos

We'll pay the _____ bills.
pelicans'
pelicans

Don't let the _____ peck.
ostrich's
ostriches

We _____ pluck the porcupine's quills.
won't
wo'nt

_____ sail on a whale.
Let's
Lets

Now unpack the _____ trunks.
elephants's
elephants'

Beware of the _____ smile.
crocodile's
crocodiles

_____ get too close to the skunks.
Don't
Do'nt

Home Connection

HOME LETTER

A letter is available to be sent home at the beginning of Unit 5. This letter informs family members that students will be learning to read and write plurals, possessives, and contractions. The at-home activity suggests that parents help their children look for contractions in environmental publications. This activity promotes interaction between student and family members while supporting students' learning of reading and writing words. A Book Corner feature suggests books that family members can look for in a local library and enjoy reading together. A letter is also available in Spanish on page 121q.

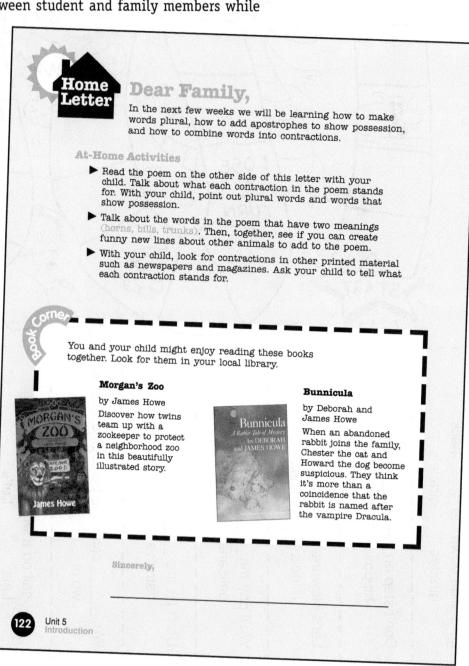

Home Letter

Dear Family,

In the next few weeks we will be learning how to make words plural, how to add apostrophes to show possession, and how to combine words into contractions.

At-Home Activities

▶ Read the poem on the other side of this letter with your child. Talk about what each contraction in the poem stands for. With your child, point out plural words and words that show possession.

▶ Talk about the words in the poem that have two meanings (horns, bills, trunks). Then, together, see if you can create funny new lines about other animals to add to the poem.

▶ With your child, look for contractions in other printed material such as newspapers and magazines. Ask your child to tell what each contraction stands for.

Book Corner

You and your child might enjoy reading these books together. Look for them in your local library.

Morgan's Zoo

by James Howe

Discover how twins team up with a zookeeper to protect a neighborhood zoo in this beautifully illustrated story.

Bunnicula

by Deborah and James Howe

When an abandoned rabbit joins the family, Chester the cat and Howard the dog become suspicious. They think it's more than a coincidence that the rabbit is named after the vampire Dracula.

Sincerely,

_____

122   Unit 5
Introduction

Carta para la casa

Estimada familia,

Durante las próximas semanas estaremos estudiando cómo formar los plurales de palabras en inglés, cómo añadir apóstrofos para indicar posesión, y cómo combinar palabras en inglés para hacer contracciones.

Actividades para hacer en casa

▶ Lean el poema en la página 121 con su hijo/a. Hablen de lo que cada contracción representa en el poema. Con su hijo/a señalen las palabras en plural y las palabras que muestran posesión.

▶ Hablen de las palabras en el poema que tienen dos significados: **horns, bills, trunks.** Luego, juntos, miren a ver si pueden crear líneas nuevas acerca de otros animales para añadírselas al poema.

▶ Con su hijo/a, busquen contracciones en otros materiales impresos, tales como periódicos y revistas. Pregúntenle qué representa cada contracción.

Rincón del libro

Su hijo/a y ustedes pueden disfrutar juntos de la lectura de estos libros. Búsquenlos en la biblioteca de su localidad.

Morgan's Zoo
por James Howe

En este cuento bellamente ilustrado, descubran cómo unos mellizos se unen al empleado del zoológico para proteger el parque zoológico del barrio.

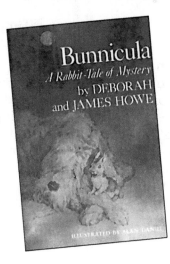

Bunnicula
por Deborah y James Howe

Cuando un conejo abandonado se une a la familia, Chester, el gato y Harold, el perro, comienzan a sospechar. Ellos creen que no es pura coincidencia que el conejo tomó su nombre de un vampiro, Drácula.

Atentamente, _____

Unit 5

Pages 121–122

Plurals, Possessives, Contractions, Syllables

Unit Focus

USING THE PAGE

- Read "At a Zany Zoo" aloud. Invite students to read along as you read the poem again.

- Talk about the activities that are possible at this zoo. Ask how this zoo is different from an ordinary zoo.

- Invite students to look at the illustration. Can they find all the activities mentioned in the poem?

- **Critical Thinking** Read aloud the questions at the bottom of page 121. Encourage students to share their speculations.

BUILDING A CONTEXT

- Ask students to name the words in the first two lines of the poem that have apostrophes. (*Let's, giraffe's, rhinos'*) Help students identify *Let's* as a contraction for *Let us* and *giraffe's* and *rhinos'* as possessives. Have them identify the objects in the poem that are possessed or owned. Point out that the poem tells about one giraffe but more than one rhino. Have students offer suggestions about how you know that.

- Erase the *'s and s'* from *giraffe* and *rhino*. Ask students to identify the number of vowels and vowel sounds in each word.

121

AT A ZANY ZOO

Let's slide down the giraffe's neck
And blow the rhinos' horns.
But don't let the ostriches peck
And don't step on the hippo's corns.

We'll pay the pelicans' bills
With cash from the kangaroo's pouch.
We won't pluck the porcupines' quills.
If we did, you'd hear us yell "Ouch!"

Let's sail on a whale for a while,
Then unpack the elephants' trunks.
But beware of the crocodile's smile
And don't get too close to the skunks.

What does the word *zany* mean? Why do you think the poem is called "At a Zany Zoo"?

Critical Thinking

Unit 5 Introduction **121**

UNIT OPENER ACTIVITIES

ANIMAL CHARACTERISTICS

Ask three volunteers to reread the poem aloud again, with each reading a stanza. Have listeners identify the animals mentioned and the part or characteristic of each the poem mentions—for example, *giraffe's neck, rhinos' horns, hippo's feet*, and so on. Talk about the importance of each animal's "possession." *Does it help the animal get food? Is it used for protection?* Encourage students to tell what they know about these animals.

ZOOMOBILE

Suggest that students make a mobile of "At a Zany Zoo." As they read the poem to list the animals to include, they should note whether their mobile should include one of each mentioned, or more than one.

ANIMAL MUSIC

Play recordings of music about animals for students to listen to. If possible, use recordings that pair whale or dolphin sounds with instrumental music, as well as "Talking to the Animals" from *Doctor Doolittle* and folk singer Bill Staines's "A Place in the Choir."

Dear Family,

In the next few weeks we will be learning how to make words plural, how to add apostrophes to show possession, and how to combine words into contractions.

At-Home Activities

▶ Read the poem on the other side of this letter with your child. Talk about what each contraction in the poem stands for. With your child, point out plural words and words that show possession.

▶ Talk about the words in the poem that have two meanings (horns, bills, trunks). Then, together, see if you can create funny new lines about other animals to add to the poem.

▶ With your child, look for contractions in other printed material such as newspapers and magazines. Ask your child to tell what each contraction stands for.

You and your child might enjoy reading these books together. Look for them in your local library.

Morgan's Zoo

by James Howe
Discover how twins team up with a zookeeper to protect a neighborhood zoo in this beautifully illustrated story.

Bunnicula

by Deborah and James Howe
When an abandoned rabbit joins the family, Chester the cat and Howard the dog become suspicious. They think it's more than a coincidence that the rabbit is named after the vampire Dracula.

Sincerely,

_____

● The Home Letter on page 122 is intended to acquaint family members with the word study skills students will be studying in the unit. Encourage students to share the letter with a family member and complete the activities together. Suggest that they also look for the books mentioned in the Book Corner at the library.

● The Home Letter can also be found on page 121q in Spanish.

CURRICULUM CONNECTIONS ✳

WRITING

Portfolio Students could write a story about how a non-zany animal reacts when it stumbles into the zany zoo. Is it bewildered, or does it join the fun? Or is the zany zoo an animal dream?

SCIENCE

Have students find out the habitat needs for each animal mentioned in the poem by finding out where its native home is and what the geography and climate are like there. Invite them to speculate how this information would help the planners creating a real zoo.

SOCIAL STUDIES

If not with cash from a kangaroo's pouch, how *are* bills paid? Have students find out how money moves—the ways financial transactions are made—including the uses of cash, checks, and electronic transfers.

BULLETIN BOARD

The zoo in the poem might be zany and unreal, but it would be fun to visit. Students could work together to design a theme park or children's playground based on the animals and activities mentioned in the poem "At a Zany Zoo."

Lesson 56

Pages 123–124

Plurals

Lesson Focus

INTRODUCING THE SKILL

- Write the words *book* and *shoe* on the board. Ask students how to change these words into the plural form. (*add s*) Tell them that the plural form of other words is formed differently.

- Call on volunteers to write *tax, buzz, branch,* and *glass* on the board. Explain that if a word ends in -ss, -z, -x, -sh, or -ch, the suffix -es is usually added to make the word plural. Have students change the words on the board to their plural forms.

- Write *mystery* and *tray*. Explain that if a word ends in a consonant and -y, the -y is changed to *i* and -es is added. If the words ends in a vowel and -y, only -s is added. Ask volunteers to write the plural forms of *mystery* and *tray*.

USING THE PAGES

Be sure students understand how to complete the exercises on pages 123 and 124. When students have completed the pages, call on a volunteer to summarize what he or she has learned about forming plurals of words.

Name _____

▶ Read each word and write its plural form on the line.

1. tax   taxes
2. buzz   buzzes
3. branch   branches
4. waltz   waltzes
5. glass   glasses
6. fox   foxes
7. wish   wishes
8. patch   patches

> **RULE**
> When a word is in its plural form, it means more than one. If a word ends in **ss, z, x, sh,** or **ch,** the suffix **es** is usually added to make the word plural.
>
> mess = mess**es**   waltz = waltz**es**
> box = box**es**   dish = dish**es**
> batch = batch**es**

▶ Read each sentence. Underline the word in the sentence that has the suffix **es**. Write its base word on the line.

9. The forecaster puts on her glasses.   glass
10. She watches the weather reports coming in.   watch
11. Ten more inches of snow fell last night.   inch
12. The mountain passes are closed due to snow.   pass
13. There are patches of ice on every road.   patch
14. The snow has caused branches to fall across roads.   branch
15. Crews use axes to chop and remove the limbs.   ax
16. The forecaster has two wishes.   wish
17. She wants bright sunshine and warm sandy beaches.   beach

Lesson 56
Plurals of words ending in ss, z, x, sh, ch   **123**

FOCUS ON ALL LEARNERS

ENGLISH LANGUAGE LEARNERS/ESL

Before students begin working, review the concept of "more than one"—*one book, two books; one glass, two glasses; one activity, two activities.* To build background for page 124, ask students about the books they enjoy reading. Point out the plurals of words they use.

VISUAL LEARNERS
LARGE GROUP

Ask volunteers to name their favorite book titles and then invite students to make up titles—serious and silly—for these subjects: cowboys, spies, mysteries, hobbies, other countries, wishes, beaches, foxes. Write their titles on the board.

KINESTHETIC/AUDITORY LEARNERS
PARTNER

Materials: colored chalk

Let students take turns offering singular nouns to a partner who writes the plural form on the board, using colored chalk to write the plural suffix. Encourage students to use some words from the lesson as well as words that need just -s.

Read each word. Write its plural form on the line.

If a word ends in **y** preceded by a consonant, change the **y** to **i** and add **es** to form the plural. If **y** is preceded by a vowel, just add **s**.

activity = activit**ies**
chimney = chimney**s**

1. fly — flies
2. mystery — mysteries
3. tray — trays
4. beauty — beauties
5. hobby — hobbies
6. medley — medleys
7. melody — melodies
8. injury — injuries

Read each sentence. Complete the sentence with the plural form of the word at the right.

9. It is fun to explore the ___libraries___ near your home. (library)
0. Which ___stories___ do you enjoy reading? (story)
1. I enjoy reading ___mysteries___. (mystery)
2. I also like books about ___spies___. (spy)
3. Some children like books about ___cowboys___. (cowboy)
4. Some people like to read about sports ___victories___. (victory)
5. My sister likes to read about lawyers and ___juries___. (jury)
6. My dad studies books about ___hobbies___. (hobby)
7. My mom reads about how to make ___pastries___. (pastry)
8. Do you enjoy books about other ___countries___? (country)

CURRICULUM CONNECTIONS

SPELLING

The following sentences can be used as a pretest for spelling words that are plurals of words ending in -ss, -z, -x, -sh, -ch, -y, -f, -fe, and -o; irregular plurals; and contractions.

1. **messes** — I made **messes** of my paintings.
2. **waltzes** — We learned two **waltzes** in dance class.
3. **boxes** — The **boxes** are stacked in the closet.
4. **dishes** — Please put the **dishes** away.
5. **batches** — Let's bake two **batches** of cookies.
6. **activities** — Tennis and swimming are healthy **activities**.
7. **wolves** — **Wolves** often spend time alone.
8. **geese** — The **geese** chased us around the lake.
9. **sheep** — There are seven **sheep** in the field.
10. **potatoes** — We ate baked **potatoes** for supper.
11. **it's** — **It's** beginning to snow.
12. **can't** — Jean **can't** come with us.

WRITING

Portfolio Ask students to continue the story of the weather forecaster on page 123. *Does the storm continue and she spend the night at the television studio? Do her wishes mysteriously come true?* When they've finished, encourage students to check to be sure they've formed the plurals correctly.

SOCIAL STUDIES

Hold a Hobby Fair at which students can share their own hobbies or invite someone they know with an unusual hobby to the class to visit. Encourage students to find out about a hobby or activity they haven't pursued but that interests them.

MUSIC

Interested students, individually or in pairs, might like to try composing simple melodies. To help them start, suggest that they listen to songs or think about how notes could mimic the sound of rain or snow falling.

AUDITORY LEARNERS

SMALL GROUP Encourage groups of three or four to take turns giving clues about nouns that end with -ss, -z, -x, -sh, -ch, and -y for group members to guess and then write the plural form. One example is *I'm thinking of animals with bushy red tails.* (foxes) Each student should have a turn.

GIFTED LEARNERS

Write these words on the board: *beach, fly, wish, hobby, country, box, glass, patch, key.* Have students work as a group to write a short mystery story, using as many of the plural forms of the words listed as possible.

LEARNERS WHO NEED EXTRA SUPPORT

When students have completed the pages, review their work with them. Help them correct any mistakes made and suggest they use each word in a sentence for reinforcement. See Daily Word Study Practice, page 204.

Lesson 57

Pages 125–126

Plurals

INFORMAL ASSESSMENT OBJECTIVES

Can students

✓ form plurals of words ending in *-f*, *-fe*, and *-o*?

✓ use the plural form of words to complete sentences?

Lesson Focus

INTRODUCING THE SKILL

- Review that plurals are formed by adding the suffix *-s* or *-es* to nouns.

- Explain that the spelling of some words must be changed to form the plural. Write *half* and *halves* on the board. Ask how the plural was formed. *(The f changed to v before -es was added.)*

- Explain that this is how the plural of most words ending in *-f* or *-fe* is formed: The *-f* or *-fe* is changed to *v* before adding *-es*. Have volunteers write the plural forms of *wolf, knife,* and *elf*.

- Write *kangaroo* on the board and ask students how to write the plural form. *(add -s)* Explain that *-s* is usually added to words ending in *-o* to make the plural, but that there are some exceptions, such as *buffaloes, tomatoes,* and *heroes*.

USING THE PAGES

- Tell students to read the sentences on page 126 carefully. To complete each, they will need to decide which form of a word from items 1–12 fits the sentence.

- When students have finished the pages, have partners review their work together.

125

Name _____

▶ **Read each word and write its plural form on the line.**

> **RULE**
> If a word ends in **f** or **fe**, usually change the **f** or **fe** to **v** and add **es** to form the plural.
> wolf = wol**ves**   wife = wi**ves**

1. half _____ halves
2. thief _____ thieves
3. life _____ lives
4. shelf _____ shelves
5. knife _____ knives
6. calf _____ calves

7. loaf _____ loaves
8. elf _____ elves
9. self _____ selves
10. leaf _____ leaves

▶ **Read each sentence. Write a word from the word bank to complete the sentence. Then write its base word on the line.**

Word Bank: shelves, hooves, wolves, thieves, lives, loaves, calves, wives, themselves

11. Farmers of long ago led very busy _____ lives _____. _____ life
12. They rose early to tend their cows and _____ calves _____. _____ calf
13. They made horseshoes for their horses' _____ hooves _____. _____ hoof
14. They put up fences to keep out animals such as _____ wolves _____. _____ wolf
15. The fox and the wolf were _____ thieves _____ that stole the farmers' chickens. _____ thief
16. The farmers' _____ wives _____ worked very hard, too. _____ wife
17. They filled the _____ shelves _____ with jars of vegetables and homemade jam. _____ shelf

Lesson 57
Plurals of words ending in f or fe **125**

✦ FOCUS ON ALL LEARNERS ✦

ENGLISH LANGUAGE LEARNERS/ESL

Before beginning page 126, show students the photo on the page and introduce them to the word *rodeo* as well as related words such as *bronco, lasso,* and *sombrero*. Encourage students to act out these words.

VISUAL LEARNERS

PARTNER   **Materials:** index cards, markers

Have pairs write the words *calf, knife, wolf, loaf, wife, tornado, kangaroo, hero, piano,* and *buffalo* on one side of cards and the plurals on the other side. Then have pairs work together to write sentences with the plural forms of the words.

AUDITORY/KINESTHETIC LEARNERS

LARGE GROUP   Have the group line up in teams in front of the board. Draw on the board a bookcase with shelves for each group. Have team members, in turn, fill their shelves by writing the plural form of the words you say. Use these words: *calf, half, hero, knife, loaf, potato, radio, shelf.*

Read each word and write its plural form on the line. Then read each sentence below and choose either the singular or plural form of a word to complete the sentence. If you are unsure of the spelling of a word, look it up in your dictionary.

RULE
If a word ends in **o**, usually add **s** to form the plurals. Some words, such as **potato**, **tomato**, and **hero**, are made plural by adding **es**.

kimono = kimono**s**

potato = potato**es**

1. kangaroo _____ kangaroos
2. rodeo _____ rodeos
3. banjo _____ banjos
4. lasso _____ lassos
5. solo _____ solos
6. sombrero _____ sombreros
7. soprano _____ sopranos
8. bronco _____ broncos
9. hero _____ heroes
10. photo _____ photos
11. igloo _____ igloos
12. patio _____ patios

13. In a _____ rodeo _____ cowhands do all sorts of tricks.
14. A singer sings a _____ solo _____ to open the show.
15. Some cowhands play tunes on _____ banjos _____ .
16. Cowhands ride bucking _____ broncos _____ .
17. These horses jump up and down like _____ kangaroos _____ .
18. Cowhands use their _____ lassos _____ to rope calves.
19. Some riders wear large _____ sombreros _____ on their heads.
20. Rodeo stars can be real _____ heroes _____ to children.

126 Lesson 57
Plurals of words ending in o

See Daily Word Study Practice, page 204.

AUDITORY LEARNERS

SMALL GROUP

Materials: index cards, marker

For each small group, make a set of word cards for the following words: *loaf, elf, shelf, life, half, knife, photo, hero, tomato, kangaroo.* Each student, in turn, picks a card from the pile and says the word and its plural form. Then the group repeats the plural form in unison.

GIFTED LEARNERS

Materials: graph paper

Using plural forms of the words from this lesson, challenge students to make a hidden-word puzzle for classmates to solve. The singular forms could be listed as puzzle clues.

LEARNERS WHO NEED EXTRA SUPPORT

Tell students that to make the plurals in the first activity on page 125, they will need to drop the -*f* or -*fe* before adding -*ves*. Suggest that they first cross out the printed -*f* or -*fe* and add -*ves* and then write the entire word on the line. See Daily Word Study Practice, page 204.

CURRICULUM CONNECTIONS

SPELLING

Materials: small cards with the letters of the alphabet on them, a bag

Draw horizontal letter spaces on the board, one for each letter of one of the spelling words (*messes, waltzes, boxes, dishes, batches, activities, wolves, geese, sheep, potatoes, it's, can't*). Have students, in turn, draw a letter card from the bag and ask, for example, "Is there a *b*?" If the letter is in the word, write it in place, and encourage the student to make a guess about the word before the next student draws. If the letter is not in the word, go on to the next student. Continue with the other spelling words.

WRITING

Portfolio Discuss with students the acts in a rodeo, including saddle and bareback bronco riding, bull riding, steer wrestling, and calf roping. Have interested students write about a real or imaginary rodeo event they would like to see—or even try— and why they would like it. Suggest that they describe the event itself, the danger involved, the training required, and any equipment or special clothing that is needed.

SCIENCE

Materials: reference books on animals

Kangaroos are marsupials, as are opossums, bandicoots, and wombats. Have students find out about these mammals, where they live, how they use their pouches, and how they defend themselves against predators.

MUSIC

Materials: reference books on music

A soprano has the highest vocal range. Have students find out the terms for voices with other ranges and rank them highest to lowest. (for example, *soprano, mezzo-soprano, contralto or alto, tenor, baritone, bass*)

Lesson 58

Pages 127–128

Plurals

INFORMAL ASSESSMENT OBJECTIVES

Can students

✔ form irregular plurals?

✔ use irregular plurals to complete sentences?

Lesson Focus

INTRODUCING THE SKILL

- Tell students that some words have unusual plurals. Write the following examples on the board: *tooth, teeth; child, children; man, men.* Then write *woman, foot,* and *goose.* Ask students if they know the plural forms. (*women, feet, geese*)

- Explain that for some words, such as *sheep* and *deer,* the singular and plural forms are the same. Help students think of other words whose singular and plural forms are the same.

- Tell students that the way to tell if one of these words is singular or plural is by looking at the context of the sentence.

    All the sheep ran through the gate.
    The sheep stamped its foot.

    Have students tell in which sentence *sheep* is plural. (*first*)

- Because these irregular plurals follow no rules or patterns, suggest that students memorize them and use the dictionary when they need help.

USING THE PAGES

Make sure students understand how to complete pages 127 and 128. When they have finished, have students discuss the ways that irregular plurals are formed.

127

Name _____

▶ **Write each plural form beside the correct singular form.**

> **RULE**
> Some words form their plurals in an unusual way.
> **goose—geese**
> **mouse—mice**

1. man _____ men
2. foot _____ feet
3. ox _____ oxen
4. woman _____ women
5. mouse _____ mice
6. child _____ children
7. goose _____ geese
8. tooth _____ teeth

oxen	mice
feet	children
mice	men
children	geese
women	teeth

▶ **Read each sentence. Write the plural form of the word in parentheses to complete the sentence.**

> **RULE**
> For some words the singular and plural forms are the same.
> **sheep deer elk**
> **salmon moose fish**

9. The _____ children _____ were learning about animals in school. (child)

10. They learned that baby _____ mice _____ are born without fur. (mouse)

11. _____ Salmon _____ swim far up rivers to lay their eggs. (Salmon)

12. Sharks have many rows of sharp _____ teeth _____ . (tooth)

13. _____ Deer _____ lose their antlers in winter and grow new ones in spring. (Deer)

14. The antlers of _____ moose _____ can spread six feet or more. (moose)

15. Moles have large _____ feet _____ that they use as shovels. (foot)

16. Most Canada _____ geese _____ fly south for the winter. (goose)

Lesson 58
Irregular plurals **127**

FOCUS ON ALL LEARNERS

ENGLISH LANGUAGE LEARNERS/ESL

Be sure students know the meaning of each of these nouns that have irregularly-formed plurals. Emphasize that they do not follow any patterns or rules, so everyone has to memorize them.

LARGE GROUP

VISUAL LEARNERS

Materials: newspaper, markers, scissors

Have students cut out from an old newspaper an article whose topic interests them. Have them read the article slowly, underlining all the plural forms of nouns. Ask students to separate the words into two lists: regular plurals and irregular plurals.

LARGE GROUP

KINESTHETIC LEARNERS

Materials: index cards, marker

Prepare cards with these words: *octopus, salmon, sheep, ox, flounder, wolf, trout, mouse, goose.* Then write *Water Animals* and *Land Animals* as headings on the board. Students choose a card and write the plural of that animal under the correct heading. Encourage them to use a dictionary as needed.

Read each clue word. Write its plural form in the puzzle.

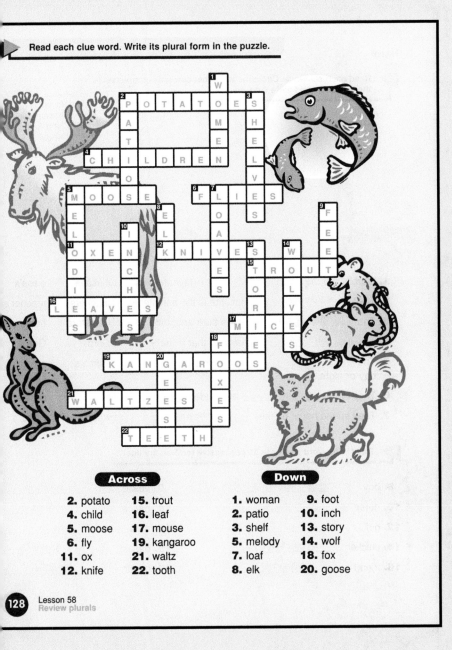

Across		Down	
2. potato	15. trout	1. woman	9. foot
4. child	16. leaf	2. patio	10. inch
5. moose	17. mouse	3. shelf	13. story
6. fly	19. kangaroo	5. melody	14. wolf
11. ox	21. waltz	7. loaf	18. fox
12. knife	22. tooth	8. elk	20. goose

128 Lesson 58
Review plurals

SPELLING

Stand in a circle with students. Choose one of the spelling words, *messes, waltzes, boxes, dishes, batches, activities, wolves, geese, sheep, potatoes, it's, can't,* to say out loud. The student on your right should start spelling the word, giving just the first letter. The next student gives the next letter, and so on, until the word has been spelled out one letter at a time. Continue until all words have been spelled.

WRITING

Portfolio Write these titles on the board.

"Why a Fox Can't Sneeze"
"The Mouse Waltz"
"Melody Flies"
"Sheep Asleep"

Have students choose one and write a short poem. Explain that the poems don't have to rhyme. Encourage students to use as many plurals as they can. Stop for a "poetry minute" throughout the day so that volunteers can share what they wrote.

MATH

Materials: measuring tape, chart paper

Have students help each other discover how tall they are. Measurements should be taken in feet and inches and can be recorded on a class chart. Help students determine the mean height for the class.

HEALTH

Materials: health books

Suggest that students find out about teeth—how many humans have, the names of the different types, and how to best care for them. Have a "tooth talk" in which students can share what they learned.

AUDITORY LEARNERS

LARGE GROUP Write *ox, mouse, child, tooth, elk, moose, foot, waltz, shelf, fly,* and *leaf* on the board. Have students clap (or snap their fingers or tap their desks) together and say first the singular form on the board and then the plural, while continuing their rhythm.

GIFTED LEARNERS

Explain that some animal groups have special names, for example, a *pride* of lions. Give students the following pairs, written in two columns of different order: *chicks, clutch; elephants, herd; whales, pod; geese, gaggle; fish, school; ants, colony.* Then have them match the animal to its group.

LEARNERS WHO NEED EXTRA SUPPORT

Materials: dictionary

Show students how to use the dictionary to help them find the plurals of words. Explain that in most dictionaries if no plural form is shown, then the plural is formed by adding *-s.* See Daily Word Study Practice, page 204.

128

Lesson 59

Pages 129–130

Possessives

> Read each sentence. Circle the word that correctly completes the sentence, and write it on the line.

RULE

The possessive form of a word is used to show that a person or animal owns, has, or possesses something. To make a singular noun show possession, add an apostrophe and an **s** (**'s**) at the end of the word.

Joan**'s** skirt   the baby**'s** bottle
the horse**'s** tail

1. Gerbils are the _____ *class's* _____ favorite pets. classes (class's)
2. The _____ *teacher's* _____ favorite is the hamster. teachers (teacher's)
3. The _____ *hamster's* _____ fur is thick and soft. hamsters (hamster's)
4. _____ *Gerbils* _____ have fur that is fuzzy. (Gerbils) Gerbil's
5. The _____ *animals'* _____ active time can be day or night. animals (animals')
6. Their _____ *cages* _____ are made of glass. (cages) cage's
7. They spend hours on their _____ *wheels* _____ . (wheels) wheel's

> Read each word and write its possessive form on the line.

8. boy _____ *boy's* _____
9. Leslie _____ *Leslie's* _____
10. nurse _____ *nurse's* _____
11. dancer _____ *dancer's* _____
12. girl _____ *girl's* _____
13. man _____ *man's* _____
14. chicken _____ *chicken's* _____
15. dentist _____ *dentist's* _____
16. friend _____ *friend's* _____
17. month _____ *month's* _____

Lesson 59
Possessives
129

INFORMAL ASSESSMENT OBJECTIVES

Can students

- form singular and plural possessives?
- identify the possessive form as singular or plural?
- use the possessive form to complete sentences?

Lesson Focus

INTRODUCING THE SKILL

- Point to your desk and say *This is the desk of the teacher.* Ask students for another way to say that the desk belongs to the teacher. *(This is the teacher's desk.)* Write *teacher's* on the board and ask students to tell how the word was changed to show possession. *(An apostrophe and -s were added.)*

- Explain that the possessive form of a word shows that one person or animal owns, has, or possesses something. To make a singular noun show possession, add an apostrophe and an *-s*.

- Ask students how to show that two desks belong to two teachers. *(teachers' desks)* Explain that when a plural noun ends in *-s*, an apostrophe is added after the *-s* to show possession.

USING THE PAGES

Make sure students understand what to do on pages 129 and 130. When they have finished working, review the lesson by correcting the papers together.

FOCUS ON ALL LEARNERS

ENGLISH LANGUAGE LEARNERS/ESL

Be sure students understand the concept of possession by demonstrating with something of yours and then something of theirs. After each possessive phrase is spoken, write it on the board and have students read what you wrote. Help them note the placement of the apostrophe.

VISUAL LEARNERS

INDIVIDUAL **Materials:** discarded magazines, scissors, glue

Students cut out and paste on paper a magazine picture of a person or object and write around it as many objects as they can that are in the possession of the person or object shown in the picture. Tell them to include, if possible, objects that are in the possession of more than one person or object.

KINESTHETIC LEARNERS

LARGE GROUP Each student chooses an object that belongs to someone or something. Point to an object and ask a volunteer to say what is possessed and who has it. (for example, *Mel's nose, the students' arms*) Then the volunteer points to his or her object for the next volunteer to identify.

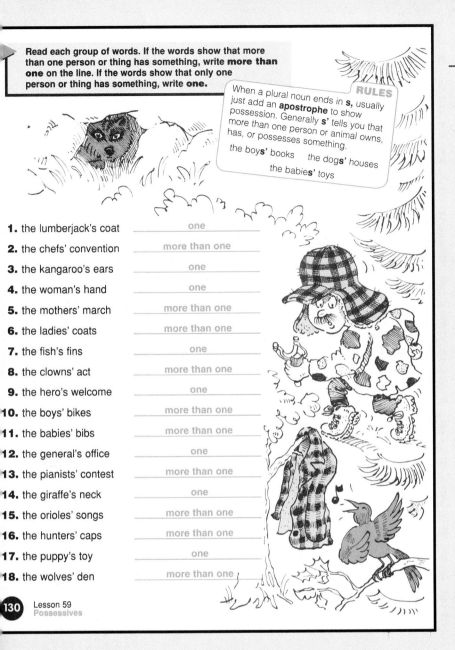

Read each group of words. If the words show that more than one person or thing has something, write **more than one** on the line. If the words show that only one person or thing has something, write **one**.

RULES

When a plural noun ends in **s**, usually just add an **apostrophe** to show possession. Generally **s'** tells you that more than one person or animal owns, has, or possesses something.

the boy**s'** books   the dog**s'** houses

the babie**s'** toys

1. the lumberjack's coat —— one
2. the chefs' convention —— more than one
3. the kangaroo's ears —— one
4. the woman's hand —— one
5. the mothers' march —— more than one
6. the ladies' coats —— more than one
7. the fish's fins —— one
8. the clowns' act —— more than one
9. the hero's welcome —— one
10. the boys' bikes —— more than one
11. the babies' bibs —— more than one
12. the general's office —— one
13. the pianists' contest —— more than one
14. the giraffe's neck —— one
15. the orioles' songs —— more than one
16. the hunters' caps —— more than one
17. the puppy's toy —— one
18. the wolves' den —— more than one

130 Lesson 59
Possessives

SPELLING

Materials: lists of the words *messes, waltzes, boxes, dishes, batches, activities, wolves, geese, sheep, potatoes, it's, can't; paper, markers*

Provide pairs with a spelling list. Have them play spelling tic-tac-toe, drawing a grid, then asking each other to spell a list word. If it is spelled correctly, the speller can mark the grid with an X or O.

WRITING

Portfolio Write *the hats of the cats, the adventure of the chickens, the shoes of the dancers, the songs of the sparrows* on the board. Students write the correct possessive for each phrase and then choose one to use as a story title. Students can illustrate their finished stories.

SOCIAL STUDIES

Materials: butcher paper, markers, crayons

Invite students to work in pairs to create Fantasy Town picture maps. Along the streets or paths, students should draw pictures of homes and label each one with the name of its owner or owners, using singular or plural possessive forms (for example: *chickens' coop, wolves' den, dentist's office, gerbil's cage, chef's bakery*). Encourage partners to take turns asking each other to locate the shortest route between two places.

ART

Materials: art materials and collage materials

Students can choose two or three of the items listed on page 130 as a basis for a collage—perhaps, for example, a clown's act that involves boys' bikes and babies' bibs! Display the collages and encourage students to compare interpretations and to see which of the items listed are represented.

AUDITORY LEARNERS

PARTNER Pairs could create a chant or rap that strings together phrases that show ownership of objects. After choosing a theme, partners can brainstorm a list of possessives that fit the theme. Ask pairs to rap or chant for the class.

GIFTED LEARNERS

Have students write a short paragraph describing their pet or a pet they would like to have. Challenge them to use as many possessives as possible, in both the singular and plural forms.

LEARNERS WHO NEED EXTRA SUPPORT

Suggest that when they complete page 130, students cover the apostrophe and the words that follow it. If the noun that shows ends in -*s*, they know that more than one person or thing is the possessor.

See Daily Word Study Practice, pages 204–205.

Lesson 60

Pages 131–132

Possessives

Can students

✔ form singular and plural possessives?

✔ identify words in the possessive form?

Lesson Focus

INTRODUCING THE SKILL

● Review that a possessive word shows that one or more persons or animals own, have, or possess something.

● Say the words *giraffe* and *dress*. Ask volunteers to write the singular and plural possessive forms of these words on the board. (*giraffe's, giraffes'; dress's, dresses'*) Ask students to explain how the different forms were written.

● Then ask a volunteer to write the words *moose* and *children*. Have students suggest how the plural possessive form of these words would be written. (*moose's, children's*) Explain that an apostrophe and *-s* are added to make the few plurals that do not end in *-s* possessive.

USING THE PAGES

Make sure students understand what to do on page 131. When students have completed the pages, have them summarize what they have learned about singular and plural possessives.

Name _____

▶ **Read each sentence. Complete the sentence with a word from the word bank.**

giraffe's	class's	porcupines'	judges'	eels'	world's
bear's	squids'	teacher's	ostrich's	birds'	dolphins'

1. The _____class's_____ science reports are due today.
2. One _____teacher's_____ class has entered a contest.
3. The _____giraffe's_____ long neck makes it the tallest animal.
4. The _____world's_____ largest desert is the Sahara.
5. A _____bear's_____ heart beat slows when hibernating.
6. The _____eels'_____ long bodies make them look like snakes.
7. The _____ostrich's_____ large body and small wings keep it from flying.
8. Some _____birds'_____ nests look like hanging baskets.
9. The _____squids'_____ tentacles are used to catch prey.
10. The _____dolphins'_____ blowholes enable them to breathe.
11. The _____porcupines'_____ quills measure up to five inches long.
12. The _____judges'_____ decisions on the winners will be final.

▶ **Write the words from the word bank at the top of the page in the correct columns.**

Singular Possessives	Plural Possessives
class's	eels'
teacher's	birds'
world's	squids'
giraffe's	dolphins'
bear's	porcupines'
ostrich's	judges'

FOCUS ON ALL LEARNERS ✳ ● ◆ ●

ENGLISH LANGUAGE LEARNERS/ESL

To build background for the story on page 131, ask students to name topics they think of when you say the word *science*—such as plants, animals, electricity, earth, oceans. Encourage them to write one or two science topics they would like to learn more about.

LARGE GROUP

VISUAL LEARNERS

On the board, write *the ___ mitt; the ___ books; the ___ office; the ___ helmet.* Have students complete each phrase with a possessive word that names someone who would use the object for his or her job. Ask them to suggest other workers and phrases to show possession.

LARGE GROUP

KINESTHETIC LEARNERS

Materials: index cards, markers, scissors

Each student cuts six cards in half and writes the name of someone or something (including plurals) on one half and the possessive form on the other. Then have them use the cards to play concentration, identifying each possessive they turn over as singular or plural.

Read the sentence in each box and draw a picture to show what the sentence means. Then circle the word or words that show possession.

1. The pretty princess drives her (neighbor's) sleigh.

2. (Ed's) shirt and the (girls') blouses are the color turquoise.

3. Two (persons') crimson cloaks and (someone's) feathered hat hung in the closet.

4. The (girls) heads were adorned with wreaths made from flower petals and (birds) feathers.

132 Lesson 60
Possessives

AUDITORY LEARNERS

SMALL GROUP Group members take turns choosing objects, writing on a piece of paper a possessive phrase identifying the chosen object, and turning the paper over. The others try to guess the possessive phrase. The spier says *hot* or *cold* depending on how close the guess is.

GIFTED LEARNERS

Challenge students to decide what the difference is in meaning between the phrases *birds' songs* and *birds song*, or another pair in which one word indicates possession and the other is a modifier.

LEARNERS WHO NEED EXTRA SUPPORT

Materials: index cards, markers

Have students write each word in the box on page 131 on a card, sort the cards into two piles, and then complete the columns at the bottom of the page with the words on the cards. See Daily Word Study Practice, pages 204–205.

CURRICULUM CONNECTIONS

SPELLING

Write the list of words, *messes, waltzes, boxes, dishes, batches, activities, wolves, geese, sheep, potatoes, it's, can't,* on the board for reference. Then write the following list of scrambled spelling words on the board for students to unscramble and write correctly: *sweazlt, peshe, tacna, sesems, toatsope, sicastveit, slevow, hissed, sit, egese, exsob, scabhet.*

WRITING

Portfolio Say *Peter Piper picked a peck of pickled peppers* and tell students that this is an example of alliteration, a repetition of an initial sound in two or more words in a phrase or sentence. Reword the sentence to show the use of a possessive form. For example: *Where can Peter Piper's pickled peppers be?* Have students write alliterative sentences that contain a possessive, offering this additional example if needed: *Nellie Needham's nice necktie is nearly new.*

SOCIAL STUDIES

Materials: reference books, geography books

The Sahara is the world's largest desert. Have students find out about the world's other deserts. Ask: *Where are they located? What are their names? Where is the smallest desert? How do geographers define a desert?* Encourage students to share what they discover.

SCIENCE

Materials: reference books on animals

Have students turn the animal items on page 131 into questions and then find the answers to them. For example: *How tall is the giraffe? How slow is the bear's heartbeat when it hibernates? What is the squids' favorite prey?*

Contractions

Lesson Focus

INTRODUCING THE SKILL

- Review with students that an apostrophe is used to show singular and plural possession in words.

- Tell students that the apostrophe is used for other purposes. Say the words *can't* and *I'm.* Ask students what type of word you are saying. *(contraction)*

- Ask volunteers to write *can't* and *I'm* on the board. Then explain that a contraction is a short way of writing two words as one. Point out the apostrophe and say that it takes the place of the missing letter or letters. Have students identify the letters missing from the contractions on the board. *(no, a)*

USING THE PAGES

Be sure students understand how to complete pages 133 and 134. After students have finished the pages, encourage pairs to discuss what they learned about contractions and share their ideas with the class.

Name

In the first column, write the two words the contraction stands for. In the second column, write the letter or letters left out of the contraction.

A **contraction** is a short way of writing two words. The two words are written together, but one or more letters are left out. An **apostrophe** stands for the missing letters.

I am = **I'm** it is = **it's**

can not = **can't**

	Words	Letter or Letters Left Out
1. haven't	have not	o
2. isn't	is not	o
3. we've	we have	ha
4. you're	you are	a
5. they'll	they will	wi
6. let's	let us	u
7. didn't	did not	o
8. I've	I have	ha

Underline the contraction in each sentence. Then write the two words it stands for on the line.

9. We're reading a book about beavers.	We are
10. We haven't read about beavers before.	have not
11. They're very interesting animals.	They are
12. A beaver's tail isn't useless.	is not
13. It's shaped like a canoe paddle.	It is
14. They'll slap their tails to warn others of danger.	They will

FOCUS ON ALL LEARNERS

ENGLISH LANGUAGE LEARNERS/ESL

Have students read the contractions in items 1-8 on page 133 before they begin working and make sure they know the words that form each.

VISUAL LEARNERS

PARTNER Pairs can each write a sentence that includes two words that could form a contraction. They exchange papers, circle the two words, and rewrite the sentence with the contraction. They repeat the activity with other sentences.

KINESTHETIC LEARNERS

LARGE GROUP Have students form teams and line up at the board. Say two words that can make a contraction. The first in each team writes the words, the second writes the contraction, the third writes the missing letters. The first team to finish earns a point. Continue with other words.

Read the words and write the contraction on the line.

1. can not	can't	2. I am	I'm
3. was not	wasn't	4. he will	he'll
5. will not	won't	6. you will	you'll
7. could not	couldn't	8. it is	it's
9. do not	don't	10. are not	aren't
11. they have	they've	12. where is	where's
13. that is	that's	14. we are	we're
15. I will	I'll	16. she is	she's
17. were not	weren't	18. should not	shouldn't

Read each sentence. Underline the words that can form a contraction. Write the contraction on the line beside the sentence.

19. <u>What is</u> a cloud? — What's
20. <u>Let us</u> think about clouds. — Let's
21. Clouds <u>are not</u> marshmallows or cotton. — aren't
22. <u>They are</u> drops of water. — They're
23. <u>That is</u> a fact. — That's
24. <u>It is</u> hard to believe this about clouds. — It's
25. Clouds <u>will not</u> always bring rain. — won't
26. <u>They will</u> sometimes bring snow or sleet. — They'll
27. A cloud <u>can not</u> move without wind. — can't
28. <u>I have</u> learned a little about clouds. — I've

134 Lesson 61
Contractions

SPELLING

Materials: spelling words *messes, waltzes, boxes, dishes, batches, activities, wolves, geese, sheep, potatoes, it's, can't* written on individual cards

Volunteers draw a card and act out that word for classmates to guess. To make a guess, a student has to write the word on the board with the correct spelling.

WRITING

Portfolio Remind students that contractions are used when writing dialogue. Ask them to imagine a scene in a play about themselves and a friend and then use contractions to help them write what each said in the scene. Before they begin, review how dialogue for plays is written.

SCIENCE

Portfolio **Materials:** weather books

Not all clouds bring rain or snow, but clouds are a help in predicting the weather. Students could make a field guide to clouds by finding out about the different kinds of clouds, drawing pictures of them, and writing captions about the weather conditions they accompany.

LANGUAGE ARTS/MATH

Have students write contraction equations for others to solve. Provide these examples: *they + are = they're; we + have = we've.* Suggest that as an extra challenge, one part of the equation can be left out for solving. For example: *they + ? = they're.*

AUDITORY LEARNERS

LARGE GROUP Have students keep their ears open for contractions heard during the day or morning and write the ones they hear on the board. Once a contraction has been written on the board, repeats could be recorded with a check. Ask students: *What are some of the most commonly used contractions?*

GIFTED LEARNERS

Materials: books, magazines

Explain that apostrophes may be used in informal written speech to indicate letters left out (*I'm waiting here 'til noon*) or in place of numbers left out (*class of '98*). Have students scan magazines and books for other such examples of an apostrophe's use.

LEARNERS WHO NEED EXTRA SUPPORT

If students have difficulty completing the first activity on page 133, write in the letter or letters that were left out to form the contraction. Students can write the words. See Daily Word Study Practice, pages 204–205.

134

Lesson 62

Pages 135–136

Syllables

INFORMAL ASSESSMENT OBJECTIVES

Can students

✔ identify the number of vowels seen and heard in a word?

✔ identify the number of syllables in a word?

✔ divide words into syllables?

Lesson Focus

INTRODUCING THE SKILL

● Ask students to define a syllable. *(a word part with one vowel sound)*

● Say these words: *gardens, lemon, music.* Ask students how many syllables each word has and how they know.

● Then call on volunteers to write the words on the board and divide them into syllables as you explain syllabication rules 5, 6, and 7 on page 136.

USING THE PAGES

● Make sure students understand what to do on pages 135 and 136. Remind them to reread the syllabication rules on page 136 if they are unsure how to divide a word into syllables.

● When students have finished the pages, call on volunteers to summarize what they know about dividing words into syllables.

Name _____

> Say each word. Write the number of vowels you see in each word on the first line. Then write the number of vowels you hear in each word on the second line.

	Vowels				Vowels	
	See	Hear			See	Hear
1. bushes	2	2		**18.** surveys	3	2
2. mysteries	4	3		**19.** halves	2	1
3. heroes	3	2		**20.** beliefs	3	2
4. glasses	2	2		**21.** teeth	2	1
5. tomatoes	4	3		**22.** waltzes	2	2
6. thieves	3	1		**23.** pianos	3	3
7. daughters	3	2		**24.** melodies	4	3
8. foxes	2	2		**25.** solos	2	2
9. geese	3	1		**26.** potatoes	4	3
10. injuries	4	3		**27.** boxes	2	2
11. sombreros	3	3		**28.** clowns	1	1
12. guesses	3	2		**29.** leaves	3	1
13. sopranos	3	3		**30.** activities	5	4
14. shelves	2	1		**31.** buzzes	2	2
15. cookies	4	2		**32.** lassos	2	2
16. wives	2	1		**33.** elves	2	1
17. scratches	2	2		**34.** patches	2	2

Lesson 62
Syllables **135**

FOCUS ON ALL LEARNERS

ENGLISH LANGUAGE LEARNERS/ESL

Because correct pronunciation of words is necessary for correct syllabication, pair each English-language learner with an English-proficient student who can help with the pronunciation.

VISUAL LEARNERS

INDIVIDUAL   **Materials:** books, magazines, newspapers

Provide each student with a printed paragraph or section. Have him or her look for and list the words in the passage that have more than one syllable and write how many syllables these words have.

KINESTHETIC LEARNERS

PARTNER   **Materials:** butcher paper, markers, number cubes, game pieces

Have each pair make a circular game track with game spaces labeled 1, 2, or 3. Then have players take turns rolling the cube to move their game pieces. To stay on a space, a player must name two words with the number of syllables shown in the space. The first player to complete the circle wins.

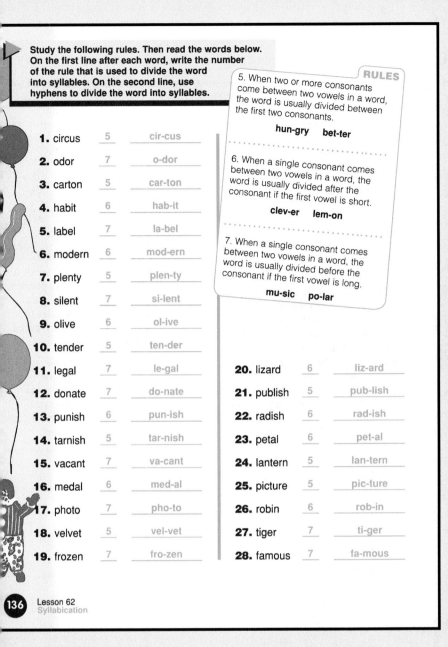

Study the following rules. Then read the words below. On the first line after each word, write the number of the rule that is used to divide the word into syllables. On the second line, use hyphens to divide the word into syllables.

RULES

5. When two or more consonants come between two vowels in a word, the word is usually divided between the first two consonants.

hun-gry   bet-ter

6. When a single consonant comes between two vowels in a word, the word is usually divided after the consonant if the first vowel is short.

clev-er   lem-on

7. When a single consonant comes between two vowels in a word, the word is usually divided before the consonant if the first vowel is long.

mu-sic   po-lar

1. circus	5	cir-cus
2. odor	7	o-dor
3. carton	5	car-ton
4. habit	6	hab-it
5. label	7	la-bel
6. modern	6	mod-ern
7. plenty	5	plen-ty
8. silent	7	si-lent
9. olive	6	ol-ive
10. tender	5	ten-der
11. legal	7	le-gal
12. donate	7	do-nate
13. punish	6	pun-ish
14. tarnish	5	tar-nish
15. vacant	7	va-cant
16. medal	6	med-al
17. photo	7	pho-to
18. velvet	5	vel-vet
19. frozen	7	fro-zen

20. lizard	6	liz-ard
21. publish	5	pub-lish
22. radish	6	rad-ish
23. petal	6	pet-al
24. lantern	5	lan-tern
25. picture	5	pic-ture
26. robin	6	rob-in
27. tiger	7	ti-ger
28. famous	7	fa-mous

Lesson 62
Syllabication

SPELLING

Materials: lists of the spelling words *messes, waltzes, boxes, dishes, batches, activities, wolves, geese, sheep, potatoes, it's, can't*

Give pairs a list of the spelling words and have them give each other a spelling "test" of the words. The tester uses each word in an oral sentence for the other to write.

WRITING

 Portfolio   **Materials:** poster paper, markers, crayons

Have students work in small groups to create a poster that illustrates the rules for dividing words into syllables. Together they can write the rules using their own words, provide example words, and develop a memory aid to help everyone remember each rule. Encourage students to combine these elements into an attractive, eye-catching design.

LANGUAGE ARTS

Explain that an analogy tells the relationship one thing has to another. For example, *Hands are to gloves as feet are to boots.* Write these on the board for students to complete.

Finger is to hand as toe is to _____. *(foot)*
Lizard is to reptile as eagle is to _____. *(bird)*
Silent is to quiet as noisy is to _____. *(loud)*

Have students write the number of syllables in each word used to complete an analogy.

PHYSICAL EDUCATION

Materials: poster paper, markers, crayons

Have students list simple stretching activities (touch toes, neck circles, and so on), make a poster for each, and design an indoor fitness routine to use when people can't go outside. Posters should have numbers identifying fitness stations. Let students do stretches in order, moving from station to station.

Technology   **AstroWord** Multisyllabic Words.
© 1998 Silver Burdett Ginn Inc. Division of Simon & Schuster.

 LARGE GROUP   ## AUDITORY LEARNERS

Say pairs of words, or groups of three words, and have students identify the syllable pattern. Some examples are *they are* (1,1); *super heroes* (2, 2); *baby's small toy* (2, 1, 1); *Old MacDonald's farm* (1, 3, 1); *two upright pianos* (1, 2, 3).

GIFTED LEARNERS

Materials: poetry books

Have students choose a short rhyming poem and identify the number of syllables in each line and determine if the poem has a rhythmic pattern. Students could try a limerick first to identify the rhythmic pattern it follows.

LEARNERS WHO NEED EXTRA SUPPORT

On page 136, have students read one syllabication rule at a time and search for words that follow that rule. See Daily Word Study Practice, page 208.

Lesson 63

Pages 137–138

Reading **Writing**

Reviewing Plurals, Possessives, Contractions, Syllables

Lesson Focus

READING

- Write the words *he's*, *she'll*, and *we've* on the board. Have students say each word and identify it as a contraction. Point to the apostrophe and ask what its purpose is. Have students name the letters that were left out when the contractions were written.

- Now say *waltz*, *goose*, *flies*, *cat*, *banjo*, and *deer*. As you say each one, ask students to identify it as singular or plural. Have volunteers write both forms of the word on the board.

- Review possessives with students. Invite them to offer examples of both singular and plural possessive forms.

- Explain that as students read a news story about the Morse code, they'll be reading many more words that are plurals, possessives, and contractions.

WRITING

Point out and explain the Morse code alphabet on page 138. As students prepare to write a coded message to a friend, remind them to refer to the Helpful Hints.

 Name _____

 Reading ▶ Read the news story. Then write your answer to the question at the end of the story.

Morse Code to Be Replaced

In 1999 the last official message in Morse code was sent over the airways. Modern technology has outgrown Samuel Morse's system of using dots and dashes to stand for letters of the alphabet.

Long ago, before radios were invented, ships' crews used flags, lanterns, and foghorns to call for help. This system only worked if the ships were near each other. Then Guglielmo Marconi invented the wireless telegraph. Using Morse's code of dots and dashes, ships could tap out messages to each other. This greatly improved safety at sea since ships didn't have to be close to each other to call for help.

Today, the touch of a button sends a distress signal that tells a ship's position, the time, and the kind of trouble it's in. Satellites orbiting the earth's poles pick up the signals and relay them to rescue stations' receivers.

By 1999 all ships had special radio beacons. If a ship sinks, the beacon will float free and continue to send out distress signals. This system has already saved the lives of more than 1,000 men, women, and children.

How do you think a ship's captain of the past would react if he were brought to the present and shown this new survival technology? Give reasons for your opinion.

_____
_____
_____
_____
_____
_____
_____

FOCUS ON ALL LEARNERS ✳ ● ◆

ENGLISH LANGUAGE LEARNERS/ESL

To build background for the article, ask students about any codes they are familiar with.

VISUAL LEARNERS

PARTNER **Materials:** a photocopy of a page from students' favorite books

Provide each pair with a copy of a page from their favorite novel. Then have them circle each plural, underline each possessive, and box each contraction. Have students analyze each word, identifying the rule that governs each formation.

KINESTHETIC LEARNERS

LARGE GROUP **Materials:** heavy paper, markers

Have students make a tic-tac-toe grid, writing *plural*, *contraction*, or *possessive* in small letters in each square. As you say *plural*, *contraction*, or *possessive*, students write an example of the word in the appropriate square. The first player with three correct examples in a row wins.

Writing

> Write a message to a friend in the space below. Then encode your message in Morse code. Exchange messages with a friend and decode the message you receive. Use the words from the word bank below.

A •—	H ••••	O ———	V •••—
B —•••	I ••	P •——•	W •——
C —•—•	J •———	Q ——•—	X —••—
D —••	K —•—	R •—•	Y —•——
E •	L •—••	S •••	Z ——••
F ••—•	M ——	T —	
G ——•	N —•	U ••—	

First, write your message.

Then, look up the code for each letter and write it.

Use slash marks to separate the code for each letter.

Don't use periods—they'd be too confusing.

Helpful Hints

wishes	I'm	codes'	hobbies	we'll
children	switches	ourselves	teacher's	can't

38 Lesson 63
Plurals, possessives, contractions, syllables: Writing

SPELLING

Write the spelling words *messes, waltzes, boxes, dishes, batches, activities, wolves, geese, sheep, potatoes, it's, can't* on the board. Provide students with the following sentences for them to complete using the correct word.

1. The stew had carrots and ____.(*potatoes*)
2. I ____ complete the puzzle.(*can't*)
3. The kitchen is messy, so I'll wash the lunch ____.(*dishes*)
4. That couple danced the ____ beautifully.(*waltzes*)
5. Those ____ have thick curly wool.(*sheep*)
6. Look at all these ____ of games.(*boxes*)
7. The pair of ____ had five pups.(*wolves*)
8. The kittens raced across the table leaving ____ of milk and juice.(*messes*)
9. Two wild ____ flew overhead.(*geese*)
10. ____ too cold to swim today.(*It's*)
11. Jo planned art ____ for us to do.(*activities*)
12. The baker made two ____ of bread.(*batches*)

SOCIAL STUDIES

Materials: navigational charts or books about maps

Explain to students that besides the Morse code, foghorns, and lighthouses, there is something else that helps boats and ships find their way—a system of buoys. Introduce students to navigational charts and how different buoys and landforms are represented on them to aid mariners.

ART/SOCIAL STUDIES

Portfolio

Materials: art paper, markers or crayons

Invite students to design a statue that honors communication in improving safety at sea. Statues can feature any kind of communication mentioned in the article or honor all of them. Encourage students to share their designs and explain how they decided on their designs.

LARGE GROUP

AUDITORY LEARNERS

As you say each phrase, have students identify the word that is a possessive and say if it is singular or plural or if more information is needed. Try these phrases: *the geese's honks; the spies' code* (more information needed, unless written); *the mouse's feet; the kangaroo's hop.*

GIFTED LEARNERS

Challenge students to write sentences in which all the words have the same number of syllables. If they get stuck, suggest that *a, an, and, the* be exceptions as well as the prepositions *over, through, before, below, above, about, among, of, into, from,* and *with.*

LEARNERS WHO NEED EXTRA SUPPORT

To encode the message on page 138, suggest that students write each letter, one at a time, on a scrap of paper and place it alongside that letter in the code box. Then they can transfer the code for the letter to the scrap paper and decode the message. See Daily Word Study Practice, pages 204–205, 208.

Lesson 64

Pages 139–140

Unit Checkup

Reviewing Plurals, Possessives, Contractions, Syllables

INFORMAL ASSESSMENT OBJECTIVES

Can students

✔ identify and use the plural form of words ending in *-ch, -f,* and *-y*?

✔ identify and use irregular plurals?

✔ identify and use singular and plural possessives?

✔ identify and use contractions?

Lesson Focus

PREPARING FOR THE CHECKUP

- Ask students to explain what a contraction is. Invite volunteers to write some examples on the board and explain how they were formed.

- Write *elf, potato, child, fox,* and *country* on the board. Have students tell how to write the plural of each word.

- Ask volunteers to write the singular and plural possessives of *elf* and *child*.

USING THE PAGES

- Be sure students understand how to complete the pages. Point out that on page 139, there are three steps: (1) deciding on the correct answer choice; (2) filling in the circle ; and (3) writing the word on the line. Remind students to answer the questions on page 140 in complete sentences.

- When students have completed the pages, have volunteers summarize what they learned about plurals, possessives, and contractions in this unit.

UNIT 5 CHECKUP

> Read each sentence. Fill in the circle next to the word that correctly completes the sentence. Write the word on the line.

1. Giant _____moose_____ are members of the deer family.
   ○ mooses
   ● moose

2. There _____hasn't_____ ever been a larger animal with antlers.
   ○ has'nt
   ● hasn't

3. Big as they are, moose can move as quietly as _____mice_____.
   ● mice
   ○ mouses

4. Moose don't have many _____enemies_____.
   ● enemies
   ○ enemys

5. _____Wolves_____ are the animals they fear most.
   ○ Wolfs
   ● Wolves

6. A moose has no front _____teeth_____ in its upper jaw.
   ● teeth
   ○ tooths

7. That means it _____can't_____ bite chunks of food.
   ○ cann't
   ● can't

8. Water _____plants'_____ soft leaves are a moose's favorite food.
   ● plants'
   ○ plants's

9. Moose also pull leaves off tree _____branches_____.
   ○ branchs
   ● branches

10. A moose can reach leaves growing twelve _____feet_____ above the ground!
    ● feet
    ○ foots

11. Sometimes moose have twin _____calves_____.
    ● calves
    ○ calfs

12. Moose _____calves'_____ legs are very long.
    ○ calve's
    ● calves'

13. A _____moose's_____ new antlers grow in May.
    ● moose's
    ○ mooses'

14. A bull moose's _____antlers_____ can weigh 85 pounds!
    ● antlers
    ○ antlers'

Lesson 64

Plurals, possessives, contractions, syllables: Checkup

139

FOCUS ON ALL LEARNERS

ENGLISH LANGUAGE LEARNERS/ESL

Build background for the sentences on page 139 by showing students photographs of a moose. Explain that moose are large animals—their shoulders can be as high as 7 1/2 feet—but they are very quiet.

SMALL GROUP

VISUAL/KINESTHETIC LEARNERS

Materials: index cards, markers

Write words of one, two, or three syllables on cards. Have each student pick a card and write the word on the board, using hyphens to divide the word into syllables.

PARTNER

KINESTHETIC LEARNERS

Materials: paper strips, markers, scissors, tape

Students each write on strips pairs of words that could be made into contractions. Then they trade strips, cut the words apart, tape the pieces together to form a contraction, and add an apostrophe in the appropriate space.

UNIT 5 CHECKUP

▶ Read the passage and answer the questions.

Tigers' Tongues and Dogs' Teeth

Paper money and coins haven't always been used as money. Stone Age people used the heads of axes for currency. The ancient Chinese used pieces of bronze cast in the shapes of things like shirts, knives, and hoes. You couldn't wear a tiny bronze shirt, but you could use it to buy a real shirt or a shirt's worth of anything else! Soldiers in Roman armies were paid in salt. In 1642, Virginia's General Assembly passed a law making tobacco the colony's only currency!

Around the world there have been many strange currencies: dogs' teeth in New Guinea, whales' teeth in the Pacific Islands, spearheads in Africa, and drums in Burma. In Thailand, tigers' tongues, claws, and teeth were used as money. Until about a hundred years ago, Asian banks issued blocks of tea as money. To make change, you'd break off pieces of the block! For many centuries, cowrie shells were accepted as money throughout much of Africa and Asia. In the French Sudan, people paid their taxes with cowries until 1907!

You can read the numbers on paper money, but long ago many people couldn't read. To help shepherds who didn't know how to read, one Welsh bank issued bank notes with pictures of sheep on them. The more sheep shown on a note, the more the note was worth!

1. What is the main idea of this passage?

Many things have been used as money.

2. What could a tiny bronze knife buy in ancient China?

It could buy a real knife or a knife's worth of something.

3. What kind of money was used in Thailand?

Tigers' tongues, claws, and teeth were used as money.

4. How did Welsh shepherds who couldn't read tell how much a bank note was worth?

The more sheep there were on a note, the more it was worth.

140 Lesson 64
Plurals, possessives, contractions, syllables: Checkup

AUDITORY LEARNERS

LARGE GROUP

Say the following words and for each one, ask students for the plural, the singular, or the plural possessive: *branch, fox, cowboy, hero, thief, goose, woman, deer, puppy,* and *rodeo.* Students should say and spell their answers.

GIFTED LEARNERS

Challenge students to look to the future and devise a new universal monetary system. Suggest that the number of syllables in the name of each bill or coin correspond in some way to the money's worth.

LEARNERS WHO NEED EXTRA SUPPORT

Materials: newspapers, books, or magazines

Provide each pair of students with a paragraph from a newspaper, book, or magazine. Have students look for and list words that contain more than one syllable. Next to each word, they can write the number of syllables. If they are unsure, they can refer to the rules on page 136. See Daily Word Study Practice, pages 204–205, 208.

ASSESSING UNDERSTANDING OF UNIT SKILLS

Student Progress Assessment Review the observational notes you made as students worked through the activities in this unit. They will help you evaluate the progress students made with identifying and writing plurals, possessives, contractions, and syllabication.

Portfolio Assessment Review the materials from the unit in students' portfolios. It may be helpful to confer with students to discuss their written work and the progress they have made since the beginning of the unit. As you review the work, evaluate how well they use these word-study skills.

Daily Word Study Practice For students who need additional practice with plurals, possessives, contractions, and syllabication, quick reviews are provided on pages 204–205, 208 in Daily Word Study Practice.

Word Study Posttest To assess students' mastery of plurals, possessives, contractions, and syllabication, use the posttest on pages 121g–121h.

Spelling Cumulative Posttest Review Unit 5 spelling words by using the following words and dictation sentences.

1.	**messes**	Let's clean up these **messes** on the counter.
2.	**waltzes**	**Waltzes** are fun to learn.
3.	**boxes**	Here are three **boxes** to keep things in.
4.	**dishes**	We bought new **dishes** last night.
5.	**batches**	She mixed two **batches** of paint.
6.	**activities**	I enjoy camp **activities**.
7.	**wolves**	Most Arctic **wolves** are white.
8.	**geese**	The **geese** flew over the lake.
9.	**sheep**	The **sheep** ran around in circles.
10.	**potatoes**	Maria peeled the **potatoes**.
11.	**it's**	**It's** a beautiful day for a walk.
12.	**can't**	Ben **can't** find his glasses.

Teacher Notes

INTRODUCING

Unit 6

Prefixes, Roots, Syllables

Student Performance Objectives

In Unit 6, students review the concept of prefixes and are introduced to new prefixes and roots and their meanings. Work on syllabication rules will be extended. As these skills are introduced or developed, students will be able to

◆ Associate the prefixes *un-*, *dis-*, *non-*, *ir-*, *il-*, *in-*, *en-*, *im-*, and *em-* with their usual meanings

◆ Associate the prefixes *ex-*, *re-*, *de-*, *co-*, *com-*, and *con-* with their usual meanings

◆ Associate the prefixes *fore-*, *pre-*, *pro-*, *super-*, *over-*, *sub-*, *under-*, *out-*, *bi-*, *tri-*, *semi-*, and *mid-* with their meanings

◆ Associate the roots *pos*, *pel*, *port*, *ject*, *duce*, *duce*, *tract*, *spec*, *spect*, and *scribe* with their meanings

◆ Use syllabication rules to divide words into syllables

Contents

Assessment Strategy Overview

Throughout Unit 6, assess students' ability to read and write words with common roots and prefixes. There are various ways to assess students' progress. You may also want to encourage students to evaluate their own work and to participate in setting goals for their own learning.

FORMAL ASSESSMENT

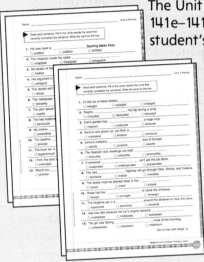

The Unit 6 Pretest on pages 141e–141f helps to assess a student's knowledge at the beginning of the unit and to plan instruction.

The Unit 6 Posttest on pages 141g–141h helps to assess mastery of unit objectives and to plan for reteaching, if necessary.

INFORMAL ASSESSMENT

The Reading & Writing pages and Unit Checkup in the student book are an effective means of evaluating students' performance.

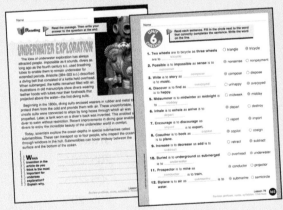

PORTFOLIO ASSESSMENT

Portfolio This logo appears throughout the teaching plans. It signals opportunities for collecting students' work for individual portfolios. You may also want to collect the following pages.

❖ Unit 6 Pretest and Posttest, pages 141e–141h

❖ Unit 6 Reading & Writing, pages 163–164

❖ Unit 6 Checkup, pages 165–166

STUDENT PROGRESS CHECKLIST

Use the checklist on page 141i to record students' progress. You may want to cut the sections apart to place each student's checklist in his or her portfolio.

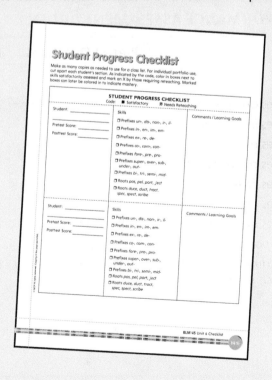

Skill	Reading & Writing Pages	Unit Checkup
Prefixes un-, dis-, non-, ir-, il-	163–164	165–166
Prefixes in-, en-, im-, em-	163–164	165–166
Prefixes ex-, re-, de-	163–164	165–166
Prefixes co-, com-, con-	163–164	165–166
Prefixes fore-, pre-, pro-	163–164	165–166
Prefixes super-, over-, sub-, under-, out-	163–164	165–166
Prefixes bi-, tri-, semi-, mid-	163–164	165–166
Roots pos, pel, port, ject	163–164	165–166
Roots duce, duct, tract, spec, spect, scribe	163–164	165–166
Syllables	163–164	165–166

Administering and Evaluating the
Pretest and Posttest

DIRECTIONS

To help you assess students' progress in learning Unit 6 skills, tests are available on pages 141e–141h. Administer the Pretest before students begin the unit. The results of the Pretest will help you identify each student's strengths and needs in advance, allowing you to structure lesson plans to meet individual needs. Administer the Posttest to assess students' overall mastery of skills taught in the unit and to identify specific areas that will require reteaching.

PERFORMANCE ASSESSMENT PROFILE

The following chart will help you identify specific skills as they appear on the tests and enable you to identify and record specific information about an individual's or the class's performance on the tests.

Depending on the results of the tests, refer to the Reteaching column for lesson-plan pages where you can find activities that will be useful for meeting individual needs or for daily word study practice.

ANSWER KEYS

Unit 6 Pretest, page 141e (BLM 41)

1. enlarged 2. dislocated 3. produced 4. immature 5. exports 6. bimonthly 7. cooperates 8. tristate 9. subsoil 10. foresight 11. semicircle 12. overheated 13. midstream

Unit 6 Pretest, page 141f (BLM 42)

14. nontoxic 15. repel 16. uncertain 17. portable 18. injection 19. conduct 20. retracted 21. prescription 22. oppose 23. porter

Unit 6 Posttest, page 141g (BLM 43)

1. entitled 2. disappear 3. undertow 4. illogical 5. extract 6. biweekly 7. copilot 8. tricycle 9. subscribes 10. forecast 11. semiannual 12. overrated 13. renew

Unit 6 Posttest, page 141h (BLM 44)

14. composer 15. dispel 16. spectators 17. transport 18. project 19. deduct 20. tractor 21. inscription 22. proposed 23. important

PERFORMANCE ASSESSMENT PROFILE

Skill	Pretest Questions	Posttest Questions	Reteaching: Focus on All Learners	Reteaching: Daily Word Study Practice
Prefixes *dis-, un-, non-, il-*	2, 14, 16	2, 4, 15	143–144, 163–164	205–206
Prefixes *in-, en-, im-*	1, 4, 18	1, 21, 23	145–146, 163–164	205–206
Prefixes *ex-, re-, de-*	5, 15, 20	5, 13, 19	147–148, 163–164	205–206
Prefixes *co-, con-, com-*	7, 19	7, 14	149–150, 163–164	205–206
Prefixes *fore-, pre-, pro-*	3, 10, 21	10, 18, 22	151–152, 163–164	205–206
Prefixes *over-, sub-, under-*	9, 12	3, 9, 12	153–154, 163–164	205–206
Prefixes *bi-, tri-, semi-, mid-*	6, 8, 11, 13	6, 8, 11	155–156, 163–164	205–206
Roots *pos, pel, port, ject*	5, 15, 17,18, 22, 23	14, 15, 17, 18, 22, 23	157–158, 163–164	206
Roots *duce, duct, tract, spect, scribe*	3, 19, 20, 21	5, 9, 16, 19, 20, 21	159–160, 163–164	206

Read each sentence. Fill in the circle beside the word that correctly completes the sentence. Write the word on the line.

1. I'd like six of these photos _____.
   ○ relarged   ○ exlarged   ○ enlarged

2. Regina _____ her hip during a jump.
   ○ unlocated   ○ dislocated   ○ bilocated

3. Carl's garden has _____ a huge crop.
   ○ reduced   ○ produced   ○ deduced

4. Sara is very grown up, but Rick is _____.
   ○ nonmature   ○ ilmature   ○ immature

5. Jenny's company _____ toys to Europe.
   ○ reports   ○ proports   ○ exports

6. The Spanish club meetings are held _____.
   ○ bimonthly   ○ comonthly   ○ foremonthly

7. If everyone _____, we'll get the job done.
   ○ cooperates   ○ underoperates   ○ preoperates

8. The new _____ highway will go through Ohio, Illinois, and Indiana.
   ○ semistate   ○ tristate   ○ overstate

9. The seeds must be planted deep in the _____.
   ○ outsoil   ○ insoil   ○ subsoil

10. Rosie had the _____ to close the windows.
   ○ desight   ○ oversight   ○ foresight

11. The students sat in a _____ around the librarian to hear the story.
   ○ supercircle   ○ semicircle   ○ precircle

12. Joel was late because his car's engine became _____.
   ○ overheated   ○ midheated   ○ subheated

13. The girl was fishing _____ most of the morning.
   ○ understream   ○ substream   ○ midstream

Go to the next page. →

> Read each sentence. Fill in the circle beside the word that completes the sentence. Write the word on the line.

14. The new antifreeze formula is _____ to animals.

○ detoxic   ○ nontoxic   ○ extoxic

15. I don't care if it rains, since my jacket can _____ water.

○ repel   ○ compel   ○ propel

16. Ramon was _____ about his family's vacation plans.

○ discertain   ○ decertain   ○ uncertain

17. My _____ calculator fits into my purse.

○ porter   ○ impossible   ○ portable

18. Sandra received an _____ to help fight her allergies.

○ injection   ○ rejection   ○ projection

19. The orchestra leader will _____ two symphonies tonight.

○ indict   ○ product   ○ conduct

20. My kitten, Bruiser, gently _____ his claws.

○ distracted   ○ retracted   ○ protracted

21. The doctor wrote a _____ to treat the patient's illness.

○ deduction   ○ injection   ○ prescription

22. How many voters _____ the new tax?

○ oppose   ○ impose   ○ depose

23. The _____ carried Mom's bags out to the car.

○ importer   ○ conductor   ○ porter

Possible score on Unit 6 Pretest is 23. Number correct _____

> Read each sentence. Fill in the circle beside the word that correctly completes the sentence. Write the word on the line.

1. His new book is _____ **Spelling Made Easy.**
○ untitled   ○ extitled   ○ entitled

2. The magician made the rabbit _____.
○ unappear   ○ disappear   ○ preappear

3. Be careful of the _____ when swimming at the shore.
○ midtow   ○ overtow   ○ undertow

4. His argument in the debate was _____.
○ unlogical   ○ ilogical   ○ illogical

5. The dentist will have to _____ that infected tooth.
○ retract   ○ protract   ○ extract

6. The newspaper is published _____.
○ biweekly   ○ coweekly   ○ foreweekly

7. The pilot asked the _____ to take over the plane's controls.
○ copilot   ○ underpilot   ○ subpilot

8. The two toddlers were fighting over one _____.
○ semicycle   ○ tricycle   ○ midcycle

9. My mother _____ to lots of medical journals.
○ prescribes   ○ inscribes   ○ subscribes

10. The weather _____ predicted snow early in the evening.
○ precast   ○ overcast   ○ forecast

11. The book fair is a _____ event.
○ superannual   ○ semiannual   ○ midannual

12. I think the food in that restaurant is _____.
○ overrated   ○ outrated   ○ subrated

13. Would you _____ my book at the library?
○ prenew   ○ renew   ○ denew

Go to the next page. →

> Read each sentence. Fill in the circle beside the word that completes the sentence. Write the word on the line.

14. Who is the _____ of that piece of music?

   ○ composer   ○ disposer   ○ imposer

15. The principal's speech helped to _____ rumors about the school closing.

   ○ compel   ○ dispel   ○ propel

16. All of the _____ were wearing the team colors.

   ○ inspectors   ○ spectators   ○ prospectors

17. It is illegal to _____ certain plants across state lines.

   ○ report   ○ deport   ○ transport

18. Actors need to _____ their voices so that they can be heard clearly.

   ○ inject   ○ reject   ○ project

19. The clerk can _____ the amount you paid from the total bill.

   ○ product   ○ induct   ○ deduct

20. We used a _____ to pull out the old stump.

   ○ distractor   ○ tractor   ○ retractor

21. The _____ in the book was signed by the author.

   ○ subscription   ○ conscription   ○ inscription

22. The mayor _____ a solution to the traffic problem.

   ○ proposed   ○ disposed   ○ deposed

23. I missed an _____ phone call while I was out.

   ○ repellent   ○ expectant   ○ important

Possible score on Unit 6 Posttest is 23. Number correct _____

Student Progress Checklist

Make as many copies as needed to use for a class list. For individual portfolio use, cut apart each student's section. As indicated by the code, color in boxes next to skills satisfactorily assessed and mark an X by those requiring reteaching. Marked boxes can later be colored in to indicate mastery.

STUDENT PROGRESS CHECKLIST

Code: ■ Satisfactory   ☒ Needs Reteaching

Student: _____	Skills	Comments / Learning Goals
_____	❑ Prefixes *un-, dis-, non-, ir-, il-*	
Pretest Score: _____	❑ Prefixes *in-, en-, im-, em-*	
Posttest Score: _____	❑ Prefixes *ex-, re-, de-*	
	❑ Prefixes *co-, com-, con-*	
	❑ Prefixes *fore-, pre-, pro-*	
	❑ Prefixes *super-, over-, sub-, under-, out-*	
	❑ Prefixes *bi-, tri-, semi-, mid-*	
	❑ Roots *pos, pel, port, ject*	
	❑ Roots *duce, duct, tract, spec, spect, scribe*	
Student: _____	Skills	Comments / Learning Goals
_____	❑ Prefixes *un-, dis-, non-, ir-, il-*	
Pretest Score: _____	❑ Prefixes *in-, en-, im-, em-*	
Posttest Score: _____	❑ Prefixes *ex-, re-, de-*	
	❑ Prefixes *co-, com-, con-*	
	❑ Prefixes *fore-, pre-, pro-*	
	❑ Prefixes *super-, over-, sub-, under-, out-*	
	❑ Prefixes *bi-, tri-, semi-, mid-*	
	❑ Roots *pos, pel, port, ject*	
	❑ Roots *duce, duct, tract, spec, spect, scribe*	

Spelling Connections

INTRODUCTION

The Unit Word List is a comprehensive list of spelling words drawn from this unit. The words are grouped by prefixes and roots studied throughout the unit. To incorporate spelling into your word study program, use the activity in the Curriculum Connections section of each teaching plan.

The spelling lessons utilize the following approach for each set of words.

1. Administer a pretest of the words that have not yet been introduced. Dictation sentences are provided.

2. Provide practice.

3. Reassess. Dictation sentences are provided.

A final test is provided at the end of the unit in Lesson 76 on page 166.

DIRECTIONS

Make a copy of Blackline Master 46 for each student. After administering the pretest for each word, give students a copy of the appropriate word list.

Students can work with a partner to practice spelling the words orally and identifying the prefix or root. You may want to challenge students to add to the list words with these or other prefixes and roots. Students can also write words of their own on *My Own Word List* (see Blackline Master 46).

Students may store their list words in an envelope in the back of their books or notebooks. You may want to suggest that students keep a spelling notebook, listing words with similar prefixes and roots. Another idea is to build word walls with students and display them in the classroom. Each section of the wall can focus on a type of word. The walls will become a good spelling resource when students are writing.

UNIT WORD LIST

Prefixes *un-, dis-, ir-, il-, en-, im-, ex-, co-, con-, pre-, pro-*
unearned
distrust
irregular
illegal
entangle
improper
export
cooperate
concern
preheat
project

Prefixes *super-, over-, sub-, under-, out-, bi-, tri-, semi-, mid-*
superhuman
oversize
subzero
underage
outside
biplane
triangle
semifinal
midyear

Roots *pos, pel, port, ject, duce, duct, tract, spec, spect, scribe*
position
propel
report
eject
reduce
conduct
tractor
spectator
inspect
describe

Name _____

Spelling   UNIT 6 WORD LIST

Prefixes un, dis, ir, il, en, im, ex, co, con, pre, pro

unearned
distrust
irregular
illegal
entangle
improper
export
cooperate
concern
preheat
project

Prefixes super, over, sub, under, out, bi, tri, semi, mid

superhuman
oversize
subzero
underage
outside
biplane
triangle
semifinal
midyear

Roots pos, pel, port, ject, duce, duct, tract, spec, spect, scribe

position
propel
report
eject
reduce
conduct
tractor
spectator
inspect
describe

My Own Word List

Word Study Games, Activities, and Technology

The following collection of ideas offers a variety of opportunities to reinforce word study skills while actively engaging students. The games, activities, and technology suggestions can easily be adapted to meet the needs of your group of learners. They vary in approach so as to consider students' different learning styles.

● **WORD WINDOWS**

Make a word window by cutting a rectangle out of the center of a sheet of tagboard as shown. Cut a slit just above and one below the window. Write a prefix such as *dis-* to the left of the window. On a strip of paper, write words and roots that combine with the prefix to make new words. As students pull the strip through the slits, have them read each word and tell its meaning.

▲ **SPIN-A-WORD**

Use tagboard and a brad to make a spinner as shown. Write one prefix in each of six sections. Have each student write a root from the unit at the top of a sheet of paper. Students take turns spinning the spinner. If the prefix combined with the root on his or her paper makes a word, the student writes down the word and its meaning. Students may be given one point for each correct word and one point for each correct meaning. The student with the most points after ten spins wins.

◆ **PREFIX SKUNK**

Make word cards for the following words: *preview, prepay, prewash, prepaid; disappear, disrespect, disagree, discover; portable, report, important, transportation; subscribe, describe, inscribe, scribble.*

Mix the cards and deal four cards to each of four players. The object of the game is to collect a hand with four word cards having the same prefix or root. Each player discards one card, placing it face down and sliding it to the player on the right. Players then pick up the new cards and again pass a card to the player on the right. The game continues in this way until one player has four words with the same prefix or root. That player then places his or her cards on the table. When the other players see that someone's cards are down, they also set their cards down. The last player to lay down his or her cards gets an *s*. The game ends when one player has the letters that spell *skunk*. The player with the fewest letters wins.

Variation: Use words with different common roots or prefixes or with words having one, two, three, and four syllables.

■ ROOT TRAIN

List the roots *pos, pel, port, ject, duce, duct, tract, spect,* and *scribe* on the board. Have students stand in a row or circle. Call out a root, such as *pos.* The first student says a word that contains that root and then names another root, for example, *position; pel.* The next student says a word containing that root and names a new root. Challenge students to see how long the "root train" can keep going without a miss.

✳ SYLLABLE BINGO

Show students how to draw a five-by-five-square grid. Have them write *FREE* in the center space and fill the other squares with the numbers 1, 2, 3, and 4 in any order they choose. Explain that the numbers will represent the number of syllables a called word has. Call words with one, two, three, or four syllables and tell students to cover the number that represents the number of syllables they hear in the word. The first student to cover five squares in a row is the winner.

Variation: Have students fill in the bingo card squares with prefixes, roots, suffixes, or unit spelling words.

● GRIDLOCK

Show students how to make a five-by-five grid as shown. Along the top, students print four roots from the unit. Along the side, they print four prefixes. Have students exchange grids and fill in as many of the squares as possible by combining the prefixes and the roots as in a multiplication grid. Students can compare grids to see whose has the most squares filled in with words.

	pel	ject	tract	duct
dis-	dispel		distract	
con-			contract	duct
pro-	propel	project	protract	product
sub-		subject	subtract	

▲ PREFIX DOMINOES

Have pairs of students choose five prefixes and make a set of twenty word card dominoes with words containing those prefixes. Have them mix up the cards and pass out six to each player, placing the rest of the dominoes in a draw pile. The first player places a domino on the table. The next player then finds a domino with the same prefix and places it next to the one on the table. If a player cannot find a match, he or she draws from the pile until one is found. The first player to play all his or her dominoes is the winner.

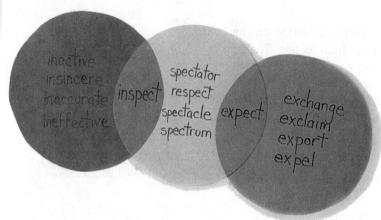

Choose words that contain both a prefix and a root studied in this unit, for example, *inspect, deduct, prescribe,* or *compose.* Draw a three-circle Venn diagram and print the words in the intersecting sections as shown. In the other parts of the diagram, have volunteers print words that contain either the prefix or the root.

● **LET'S PLAY CHECKERS**

Duplicate the game board on Blackline Master 47 and distribute one game board to each pair of students. Each student must have twelve matching playing pieces, such as checkers, coins, or paper disks. Students play the game according to the rules of checkers, except that when they land on a space, they must say a word that contains the root or prefix printed in that space. A player may challenge another player's word, using a dictionary to support the challenge. A player who is successfully challenged loses a turn. Play continues until one player has captured all of the other player's checkers.

Technology

The following software products are designed to improve students' comprehension skills.

Undersea Reading for Meaning   Students in grades 2–8 take on the role of divers who must recover five artifacts from a sunken ship. To do so, they must outsmart a giant octopus by reading short passages and answering comprehension questions that involve these skills: predicting outcomes, drawing conclusions, determining cause and effect, and drawing inferences.
**GAMCO Educational Materials/
    Siboney Learning Group
P.O. Box 1911
Big Spring, TX 79721
(800) 351-1404

Pickleface and Other Stories   The adventures of Jodi and her friends are designed to engage students in grades 4–6 while helping to build comprehension skills. Activities call for making inferences and predictions, distinguishing fact from opinion, and expanding vocabulary.

**Hartley Coursewear
9920 Pacific Heights Boulevard
Suite 500
San Diego, CA 92121
(800) 247-1380

Captain Zog's Main Idea   Robots help defend players in grades 2-8 from the fearsome Captain Zog. To give the robots the ammunition they need, students must identify the main idea by reading passages (135 in all) about a range of subjects.
**GAMCO Educational Materials/
    Siboney Learning Group
P.O. Box 1911
Big Spring, TX 79721
(800) 351-1404

Name _____

Let's Play Checkers

ex		re		scribe		con	
	tract		port		ject		spect
fore		pre		pro		tri	
	dis		in		em		im
co		ex		re		con	
	semi		over		sub		bi
duce		pos		pel		duct	
	pre		en		in		dis

Home Connection

A letter is available to be sent home at the beginning of Unit 6. This letter informs family members that students will be learning to read and write words with common prefixes and roots. The at-home activities encourage parents to help their children draw a picture with hidden objects in it and to identify any prefixes or roots in the names of the objects, as well as to look for prefixes and roots in books, magazines and newspapers. These activities promote interaction between student and family members while supporting students' learning of reading and writing words. A Book Corner feature suggests books that family members can look for in a local library and enjoy reading together. A letter is also available in Spanish on page 141q.

Home Letter

Dear Family,

As we work through this unit, we will be studying roots and prefixes—word parts that are added to the beginning of base words and roots to form new words.

At-Home Activities

▶ Ask your child to show you the pictures on the other side of this letter. (conductor, triangle, biplane, tripod, submarine, bicycle, superhero, tricycle, tractor, binoculars, triplets, propeller) Identify the prefixes and roots in the names of the items. (super-, bi-, tri-, sub-, con-, pro-, pel, duct, tract)

▶ With your child, look in magazines, newspapers, or homework papers for other words with prefixes and roots. Make a list of the words you find.

▶ Encourage your child to draw a picture with objects in it that begin with different prefixes and have you identify them.

Book Corner

You and your child might enjoy reading these books together. Look for them in your local library.

Doctor Coyote—A Native American Aesop's Fables

by John Bierhorst

Brilliantly retold fables and soft watercolor illustrations make a collection of entertaining and thought–provoking tales.

Jennifer-the-Jerk Is Missing

by Carol Gorman

A nerdy brat and his babysitter form an unlikely team in a suspenseful pursuit of kidnappers.

Sincerely,

_____

142 Unit 6
Introduction

Carta para la casa

Estimada familia,

A medida que trabajamos en esta unidad, estaremos estudiando raíces y prefijos: partes de palabras que se añaden al principio de las palabras base y las raíces de las palabras en inglés para crear palabras nuevas.

Actividades para hacer en casa

▶ Pídanle a su hijo/a que les muestre las imágenes en la página 141 de su libro: **conductor (conductor)**, **triangle (triángulo)**, **biplane (aeroplano)**, **trip (travesía)**, **submarine (submarino)**, **bicycle (bicicleta)**, **superhero (superhéroe)**, **tractor (tractor)**, **binoculars (binoculares)** **triplets (trillizos)**, **explosives (explosivos)**. Identifique los prefijos y las raíces en los nombres de los artículos **(super-, bi-, tri-, sub-, con-, ex-, over-, duct, tract)**.

▶ Animen a su hijo/a a hacer un dibujo con objetos escondidos en él.

▶ Con su hijo/a, busquen en revistas, periódicos o entre los papeles de las tareas, palabras en inglés con estos y otros prefijos y raíces.

Rincón del libro

Su hijo/a y ustedes pueden disfrutar juntos de la lectura de estos libros. Búsquenlos en la biblioteca de su localidad.

Doctor Coyote—A Native American Aesop's Fables
por John Bierhorst

Fábulas contadas de nuevo con suaves ilustraciones en acuarela que crean una colección de cuentos entretenidos y que causan reflexión.

Jennifer-the-Jerk Is Missing
por Carol Gorman

Un niño bitongo y malcriado y su niñera forman un equipo inusitado en la emocionante persecusión de unos secuestradores.

Atentamente,_____

Unit 6

Pages 141–142

Prefixes, Roots, Syllables

ASSESSING PRIOR KNOWLEDGE

To assess students' prior knowledge of prefixes, roots, and syllables, use the pretest on pages 141e–141f.

Unit Focus

USING THE PAGE

- Have students look at the picture on page 141 and talk about the scene. Then ask them to find the tricycle.
- Explain that many words begin with a word part that adds meaning—for example, *tri-* in *tricycle* means "three." Ask how many wheels are on a tricycle.
- Lead students to see that each part of a word adds meaning. Give a few other examples from the picture.
- **Critical Thinking** Read the questions aloud and invite students to share their responses.

BUILDING A CONTEXT

- Write on the board *bi-, sub-, super-, ex-*. Explain that these are prefixes—word parts that come at the beginning of a word and change its meaning. Ask volunteers to find an item in the picture whose name begins with each prefix.
- Write *tract, duct, pos,* and *pel* and explain that these are roots—word parts to which prefixes and suffixes can be added to make words. Add prefixes to make *retract, deduct, compos(e),* and *expel.* Have students circle each prefix and tell you what they think each word means.
- Explain that each of these prefixes added a syllable to the word. Ask how many syllables each word has. Now add suffixes to make *retraction, deducted, composition,* and *expelled.* Ask volunteers to say each word and tell you how many syllables it has.

UNIT 6 **Prefixes, Roots, Syllables**

What do you think the prefixes *bi* and *tri* mean? How are they alike?

Critical Thinking

Find the following items in the picture: a conductor, a triangle, a biplane, a tripod, a submarine, a bicycle, a superhero, a tricycle, a tractor, binoculars, triplets, and a propeller.

© MCP All rights reserved. Copying strictly prohibited.

UNIT OPENER ACTIVITIES

ALL KINDS OF PARADES

Have students look at the picture on page 141 again and suggest the kinds of celebrations that include parades. *(holidays, athletic contests, religious observances, landmark successes, and so on)* Allow time for volunteers to tell about parades they've seen in person or on television.

PREFIX HUNT

Write *tri-* on the board and ask students to find all the items in the picture on page 141 whose names start with *tri-* and circle them in one color. Repeat with other prefixes and roots, having students use different colors. On a separate piece of paper, students can also add other words they know that contain the prefix or root.

LITERATURE LOOKOUT

Invite students to search the library for interesting book titles that contain words with prefixes. Set up a display corner and encourage students to read the books independently.

Dear Family,

As we work through this unit, we will be studying roots and prefixes—word parts that are added to the beginning of base words and roots to form new words.

At-Home Activities

► Ask your child to show you the pictures on the other side of this letter. (conductor, triangle, biplane, tripod, submarine, bicycle, superhero, tricycle, tractor, binoculars, triplets, propeller) Identify the prefixes and roots in the names of the items. (super-, bi-, tri-, sub-, con-, pro-, pel, duct, tract)

► With your child, look in magazines, newspapers, or homework papers for other words with prefixes and roots. Make a list of the words you find.

► Encourage your child to draw a picture with objects in it that begin with different prefixes and have you identify them.

Book Corner

You and your child might enjoy reading these books together. Look for them in your local library.

**Doctor Coyote—
A Native American
Aesop's Fables**

by John Bierhorst

Brilliantly retold fables and soft watercolor illustrations make a collection of entertaining and thought-provoking tales.

**Jennifer-the-Jerk
Is Missing**

by Carol Gorman

A nerdy brat and his babysitter form an unlikely team in a suspenseful pursuit of kidnappers.

Sincerely,

_____

BULLETIN BOARD

For a bulletin board entitled "How Many?" have students brainstorm a list of nouns with the prefixes *uni-, bi-, tri-,* or *quad-/quart-*. Then have students select a noun and illustrate it. Display all pictures on the board arranged according to prefix.

● The Home Letter on page 142 is intended to acquaint family members with the word study skills students will be studying in the unit. Students can tear out page 142 and take it home. You may want to suggest that they complete the activities on the page with a family member. Encourage students to look for the books pictured on the page in the library and read them with family members.

● The Home Letter can also be found on page 141q in Spanish.

CURRICULUM
CONNECTIONS

WRITING

Portfolio **Materials:** reference books about nineteenth-century America

Explain that long ago, before movies, radio, television, and video games, it was often the most exciting day of the year when the circus came to town. Everyone would rush out to watch the colorful parade of performers and animals as they marched from their circus wagons or circus train to the field where the circus tent would be set up. Ask students to imagine that they live in a small town in nineteenth-century America. Have them write a description of a circus parade.

SCIENCE

Materials: binoculars, telescope

Provide a pair of binoculars and a small telescope of the same magnification. Take students outdoors and have them look through both instruments and compare the two experiences. What is different about what they see when using both eyes compared with when they use one eye?

MUSIC

Play some lively parade music, such as a Sousa march, and have students write a sentence about how the music makes them feel or what images it evokes. Let students march around the room to the music. Start them off on the same foot and have them try to keep in step.

Lesson 65

Pages 143–144

Prefixes un-, dis-, non-, ir-, il-

Lesson Focus

INTRODUCING THE SKILL

- Ask students to explain what a base word is. (*a word to which a suffix may be added*)

- Tell students that they can also add a prefix to a base word. Define a prefix as a word part added at the beginning of a base word to change the base word's meaning or form a new word.

- Write these words on the board: *unclear, dislike, nonstop, irrelevant, illiterate.* Ask students to name the base words and the prefixes.

- Have volunteers circle the prefixes. Explain that *un-, dis-, non-, ir-,* and *il-* usually mean "not." Encourage students to define the words, using *not.*

USING THE PAGES

- Make sure students understand the directions. Have a volunteer read aloud the definitions on page 143 and the rule on page 144 before students begin each page.

- After both pages have been completed, have students discuss what they have learned about prefixes that mean "not."

143

Name

▶ Read each word and circle the prefix **un, dis,** or **non.**

1. (non)partisan
2. (un)clear
3. (un)kind
4. (non)stop
5. (un)dress
6. (non)sense
7. (non)essential
8. (un)fold
9. (non)restrictive
10. (dis)like
11. (dis)cover
12. (un)opened
13. (dis)appear
14. (un)familiar
15. (dis)interested
16. (non)fiction
17. (non)productive
18. (un)pleasant
19. (dis)close
20. (non)existent

DEFINITIONS

A **base word** is a word to which a prefix or suffix may be added to form a new word. A **prefix** is a word part that is added at the beginning of a base word to change the base word's meaning or form a new word.

Un, dis, and **non** are prefixes that usually mean **not.**

unearned = not earned

distrust = not trust

nonprofit = not profit

▶ Read each sentence. Complete the sentence by adding a prefix to the base word in parentheses.

21. These books are _____**unfamiliar**_____ to me. (familiar)
22. I'd like to _____**discover**_____ what they're about. (cover)
23. I like reading _____**nonfiction**_____ books. (fiction)
24. I can read a book _____**nonstop**_____ if it's good. (stop)
25. I don't _____**dislike**_____ reading any kind of book. (like)
26. Reading is never _____**unpleasant**_____ for me. (pleasant)

FOCUS ON ALL LEARNERS ✳ ● ◆ ●

ENGLISH LANGUAGE LEARNERS/ESL

Show students a nature book and a novel. Ask them to tell what the difference is between a fiction book and a nonfiction book. Have volunteers tell which kind they prefer to read and ask someone to explain what the prefix *non-* means in *nonfiction.*

VISUAL LEARNERS

Write these incorrect words: *nonpleasant, disresponsible, irrestrictive, unlogical, ilappear.* Invite students to separate the mixed-up prefixes from the base words and then rewrite the words with the correct prefixes. Call on volunteers to use each word in a sentence.

KINESTHETIC LEARNERS

Materials: index cards, markers

Make cards for four words with each prefix *un-, dis-, non-, ir-, il-.* Have students play concentration. If two words with the same prefix are turned up, the player keeps the cards. If not, the words are replaced.

Read each word and circle its prefix.

> **RULE**
> The prefixes **ir** and **il** mean **not**.
> **ir**regular = not regular
> **il**legal = not legal

1. (ir)removable
2. (il)literate
3. (ir)responsible
4. (ir)rational
5. (il)ogical
6. (ir)resistible
7. (ir)relevant
8. (il)legible
9. (ir)reversible

Read the sentences below. Use the information in each sentence to help you write the meaning of the word in boldface print.

10. An argument that is logical makes sense. What is an **illogical** argument?
It is an argument that does not make sense.

11. Something that is relevant has to do with the subject being discussed. What is something that is **irrelevant?**
It is something that has nothing to do with the subject being discussed.

12. If a person's writing is legible, it is easy to read. What is **illegible** writing?
It is writing that is very difficult to read.

13. A person who is literate is able to read and write. What is an **illiterate** person?
It is a person who is not able to read and write.

14. A person who is responsible can be depended upon and shows a strong sense of duty. What is an **irresponsible** person?
It is a person who cannot be depended upon.

15. Something that is removable is able to be removed. What is something that is **irremovable**?
It is something that cannot be removed.

CURRICULUM CONNECTIONS

SPELLING

The following sentences can be used as a pretest for spelling words that have the prefixes *un-, dis-, non-, ir-, il-, in-, en-, im-, em-, ex-, re-, de-, co-, com-, con-, fore-, pre-,* and *pro-*.

1. **distrust** — Do you trust me or **distrust** me?
2. **unearned** — I can't accept **unearned** money.
3. **irregular** — I paid less for **irregular** socks.
4. **improper** — It's **improper** to stare at people.
5. **entangle** — Seaweed can **entangle** a swimmer.
6. **export** — Many nations **export** toys to the U.S.
7. **cooperate** — To **cooperate** is to work together.
8. **concern** — Dad's illness is our main **concern**.
9. **project** — Did you finish the **project**?
10. **preheat** — I **preheat** the oven before baking.
11. **illegal** — Should it be **illegal** to smoke?

WRITING

Invite students to make a list of everyday things that they find unpleasant. Have them include a prefix from the lesson in each item. See who can make the longest list.

PHYSICAL EDUCATION

Ice is nothing but water in nonliquid form! But without it, several exciting sports would not exist: ice hockey, ice dancing, figure skating, speed skating, curling, and ice boating. Have small groups of students each research one of these sports and give a short oral report.

SOCIAL STUDIES

 Portfolio Have students use on-line encyclopedias to find out about Mohandas Gandhi and what he accomplished through nonviolent resistance.

Technology **AstroWord** Prefixes.
© 1998 Silver Burdett Ginn Inc.
Division of Simon & Schuster.

AUDITORY LEARNERS

LARGE GROUP Read aloud the following base words, have volunteers add a prefix from this lesson to form a correct word, and then say the word: *happy (un-), like (dis- or un-), existent (non-), regular (ir-), legal (il-), likely (un-), cover (un- or dis-), legible (il-).*

GIFTED LEARNERS

Invite students to look through a dictionary and find ten words not used in this lesson that begin with the prefixes *un-, dis-, non-, ir-,* and *il-*. Ask students to restrict their lists to words they can define using the *not* meaning of the prefix. Encourage students to use each word in a sentence.

LEARNERS WHO NEED EXTRA SUPPORT

Point out to students that when these prefixes are added to a base word, they usually form a word that means the opposite of the base word, such as *happy, unhappy* or *existent, nonexistent*. See Daily Word Study Practice, pages 205–206.

Lesson 66

Pages 145–146

Prefixes in-, en-, im-, em-

INFORMAL ASSESSMENT OBJECTIVES

Can students

✔ recognize and identify the meanings of the prefixes *in-*, *en-*, *im-*, and *em-*?

✔ distinguish among the prefixes *in-*, *en-*, *im-* and *em-* when added to base words?

Lesson Focus

INTRODUCING THE SKILL

● Review that prefixes are word parts added at the beginning of base words.

● Write *impossible, enlarge, embitter,* and *inaccurate* on the board. Encourage students to identify the prefixes and the base words. Call on volunteers to circle the prefixes.

● Encourage students to suggest a meaning for each prefix. Then explain that *im-* and *in-* can mean "not," and that *em-* and *en-* mean "to cause to be" or "to make." Have students define each word, based on the meanings of the prefix and the base word.

USING THE PAGES

● Make sure students know what to do on pages 145 and 146. After they complete the pages, discuss what they have learned about the prefixes.

● **Critical Thinking** Read aloud the question at the bottom of page 146 and invite students to share their responses. Encourage them to talk about what was most fascinating about Tutankhamen's tomb and why.

Name _____

▶ **Read each word and circle its prefix.**

1. (in)flexible
2. (en)titled
3. (en)large
4. (in)effective
5. (im)patient
6. (im)possible
7. (em)bitter
8. (in)accurately
9. (en)code
10. (en)danger
11. (en)case
12. (im)perfect

> **RULE**
> The prefixes **im** and **in** can also mean **not**. The prefixes **em** and **en** mean **cause to be** or **to make**.
> **im**proper = not proper
> **in**curable = not curable
> **em**power = to make powerful
> **en**tangle = to make tangled

▶ **Rewrite each sentence below. Use one of the words from above to replace the underlined words.**

13. The agent will <u>put</u> the secret message <u>in code</u>.

   The agent will encode the secret message.

   _____

14. Then the message will <u>not</u> be <u>possible</u> for just anyone to read.

   Then the message will be impossible for

   just anyone to read.

15. We don't want to <u>not accurately</u> encode the message.

   We don't want to inaccurately encode the message.

   _____

16. That might <u>put</u> someone in <u>danger</u>.

   That might endanger someone.

   _____

Lesson 66
Prefixes in-, en-, im-, em- **145**

FOCUS ON ALL LEARNERS

ENGLISH LANGUAGE LEARNERS/ESL

To build background for the article on page 146, ask students if they have ever read a book or seen a show on television about finding the treasures of ancient Egypt. Define key words and difficult words such as *archaeologist, pharaoh,* and *irrational.*

VISUAL LEARNERS

PARTNER Ask pairs of students to work together to define each word based on the meanings of the base word and prefix: *enrage, imperfect, empower, enable, immature, inactive, enclosed, encourage, enacted, embedded, insincere.* Have partners confirm their definitions in a dictionary.

KINESTHETIC LEARNERS

LARGE GROUP **Materials:** colored chalk

   Write these incomplete words on the board and have volunteers use colored chalk to write *em-, im-, in-,* or *en-* to complete each word: *__lighten, __correct, __gulfed, __battled, __polite, __dangered, __complete, __possible, __rich.* Have students in turn use the word in a sentence of their own.

Read the passage. Underline each word that has one of these prefixes: **un, dis, non, ir, il, im, in, em, en**. Then answer the questions below.

Uncovered Treasures of a Boy King

For centuries, people searched for underdiscovered burial places of Egypt's pharaohs. Few had been left undisturbed. Yet incredibly, one tomb in the Royal Valley went untouched. This was the now-famous tomb of King Tutankhamen, discovered in 1922. King Tut, as he is often called, was an unimportant and almost unknown ruler who died in 1352 B.C. at the age of 19. Yet because Tut's tomb was found nearly intact, unlike most others, it remains the world's most exciting archaeological discovery.

No one encouraged British archaeologist Howard Carter in his search for King Tut's tomb. Most people felt that finding the tomb was impossible. They thought that Carter's insistence was irrational nonsense. Yet Carter would not be discouraged. After six years of digging, he finally unearthed the door of the tomb. He was not disappointed by the discoveries he made. Entombed with the young king were incredible treasures.

Perhaps the greatest treasure of all was the king's embalmed mummy, which was enclosed in a series of cases. The final one was solid gold! When the coffins were unsealed, Carter said, "The very air you breathe, unchanged through the centuries, you share with those who laid the mummy to its rest."

Why was the discovery of King Tutankhamen's tomb so special?

Critical Thinking

1. Why did people try to discourage Carter from searching for the tomb? _They thought finding it was impossible._

2. What word tells you that Carter was delighted by what he saw? _enchanted_

3. What does *unearthed* mean? _It means to be dug up out of the earth._

4. What did Carter do when he unsealed the coffins? _He opened them up._

146 Lesson 66
Review prefixes un-, dis-, non-, ir-, il-, im-, in-, em-, en-

---

LARGE GROUP

AUDITORY/VISUAL LEARNERS

Write the words at the top of page 145 on the board, adding *embolden* and *empower* to the list. Say *im-*, *em-*, *en-*, and *in-* in random order, pronouncing each prefix distinctly. After each prefix, have a volunteer circle a word on the board that starts with that prefix.

GIFTED LEARNERS

Invite students to write a paragraph on one of these topics: (1) an idea that would *empower* people to make positive changes; (2) how to be happy in an *imperfect* world; (3) the traits needed by a person hoping for a career in law *enforcement*.

LEARNERS WHO NEED EXTRA SUPPORT

Tell students that the prefixes *em-* and *im-* usually come before base words that start with *b*, *p*, or *m*, while *en-* and *in-* come before base words beginning with other consonants. See if they can offer examples of each. See Daily Word Study Practice, pages 205–206.

SPELLING

Make two cards for each spelling word, one with the prefix and one with the base or root. (Words: *distrust, unearned, irregular, improper, entangle, export, cooperate, concern, project, preheat, illegal*) Have small groups of students use the cards to play Concentration. If they turn up two cards that make a spelling word, they keep the cards. The student with the most cards at the end of the game wins.

WRITING

Portfolio Tell students that the word *embroider* comes from an old French word for fancy sewing, *broder*, plus the prefix *em-*. Display some pictures of embroidery. Explain that *embroider* also means "to embellish the truth"—to exaggerate to make an ordinary story more interesting. Have students write about something that happened to them, but ask them to embroider the story to make an ordinary event more interesting to the listener.

LANGUAGE ARTS

Materials: construction paper, scissors, brad

Invite students to make a code buster. Have them cut out two circles of unequal size and use a brad to fasten them together at the center. Have students write the alphabet around the edge of the outer circle and a mixed-up alphabet around the inner circle, lining up the letters on the two circles. Then have them use the inner letters as the code for the outer letters. Have students encode their messages for classmates to decode.

MATH

Tell students that a department store is having a 20%-off sale on imperfect sneakers that came from the factory with a slight flaw. Have students calculate how much they will pay for sneakers that, if perfect, would cost $50, $75, and $110. (*$40, $60, $88*) Let them make up problems about discounts on imperfect jeans and sporting goods and solve each other's math problems.

AstroWord Prefixes.
© 1998 Silver Burdett Ginn Inc. Division of Simon & Schuster.

Lesson 67
Pages 147–148

Prefixes ex-, re-, de-

INFORMAL ASSESSMENT OBJECTIVES

Can students

✓ recognize and identify the meanings of the prefixes *ex-*, *re-*, and *de-*?

✓ distinguish among the prefixes *ex-*, *re-*, and *de-* when these are added to base words?

Lesson Focus

INTRODUCING THE SKILL

- Review that a prefix changes a base word's meaning or creates a new word.

- Introduce the prefixes *ex-*, *re-*, and *de-* by writing them on the board and explaining that *ex-* usually means "out from" or "beyond;" *re-* usually means "again" or "back;" and *de-* usually means "down from," "away from," or "the opposite of" the base word.

- Call on volunteers to write the words *rebuild*, *deplane*, and *exchange*. Ask others to underline the base words and circle the prefixes. Invite students to define each word, using the meaning of the prefix.

USING THE PAGES

- Point out the riddle at the bottom of page 147 and explain that the numbered letters in the activity solve the riddle. Remind students to use complete sentences to answer the questions on page 148.

- After both pages have been completed, ask a volunteer to explain what the class has learned about *ex-*, *re-*, and *de-*.

> Read each clue. Find the word in the word bank that matches the clue and write it on the lines. Then write the letters in order from 1–11 in the spaces below to answer the riddle.

RULE

Ex is a prefix that usually means **out from** or **beyond**. **Re** is a prefix that usually means **again** or **back**. **De** is a prefix that usually means **down from**, **away from**, or **the opposite**.

export = to send goods from one country to another

repay = to pay again or to pay back

depress = to press down

expense	defend	recount
destroy	repay	reunite
excavate	dethrone	rebound
	expand	

1. pay again or pay back — r e p a y (6 under y)

2. put off a throne — d e t h r o n e (10 under n)

3. spring back — r e b o u n d (7 under o, 3 under u)

4. hollow out — e x c a v a t e (1 under a)

5. count again — r e c o u n t (5 under n)

6. tear down; ruin — d e s t r o y (11 under y)

7. cost; charge — e x p e n s e (9 under s)

8. keep safe; protect — d e f e n d (2 under f)

9. bring together again — r e u n i t e (8 under t)

10. grow larger — e x p a n d (4 under a)

What do you call a rabbit that tells jokes?

a f u n n y b u n n y

Riddle

FOCUS ON ALL LEARNERS

ENGLISH LANGUAGE LEARNERS/ESL

Point out to students whose first language is Spanish that they already know these prefixes because they are common in Spanish. For example, they are found in words such as *excavar* (to dig out), *deprimir* (to press down), and *retrasar* (to set back).

VISUAL LEARNERS

SMALL GROUP On the board, list *dethrone, rewash, recharge, refill, exchange, defrost, derail, extend*. Have small groups write "What am I?" riddles whose answers are words in the list, and then trade riddles and guess the answers. (For example, *I'm what you do to a bad king. What am I?* <u>dethrone</u>)

KINESTHETIC LEARNERS

PARTNER **Materials:** index cards, marker, scissors

Make word cards for words that begin with *ex-*, *re-*, and *de-*, and cut them apart after the prefix. Give all the pieces to a pair of students to reassemble into words. Use these words: *explode, detour, exclaim, restate, reheat, defense, refresh, extract, debug*.

Read each sentence. Think about the meaning of the underlined word. Then follow the directions in the sentence.

1. Tell why you might <u>return</u> something to a store.

   Answers will vary.

2. Write about a time you wanted to <u>exchange</u> something with a friend.

3. Tell what you would do to <u>decode</u> a message.

4. Explain how a cook might <u>defrost</u> some frozen meat.

5. Tell why someone might <u>rewash</u> a bicycle.

6. Write a short news spot telling how the police <u>recaptured</u> a gorilla who escaped from the zoo.

7. List three things that can <u>explode</u>.

8. Tell two reasons why drivers might have to take a <u>detour</u> instead of their normal route.

DETOUR

AUDITORY LEARNERS

LARGE GROUP Say *ex-*, *re-*, and *de-* in random order. Each time, call on a student to say a complete word with that prefix and write it on the board. Continue until every student has had a turn.

GIFTED LEARNERS

Materials: dictionary that gives etymologies

Have students look up the following words in a dictionary that gives etymologies and explain the meaning of each, including how the meaning of the prefix affects the meaning of the word: *extract, extricate, exult, extol, expatriate, excerpt, expectorant, extrude.*

LEARNERS WHO NEED EXTRA SUPPORT

Write *ex-*, *re-*, and *de-* with common roots, defining each word to show the differences among the meanings. Examples are: *extract* (take <u>out</u>), *detract* (take <u>away</u>), *retract* (take <u>back</u>); *export* (send <u>out</u>), *deport* (send <u>away</u>), *report* (send <u>back</u>). Have students give additional examples. See Daily Word Study Practice, pages 205–206.

CURRICULUM CONNECTIONS

SPELLING

Write the following paragraph on the board, omitting the underlines. Have students proofread the paragraph, competing with one another to be first to find each misspelled spelling word.

Frank is in the <u>eksport</u> business, selling ovens you don't have to <u>preheat</u>. He has to <u>coperate</u> with traders from other nations. There can be no <u>disetrust</u> between them, or an important business <u>prodject</u> could be ruined. Frank's main <u>conscern</u> is not to <u>intangle</u> himself in any <u>ileggal</u> dealings or do anything <u>immproper</u> or <u>iregular</u>. He doesn't want the respect between him and his colleagues to be <u>unnerned</u>.

WRITING

Portfolio Have students write a brief summary of a historical event in U.S. history. Encourage them to use as many words with prefixes *ex-*, *de-*, and *re-* as they can in their writing. You might have students brainstorm words before they start writing.

ART

Show students a few examples of bookplates. Explain that a bookplate is a sticker that a book owner pastes inside the front cover of a book to show who the owner is. Tell them that many bookplates have at the top the Latin words *Ex libris*, meaning "from the library of," followed by a blank where the owner writes his or her name. Let students design their own bookplates, beginning with *Ex libris*.

SCIENCE

Write on the board the names of these computer keys and have volunteers explain what happens when they are depressed: DELETE (takes away words or letters); RETURN (moves the cursor to the beginning of the next line). Have students type sentences on a computer and practice deleting words, replacing them with others, and returning the cursor.

Technology **AstroWord** Prefixes.
© 1998 Silver Burdett Ginn Inc.
Division of Simon & Schuster.

Lesson 68

Pages 149–150

Prefixes co-, com-, con-

INFORMAL ASSESSMENT OBJECTIVES

Can students

✓ recognize and identify the meanings of the prefixes *co-*, *com-*, and *con-*?

✓ distinguish among the prefixes *co-*, *com-*, and *con-*?

Lesson Focus

INTRODUCING THE SKILL

- Tell students that some prefixes that can be added to words have the same or very nearly the same meaning.

- Write the prefixes *co-*, *com-*, and *con-* on the board. Explain that these prefixes can mean "with" or "together."

- Call on volunteers to write the words *compress*, *condense*, and *cooperate*. Have students circle the prefixes and name the base word. Have students suggest a meaning for each word, using the prefix and what they know about the meaning of the base word.

USING THE PAGES

- Explain that page 149 introduces three new prefixes and that page 150 reviews the new prefixes in addition to those from the previous lesson.

- After students have completed the pages, ask volunteers to tell what they have learned about *co-*, *com-*, and *con-*.

- **Critical Thinking** Invite students to discuss their respones to the question at the bottom of page 150. Make sure they support their opinions with reasons.

149

Name _____

▶ Look at each picture and circle the word that describes it.

> **RULE**
> **Co, com,** and **con** are prefixes that can mean **with** or **together.**
> **co**operate = to work with others
> **com**press = to press together
> **con**verse = to talk with others

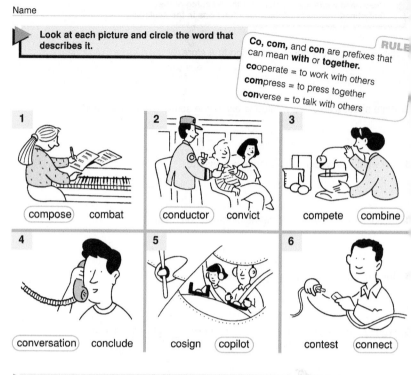

1	2	3
(compose) combat	(conductor) convict	compete (combine)

4	5	6
(conversation) conclude	cosign (copilot)	contest (connect)

▶ Circle the prefix in each word. Then write a short definition of the word.

7. **co**author _____ an author who works with another author

8. **con**join _____ to join together or with

9. **com**pact _____ to pack together or with

10. **co**exist _____ to exist together or with

11. **com**pile _____ to gather together or with

12. **co**pilot _____ a pilot who works with another pilot

© MCP All rights reserved. Copying strictly prohibited.

FOCUS ON ALL LEARNERS

ENGLISH LANGUAGE LEARNERS/ESL

To build background for the story on page 150, talk with students about scout troops. Explain that these groups are for both boys and girls. Discuss some of the skills students learn and activities they do as scout members, including doing good work for the community.

VISUAL LEARNERS

PARTNER Provide pairs of students with simple definitions like the following and have them write a *co-*, *com-*, or *con-* word with that meaning: a group of people who work together to do certain things (*committee*), to go along with (*conform*), to live peacefully with others (*coexist*).

KINESTHETIC LEARNERS

LARGE GROUP **Materials:** index cards, markers

Make cards for *co-*, *com-*, and *con-* for each student. Write a list of incomplete words like these on the board: *mit, tract, star, trol, plain, fuse, bine, test*. Have students hold up the correct prefix as you point to each word.

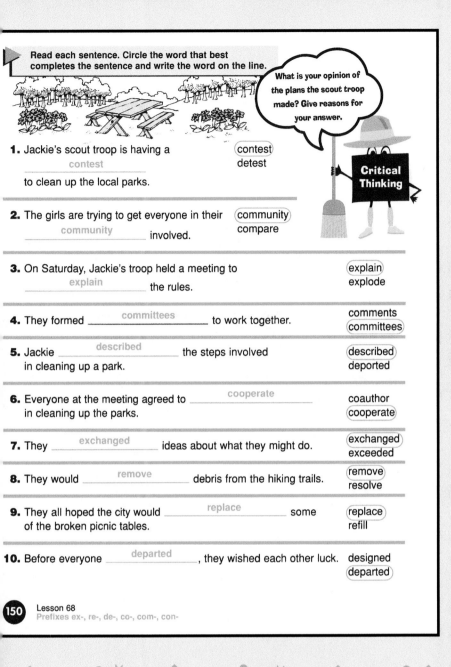

Read each sentence. Circle the word that best completes the sentence and write the word on the line.

What is your opinion of the plans the scout troop made? Give reasons for your answer.

Critical Thinking

1. Jackie's scout troop is having a ___contest___ to clean up the local parks.

   (contest) / detest

2. The girls are trying to get everyone in their ___community___ involved.

   (community) / compare

3. On Saturday, Jackie's troop held a meeting to ___explain___ the rules.

   (explain) / explode

4. They formed ___committees___ to work together.

   comments / (committees)

5. Jackie ___described___ the steps involved in cleaning up a park.

   (described) / deported

6. Everyone at the meeting agreed to ___cooperate___ in cleaning up the parks.

   coauthor / (cooperate)

7. They ___exchanged___ ideas about what they might do.

   (exchanged) / exceeded

8. They would ___remove___ debris from the hiking trails.

   (remove) / resolve

9. They all hoped the city would ___replace___ some of the broken picnic tables.

   (replace) / refill

10. Before everyone ___departed___, they wished each other luck.

    designed / (departed)

150 Lesson 68
Prefixes ex-, re-, de-, co-, com-, con-

CURRICULUM CONNECTIONS

SPELLING

Make a card for each student with a spelling word on each. (*preheat, project, illegal, export, improper, concern, distrust, cooperate, entangle, unearned, irregular*) On some cards, spell the words correctly; on others, spell them incorrectly. Shuffle the cards and give one to each student. On your signal, have students go to two areas—*Correct* and *Incorrect*. Check the cards in each group. Anyone in the wrong group is out of the game. Play again.

WRITING

Encourage pairs of students to write a brief conversation that two scouts might have during a campout. Ask students to try to use a few words with *co-*, *com-*, or *con-* in their conversations. Let each pair present its conversation for the class.

SCIENCE

Portfolio

Explain that the word *conductor* has several meanings, including "a person who takes fares on a train" and "a person who leads an orchestra." A third meaning has to do with electricity. Have students find out about this kind of conductor and write a paragraph naming some materials that are good and poor conductors of electricity.

LANGUAGE ARTS

Have students sort these words by prefix and then by the letter after the prefix: *combine, condense, concur, comment, connect, contest, convince, concern, confine, combat, conquest, command, condone, console, compare, congregate, conquer, confuse, company, conjure, complete, control, connive, constant, commune, complain, convenient, conjunction, congested.* See if students can deduce a rule for when to use each prefix. (*Com-* precedes b, m, or p; *con-* precedes the other consonants.)

Technology

AstroWord Prefixes.
© 1998 Silver Burdett Ginn Inc.
Division of Simon & Schuster.

AUDITORY LEARNERS

SMALL GROUP

Have a leader read the prefixes *co-*, *com-*, and *con-* in mixed order and ask other group members to say a complete a word for each one. Examples: *co—cooperate; com—complete; con—conspiracy; com-command; co—coauthor.*

GIFTED LEARNERS

Materials: dictionaries that give etymologies

Have students research the prefixes *co-*, *com-*, and *con-* to find out what language they come from and what they mean in that language. (*Latin; same meaning as in English*)

LEARNERS WHO NEED EXTRA SUPPORT

Point out to students that the use of *con-* or *com-* often depends on how easy the word is to say. For example, it's easier to say *complain* than *conplain* and *connect* than *comnect*. Encourage students to give other examples. See Daily Word Study Practice, pages 205–206.

Lesson 69

Pages 151–152

Prefixes fore-, pre-, pro-

✳ • • ◆ • ✳ • ◆ • ● •

INFORMAL ASSESSMENT OBJECTIVES

Can students

✓ recognize and identify the meanings of the prefixes *fore-*, *pre-*, and *pro-*?

✓ distinguish among the prefixes *fore-*, *pre-*, and *pro-* when added to base words?

Lesson Focus

INTRODUCING THE SKILL

● Write these prefixes on the board: *fore-*, *pre-*, *pro-*. Then read aloud each of the following words and have students select one of the prefixes to make a new word: *see, test, heat, noun, cast (foresee, pretest, preheat, pronoun, forecast).*

● Ask students to suggest what the prefixes mean. Explain that *fore-* means "before" or "in the front"; *pre-* means "before" or "ahead of time"; and *pro-* means "for," "in favor of," or "forward."

● Have students define the words based on the meanings of the prefixes. *(to see before, to test before, to heat ahead of time, for a noun, to cast, or say, what will happen ahead of time)*

USING THE PAGES

Make sure everyone understands what to do on pages 151 and 152. When students have completed both pages, ask a volunteer to summarize what he or she learned about prefixes *fore-*, *pre-*, and *pro-*.

151

Name _____

▶ **Read each word and circle its prefix.**

> **RULES**
> The prefixes **fore**, **pre**, and **pro** have slightly different meanings.
> **fore**warn = to warn before something happens
> **pre**heat = to heat ahead of time
> **pro**ject = to throw forward

1. (fore)arm
2. (pre)fix
3. (pre)view
4. (pro)pel

5. (pro)noun
6. (fore)noon
7. (pre)pare
8. (fore)head

9. (pro)duce
10. (fore)fathers
11. (fore)sight
12. (pre)pay

▶ **Read each sentence. Fill in the circle beside the word that best completes the sentence. Write the word on the line.**

13. Maria has _____proclaimed_____ that she will be a great tennis player.
   ○ prorated　　○ prepaid　　● proclaimed

14. Every day she practices her _____forehand_____ and backhand shots.
   ○ forefather　　● forehand　　○ project

15. She is working hard to _____prepare_____ for a big tournament.
   ○ propel　　● prepare　　○ foresee

16. Today she must play a _____preliminary_____ match to qualify for the tournament.
   ● preliminary　　○ prefix　　○ prevention

17. Maria's coach _____forewarned_____ her that the competition would be stiff.
   ○ produced　　● forewarned　　○ pretended

18. However, her coach _____predicts_____ that she will make the tournament.
   ● predicts　　○ prevents　　○ preserves

Lesson 69
Prefixes fore-, pre-, pro-　**151**

FOCUS ON ALL LEARNERS ✳ • ◆ •

ENGLISH LANGUAGE LEARNERS/ESL

As background for the story on page 151, ask students if they have ever played tennis or watched a tennis match. Have a volunteer explain how the game is played. Ask someone to pantomime a forehand stroke and a backhand stroke.

VISUAL LEARNERS

LARGE GROUP

Have the class form three teams. Assign each team *fore-*, *pre-*, or *pro-*. Encourage teams to write within a specified time as many words as they can with their assigned prefix. Have them use a dictionary if they need help. Invite teams to share their lists.

KINESTHETIC LEARNERS

SMALL GROUP

Materials: index cards, markers

Make each group one card for *pre-* and one for *pro-*. Provide these partial words: __vent, __heat, __ject, __claim, __serve, __pose, __fer, __vide, __dict, __duce, __gram, __tect, __tend. Have students take turns holding a card before a root to form a word.

Read each clue. Find the word in the word bank that matches the clue. Then write the word in the crossword puzzle. There are more words in the list than you need.

forecast	forewarned	protect	promote	professional
pretend	presented	prepay	produce	forearm
preserve	forefathers	propose	protest	prepare

Across

2. to guard against harm or danger
3. to prepare food for later use by canning, pickling, or salting
5. to make an offer of marriage
7. a person who works in an occupation that requires special education and training
9. to raise to a higher rank or grade
10. to make believe as in a play
11. to give money ahead of time

Down

1. to tell or try to tell how something will turn out
3. to make something ready before the time that it is needed
4. to get ready for trouble before it comes
6. to speak out against, to object
7. shown
8. advised in advance

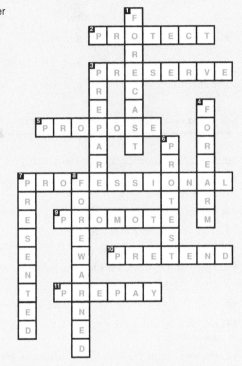

SPELLING

The following sentences can be used as a spelling posttest for words that have the prefixes *un-, dis-, non-, ir-, il-, in-, en-, im-, em-, ex-, re-, de-, co-, com-, con-, fore-, pre-,* and *pro-.*

1. **irregular**   Cement has an **irregular** surface.
2. **preheat**   **Preheat** the oven to 400°F.
3. **unearned**   Our trust in him is **unearned**.
4. **project**   Try to **project** your voice.
5. **entangle**   A cat can **entangle** itself in yarn.
6. **illegal**   It's **illegal** to park there.
7. **cooperate**   If we **cooperate**, we can win.
8. **export**   What products does the U.S. **export**?
9. **distrust**   We should **distrust** him for his lies.
10. **improper**   It's **improper** to say "Hey, you."
11. **concern**   It is none of your **concern**.

WRITING

 Write these proverbs on the board.

Forewarned is forearmed.

Prejudice is the child of ignorance.

Never make a promise you can't keep.

Have students discuss what they think each saying means. Then have each student draw a comic strip with speech balloons that illustrates the meaning of one saying.

SCIENCE/ART

Display a drawing or photograph of a lion and point out the following parts: forehead, forelock, forefoot, foreleg, forequarters.

SOCIAL STUDIES

Copy and distribute the preamble to the U.S. Constitution. Have volunteers read it aloud and then have students discuss its meaning.

 AstroWord Prefixes.
© 1998 Silver Burdett Ginn Inc.
Division of Simon & Schuster.

AUDITORY LEARNERS

 PARTNER   Have students ask a partner questions whose answers are words with *fore-, pre-,* and *pro-*; for example, *What's the front of your head, with* fore-? *(forehead) What's an early look at a movie, with* pre-? *(preview) What's the spinning part that pushes a plane forward, with* pro-? *(propeller)* Have partners switch roles, asking questions and giving answers.

GIFTED LEARNERS

Challenge students to write several different sentences that each contain one word with *fore-*, one word with *pre-*, and one word with *pro-*; for example, *I foresaw that I would have to prepare carefully for the program.*)

LEARNERS WHO NEED EXTRA SUPPORT

Review how to do a crossword puzzle before students begin working on page 152. You may want to model completing a few example words on the board. See Daily Word Study Practice, pages 205–206.

Lesson 70
Pages 153–154

Prefixes super-, over-, sub-, under-, out-

Can students

✔ recognize and identify the meanings of the prefixes *super-*, *over-*, *sub-*, *under-*, and *out-*?

✔ distinguish among the prefixes *super-*, *over-*, *sub-*, *under-*, and *out-* when added to base words?

Lesson Focus

INTRODUCING THE SKILL

- Have volunteers write *cook* and *woman* on the board. Add the prefixes *over-* and *super-* to make *overcook* and *superwoman*. Ask students to suggest meanings for the prefixes. Explain that *super-* and *over-* mean "over," "above," "extra," or "too much."

- Ask students what word means the opposite of *overcook*. Write *undercook* and ask students to suggest a meaning for the prefix. Explain that the prefixes *under-* and *sub-* mean "under," "below," "beneath," or "not quite."

- Write the word *outside*. Tell students that *out-* means "outside," "away from," "better than," or "more than."

USING THE PAGES

- Make sure students know what to do on pages 153 and 154.

- **Critical Thinking** Ask a volunteer to read the story again, then have the class discuss their responses to the question at the bottom of page 154.

153

▶ **Read each word and circle its prefix.**

> **RULE**
> **Super** and **over** are prefixes that mean **over, above, extra,** or **too much.**
> **super**human = having a nature above human beings
> **over**size = greater than normal size

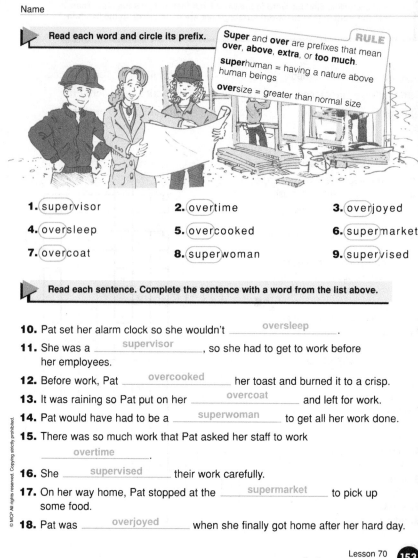

1. (super)visor
2. (over)time
3. (over)joyed
4. (over)sleep
5. (over)cooked
6. (super)market
7. (over)coat
8. (super)woman
9. (super)vised

▶ **Read each sentence. Complete the sentence with a word from the list above.**

10. Pat set her alarm clock so she wouldn't _____oversleep_____.
11. She was a _____supervisor_____, so she had to get to work before her employees.
12. Before work, Pat _____overcooked_____ her toast and burned it to a crisp.
13. It was raining so Pat put on her _____overcoat_____ and left for work.
14. Pat would have had to be a _____superwoman_____ to get all her work done.
15. There was so much work that Pat asked her staff to work _____overtime_____.
16. She _____supervised_____ their work carefully.
17. On her way home, Pat stopped at the _____supermarket_____ to pick up some food.
18. Pat was _____overjoyed_____ when she finally got home after her hard day.

FOCUS ON ALL LEARNERS

ENGLISH LANGUAGE LEARNERS/ESL

Ask students who Superman is and have someone explain how he is different from an ordinary man. Have students pantomime as you act out a few words on these pages, such as *overjoyed*, *underneath*, *supervisor*, and *outburst*.

VISUAL LEARNERS

PARTNER **Materials:** dictionaries

Write these words on the board: *supersensitive*, *overanxious*, *subtopic*, *underappreciated*, *outperform*, *overdo*, *subsequent*, *underage*, *outcast*. Have partners agree on what they think each means and then check the definition in a dictionary.

KINESTHETIC LEARNERS

INDIVIDUAL Have students draw a picture illustrating the meaning of one of these words and then write a caption or voice balloon including the word: *supermodel*, *underground*, *subzero*, *outdo*, *overcast*, *subconscious*, *underdog*.

Read the story. Underline the words that have the prefixes **sub**, **under**, and **out**. Then answer the questions, using as many of the underlined words as you can.

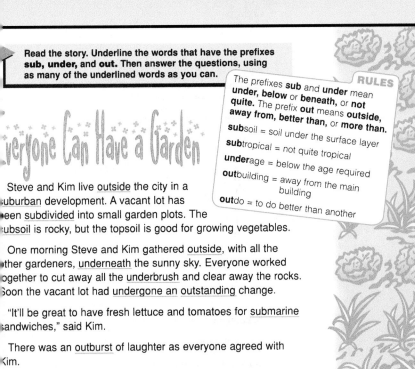

RULES

The prefixes **sub** and **under** mean **under**, **below** or **beneath**, or **not quite**. The prefix **out** means **outside**, **away from**, **better than**, or **more than**.

subsoil = soil under the surface layer

subtropical = not quite tropical

underage = below the age required

outbuilding = away from the main building

outdo = to do better than another

veryone Can Have a Garden

Steve and Kim live <u>outside</u> the city in a suburban development. A vacant lot has been <u>subdivided</u> into small garden plots. The subsoil is rocky, but the topsoil is good for growing vegetables.

One morning Steve and Kim gathered <u>outside</u>, with all the other gardeners, <u>underneath</u> the sunny sky. Everyone worked together to cut away all the <u>underbrush</u> and clear away the rocks. Soon the vacant lot had <u>undergone</u> an <u>outstanding</u> change.

"It'll be great to have fresh lettuce and tomatoes for <u>submarine</u> sandwiches," said Kim.

There was an <u>outburst</u> of laughter as everyone agreed with Kim.

1. Where do Kim and Steve live? Kim and Steve live outside the city in a surburban development.

2. What part of the ground is rocky? The subsoil is rocky.

3. What is underbrush? Underbrush is bushes that grow beneath trees.

4. Why did everyone laugh when Kim mentioned lettuce and tomatoes? Answers may vary.

How can you tell that Steve and Kim's neighbors all like one another?

Critical Thinking

(154) Lesson 70
Prefixes sub-, under-, out-

SPELLING

The following sentences can be used as a spelling pretest for words that have the prefixes *super-, over-, sub-, under-, out-, bi-, tri-, semi-, mid-;* and the roots *pos, pel, port, ject, duce, duct, tract, spec, spect, scribe.*

1. **oversize** — I couldn't pass the **oversize** truck.
2. **position** — What team **position** does Joe play?
3. **underage** — If I'm too young, I'm **underage**.
4. **subzero** — **Subzero** weather is very cold.
5. **biplane** — A **biplane** has two main wings.
6. **triangle** — Tara plays the **triangle** in the band.
7. **midyear** — June comes at **midyear**.
8. **propel** — Jet engines will **propel** the plane.
9. **superhuman** — He has **superhuman** strength.
10. **conduct** — **Conduct** yourself well.
11. **inspect** — The detectives **inspect** the evidence.

WRITING

Portfolio Ask students to write a paragraph that describes the neighborhood they live in and identifies it as an urban area, a suburban area, or a rural area. Encourage students to include in their paragraphs as many words with the lesson prefixes as they can.

SCIENCE

The Siberian tiger, the largest living cat in the world, is an endangered subspecies of tiger. Of the eight tiger subspecies, three are now extinct and the remaining five are endangered. There are estimated to be only 200 Siberian tigers left in the wild. Have students find out about this animal or another endangered subspecies.

Technology

AstroWord Prefixes.
© 1998 Silver Burdett Ginn Inc.
Division of Simon & Schuster.

LARGE GROUP

AUDITORY LEARNERS

Write the lesson prefixes on the board. Read aloud a list of base words. For each, have a volunteer choose a prefix and say the entire word. Use these words: *tired (overtired), confident (overconfident), star (superstar), category (subcategory), burst (outburst).*

GIFTED LEARNERS

Materials: dictionaries

Tell students that browsing in a dictionary can expand one's working vocabulary. Have them look for interesting words with the lesson prefixes, such as *supercilious, overweening, underling,* and *outflank,* write ten words they didn't already know, and use each in a sentence.

LEARNERS WHO NEED EXTRA SUPPORT

Draw a horizontal rule on the board. Invite students to come up and write words you dictate either above or below the rule, depending on the prefix of the word. See Daily Word Study Practice, pages 205–206.

Lesson 71
Pages 155–156

Prefixes bi-, tri-, semi-, mid-

✳ ● ◆ ● ● ✳ ● ◆ ● ●

INFORMAL ASSESSMENT OBJECTIVES

Can students

✔ recognize and identify the meanings of the prefixes *bi-*, *tri-*, *semi-*, and *mid-*?

✔ distinguish among the prefixes *bi-*, *tri-*, *semi-*, and *mid-* when added to base words?

Lesson Focus

INTRODUCING THE SKILL

● Explain that some prefixes can indicate number, amount, or location.

● Say the following: *A triangle has three points . A biplane has two wings.* Then write *biplane* and *triangle* on the board. Ask students to identify the prefixes and suggest meanings based on the sentences.

● Then say, *Our family has a semiannual party, every six months. The last party was midyear, in June.* Ask students to name the words with prefixes. Write the words and encourage students to define them. (*every half year, middle of the year*)

● Explain that *semi-* means "half" or "partly," while *mid-* means "the middle part of."

USING THE PAGES

Make sure students know what to do on pages 155 and 156. After they complete the pages, encourage students to discuss what they learned about words with the prefixes *bi-*, *tri-*, *semi-*, and *mid-*.

155

▶ Twelve words containing the prefixes **bi-** and **tri-** are hidden in the puzzle. Some of the words go across, and some go down. Circle each word and write it next to its definition.

RULES

The prefix **bi** usually means **two**. The prefix **tri** usually means **three**.

biplane = an airplane with two sets of wings

triangle = a figure with three angles

```
o  b  i  m  o  n  t  h  l  y
b  i  p  o  l  a  r  i  t  c
i  c  u  t  t  r  i  p  o  d
w  y  t  r  i  d  e  n  t  t
e  c  b  i  v  w  n  t  l  r
e  l  m  a  n  x  n  y  b  i
k  e  r  d  k  n  i  j  i  p
l  p  f  e  l  r  a  s  p  l
y  q  b  i  v  a  l  v  e  e
t  r  i  c  y  c  l  e  d  t
```

1.	biweekly	happening every two weeks
2.	triad	group of three
3.	tricycle	vehicle with three wheels
4.	biped	animal with two feet
5.	triennial	happening every three years
6.	bipolar	having two poles
7.	bimonthly	happening every two months
8.	tripod	item having three legs
9.	bicycle	vehicle with two wheels
10.	trident	spear with three prongs
11.	triplet	one of three children born at the same time of the same mother
12.	bivalve	shellfish with two shells

Lesson 71
Prefixes bi-, tri- **155**

FOCUS ON ALL LEARNERS ✳ ● ◆ ●

ENGLISH LANGUAGE LEARNERS/ESL

To help Spanish-speaking students feel comfortable with this lesson, ask them to name Spanish words they know that have the prefixes *semi-*, *bi-*, *tri-*, and *mid-* (*media*); for example, *semicírculo (semicircle)*, *bicicleta (bicycle)*, *medianoche (midnight)*.

LARGE GROUP

VISUAL LEARNERS

Write on the board two columns: (1) *bi-, bi-, tri-, tri-, semi-, semi-, mid-, mid-;* (2) *air, circle, centennial, nity, cycle, plets, winter, tropical.* Have volunteers draw a line from a prefix to a word part to form a word. (Note: *Bi-* and *tri-* can be joined to both *centennial* and *cycle.*)

SMALL GROUP

KINESTHETIC LEARNERS

Materials: colored chalk

Have group members come to the board to do the following: (1) Draw a yellow square *midway* across the chalkboard; (2) Draw a green circle and *bisect* it; (3) Color one of the *semicircles* white; (4) Draw a *trio* of red dots in the other *semicircle*; (5) Draw a blue *triangle* next to the square.

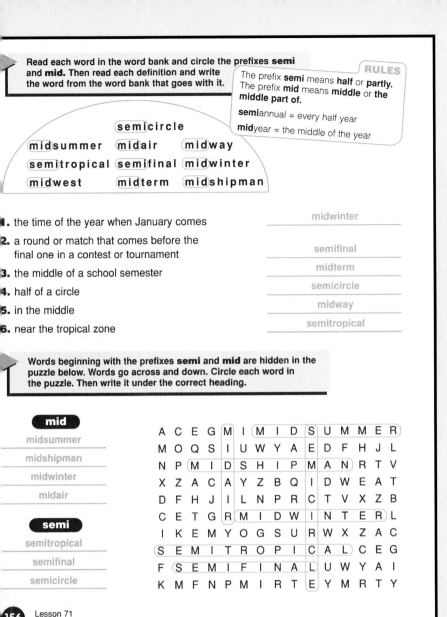

Read each word in the word bank and circle the prefixes **semi** and **mid**. Then read each definition and write the word from the word bank that goes with it.

RULES

The prefix **semi** means **half** or **partly**. The prefix **mid** means **middle** or **the middle part of**.

semiannual = every half year
midyear = the middle of the year

semicircle
midsummer   midair   midway
semitropical   semifinal   midwinter
midwest   midterm   midshipman

1. the time of the year when January comes _____midwinter_____

2. a round or match that comes before the final one in a contest or tournament _____semifinal_____

3. the middle of a school semester _____midterm_____

4. half of a circle _____semicircle_____

5. in the middle _____midway_____

6. near the tropical zone _____semitropical_____

Words beginning with the prefixes **semi** and **mid** are hidden in the puzzle below. Words go across and down. Circle each word in the puzzle. Then write it under the correct heading.

mid
midsummer
midshipman
midwinter
midair

```
A C E G M I M I D S U M M E R
M O Q S I U W Y A E D F H J L
N P M I D S H I P M A N R T V
X Z A C A Y Z B Q I D W E A T
D F H J I L N P R C T V X Z B
C E T G R M I D W I N T E R L
I K E M Y O G S U R W X Z A C
S E M I T R O P I C A L C E G
F S E M I F I N A L U W Y A I
K M F N P M I R T E Y M R T Y
```

semi
semitropical
semifinal
semicircle

156 Lesson 71
Prefixes semi-, mid-

CURRICULUM CONNECTIONS

SPELLING

Write these two lists on the board. Have volunteers come up and draw lines to connect the parts that make a spelling word. Column 1: *bi-, con-, in-, mid-, over-, pos-, pro-, sub-, super-, tri-, under-*; Column 2: *age, angle, duct, human, pel, plane, ition, size, spect, year, zero.*

WRITING

Portfolio   Share this information with students: Benjamin Franklin got really tired of switching from his distance eyeglasses to his reading glasses, so he invented bifocals—spectacles (or eyeglasses, as they're now called) with two different lenses in the same frame. Have students think of a way to improve something they use all the time. Ask them to write a paragraph describing their idea.

SCIENCE

Invite students to research kinds of trucks and find out why the big tractor-trailer—the standard vehicle of the trucking industry—is nicknamed a semi. What is *semi* short for? (*semitrailer truck*) How can something so huge have a name that begins with a prefix meaning "half"? (*The trailer has wheels at only one end; the other end attaches to the tractor.*) Have interested students draw a picture of a semi, labeling the parts and showing how it works.

ART/LANGUAGE ARTS

Encourage students to find out about one of the following items and draw a picture showing it.

1. The French flag is called the tricolor.

2. The Roman god of the sea, Neptune, carries a trident.

3. There are three athletic events in a triathlon.

Technology

AstroWord Prefixes.
© 1998 Silver Burdett Ginn Inc.
Division of Simon & Schuster.

156

Lesson 72

Pages 157–158

Roots *pos, pel, port, ject*

Can students

✓ identify words that contain the roots *pos, pel, port, ject?*

✓ define words that contain the roots *pos, pel, port, ject?*

Lesson Focus

INTRODUCING THE SKILL

● Review that prefixes and suffixes are word parts added to change a word's meaning or form new words.

● Introduce the concept of roots by writing the words *expel* and *compose* on the board. Ask students to name the prefixes. Then focus on the roots *pel* and *pos*. Explain that a root is a word part that has meaning but cannot stand alone; a prefix or suffix may be added to a root to form a word. Tell students that *pos* usually means "put" or "place," and *pel* usually means "push" or "drive."

● Encourage students to suggest meanings for each word based on what they know about the prefix and the root. (*push out from, put together*)

● Follow the same procedure for the words *porter* and *project* and the roots *port* and *ject*. Explain that *port* means "carry" and *ject* means "throw."

USING THE PAGES

Make sure students know what to do on pages 157 and 158. After they have finished, invite them to discuss the roots *pos, pel, port,* and *ject.*

157

Name _____

> Read the following words. Circle each word that contains the root **pos**. Underline each word that contains the root **pel**.

> **DEFINITION**
> A **root** is a word part to which a prefix or suffix may be added to change its meaning. **Pos** usually means **put** or **place**. **Pel** usually means **push** or **drive**.
>
> **pos**ition = the way in which a person or thing is placed or arranged
>
> pro**pel** = to push or drive forward

1. (posed)   2. expel
3. (impose)   4. (dispose)
5. (compose) 6. repellent
7. compel   8. dispel
9. (repose)   10. (expose)

> Read each sentence. Circle the meaning of the underlined word.

11. Nan's mom <u>expelled</u> Nan's cat from the kitchen for jumping on the table.
    (a. forcibly removed)   b. politely excused

12. She <u>proposed</u> that the cat be banned from the kitchen at mealtimes.
    (a. suggested)   b. invited

13. Nan agreed and promised that the cat would not <u>impose</u> on her again.
    a. help   (b. bother)

14. With the cat problem <u>dispelled</u>, Nan could get back to her homework.
    a. surrounded   (b. made to disappear)

15. The only one <u>opposed</u> to the new rule was the cat.
    (a. to be against)   b. to be polite

Lesson 72
Roots *pos, pel*   **157**

FOCUS ON ALL LEARNERS

ENGLISH LANGUAGE LEARNERS/ESL

To build background for the story on page 158, ask if anyone has ever visited a factory to see how a product is made or if they know someone who works on an assembly line. Have volunteers tell what they think it would be like to work on an assembly line.

VISUAL/AUDITORY LEARNERS

SMALL GROUP

Materials: dictionary

Write the following words on the board: *reject, impose, dispel, export, compel.* Have volunteers read aloud dictionary definitions without naming the word. Encourage students to identify the word being defined.

KINESTHETIC LEARNERS

PARTNER   **Materials:** index cards, markers

Make cards for *im-, re-, com-, de-, ex-, dis-, in-, pro-, sub-* and for *pos, port, pel, ject* and then give a full set to each pair of students. Have partners work with one root at a time, combining it with as many prefixes as possible to make real words.

Read each word and circle its root.

1. import 2. rejection 3. projectile
4. eject 5. porter 6. report
7. injection 8. project 9. transportation

> **HINT**
> Here are some roots, or word parts, that appear in many English words. **Port** means **carry**. **Ject** means **throw** or **force**.
>
> **port**able = able to be carried
> **eject** = to force out

Read each sentence. Circle the word that best completes the sentence and write the word on the line.

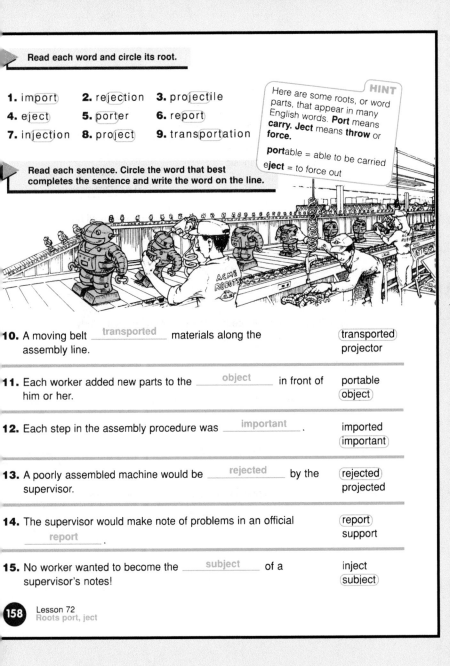

10. A moving belt ___transported___ materials along the assembly line.
    - transported
    - projector

11. Each worker added new parts to the ___object___ in front of him or her.
    - portable
    - object

12. Each step in the assembly procedure was ___important___ .
    - imported
    - important

13. A poorly assembled machine would be ___rejected___ by the supervisor.
    - rejected
    - projected

14. The supervisor would make note of problems in an official ___report___ .
    - report
    - support

15. No worker wanted to become the ___subject___ of a supervisor's notes!
    - inject
    - subject

158 Lesson 72
Roots port, ject

AUDITORY LEARNERS

LARGE GROUP

Read these sentences, pausing at the blanks to let students complete the word: *Joe asks Sue to marry him; he pro_(poses)_ . Pete is a bus driver; he provides trans_(portation)_ . Ahmed is sick; his doctor gives him an in_(jection)_ . Rub this lotion on your arms; it's mosquito re_(pellent)_ .*

GIFTED LEARNERS

Have students add the unit prefixes to *pos, port, pel,* and *ject* to build new words; for example, *pos—repose, compose, impose, expose, dispose; port—import, export, report, deport; pel—impel, expel, repel, compel, propel; ject—reject, dejected, inject, project, subject, eject.*

LEARNERS WHO NEED EXTRA SUPPORT

Materials: index cards, marker

Make cards for the following words: *injection, subject, reject, project, transport, portable, important, reporter, propose, impose, repose, repel, compel, expelled, propel.* Shuffle the cards and have students sort them by root. See Daily Word Study Practice, page 206.

CURRICULUM CONNECTIONS

SPELLING

Provide pairs with a list of the spelling words (*midyear, position, underage, propel, conduct, superhuman, eject, biplane, subzero, oversize, inspect, triangle*) and have them take turns quizzing each other on the spelling of each word. Words can be spelled orally or written. Encourage the tester to use each word in a context sentence.

WRITING

Portfolio How did Nan's cat feel after being ejected from the kitchen? Did it feel rejected? dejected? Have students write a letter from the cat to Nan's mom, expressing its feelings. The cat should use several words with *pos, pel, ject* and *port.* Review the letter form, if necessary.

MUSIC/LANGUAGE ARTS

Materials: recordings of classical music

Discuss famous composers of classical music, encouraging students to suggest names of any composers they know. Tell students that you will play a recording and give them the composer's name. Invite students to close their eyes and let themselves visualize the images or feel the emotions the composer was expressing. Then have students write a brief poem or paragraph describing how the music makes them feel.

SOCIAL STUDIES

To teach about imports, ask students to list several of their family's belongings whose tags identify country of origin (clothing, sporting goods, sneakers, backpacks, toys, and so on), writing down each item and where it was made. Have students combine their lists into a class table. What countries do most imports that students use come from? Do certain categories come from particular areas of the world?

AstroWord Prefixes.
© 1998 Silver Burdett Ginn Inc.
Division of Simon & Schuster.

158

Lesson 73

Pages 159–160

Roots *duce, duct, tract, spec, spect, scribe*

Lesson Focus

INTRODUCING THE SKILL

● Review the definition of a root. *(a word part that can have prefixes and suffixes added to it to create words)*

● Write *conduct, induce, distract, specify, inspect,* and *inscribe* on the board. Ask volunteers to underline each prefix or suffix. Then focus on the roots. Explain that *duct* or *duce* means "lead;" *tract* means "pull" or "draw"; *spec* or *spect* can mean "examine," "see," or "look"; and *scribe* means "write."

● Based on what students know about these roots, encourage them to suggest meanings for the words on the board. *(lead or guide, lead to do something, draw attention away, tell in detail, look at carefully, write something)*

USING THE PAGES

● Go over the directions for pages 159 and 160. Remind students to use complete sentences in answering the first four questions.

● After students have completed both pages, ask a volunteer to summarize what he or she has learned about roots.

159

Name _____

▶ Read each sentence. Underline each word that has the root **duct, duce,** or **tract** and write the meaning of the word on the line.

> **HINT**
> Here are three more roots that appear in many English words. **Duct** or **duce** usually means *lead.* **Tract** means to *pull* or *draw.*
> con**duct** = to lead or guide
> in**duce** = to lead to do something
> dis**tract** = to draw one's attention away

1. Sam needed to finish his homework but was distracted by loud music.
To be distracted is to be drawn
in another direction.

2. He found his brother in the garage conducting his rock-and-roll band.
Conducting means leading.

3. The band had signed a contract to play at a school dance on Saturday.
A contract is an agreement between two or more parties.

4. Sam asked if they could reduce the noise level so he could study.
To reduce is to make smaller by taking away from.

▶ Read the words and the definitions. Write the number of each word on the line beside its definition.

5. deduct	7	to bring into view
6. conductor	9	to take or pull back
7. produce	10	to present one person to another
8. tractor	5	to subtract or take away from
9. retract	6	person who leads
10. introduce	11	to pull toward
11. attract	8	machine used for pulling

Lesson 73
Roots duce, duct, tract
159

FOCUS ON ALL LEARNERS

ENGLISH LANGUAGE LEARNERS/ESL

Because several languages have many words from Latin, some of your English language learners may be familiar with one or more of these roots. Have Spanish, French, or Italian speakers say words from their first language that share these roots and talk about the meanings.

VISUAL LEARNERS

LARGE GROUP

Write *duce, duct, tract, spec, spect,* and *scribe* on the board and some incomplete words from the lesson: *con__or* (tract or duct), *re__* (duce, tract, or spect), *at__* (tract), *__ator* (spect), *sub__* (tract or scribe), *__ify* (spec). Have volunteers supply roots that fit.

KINESTHETIC LEARNERS

SMALL GROUP

Materials: a pen, a piece of rope, a pair of eyeglasses (or a picture of each); a bag

Put the three items in the bag. Have students take turns grabbing one item. If it's the pen, they must say a word with *scribe*; if it's the glasses, they must say a word with *spec* or *spect*; if it's the rope, they must say a word with *tract, duce,* or *duct.*

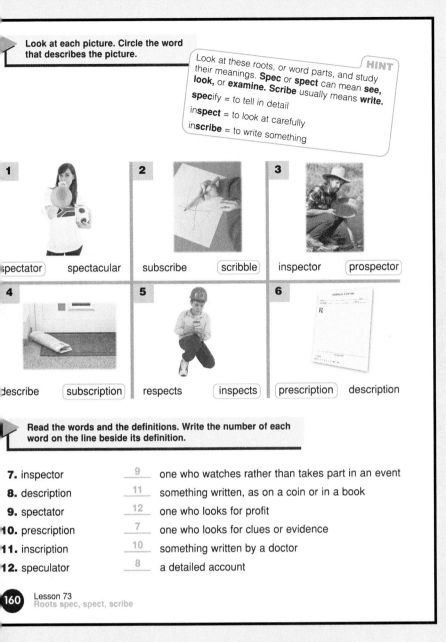

Look at each picture. Circle the word that describes the picture.

> **HINT**
> Look at these roots, or word parts, and study their meanings. **Spec** or **spect** can mean **see, look,** or **examine. Scribe** usually means **write.**
> **spec**ify = to tell in detail
> in**spect** = to look at carefully
> in**scribe** = to write something

1 spectator   spectacular

2 subscribe   (scribble)

3 inspector   (prospector)

4 describe   (subscription)

5 respects   (inspects)

6 (prescription)   description

Read the words and the definitions. Write the number of each word on the line beside its definition.

7. inspector
8. description
9. spectator
10. prescription
11. inscription
12. speculator

9 one who watches rather than takes part in an event
11 something written, as on a coin or in a book
12 one who looks for profit
7 one who looks for clues or evidence
10 something written by a doctor
8 a detailed account

AUDITORY LEARNERS

LARGE GROUP

Read these words aloud and call on students to name the root: *subscribe, spectacles, description, conduct, tractable, deduction, specimen, reducing, disrespect, distraction.* Ask them to enunciate carefully so that you can hear the difference between *spec* and *spect.*

GIFTED LEARNERS

Have students list as many additional words as they can with the roots and then discuss how the root and any prefixes or suffixes contribute to the meaning of each word. Let students use dictionaries if they wish.

LEARNERS WHO NEED EXTRA SUPPORT

Because there are several roots to think about in this lesson, you may want to have students work on only one or two of the activities. Explain that other roots work in the same way. See Daily Word Study Practice, page 206.

CURRICULUM CONNECTIONS

SPELLING

Materials: index cards, markers

Make two sets of word cards for the spelling words *superhuman, conduct, eject, propel, biplane, underage, subzero, position, oversize, triangle, midyear,* and *inspect.* Cut each spelling word into its parts (prefix and base or root; cut *position* after *pos*) and mix each set of cards on a separate table. Divide the class into six teams. When you say *Go!* have two teams race to see which can reassemble all the words faster. Play again until all teams have played, and then have a playoff for the championship.

WRITING

Portfolio Discuss what a contract is, and then have students work together to write a contract between a school group and a rock band they have hired to play at an imaginary school concert.

LANGUAGE ARTS

Tell students the rules for making introductions: (1) The first introduction should be made to the more important person; (2) The first introduction should be made to the older person. Have students role-play and then discuss the introduction of a student's grandmother and a school friend, a new student and the school principal, the President and someone's great-grandmother.

SOCIAL STUDIES

Explain that *manuscript* literally means "written by hand" and show pictures of illuminated manuscripts. Explain that before the printing press, all books were hand-lettered. Most of this work was done by monks in a room called a scriptorium. It could take years to make one copy of a book. Ask students to imagine that a medieval monk has time-traveled 700 years to visit the modern-day world. Talk about what things in our world would most amaze him— for example, newspapers, copy machines, paperback books, computers.

Technology **AstroWord** Prefixes.
© 1998 Silver Burdett Ginn Inc.
Division of Simon & Schuster.

Lesson 74

Pages 161–162

Syllables

INFORMAL ASSESSMENT OBJECTIVES

Can students

✓ recognize prefixes, suffixes, and base words?

✓ identify the number of syllables in words with prefixes and suffixes?

Lesson Focus

INTRODUCING THE SKILL

- Ask students how they would divide a word with a prefix or a suffix added to the base word.

- Say the words *softness, compel, overnight,* and *triangle.* Ask students to name the number of syllables in each word and tell how they know.

- Have students write the words on the board and divide them into syllables. (*soft-ness, com-pel, o-ver-night, tri-an-gle*)

- Ask if other syllabication rules could apply. (*compel: divide between two consonants; overnight: divide before a consonant after a long vowel sound; triangle: divide between two vowels sounded separately, divide before the consonant preceding* le)

USING THE PAGES

- Remind students that on page 161 they are to count the number of vowel *letters* in the word and then the number of vowel *sounds.* Suggest that they say each word to hear the vowel sounds.

- After page 162 has been completed, ask a volunteer to review how to divide a word that has a prefix.

Name

▶ Read each word. Write the number of vowels you see in each word. Then write the number of vowel sounds you hear.

	Vowels				**Vowels**	
	See	**Hear**			**See**	**Hear**
1. discomfort	3	3	18. inscription	4	3
2. supermarket	4	4	19. pronoun	3	2
3. demerit	3	3	20. enclose	3	2
4. triangle	3	3	21. bicycle	3	3
5. overseas	4	3	22. forenoon	4	2
6. nonresident	4	4	23. disappear	4	3
7. outcast	3	2	24. midnight	2	2
8. explode	3	2	25. recover	3	3
9. uncertain	4	3	26. contestant	3	3
10. preview	3	2	27. illegal	3	3
11. retract	2	2	28. objection	4	3
12. inspection	4	3	29. embitter	3	3
13. underweight	4	3	30. depress	2	2
14. combine	3	2	31. unhealthy	4	3
15. irregular	4	4	32. portable	3	3
16. repellent	3	3	33. coexist	3	3
17. semicircle	4	4	34. submarine	4	3

Lesson 74
Syllables **161**

FOCUS ON ALL LEARNERS ✳ ● ◆ ●

ENGLISH LANGUAGE LEARNERS/ESL

Take a few minutes before students begin page 161 to go over the words with them. Discuss the meaning of each word and then have students pronounce it with you, listening for the number of vowel sounds.

VISUAL LEARNERS

PARTNER Have each student write five sentences using words from this lesson, underlining the lesson word. Have partners trade sentences and divide the underlined words into syllables.

KINESTHETIC LEARNERS

SMALL GROUP **Materials:** number cube, tape, marker

Tape one of these prefixes to each face of a number cube: *re-, ir-, con-, ex-, sub-, under-.* Have students take turns rolling the cube and saying and writing a word with the prefix that comes up. The next student rolls the cube for a new prefix. Play again with six more prefixes.

Read each word. Use hyphens to divide it into syllables.

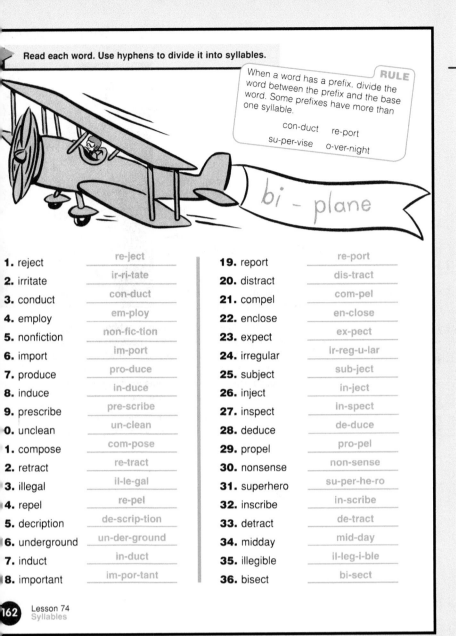

RULE

When a word has a prefix, divide the word between the prefix and the base word. Some prefixes have more than one syllable.

con-duct   re-port
su-per-vise   o-ver-night

bi - plane

1. reject	re-ject	19. report	re-port
2. irritate	ir-ri-tate	20. distract	dis-tract
3. conduct	con-duct	21. compel	com-pel
4. employ	em-ploy	22. enclose	en-close
5. nonfiction	non-fic-tion	23. expect	ex-pect
6. import	im-port	24. irregular	ir-reg-u-lar
7. produce	pro-duce	25. subject	sub-ject
8. induce	in-duce	26. inject	in-ject
9. prescribe	pre-scribe	27. inspect	in-spect
10. unclean	un-clean	28. deduce	de-duce
11. compose	com-pose	29. propel	pro-pel
12. retract	re-tract	30. nonsense	non-sense
13. illegal	il-le-gal	31. superhero	su-per-he-ro
14. repel	re-pel	32. inscribe	in-scribe
15. decription	de-scrip-tion	33. detract	de-tract
16. underground	un-der-ground	34. midday	mid-day
17. induct	in-duct	35. illegible	il-leg-i-ble
18. important	im-por-tant	36. bisect	bi-sect

162 Lesson 74
Syllables

SPELLING

Materials: index cards, markers

Make letter cards for each spelling word. Give each of two volunteers the letter cards for two words, shuffled together. Have the two students race to see who can unscramble the letters to form their two words correctly along the chalk ledge first. Repeat with other students and other spelling words until all words have been spelled correctly.

WRITING

Portfolio Science-fiction writers often dream up a future that really comes true! Long ago, in 1870, the British writer Jules Verne wrote *Twenty Thousand Leagues Under the Sea.* This novel describes adventures on an undersea vessel very much like a modern submarine. Have students write a description of an invention that might exist far in the future. Students can also work on a detailed diagram of their invention.

ART/SOCIAL STUDIES

In 1903, on a sand dune near Kitty Hawk, North Carolina, Wilbur and Orville Wright made the first successful flight of a motor-driven aircraft. Their plane was a biplane called *Flyer I.* Encourage students to locate a picture of *Flyer I* and make a drawing of the Wright brothers' first flight.

SOCIAL STUDIES

Materials: encyclopedia

Encourage students to use an encyclopedia to read about nuclear submarines. Then have them imagine what it would be like to live and work on one during a long undersea voyage. Have them list the things they think they would like and not like about it.

AstroWord Multisyllabic Words. © 1998 Silver Burdett Ginn Inc. Division of Simon & Schuster.

AUDITORY LEARNERS

LARGE GROUP Read the following words, pausing after each one, and have students raise their hands if a word has a two-syllable prefix: *unknown, deduction, supervise, returning, underground, impression, exciting, semicircle, prepaid, superfine, command, overtired.*

GIFTED LEARNERS

Materials: index cards, marker, paper

Have students try to stump one another by choosing several words from the unit so far, writing them on cards, and dividing them into syllables, either correctly or incorrectly. Another student must decide if the word is correctly divided and if not, how to divide it correctly.

LEARNERS WHO NEED EXTRA SUPPORT

You might suggest that, for page 162, students first circle the prefix in each word and then decide where to divide the word. See Daily Word Study Practice, page 208.

Lesson 75

Pages 163–164

 **R**eading **W**riting

Reviewing Prefixes, Roots, and Syllables

INFORMAL ASSESSMENT OBJECTIVES

Can students

✓ read a passage containing words with prefixes, roots, and various numbers of syllables?

✓ write a story containing words with prefixes, roots, and various numbers of syllables?

Lesson Focus

READING

- Say the words *underwater, overhead, submarine, impossible,* and *uncomfortable.* Have volunteers write each word on the board and tell you what is the same about all the words. (*They all have prefixes.*)

- Write *inject, report,* and *conduct.* Have someone circle the root in each word and identify each prefix. Then have a volunteer add a suffix to each word and tell how many syllables it now has. Ask another student to divide each word into syllables.

- Explain that as students read the passage about underwater exploration, they will be reading many more words with prefixes, roots, and different numbers of syllables.

WRITING

Explain that on page 164, students will write a story about an imaginary underwater trip. Before students begin writing, have them refer to the Helpful Hints.

Name _____

 Reading ▶ Read the passage. Then write your answer to the question at the end.

UNDERWATER EXPLORATION

The idea of underwater exploration has always attracted people. Impossible as it sounds, divers as long ago as the fourth century B.C. used breathing tubes to enable them to remain underwater for extended periods. Aristotle (384–322 B.C.) described a diving bell that consisted of a kettle held overhead. When submerged, the kettle remained filled with air. Illustrations in old manuscripts show divers wearing leather hoods with tubes near their foreheads that projected above the water—the first diving suits.

Beginning in the 1800s, diving suits encased wearers in rubber and metal to protect them from the cold and provide them with air. These uncomfortable, unsafe suits were connected to ships by long hoses through which air was propelled. Later, a tank worn on a diver's back was invented. This enabled a diver to swim without restriction. Recent improvements in diving gear enable divers to enjoy the incredible beauty of the underwater world in comfort.

Today, scientists explore the ocean depths in special submarines called submersibles. These can transport up to four people, who inspect the ocean through windows in the hull. Submersibles can hover midway between the surface and the bottom of the ocean.

Which invention in the article do you think is the most important for undersea exploration? Explain why.

_____
_____
_____
_____
_____
_____

FOCUS ON ALL LEARNERS ✳ • ◆ •

ENGLISH LANGUAGE LEARNERS/ESL

To familiarize students with the undersea setting, have individuals tell about any television programs they may have seen about underwater exploration. How do scientists move around underwater? What kinds of creatures live in that environment?

VISUAL LEARNERS

PARTNER Have pairs of students reread the passage on page 163 and work together to list three words from it with each of these prefixes: *sub-, ex-, re-, pro-, en-.* Examples are *submersible, submerged, submarines; exploration, extended, explore; remained, restriction, recent; projected, provide, propelled; encased, enabled, enjoy.*

KINESTHETIC LEARNERS

INDIVIDUAL **Materials:** drawing paper, markers or pencils

Have each student make stick-figure drawings to show the action represented by each of the following roots from this unit: *pel (push), tract (pull/draw), duce/duct (lead), port (carry), spec/spect (see/look), scribe (write), ject (throw), pos (place/put).* Have students exchange papers and guess the root depicted.

Writing

Write a story about an underwater trip. Describe how you would go, with a scuba tank or in a submersible. What do you think you would see? The words in the word bank may help you.

Helpful Hints

Think of a good title for your story.

Who are the main characters?

What happens to them?

Use active verbs to make your writing interesting.

Include details.

unexpected	midway	conclude
depart	unforeseen	nonstop
impatiently	reassure	binoculars
	outline	

SPELLING

The following sentences can be used as a spelling posttest for words that have the prefixes *super-, over-, sub-, under-, out-, bi-, tri-, semi-, mid-;* and the roots *pos, pel, port, ject, duce, duct, tract, spec, spect, scribe.*

1. **position** — I'm not in a **position** to promise.
2. **superhuman** — She made a **superhuman** effort.
3. **conduct** — Does aluminum **conduct** heat well?
4. **eject** — Dad tried to **eject** me from his chair.
5. **propel** — I **propel** my bike with my feet.
6. **biplane** — A **biplane** has two sets of wings.
7. **underage** — We are **underage** for that movie.
8. **subzero** — Below zero is the same as **subzero**.
9. **oversize** — **Oversize** shirts are very popular now.
10. **triangle** — A **triangle** has three sides.
11. **midyear** — My brother has **midyear** exams.
12. **inspect** — **Inspect** the dogs for ticks.

PHYSICAL EDUCATION/ SCIENCE/ART

Materials: posterboard, markers, crayons

Snorkeling is an excellent way for youngsters to explore the undersea world before they are 12 and old enough to scuba dive. Have students find out what equipment is needed for snorkeling (*mask, snorkel, fins, vest*) and what some safety rules are for snorkeling. (*know how to swim, use the buddy system, avoid getting cold, have a dive plan, check water conditions before diving*) Invite them to make and illustrate a poster about safe snorkeling.

AstroWord Prefixes; Multisyllabic Words. © 1998 Silver Burdett Ginn Inc. Division of Simon & Schuster.

AUDITORY LEARNERS

SMALL GROUP

Materials: index cards, markers

Make cards for these prefixes and roots: *ex-, re-, de-, sub-, in-, im-, pre-, pro-, com-, con-, re-, ex-, dis-, pel, tract, duce, duct, port, spec, spect, scribe, ject, pos.* Have small groups of students form as many words as they can using the cards. Appoint one student to write the words in a list.

GIFTED LEARNERS

Materials: grid paper

Invite pairs of students to create a crossword puzzle using words from this unit. Ask partners to solve each other's puzzles to make sure they are numbered correctly and that the clues are sufficiently clear. Then have them exchange their puzzles with another pair and solve.

LEARNERS WHO NEED EXTRA SUPPORT

To check comprehension, ask students to retell some of the information in the passage on page 163 in their own words before beginning their own writing on page 164. See Daily Word Study Practice, pages 205–206, 208.

Lesson 76

Pages 165–166

Unit Checkup

Reviewing Prefixes, Roots, and Syllables

✳ • ◆ • ● • ✳ ◆ • ● • ●

INFORMAL ASSESSMENT OBJECTIVES

Can students

✔ identify prefixes, roots, and the number of syllables in words?

✔ read words that contain prefixes, roots, and varying numbers of syllables?

Lesson Focus

PREPARING FOR THE CHECKUP

● Ask a volunteer to define *prefix.* (*a word part added at the beginning of a word to change the meaning of the root or base word*) Invite students to give you examples of words with these prefixes: *un-, en-, de-, super-.* Write their suggestions on the board.

● Ask for someone to define *root.* (*a word part that can have prefixes and suffixes added to it to create words*) Write *ject, spect,* and *pel* on the board and ask students to add a prefix to each and write the word. Review the meanings of the roots taught in this unit.

● Write *respectful, injection, extracting,* and *undersea* on the board and have volunteers underline each root. Then ask them to circle each prefix and suffix.

● Have students write each word and use hyphens to divide it into syllables.

USING THE PAGES

Make sure everyone knows what to do on pages 165 and 166. When students have completed the pages, have several volunteers summarize what they learned in the unit.

165

UNIT 6 CHECKUP — Read each sentence. Fill in the circle next to the word that correctly completes the sentence. Write the word on the line.

1. **Two wheels** are to **bicycle** as **three wheels** are to _____**tricycle**_____.
   ○ triangle ● tricycle

2. **Possible** is to **impossible** as **sense** is to _____**nonsense**_____.
   ● nonsense ○ nonpayment

3. **Write** is to **story** as _____**compose**_____ is to **music.**
   ● compose ○ dispose

4. **Discover** is to **find** as _____**overjoyed**_____ is to **happy.**
   ○ unhappy ● overjoyed

5. **Midsummer** is to **midwinter** as **midnight** is to _____**midday**_____.
   ○ midweek ● midday

6. **Inhale** is to **exhale** as **arrive** is to _____**depart**_____.
   ● depart ○ destroy

7. **Encourage** is to **discourage** as _____**import**_____ is to **export.**
   ○ report ● import

8. **Coauthor** is to **book** as _____**copilot**_____ is to **plane.**
   ● copilot ○ cosign

9. **Increase** is to **decrease** as **add** is to _____**subtract**_____.
   ○ retract ● subtract

10. **Buried** is to **underground** as **submerged** is to _____**underwater**_____.
    ○ overhead ● underwater

11. **Prospector** is to **mine** as _____**conductor**_____ is to **train.**
    ● conductor ○ projector

12. **Biplane** is to **air** as _____**submarine**_____ is to **water.**
    ● submarine ○ semicircle

Lesson 76
Review prefixes, roots, syllables: Checkup **165**

FOCUS ON ALL LEARNERS ✳ • ● • ●

ENGLISH LANGUAGE LEARNERS/ESL

Ask if anyone has ever passed on outgrown clothing to a younger sibling. Explain that this is one way of recycling. Ask students what else their family recycles and what they throw away. Discuss ways students could help reduce the amount of trash their household produces in one day.

VISUAL LEARNERS

INDIVIDUAL Have students list several words containing the suffixes and roots they learned in this unit. Encourage them to use the list to write a paragraph about a recycling project in their home, school, or community. Suggest that students brainstorm for words before they begin writing.

KINESTHETIC LEARNERS

SMALL GROUP **Materials:** three boxes, index cards, markers, scissors

Label each box *prefixes, suffixes,* or *roots.* Make word cards for several words with all three parts. Have students cut the words between the parts and "recycle" the parts by placing them in the appropriate "recycling bins." Then have them reuse the parts to build new words.

UNIT 6 CHECKUP

> Read the passage and answer the questions.

Reduce, Reuse, Recycle

Our planet's natural resources can never be replaced. Although many of the world's environmental problems may seem overwhelming and impossible to combat, we can prevent further destruction. Here are a few ideas to enable you to conduct a war on waste.

Reduce Many things come packaged in unnecessary layers. When we unwrap and remove a purchase, we discard the packaging. Plastic packaging is produced from oil extracted from underground wells. That oil can never be reused or replaced. Discarded as trash, plastic takes centuries to decompose. What can you do?
► Refuse to purchase products that employ excessive packaging.

Reuse People have always reused things to create new ones. Stone Age people didn't discard broken stone tools. They reshaped them into new tools. What can you do?
► Buy eggs in cardboard cartons. Reuse the cartons for art projects.

Recycle Glass, metal, paper, and some kinds of plastic can be recycled. Many communities encourage or even require residents to recycle these reusable materials. What can you do?
► Collect recyclable materials and take them to your local recycling center.

1. What three words are the keys to helping save the earth?
   reduce, reuse, recycle

2. What is the problem with many things we purchase?
   They come packaged in unnecessary layers.

3. How can people reduce waste?
   They can refuse to purchase products that employ excessive packaging.

4. What kinds of materials can be recycled?
   Glass, metal, paper, and some kinds of plastics can be recycled.

166 Lesson 76
Review prefixes, roots, syllables: Checkup

AUDITORY LEARNERS

LARGE GROUP Make up riddles and present them orally. Pause after each clue to let students guess the word. If nobody guesses, give easier clues until someone does; for example, *I mean sad. I have the root ject. I have three syllables. I have the prefix de-. I end with -ed. I am spelled d-e-j-e-c-t-e-d.*

GIFTED LEARNERS

Provide each student with six words such as the following: *reject, tripod, underpaid, midwest, illegal, semisweet.* Challenge them to create analogies like those on page 165, giving two choices for each missing word. Have students exchange papers and complete each other's analogies.

LEARNERS WHO NEED EXTRA SUPPORT

Review what an analogy is. Present one or two simple examples on the board. Talk about the kinds of relationships the words in an analogy can have—for example: synonyms, antonyms, part-whole, cause-effect, action-actor, container-contained. See Daily Word Study Practice, pages 205–206, 208.

ASSESSING UNDERSTANDING OF UNIT SKILLS

Student Progress Assessment You may wish to review the observational notes you made as students worked through the activities in this unit. Your notes will help you evaluate the progress students made with prefixes, roots, and syllables.

Portfolio Assessment Review the materials that students have collected in their portfolios. You may wish to have interviews with students to discuss their written work and the progress they have made since the beginning of the unit. As you review students' work, evaluate how well they use the word study skills.

Daily Word Study Practice For students who need additional practice with prefixes, roots, and syllables, quick reviews are provided on pages 205–206, 208 in Daily Word Study Practice.

Word Study Posttest To assess students' mastery of prefixes, roots, and syllables, use the posttest on pages 141g–141h.

Spelling Cumulative Posttest Review Unit 6 spelling words by using the following words and dictation sentences.

1.	**improper**	It's **improper** to talk during a concert.
2.	**distrust**	I sense that you **distrust** me.
3.	**illegal**	It's **illegal** to drive through a stop sign.
4.	**export**	Wheat is a main **export** of the U.S.
5.	**superhuman**	What she did for us is **superhuman**.
6.	**inspect**	**Inspect** these cars for any defects.
7.	**cooperate**	We'll **cooperate** with you.
8.	**subzero**	Stay indoors in **subzero** weather.
9.	**entangle**	Twigs can **entangle** your hair.
10.	**eject**	The guide will **eject** those loud boys from the museum.
11.	**biplane**	At the air show we saw a **biplane**.
12.	**propel**	High winds **propel** tumbleweeds.
13.	**triangle**	My yard is shaped like a **triangle**.

Teacher Notes

Contents

Student Performance Objectives

In Unit 7, students will review and extend their recognition of synonyms, antonyms, and homonyms. Students will review and extend dictionary skills involving the use of guide words, entry words, and the pronunciation key. As these skills are developed, students will be able to

◆ Identify pairs of synonyms, antonyms, and homonyms

◆ Recognize and understand functions of guide words and entry words in the dictionary

◆ Locate words in the dictionary

◆ Recognize and understand multiple meanings of words (homographs)

◆ Recognize and understand the pronunciation key

Assessment Strategy Overview

Throughout Unit 7, assess students' ability to read and write synonyms, antonyms, homonyms, and to use dictionary skills. There are various ways to assess students' progress. You may also want to encourage students to evaluate their own work and to participate in setting goals for their own learning.

FORMAL ASSESSMENT

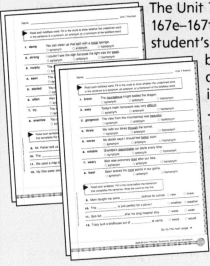

The Unit 7 Pretest on pages 167e–167f helps to assess a student's knowledge at the beginning of the unit and to plan instruction.

The Unit 7 Posttest on pages 167g–167h helps to assess mastery of unit objectives and to plan for reteaching, if necessary.

INFORMAL ASSESSMENT

The Reading & Writing pages and Unit Checkup in the student book are an effective means of evaluating students' performance.

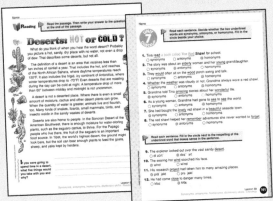

Skill	Reading & Writing Pages	Unit Checkup
Synonyms	189–190	191–192
Antonyms	189–190	191–192
Homonyms	189–190	191–192
Alphabetical Order	189–190	191–192
Guide Words	189–190	191–192
Definitions	189–190	191–192
Homographs	189–190	191–192
Different Spellings	189–190	191–192
Pronunciation Key	189–190	191–192
Accent Marks	189–190	191–192

PORTFOLIO ASSESSMENT

Portfolio This logo appears throughout the teaching plans. It signals opportunities for collecting students' work for individual portfolios. You may also want to collect the following pages.

❖ Unit 7 Pretest and Posttest, pages 167e–167h

❖ Unit 7 Reading & Writing, pages 189–190

❖ Unit 7 Checkup, pages 191–192

STUDENT PROGRESS CHECKLIST

Use the checklist on page 167i to record students' progress. You may want to cut the sections apart to place each student's checklist in his or her portfolio.

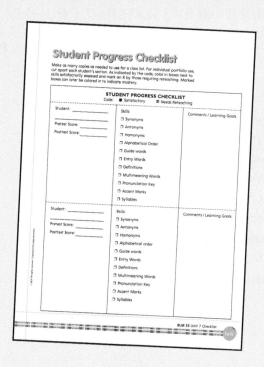

Administering and Evaluating the
Pretest and Posttest

DIRECTIONS

To help you assess students' progress in learning Unit 7 skills, tests are available on pages 167e–167h. Administer the Pretest before students begin the unit. The results of the Pretest will help you identify each student's strengths and needs in advance, allowing you to structure lesson plans to meet individual needs. Administer the Posttest to assess students' overall mastery of skills taught in the unit and to identify specific areas that will require reteaching.

PERFORMANCE ASSESSMENT PROFILE

The following chart will help you identify specific skills as they appear on the tests and enable you to identify and record specific information about an individual's or the class's performance on the tests.

Depending on the results of the tests, refer to the Reteaching column for lesson-plan pages where you can find activities that will be useful for meeting individual needs or for daily word study practice.

ANSWER KEYS

Unit 7 Pretest, page 167e (BLM 49)

1. synonym
2. antonym
3. synonym
4. homonym
5. antonym
6. synonym
7. synonym
8. antonym
9. new
10. weather
11. weak
12. wood

Unit 7 Pretest, page 167f (BLM 50)

13. hard 3, happen 1, hatch 4, harbor 2
14. marry 3, marvel 4, marble 1, market 2
15. fancy / feather
16. fault
17. desert[1]
18. street
19. desert[2]

Unit 7 Posttest, page 167g (BLM 51)

1. synonym
2. antonym
3. synonym
4. homonym
5. antonym
6. synonym
7. synonym
8. antonym
9. plain
10. scent
11. route
12. peeks

Unit 7 Posttest, page 167h (BLM 52)

13. diary 2, dinosaur 3, diaper 1, ditch 4
14. frighten 4, fresh 3, freckle 1, freeze 2
15. idiot / illness
16. magnet
17. iguana
18. lead[1]
19. lead[2]

PERFORMANCE ASSESSMENT PROFILE

Skill	Pretest Questions	Posttest Questions	Reteaching: Focus on All Learners	Reteaching: Daily Word Study Practice
Synonyms	1, 3, 6, 7	1, 3, 6, 7	169–170, 189–190	206–207
Antonyms	2, 5, 8	2, 5, 8	171–172, 189–190	206–207
Homonyms	4, 9, 10, 11, 12	4, 9, 10, 11, 12	173–174, 189–190	206–207
Alphabetical Order	13, 14	13, 14	175–176, 189	207–208
Guide Words	15	15	177–178, 190	207–208
Definitions	19	19	179–182	207–208
Multimeaning Words	19	19	181–182, 189–190	207–208
Pronunciation Key	18	18	183–186	208
Accent Marks	17	17	187–188	208
Syllables	16	16	188	208

> Read each boldface word. Fill in the circle to show whether the underlined word in the sentence is a synonym, an antonym, or a homonym of the boldface word.

1. brave   The <u>courageous</u> knight battled the dragon.
○ synonym   ○ antonym   ○ homonym

2. easy   Today's math homework was very <u>difficult</u>.
○ synonym   ○ antonym   ○ homonym

3. gorgeous   The view from the mountaintop was <u>beautiful</u>.
○ synonym   ○ antonym   ○ homonym

4. threw   We rode our bikes <u>through</u> the tunnel.
○ synonym   ○ antonym   ○ homonym

5. worse   My doctor says I should feel <u>better</u> soon.
○ synonym   ○ antonym   ○ homonym

6. reliable   Grandpa's <u>dependable</u> car starts every time.
○ synonym   ○ antonym   ○ homonym

7. weary   Blair was extremely <u>tired</u> after our hike.
○ synonym   ○ antonym   ○ homonym

8. least   Sean scored the <u>most</u> points in our game.
○ synonym   ○ antonym   ○ homonym

> Read each sentence. Fill in the circle before the homonym that completes the sentence. Write the word on the line.

9. Mom bought me some _____ clothes for school. ○ new   ○ knew

10. This _____ is just perfect for a picnic!   ○ whether   ○ weather

11. Bob felt _____ after his long hospital stay.   ○ weak   ○ week

12. Tracy built a birdhouse out of _____ at camp.   ○ wood   ○ would

Go to the next page. →

> Put each set of words in alphabetical order. Fill in the circle that shows what number the word is in that order.

13. hard   ○ 1   ○ 2   ○ 3   ○ 4   **14.** marry   ○ 1   ○ 2   ○ 3   ○ 4

happen   ○ 1   ○ 2   ○ 3   ○ 4   marvel   ○ 1   ○ 2   ○ 3   ○ 4

hatch   ○ 1   ○ 2   ○ 3   ○ 4   marble   ○ 1   ○ 2   ○ 3   ○ 4

harbor   ○ 1   ○ 2   ○ 3   ○ 4   market   ○ 1   ○ 2   ○ 3   ○ 4

> Read the dictionary entries. Then read each question below. Fill in the circle before the answer to the question.

desert¹ (de zʉrt´) **v.** to leave, abandon someone or something

desert² (dez´ ərt) **n. 1** a dry, sandy region with little or no plant life **2** a wild region

dessert (də zʉrt´) **n.** something sweet served at the end of a meal

fault (fôlt) **n. 1** flaw **2** a mistake **3** blame for some thing wrong **4** a crack in rock layers

miser (mī´ z ər) **n.** a greedy, stingy person who hoards money for its own sake

photo (fōt´ ō) **n.** shortened form of PHOTOGRAPH

street (strēt) **n. 1** a public road in a town, esp. a paved one **2** such a road with its sidewalks and buildings

15. What guide words would be on a dictionary page containing the word **fault**?

   ○ fawn / fellow   ○ fancy / feather   ○ farther / faucet

16. What entry word has only one syllable?

   ○ fault   ○ photo   ○ dessert   ○ miser

17. What entry word has an accent mark on the last syllable?

   ○ photo   ○ miser   ○ desert¹   ○ desert²

18. What entry word has the same sound as the underlined letters in the boldface word?

sl<u>ee</u>p   ○ desert   ○ street   ○ miser

19. What entry word completes the sentence?

The spines of a cactus protect it from ____ animals.

   ○ desert¹   ○ fault   ○ desert²   ○ dessert

Possible score on Unit 7 Pretest is 19. Number correct _____.

► Read each boldface word. Fill in the circle to show whether the underlined word in the sentence is a synonym, an antonym, or a homonym of the boldface word.

1. damp   You can clean up that spill with a <u>moist</u> sponge.
○ synonym   ○ antonym   ○ homonym

2. strong   I couldn't see the sign because the light was too <u>weak</u>.
○ synonym   ○ antonym   ○ homonym

3. noisily   The candidate <u>loudly</u> proclaimed his victory.
○ synonym   ○ antonym   ○ homonym

4. seen   The ambulance arrived at the <u>scene</u> of the accident.
○ synonym   ○ antonym   ○ homonym

5. started   You should have <u>finished</u> your homework by now.
○ synonym   ○ antonym   ○ homonym

6. often   Alex <u>frequently</u> visits his grandmother in New York.
○ synonym   ○ antonym   ○ homonym

7. try   The hikers should not <u>attempt</u> to cross that flooded stream.
○ synonym   ○ antonym   ○ homonym

8. enemies   You can depend on your <u>friends</u> for support.
○ synonym   ○ antonym   ○ homonym

► Read each sentence. Fill in the circle before the homonym that completes the sentence. Write the word on the line.

9. Mr. Fisher told us to write on _____ paper.   ○ plain   ○ plane

10. The _____ of the flowers filled the room.   ○ sent   ○ scent

11. We used a map to plan our _____.   ○ route   ○ root

12. My little sister always _____ at her presents.   ○ peeks   ○ peaks

Go to the next page. →

> Put each set of words in alphabetical order. Fill in the circle that shows what number the word is in that order.

13. diary   ○ 1   ○ 2   ○ 3   ○ 4   **14.** frighten   ○ 1   ○ 2   ○ 3   ○ 4

dinosaur   ○ 1   ○ 2   ○ 3   ○ 4   fresh   ○ 1   ○ 2   ○ 3   ○ 4

diaper   ○ 1   ○ 2   ○ 3   ○ 4   freckle   ○ 1   ○ 2   ○ 3   ○ 4

ditch   ○ 1   ○ 2   ○ 3   ○ 4   freeze   ○ 1   ○ 2   ○ 3   ○ 4

> Read the dictionary entries. Then read each question below. Fill in the circle before the answer to the question.

iguana (i gwä´ nə) *n.* a large tropical American lizard
lead[1] (lēd) *v.* **1.** to show the way **2.** to be the first or ahead of others **3.** to form a route or passage **4.** to direct or conduct **5.** to experience; live
lead[2] (led) *n.* **1.** a heavy gray metal **2.** a material used in pencils for writing

led (led) *v.* **1.** the past tense of **lead**; showed, guided
magnet (mag´nit) *n.* **1.** a piece of metal that attracts iron and steel **2.** someone or something that attracts other things

15. What guide words would be on a dictionary page containing the word **iguana**?
    ○ idiot / illness   ○ iceberg / ignite   ○ igloo / ignore

16. What entry word has two syllables?
    ○ iguana   ○ lead   ○ led   ○ magnet

17. What entry word has an accent mark on the second syllable?
    ○ magnet   ○ lead   ○ iguana   ○ led

18. What entry word has the same sound as the underlined letters in the boldface word?
be<u>a</u>ch   ○ led   ○ lead[1]   ○ magnet

19. What entry word completes the sentence?
The heavy box was made out of ___.
    ○ lead[1]   ○ led   ○ lead[2]

Possible score on Unit 7 Posttest is 19. Number correct _____.

Student Progress Checklist

Make as many copies as needed to use for a class list. For individual portfolio use, cut apart each student's section. As indicated by the code, color in boxes next to skills satisfactorily assessed and mark an X by those requiring reteaching. Marked boxes can later be colored in to indicate mastery.

STUDENT PROGRESS CHECKLIST
Code: ■ Satisfactory   ☒ Needs Reteaching

| Student: _____
_____

Pretest Score: _____

Posttest Score: _____ | Skills
❏ Synonyms
❏ Antonyms
❏ Homonyms
❏ Alphabetical Order
❏ Guide words
❏ Entry Words
❏ Definitions
❏ Multimeaning Words
❏ Pronunciation Key
❏ Accent Marks
❏ Syllables | Comments / Learning Goals |
| Student: _____
_____

Pretest Score: _____

Posttest Score: _____ | Skills
❏ Synonyms
❏ Antonyms
❏ Homonyms
❏ Alphabetical order
❏ Guide words
❏ Entry Words
❏ Definitions
❏ Multimeaning Words
❏ Pronunciation Key
❏ Accent Marks
❏ Syllables | Comments / Learning Goals |

Spelling Connections

INTRODUCTION

The Unit Word List is a list of spelling words drawn from this unit. The words are grouped by synonyms, antonyms, and homonyms. To incorporate spelling into your word study program, use the activity in the Curriculum Connections section of each teaching plan.

The spelling lessons utilize the following approach for each phonemic element.

1. Administer a pretest of all the words that have not yet been introduced. Dictation sentences are provided.

2. Provide practice.

3. Reassess. Dictation sentences are provided.

A final test is provided at the end of the unit on page 192.

DIRECTIONS

Make a copy of Blackline Master 54 for each student. After administering the pretest for each word, give students a copy of the appropriate word list.

Students can work with a partner to practice spelling the words orally and identifying the phonemic element in each word. You may want to challenge students to add to the list other synonyms, antonyms, and homonyms. Students can also write words of their own on *My Own Word List* (see Blackline Master 54).

Students may store their list words in envelopes or plastic zipper bags in the back of their books or notebooks. You may want to suggest that students keep a spelling notebook, listing synonyms, antonyms, and homonyms. Another idea is to build word walls with students and display them in the classroom. Each section of the wall can focus on words with a single word study element. The walls will become a good resource for spelling when students are writing.

UNIT WORD LIST
Synonyms
courageous
brave
Antonyms
bitter
sweet
Homonyms
threw
through
whether
weather

Spelling UNIT 7 WORD LIST

Synonyms

courageous
brave

Antonyms

bitter
sweet

Homonyms

threw
through
whether
weather

My Own Word List

Word Study Games, Activities, and Technology

The following collection of ideas offers a variety of opportunities to reinforce word study skills while actively engaging students. The games, activities, and technology suggestions can easily be adapted to meet the needs of your group of learners. They vary in approach so as to consider students' different learning styles.

● **GUIDE-WORD FOOTBALL KICK**

Cut two footballs out of construction paper. On the chalkboard, draw a football field marked off in ten-yard increments from the goal line to the 50-yard line and then to the opposite goal line. Tape the two footballs at one goal line. Divide the class into two teams and explain that each team will get ten chances to kick its football and reach the other goal.

Write the following sets of guide words on the board: *ball/bar, clear/closet, dress/duck, fix/fleet, heap/help, kick/knock, launch/lean, mark/mate, pack/palm, rhyme/ring, radio/range, rod/rot, small/strip, stack/start, tip/top*. Have Team 1 write three entry words that would appear on a dictionary page between any guide-word pair shown. If the team is correct, its football is moved ten yards forward. Then Team 2 gets a turn. If a team cannot think of three entry words or if the words are incorrect, the football stays in place. The team to reach the opposite goal wins.

▲ **GUIDE-WORD SHUFFLE**

On word cards, list four pairs of guide words, such as *small/smell, driver/duck, lizard/llama, age/air*. For each pair of guide words, make seven cards for words that fall alphabetically between the two words. Place the guide-word cards face down in a pile and deal out all of the word cards to players. To begin play, turn up one of the guide-word cards. Players take turns laying down a word from their hand that falls between the guide words shown. If a player does not have a word, he or she skips the turn. When all the words for that set of guide words have been played, another guide-word card is turned over, and the procedure is repeated. The first player to lay down all of his or her cards wins.

◆ **HOMOGRAPH SENTENCES**

From the dictionary, select a word that has more than one meaning—for example, *squash*. Invite students to write one sentence using at least two of the meanings given in the dictionary—for example, *Please squash the squash for tonight's dinner before you leave to play squash*. Have students choose one of their sentences to illustrate for a bulletin-board display.

Variation: List pairs of homophones on the board. Challenge students to look up both words in the dictionary and write and illustrate sentences that contain both homophones.

■ THE NAME GAME

Use students' own names to practice dictionary skills. When selecting students to line up, leave the room, or help with a classroom chore, use categories such as the following as a means of selection: *Will all students whose first names fall between the guide words* Alex *and* Arnold *please line up? Will all students whose last names are accented on the* second *syllable please line up? Will Group 1 please line up in alphabetical order?*

✳ GUIDE-WORD RACE

Divide the class into two or three teams and give each team a dictionary. Call out a word. One player from each team looks up the word in the dictionary. As soon as the word is found, the team members raise their hands and the player gives the guide words on the page where the word is located. The first team to raise their hands and give the correct guide words gets a point. The first team to gain ten points wins.

● DOUBLE TROUBLE

On the chalkboard, draw an apple with arms holding a bowling ball. Ask, *Have you ever seen a fruit bowl?* Ask students to give other examples of homographs whose double meanings could be illustrated in a silly way, such as a *school of fish* or an *elephant's trunk*. Have students draw and label their silly pictures on drawing paper. Bind the illustrations into a class book entitled "Double Trouble."

an elephant's trunk

▲ DICTIONARY OF EXTRAORDINARY WORDS

Challenge students to make their own dictionaries of extraordinary words. Encourage them to peruse dictionaries to find 10–20 words that have interesting pronunciations or meanings. Have them write the words on index cards and place the index cards in alphabetical order. Then have them copy the words onto sheets of paper, giving the pronunciation and a short definition for each word. Encourage students to illustrate their dictionary entries wherever possible. Have students write guide words at the top of each page of their dictionaries

◆ NAMES AND PLACES

Have students use almanacs or other reference books to brainstorm names of people, places, or other words associated with a current topic of study. Write the cumulative list on the board and challenge students to rewrite the list in alphabetical order.

■ ANTONYM-SYNONYM CROSSWORDS

Give students sheets of graph paper and challenge them to make their own crossword puzzles with antonyms and synonyms as clues. Begin by making a list of ten pairs of antonyms and ten pairs of synonyms. Show students how to choose a word from each pair and "cross it" with other words by writing the letters in the squares of the graph paper. Then demonstrate how to number the words and list clues such as "an antonym for *wrong*" or "a synonym for *happy*." Encourage students to make puzzles from their own lists of antonyms and synonyms and exchange their puzzles with a partner to solve.

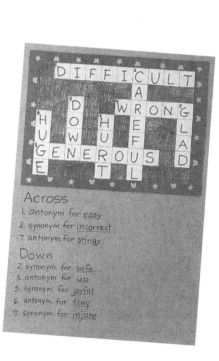

✳ I DOUBT IT!

Divide the class into two teams. Write a homograph such as *bow* on the board. The first player from Team 1 uses the word in a sentence. Team 2 has ten seconds to decide if the word is used correctly. If the team decides it has not been used correctly, they shout *I doubt it!* The team that is correct wins a point. The first team to gain ten points wins.

● TAKEOFF!

Cut two airplanes out of construction paper. Draw a vertical scale to 500 marked off in increments of fifty feet on the board. Tape the planes at zero. Write each of these word pairs on a separate piece of paper and put them in a container.

<u>Synonyms</u>: *simple, plain; like, enjoy; ill, sick; short, brief; harm, hurt; rare, scarce; take, seize.* <u>Antonyms</u>: *dull, sharp; cry, laugh; polite, rude; wide, narrow; above, below; far, near; ask, tell.* <u>Homonyms</u>: *ate, eight; berry, bury; buy, bye; chews, choose; main, mane; horse, hoarse; doe, dough; heel, heal.*

Divide the class into two teams. Have Team 1 draw a word pair and identify the words as synonyms, antonyms, or homonyms. If the team is correct, their airplane moves 50 feet up the scale. If the team is incorrect, the airplane moves the airplane 50 feet down. The first team to reach 500 feet achieves "Takeoff!" and wins.

▲ DICTIONARY CODE

Write the following secret message on the board: *This mes´ij is in top sē krit cōd.* Ask a volunteer to use the pronunciation key in a dictionary to "decode" the message. Divide the class into pairs and challenge each pair to write coded messages to each other. Then have them exchange and decode their messages. As students become more adept at reading dictionary pronunciations, begin each day by writing "coded" instructions about the day's activities on the board. Encourage students to "decode" the message to find out about the day ahead.

◆ SYNONYM-ANTONYM BIKE RACE

Make a spinner by using a brad to fasten an arrow to a circle made of cardboard. Divide the circle into three sections and number them 1, 2, and 3. Draw bicycles on small construction-paper squares of different colors. Duplicate and distribute Blackline Master 55 to small groups of students.

Have students place their bikes on Start. Direct the first student to spin the arrow and move the number of spaces shown. Have the player name a synonym or an antonym for the word in the space. If correct, the player's bike stays in the space. If incorrect, the bike moves back to its previous position. The first player to reach Finish wins.

Technology

The following software products are designed to provide practice in dictionary skills.

Macmillan Dictionary for Children This multimedia dictionary for students ages 6-12 features over 12,000 words, 1,000 pictures, and 400 sound effects. Some of the pages include hyperlinks that offer connections to semantically related words or word derivations. Several word games are included.
** Simon & Schuster Interactive
P.O. Box 2002
Aurora, CO 80040-2002
(800) 910-0099

Reading Blaster Through hundreds of word-skill games, third graders through sixth graders can practice writing words in alphabetical order, spelling, detecting synonyms and antonyms, and following directions.
** Davidson & Associates, Inc.
19840 Pioneer Avenue
Torrance, CA 90503
(800) 545-7677

Synonym - Antonym Bike Race

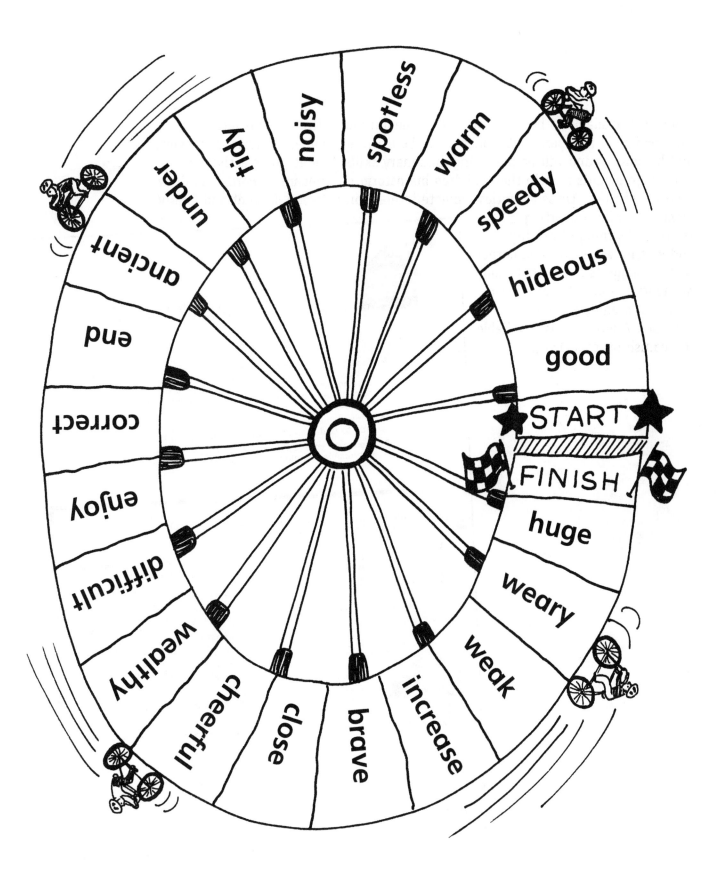

Home Connection

HOME LETTER

A letter is available to be sent home at the beginning of Unit 7. This letter informs family members that students will be learning about synonyms, antonyms, and homonyms and will be practicing dictionary skills. The at-home activities encourage parents to help their children brainstorm multimeaning words and draw pictures of them. These activities promote interaction between student and family members while supporting students' learning of reading and writing words. A Book Corner feature suggests books that family members can look for in a local library and enjoy reading together. A letter is also available in Spanish on page 167q.

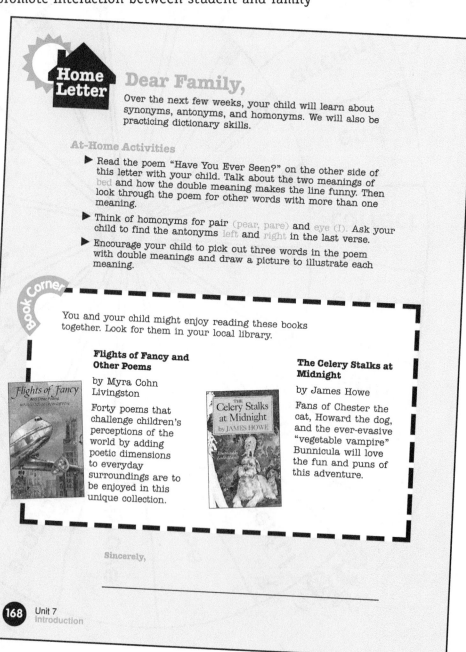

Home Letter

Dear Family,

Over the next few weeks, your child will learn about synonyms, antonyms, and homonyms. We will also be practicing dictionary skills.

At-Home Activities

▶ Read the poem "Have You Ever Seen?" on the other side of this letter with your child. Talk about the two meanings of bed and how the double meaning makes the line funny. Then look through the poem for other words with more than one meaning.

▶ Think of homonyms for pair (pear, pare) and eye (I). Ask your child to find the antonyms left and right in the last verse.

▶ Encourage your child to pick out three words in the poem with double meanings and draw a picture to illustrate each meaning.

Book Corner

You and your child might enjoy reading these books together. Look for them in your local library.

Flights of Fancy and Other Poems

by Myra Cohn Livingston

Forty poems that challenge children's perceptions of the world by adding poetic dimensions to everyday surroundings are to be enjoyed in this unique collection.

The Celery Stalks at Midnight

by James Howe

Fans of Chester the cat, Howard the dog, and the ever-evasive "vegetable vampire" Bunnicula will love the fun and puns of this adventure.

Sincerely,

_____

168 Unit 7
Introduction

Carta para la casa

Estimada familia,

En las próximas semanas, su hijo/a aprenderá acerca de sinónimos, antónimos y homónimos en inglés. También practicaremos el uso del diccionario.

Actividades para hacer en casa

▶ Lean el poema "**Have You Ever Seen?**" (**¿Alguna vez has visto...?**) en la página 167 de su libro. Hablen de los dos significados de **bed** (**cama**) y de cómo el significado doble hace que el cuento sea cómico. Luego repasen el poema en busca de otras palabras que tengan más de un significado.

▶ Piensen en homónimos de **pair** (**pareja**): **pear**, **pare** (**pera, cortar**) y de **eye** (**ojo**): **I** (**yo**). Pídanle a su hijo/a que busque los antónimos **left** (**izquierda**) y **right** (**derecha**) en el último verso.

▶ Animen a su hijo/a a señalar tres palabras en el poema que tengan dos significados y a hacer un dibujo que ilustre cada significado.

Rincón del libro

Su hijo/a y ustedes pueden disfrutar juntos de la lectura de estos libros. Búsquenlos en la biblioteca de su localidad.

Flights of Fancy and Other Poems
por Myra Cohn Livingston

Estos cuarenta poemas confrontan las percepciones de los niños acerca del mundo agregando una dimensión poética al entorno de todos los días.

The Celery Stalks at Midnight
por James Howe

A los fanáticos de Chester, el gato, y de Harold, el perro, y del siempre evasivo "vampiro de vegetales" Bunnicula, les encantará lo divertido que son los juegos de palabras de esta aventura.

Atentamente, _____

Unit Focus

USING THE PAGE

- Read "Have You Ever Seen?" aloud.

- Invite students to read along as you
  read the poem again. Ask students to
  look at the pictures and identify the
  words illustrated in each picture.

- **Critically Thinking** Have a volunteer
  read aloud the sentences in the
  balloon. Then call on students to tell
  how each word is used in the poem
  and then give a second meaning for
  each word.

BUILDING A CONTEXT

- Write the word pairs *peep, look* and
  sound, noise on the board. Have
  students tell you what they notice
  about each pair. (*They mean the same
  or almost the same thing.*)

- Write the word pairs *left, right* and
  dark, light. Ask students what they
  notice. (*The words in each pair are
  opposites.*)

- Repeat with *write, right; hair, hare;
  seen, scene.* (*The words sound the same
  but are spelled differently and have
  different meanings.*)

- Now repeat with *head, head.* (*The
  words are spelled the same and sound
  the same but have different meanings.*)

- Ask students how they could find out
  the different meanings of a word. (*They
  could use the dictionary.*) Ask how they
  could find out how to pronounce a
  word. (*They could use the dictionary.*)

167

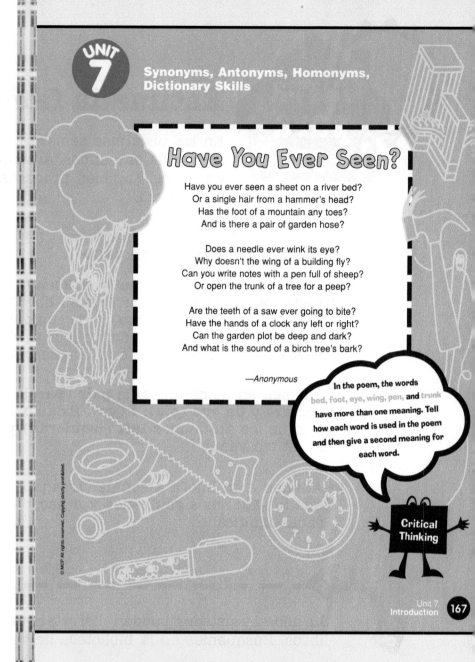

Have You Ever Seen?

Have you ever seen a sheet on a river bed?
Or a single hair from a hammer's head?
Has the foot of a mountain any toes?
And is there a pair of garden hose?

Does a needle ever wink its eye?
Why doesn't the wing of a building fly?
Can you write notes with a pen full of sheep?
Or open the trunk of a tree for a peep?

Are the teeth of a saw ever going to bite?
Have the hands of a clock any left or right?
Can the garden plot be deep and dark?
And what is the sound of a birch tree's bark?

—Anonymous

In the poem, the words
bed, foot, eye, wing, pen, and trunk
have more than one meaning. Tell
how each word is used in the poem
and then give a second meaning for
each word.

**Critical
Thinking**

Unit 7
Introduction **167**

UNIT OPENER ACTIVITIES

HUMOR IN WORDS

Reread the poem, asking students to pay special attention to
the humor that results when words are used in unexpected
ways. Ask students these jokes: *When is a car not a car? (when
it turns into a driveway) How do you stop a rhino from charging?
(take away his credit cards)* Invite students to share other jokes
they know whose humor is based on words having more than
one meaning.

HOMOGRAPH HUNT

Explain that words that are spelled the same but have different
meanings are homographs. Elicit familiar examples, such as *saw*
and *peep.* Invite small groups of students to hunt through a
dictionary for three pairs of homographs.

CARTOON HUMOR

Challenge students to write a funny sentence that has a
homonym or a homograph and then draw a cartoon to show the
humor in it. Offer the following examples: *I washed my hare
this morning. (girl bathing a rabbit) The horse draws the plow.
(horse sketching a plow)*

Home Letter

Dear Family,

Over the next few weeks, your child will learn about synonyms, antonyms, and homonyms. We will also be practicing dictionary skills.

At-Home Activities

▶ Read the poem "Have You Ever Seen?" on the other side of this letter with your child. Talk about the two meanings of *bed* and how the double meaning makes the line funny. Then look through the poem for other words with more than one meaning.

▶ Think of homonyms for pair (pear, pare) and eye (I). Ask your child to find the antonyms left and right in the last verse.

▶ Encourage your child to pick out three words in the poem with double meanings and draw a picture to illustrate each meaning.

You and your child might enjoy reading these books together. Look for them in your local library.

Flights of Fancy and Other Poems

by Myra Cohn Livingston

Forty poems that challenge children's perceptions of the world by adding poetic dimensions to everyday surroundings are to be enjoyed in this unique collection.

The Celery Stalks at Midnight

by James Howe

Fans of Chester the cat, Howard the dog, and the ever-evasive "vegetable vampire" Bunnicula will love the fun and puns of this adventure.

Sincerely,

_____

BULLETIN BOARD

Have the class brainstorm a list of words that have both a synonym and an antonym. Have them write the words on colored cards, illustrate them, and arrange them on a bulletin board entitled "Same and Opposite."

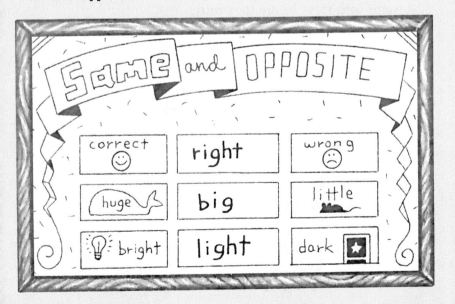

HOME CONNECTIONS

● The Home Letter on page 168 is intended to acquaint family members with the word study skills students will be studying in the unit. Students can tear out page 168 and take it home. You may want to suggest that they complete the activities on the page with a family member. Encourage students to look for the books pictured on page 168 in the library and read them with family members.

● The Home Letter can also be found on page 167q in Spanish.

CURRICULUM CONNECTIONS

WRITING

Portfolio Ask students to try writing another verse to the poem "Have You Ever Seen?" Have them brainstorm double-meaning words such as *wave, light, fine, note, ring, ruler, nail, date,* and *bank* to help them get started.

SCIENCE

Materials: reproductions of da Vinci's mirror writing, mirrors

Many famous people throughout history have been left-handed. Perhaps the most famous of all is Leonardo da Vinci, the Italian painter, scientist, and inventor. Da Vinci kept notebooks in mirror writing—writing that looks normal only when viewed in a mirror. Provide some small mirrors and show students some examples of da Vinci's mirror writing. Invite students to choose a line from the poem on page 167 and try to write it in mirror writing.

LANGUAGE ARTS

When a word has two meanings, one of them probably developed because the thing being named reminded people of something they already had a name for. Have students discuss which of each pair of meanings probably came first, and why: *eye* (*of a person, of a needle*); *head* (*of a person, of a hammer*); *foot* (*of a person, of a mountain*); *teeth* (*of a person, of a saw*); *hands* (*of a person, of a clock*); *wing* (*of a bird, of a building*). Encourage students to give their own examples of double-meaning words and then speculate about the origin of each.

Lesson 77

Pages 169–170

Synonyms

Lesson Focus

INTRODUCING THE SKILL

- Tell students that when they write a story, they should use a variety of words to describe events and add interest to their writing. One way to do this is to use synonyms.

- Write these word pairs on the board: *unhappy, sad; glad, happy*. Ask students what each pair has in common. (*similar meanings*)

- Explain that synonyms are words that have the same or almost the same meaning. Encourage students to think of additional synonyms for *sad* and *glad*. (*gloomy, joyful*)

- Tell students that knowing synonyms will help them avoid repeating the same word and make their writing more interesting. Write *She ran down the street and ran around the corner.* Have students suggest other words for *ran*. (*hurried, rushed*)

USING THE PAGES

Ask a volunteer to read the directions for each activity on pages 169 and 170 aloud before students begin it. Field any questions about what students are to do. After the pages have been completed, have a volunteer review what a synonym is and ask for examples of synonyms.

169

Name

▷ Circle the words in the puzzle that are synonyms for the numbered words. Write the words you find.

> **DEFINITION**
> Synonyms are words that have the same or almost the same meaning.
> sad—unhappy   glad—happy

```
n e a t b q p
g h a r m u r
r c g i j i h
i n s p e c t
n a q u z k o
```

1. journey   trip
2. tidy   neat
3. rapid   quick
4. hurt   harm
5. examine   inspect
6. smile   grin

▷ Read the passage. Write a synonym from the word bank below for each word in parentheses to complete each sentence.

strength	providing	simply	saying	quantity	varying
speech	create	whole	used	ideas	speed

Without _____saying_____ a word, the Mazateco people of Mexico can carry on
     1. (speaking)

_____whole_____ conversations. They do this _____simply_____ by whistling!
  2. (entire)   3. (just)

This unusual form of _____speech_____ _____used_____ only by the men
      4. (language)   5. (employed)

of the tribe. They get across _____ideas_____ by _____varying_____ the
      6. (thoughts)   7. (changing)

_____speed_____, pitch, and _____strength_____ of the whistles. Traders
  8. (quickness)   9. (force)

can _____create_____ deals by _____providing_____ exact details of
   10. (make)   11. (giving)

_____quantity_____ and price without saying a word!
  12. (amount)

Lesson 77
Synonyms
169

FOCUS ON ALL LEARNERS

ENGLISH LANGUAGE LEARNERS/ESL

Tell students they can remember that synonyms are words that have similar meanings because *synonyms* and *similar* both begin with *s*. The second activity on page 170 may be difficult for English language learners. You may want to unscramble the words with them before they write.

VISUAL LEARNERS

LARGE GROUP

Write on the board *tired, fast, eyeglasses, enjoy, note, loyal, make-believe, letter, faithful, spectacles, quick, like, exhausted,* and *fantasy*. Invite a volunteer to choose a word and say a sentence using it. Have another student repeat the sentence, using a synonym from the board.

KINESTHETIC LEARNERS

PARTNER   **Materials:** index cards, markers

Make word cards for *leave, depart, baby, infant, replied, answered, brook, stream, correct, right, mistake, error, flower, blossom, sure, certain, bush, shrub, thin,* and *lean*. Have pairs play concentration. The player with the most synonym pairs wins.

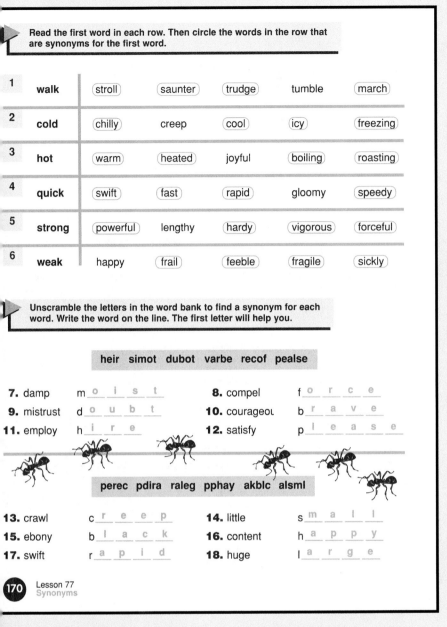

Read the first word in each row. Then circle the words in the row that are synonyms for the first word.

1	walk	(stroll)	(saunter)	(trudge)	tumble	(march)
2	cold	(chilly)	creep	(cool)	(icy)	(freezing)
3	hot	(warm)	(heated)	joyful	(boiling)	(roasting)
4	quick	(swift)	(fast)	(rapid)	gloomy	(speedy)
5	strong	(powerful)	lengthy	(hardy)	(vigorous)	(forceful)
6	weak	happy	(frail)	(feeble)	(fragile)	(sickly)

Unscramble the letters in the word bank to find a synonym for each word. Write the word on the line. The first letter will help you.

heir	simot	dubot	varbe	recof	pealse

7. damp   m o i s t   8. compel   f o r c e
9. mistrust   d o u b t   10. courageou   b r a v e
11. employ   h i r e   12. satisfy   p l e a s e

perec	pdira	raleg	pphay	akblc	alsml

13. crawl   c r e e p   14. little   s m a l l
15. ebony   b l a c k   16. content   h a p p y
17. swift   r a p i d   18. huge   l a r g e

SPELLING

The following sentences can be used as a pretest for spelling words that are synonyms, antonyms, and homonyms.

1. **courageous**   Firefighters are **courageous**.
2. **brave**   The soldier was **brave** in battle.
3. **bitter**   Ugh! This medicine tastes **bitter**!
4. **sweet**   After supper we like a **sweet** treat.
5. **threw**   I **threw** my ball against the wall.
6. **through**   Dad drove **through** the tunnel.
7. **whether**   I can't tell **whether** it is raining.
8. **weather**   Rain is fine **weather** for ducks.

WRITING

Portfolio Explain that when writing dialogue, writers have to use words like *he said* and *she said* to let the reader know who is speaking. However, to vary their language, writers can sometimes use synonyms for *said*, such as *whispered*, *asked*, and *exclaimed*. Have students list as many synonyms for *said* as they can and then write a short dialogue using some of their words.

MATH

The words *mean* and *median* are used as synonyms in everyday English. However, in math they are not synonyms. Have students find out the mathematical difference between *mean* and *median* and come up with a set of numbers whose mean and median are different; for example, *Five girls shoot 3, 4, 5, 8, and 10 baskets. The mean (quotient obtained by dividing the sum by the number of figures) is 6 baskets; the median (middle value) is 5 baskets.*

ART/LANGUAGE ARTS

Materials: posterboard, paints, index cards

Red, crimson, scarlet, vermilion, rose, maroon—these are all synonyms for *red*. However, color synonyms don't have exactly the same meaning. Have students find or paint an example of each color, paste each example on a card, and arrange the cards to create a poster.

AUDITORY LEARNERS

SMALL GROUP Invite groups of four students to play the "synonym game." Provide these words: *little, big, happy, sad, walk, eat, fast, hot, cold*. Have a group member say each word aloud and have the rest of the group say as many synonyms as they can. Set a time limit. Award one point for each correct answer.

GIFTED LEARNERS

Materials: copies of pages from a story, thesauruses

Provide each student with a copy of a different page from a story. Challenge them to use a thesaurus to find synonyms for as many words on the page as possible. Have them list their synonym pairs and then combine their lists with other students.

LEARNERS WHO NEED EXTRA SUPPORT

Materials: thesauruses

Model how to use a thesaurus to find synonyms and encourage students to find more synonyms for the words in the lesson. You may want to let some students use a thesaurus as they work on the lesson. See Daily Word Study Practice, pages 206–207.

Lesson 78

Pages 171–172

Antonyms

INFORMAL ASSESSMENT OBJECTIVES

Can students

- [ ] identify antonyms?
- [ ] choose between antonyms to complete sentences?

Lesson Focus

INTRODUCING THE SKILL

- Review synonyms with students by asking them to define *synonym* and offer examples of synonym pairs.

- Call on a volunteer to write *large* on the board. Ask students to name words that mean the opposite. Explain that words that are opposite in meaning are called antonyms.

- Have volunteers write these words on the board: *cold, fast, sad, full, hard.* Call on other students to write an antonym for each word.

- Use examples, such as *tree, car,* and *squirrel,* to help students understand that not all words have an antonym. Then invite students to offer additional examples of word pairs that are antonyms and list them on the board.

USING THE PAGES

Be sure students understand what to do on pages 171 and 172. When they have completed the pages, review what students learned about antonyms as you correct the papers together.

Name _____

▶ Read the first word in each row. Then circle the words in the row that are antonyms of the first word.

> **DEFINITION**
> **Antonyms** are words that are opposite or almost opposite in meaning.
>
> happy—sad   large—small

1	slow	(quick)	happy	(fast)	(rapid)	(swift)
2	sweet	(sour)	(tart)	(bitter)	sugary	(unsweet)
3	weak	(strong)	(hardy)	powerless	(powerful)	(forceful)
4	safe	secure	(uncertain)	(insecure)	(unsafe)	unprotected
5	forbid	(allow)	refuse	(permit)	(tolerate)	(approve)
6	distrust	(trust)	(faith)	(belief)	disbelief	(confidence)

▶ Read each pair of sentences. Find the word in the first sentence that is an antonym of a word in the second sentence. Underline the two words.

7. Leah had just started skating and found it difficult.
8. Ted had been skating for years and made it look easy.

9. Ted felt that Leah was getting much better at skating.
10. Every time Leah fell, she felt she was just getting worse.

11. It was early when they started skating.
12. Leah and Ted skated until late in the day.

13. Around four o'clock Ted and Leah became tired.
14. Then they went home to get rested.

Lesson 78
Antonyms

171

FOCUS ON ALL LEARNERS

ENGLISH LANGUAGE LEARNERS/ESL

Before students begin working, make sure they understand the concept of opposite by demonstrating happiness and sadness with facial expressions or by locating objects that are large and small. Review the vocabulary in the first exercise on page 171 and in the box on page 172.

VISUAL LEARNERS

PARTNER Write *damp, courageous, tall, thin, lost, rough, simple, straight,* and *repair* on the board. Have students write sentences for the words, trade papers with a partner, and rewrite each other's sentences, substituting an antonym for each listed word.

KINESTHETIC LEARNERS

LARGE GROUP Have students form two teams and line up at the board. As you say each of the following words, a member of each team writes the word's antonym on the board: *loud, lead, rough, tidy, loose, young, same, arrive, ripe, heavy.* Each correctly written word earns the team a point.

> Find the antonym in the word bank for each of the following words. Write each antonym on the line beside the word.

| tasty | quiet | joyful | follow | narrow | frown | hard | fresh |

1. soft   h a r d
2. bland   t a s t y
3. noisy   q u i e t
4. wide   n a r r o w
5. smile   f r o w n
6. unhappy   j o y f u l
7. stale   f r e s h
8. lead   f o l l o w

> Read each sentence and the pair of words that follows. Choose the word that best completes the sentence and write the word on the line.

9. For the first time the usually honest boy was _____untruthful_____ about his behavior.
   untruthful
   truthful

10. He said he would take the fastest way home, but he took the _____slowest_____.
   quickest
   slowest

11. His mother was unhappy with him but was _____overjoyed_____ to see he was safe.
   disappointed
   overjoyed

12. The hungry boy devoured his food and was soon _____full_____.
   full
   empty

13. Then he took off his dirty clothes and put on some _____clean_____ pajamas.
   soiled
   clean

14. Feeling tired, he went to bed so he would be _____rested_____ the next day.
   rested
   exhausted

172   Lesson 78
Antonyms

AUDITORY LEARNERS

PARTNER On the board, write the words *loud, lead, rough, tidy, loose, young, same, arrive, ripe, heavy*. One student says a sentence with one of the words; the other responds with another sentence, using the word's antonym.

GIFTED LEARNERS

Encourage students to create an antonym section in their personal word banks. Remind them that some words have more than one antonym, and that multimeaning words may have an antonym for one meaning but not for the other—for example, *green*, meaning "unripe" does; *green*, the color, does not.

LEARNERS WHO NEED EXTRA SUPPORT

Work with students as they begin page 171, helping them identify all the antonyms in the row. Be sure they understand that they will look for more than one antonym. See Daily Word Study Practice, pages 206–207.

SPELLING

Write the spelling words *courageous, brave, bitter, sweet, threw, through, whether, weather* on the board. Students choose a word and make up a sentence clue for classmates to complete: For example: *A yummy dessert is so _____. (sweet)*

WRITING

Portfolio Have students imagine they have landed in a place where everything is opposite from what it is at home. Ask them to write a description contrasting the unfamiliar place with the familiar one by describing the differences. Remind students to use antonyms in their descriptions.

LANGUAGE ARTS

Materials: paper, markers

To play "antonym bingo," students fold papers into 16 squares (4 across, 4 down) and write these words in the squares in any order: *slow, sweet, weak, distrust, open, noisy, tiny, delay, destroy, raise, easy, generous, cheap, careful, allow, push*. Then, as you say each of the following words, students should cross off its antonym: *fast, close, construct, careless, expensive, sour, quiet, lower, enormous, strong, difficult, forbid, trust, hasten, stingy, pull*. The first person to cross out the words across, down, or diagonally is the winner.

MATH

Students can create a list of math terms that are opposites, writing the ones they find on the board—for example, *multiply, divide; add, subtract; plus, minus; greater than, less than; positive, negative*.

AstroWord, Vocabulary.
© 1998 Silver Burdett Ginn Inc.
Division of Simon & Schuster.

Lesson 79

Pages 173–174

Homonyms

Can students

- recognize homonyms?
- associate pictures with homonyms?
- choose between homonyms to complete sentences?

Lesson Focus

INTRODUCING THE SKILL

- Introduce homonyms by reading aloud these sentences: *I had a great time. My mom asked me to grate some cheese.* Ask what the sentences have in common. (*words that sound the same*)

- Write the sentences on the board and underline *great* and *grate*. Ask students how the two words are alike and different. (*sound alike; have different spellings and meanings*)

- Explain that *great* and *grate* are homonyms, words that sound alike but have different meanings and usually have different spellings.

- Write these words on the board and invite volunteers to write a homonym for each one: *knew, hear, to, buy, won.* (*new, here, two or too, by or bye, one*)

USING THE PAGES

- Make sure students understand what to do before they begin each activity.

- After students have completed both pages, call on a volunteer to give some examples of homonyms and spell each one.

173

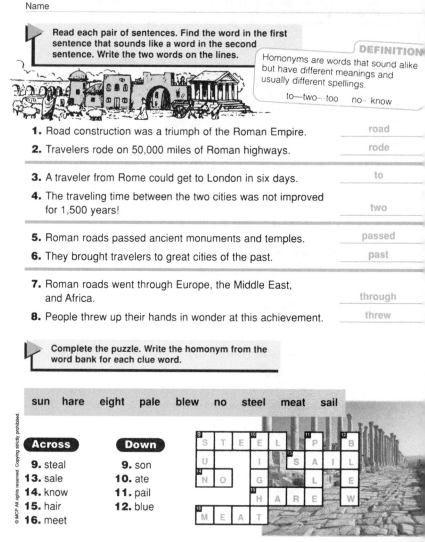

Name _____

Read each pair of sentences. Find the word in the first sentence that sounds like a word in the second sentence. Write the two words on the lines.

DEFINITION
Homonyms are words that sound alike but have different meanings and usually different spellings.
to—two··too   no·· know

1. Road construction was a triumph of the Roman Empire.   road
2. Travelers rode on 50,000 miles of Roman highways.   rode

3. A traveler from Rome could get to London in six days.   to
4. The traveling time between the two cities was not improved for 1,500 years!   two

5. Roman roads passed ancient monuments and temples.   passed
6. They brought travelers to great cities of the past.   past

7. Roman roads went through Europe, the Middle East, and Africa.   through
8. People threw up their hands in wonder at this achievement.   threw

Complete the puzzle. Write the homonym from the word bank for each clue word.

| sun | hare | eight | pale | blew | no | steel | meat | sail |

Across
9. steal
13. sale
14. know
15. hair
16. meet

Down
9. son
10. ate
11. pail
12. blue

Lesson 79
Homonyms
173

FOCUS ON ALL LEARNERS

ENGLISH LANGUAGE LEARNERS/ESL

To build background for the story on page 173, ask volunteers to tell what they know about the ancient Romans. Show pictures of Roman roads, buildings, and aqueducts, if available. Talk about the Romans' technical ability.

VISUAL LEARNERS

PARTNER   Distribute one of these words and sentences to each pair of students: *hear, here; one, won; week, weak; After my illness, I felt _____ all _____; My team _____ by _____ point; I can _____ the noise over _____.* Have partners complete the sentences and write more like them for classmates to complete.

KINESTHETIC LEARNERS

LARGE GROUP   **Materials:** index cards, markers

Using the homonyms in the lesson and others if needed, make a word card for each student. Distribute them and on your signal, have everyone find the classmate with the homonym for his or her word. Have the two paired students write a sentence for each homonym.

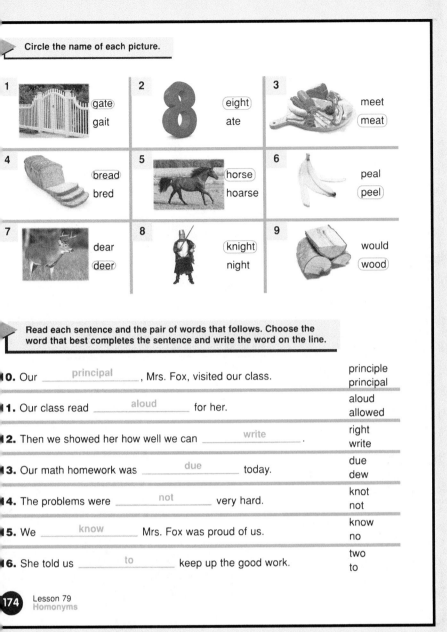

Circle the name of each picture.

1. (gate) / gait
2. 8 — (eight) / ate
3. meet / (meat)
4. (bread) / bred
5. (horse) / hoarse
6. peal / (peel)
7. dear / (deer)
8. (knight) / night
9. would / (wood)

Read each sentence and the pair of words that follows. Choose the word that best completes the sentence and write the word on the line.

10. Our ___principal___, Mrs. Fox, visited our class. — principle / principal
11. Our class read ___aloud___ for her. — aloud / allowed
12. Then we showed her how well we can ___write___. — right / write
13. Our math homework was ___due___ today. — due / dew
14. The problems were ___not___ very hard. — knot / not
15. We ___know___ Mrs. Fox was proud of us. — know / no
16. She told us ___to___ keep up the good work. — two / to

SPELLING

The following sentences can be used as a spelling posttest for synonyms, antonyms, and homonyms.

1. **sweet** — It was **sweet** of you to come.
2. **brave** — America is the home of the **brave.**
3. **weather** — We play outside in good **weather.**
4. **courageous** — Police officers are **courageous.**
5. **threw** — I **threw** the apple core in the trash.
6. **bitter** — Some cooking herbs taste **bitter.**
7. **whether** — I'll cheer **whether** you win or not.
8. **through** — Can you see **through** this telescope?

WRITING

Portfolio Invite students to write a silly story using incorrect homonyms; for example, *Won knight, sum cowboys road two town in the rein.* Have students read their story aloud to a partner and then switch stories. Have the partner read the story again silently, identify each incorrect homonym, and write the correct one.

LANGUAGE ARTS

Explain that many jokes rely on homonyms for their humor.

1. "I hurt my toe last night." "What did you do?" "I called a toe truck."
2. "What's the best day to hold a parade?" "March fourth."
3. "In what country are sports scores always even?" "Thailand."

Have students recall or create a joke based on a pair of homonyms.

MATH

Ask students to spell out numbers one through ten and write homonyms for words that have them. (*one, won; two, to, too; four, for, fore; eight, ate*) Then write on the board *Our team ___1___ the big race!* Have a volunteer erase the numeral and write the word that fits. (*won*)

AUDITORY LEARNERS

LARGE GROUP Have the class form two teams. Say aloud a word from the lesson. The first team to write a homonym for it earns a point for the team. Continue saying words aloud and having students write homonyms until everyone has had a turn. The team with more points wins.

GIFTED LEARNERS

Tell students that hundreds of words have homonyms. Challenge them to list as many homonym pairs and trios as they can within a time limit. You may wish to have students compete. If so, grant one point for each homonym pair and five points for each homonym trio.

LEARNERS WHO NEED EXTRA SUPPORT

Materials: index cards, markers

Find or draw pictures to illustrate several homonym pairs and put them on cards. Examples include *blue, blew; tow, toe; pear, pair; sun, son.* Label the cards. Provide sentences with missing homonyms and have students choose the correct card for the blank. See Daily Word Study Practice, pages 206–207.

Lesson 80
Pages 175–176

Alphabetical Order

INFORMAL ASSESSMENT OBJECTIVES

Can students

✔ alphabetize words to the second and third letter?

✔ identify general sections of the dictionary for a specific entry?

Lesson Focus

INTRODUCING THE SKILL

- Write these two sets of words on the board: *1. cellar, catch, class, chime; 2. ground, green, grate, grid.* Have students name the beginning letter in each word in the first set. *(c)*

- Ask students how they would put the words in order if the first letters are the same. Call on a volunteer to write the first set of words in order.

- Have students look at the second set of words. Help them conclude that because each word begins with *gr*, they must look at the third letter of each word to determine the alphabetical order.

- Ask students how words are arranged in a dictionary. Then suggest that they think of a dictionary in sections *A–C, D–L, M–R, S–Z.* Say the following words and have students identify the section each would be in: *green, outside, answer, youth.*

USING THE PAGES

Make sure students know what to do on pages 175 and 176.

When they have completed the pages, suggest that pairs discuss what they learned about alphabetical order.

175

Name _____

 ▶ Write the words in each group in alphabetical order.

1. pearl — part
pin — pearl
powder — photo
part — pin
photo — powder

2. door — date
duty — digest
date — door
drain — drain
digest — duty

3. llama — lizard
lucky — llama
lodge — lodge
lying — lucky
lizard — lying

▶ Write the names of the animals in the word bank in alphabetical order. Use the dictionary to find out about the animals you do not know.

panda	peacock
parrot	porpoise
rhinoceros	rabbit
raccoon	raven
toucan	tortoise
tiger	turtle

4. panda
5. parrot
6. peacock
7. porpoise
8. rabbit
9. raccoon
10. raven
11. rhinoceros
12. tiger
13. tortoise
14. toucan
15. turtle

Lesson 80
Alphabetical order
175

FOCUS ON ALL LEARNERS

ENGLISH LANGUAGE LEARNERS/ESL

Review the alphabet with students. Although they do not need to know the meaning of the words to complete the first three activities, encourage them to practice their dictionary skills by looking up words they do not know.

VISUAL LEARNERS

PARTNER **Materials:** dictionary, paper

Invite pairs to take turns finding words in the dictionary and reading them to their partners, who will write in which section the word is located before verifying the section with the dictionary. Encourage pairs to continue for several turns.

KINESTHETIC LEARNERS

PARTNER **Materials:** index cards, marker, stopwatch or clock with second hand

Prepare alphabet cards. Have students shuffle the cards and take turns seeing how fast they can arrange them in alphabetical order. The partner acts as timekeeper.

Read each word and figure out in which section of the dictionary you would find this word. Use the picture in the box to help you. Then write the word first, second, third, or fourth on the line next to each word.

DICTIONARY TIP
The words in a dictionary are listed in alphabetical order from **A** to **Z**.

1. banquet _____first_____
2. impostor _____second_____
3. frontier _____second_____
4. turret _____fourth_____
5. privilege _____third_____
6. repeal _____third_____

See how quickly you can find these words in the dictionary. Then write each word on the line beside its definition.

petunia	visibility	barnacle	crest
jerkin	abacus	redwood	easel

7. used for doing math quickly without writing _____abacus_____
8. a standing frame for holding an artist's painting _____easel_____
9. a short, tight jacket often without sleeves _____jerkin_____
10. a plant with flowers of various colors _____petunia_____
11. a giant evergreen tree found in California and Oregon _____redwood_____
12. a small sea animal with a shell which fastens itself to rocks and the bottom of boats _____barnacle_____
13. the distance within which things are visible _____visibility_____
14. a tuft of feathers or fur on the head of some birds and animals _____crest_____

176 Lesson 80
Locating words in the dictionary

SPELLING

The following sentences could be used as a pretest for spelling words to review level skills.

1. **third** — Mr. Ray teaches **third** grade.
2. **knight** — The **knight** wore shiny armor.
3. **angriest** — She's **angriest** when she's tired.
4. **instrument** — I play a musical **instrument**.
5. **unusual** — The house was **unusual**.
6. **desert** — Wind blew across the **desert**.
7. **soil** — The garden **soil** was perfect for roses.
8. **respell** — Please **respell** this word.
9. **employ** — Ms. Lee likes to **employ** teenagers.
10. **poisonous** — Not all snakes are **poisonous**.

WRITING

Portfolio **Materials:** classroom books

Suggest that students list the names of eight classroom books and their authors, then rewrite the list, alphabetizing the titles by the author's last name, using this form: White, E.B. *Charlotte's Web.*

ART

Materials: art paper, markers or crayons

Invite students to work in small groups to create a treasure map. The way to find the treasure from a starting point is to follow the landmark clues in alphabetical order. To begin, suggest that they imagine what their treasure land looks like and that they make an alphabetical list of landmarks that would be there.

MATH/ART

Materials: picture of an abacus, reference books, string, a box, beads

Show students a picture of an abacus and tell them that the abacus, developed in China in the sixth century, is the oldest form of computer. Students could learn more about the abacus and create a simple one using string, beads, and a box for a frame. Challenge students to do simple additions on their homemade abacus.

AUDITORY LEARNERS

LARGE GROUP Say a word and randomly name a section of the dictionary. Students should tell you if the word would be in that section, an earlier section, or a later section. You might use these words: *plop, honk, crunch, zip, buzz, clang, chirp, murmur, rustle, beep, ding, squeal, thump.*

GIFTED LEARNERS

Challenge students to collect words that are the same to the fifth or sixth letter, such as *flounce* and *flounder, discount* and *discourage.*

LEARNERS WHO NEED EXTRA SUPPORT

Suggest that students make groups of the words in the word bank on page 175 that begin with the same letter and alphabetize those smaller groups before writing the whole list. See Daily Word Study Practice, page 207.

Lesson 81

Pages 177–178

Dictionary Guide Words

INFORMAL ASSESSMENT OBJECTIVES

Can students

✓ recognize words in alphabetical order?

✓ locate words in the dictionary, using guide words as references?

Lesson Focus

INTRODUCING THE SKILL

Materials: dictionary

- Open a dictionary and display a page. Ask students to name what they see at the top. *(two boldfaced words)* Explain that these are guide words, words that show the first and last words on a page. Explain that the other words on the page are in alphabetical order between the two guide words.

- Write these lists of words on the board in random order: *goal, gobble, goddess, goggle, gold, gorge; kickoff, kidney, kilo, kind, kiss, kiwi.* Call on volunteers to rewrite each group of words in alphabetical order.

- Then have students imagine that each group represents the entry words for a dictionary page. Ask which words in each group would be the guide words. *(goal, gorge; kickoff, kiwi)*

USING THE PAGES

Make sure students understand how to complete pages 177 and 178. When they have finished, encourage them to review their answers with a partner and discuss what they learned about guide words.

Name _____

> Look at each pair of guide words and the words below them. Cross out any words that would not be found on the same page as those guide words. Then write the remaining words in alphabetical order on the lines.

DEFINITION
Guide words are found at the top of each dictionary page. The guide words tell you the first and last word on each page. The remaining words on the dictionary page are in alphabetical order between the two guide words.

1   fluffy · fold

fly	fly
foil	focus
~~foot~~	foil
focus	

2   muddle · napkin

nap	mystery
much	nap
mystery	
~~nation~~	

3   safety · sauce

salad	salad
satisfy	salt
salt	satisfy
~~sad~~	

4   oar · oft

object	object
office	occur
occur	office
~~out~~	

5   penny · pizza

plain	people
people	perfect
piano	piano
perfect	

6   job · jug

jog	jog
~~jut~~	join
jolt	jolt
join	

> Look at each pair of guide words. Circle the words that would be on the same page as the guide words. Then number the circled words in each column in alphabetical order.

7   ant · apple

2	(apart)
	apt
3	(apologize)
1	(any)

8   dose · drake

2	(down)
3	(doze)
1	(dot)
	dream

9   machine · make

3	(major)
	male
1	(magazine)
2	(maid)

Lesson 81
Dictionary guide words   **177**

FOCUS ON ALL LEARNERS

ENGLISH LANGUAGE LEARNERS/ESL

Materials: dictionary

Review the lesson with students. Help individuals use the guide words to locate words of their choosing in the dictionary.

VISUAL/KINESTHETIC LEARNERS

PARTNER

Materials: dictionary

Encourage each student in a pair to use a dictionary to write in random order ten entry words from one page. Tell students to exchange papers, alphabetize the list, and identify the guide words. Then have them trade papers again for checking.

KINESTHETIC LEARNERS

INDIVIDUAL   **Materials:** paper, paper strips, markers, tape

Post five pairs of guide words around the room. Have each student write one word on a paper strip that would appear on a dictionary page with each set of guide words and tape it to the appropriate posted pair.

> Read the words in the word bank. Then read the pairs of guide words below. Find three words in the word bank that would be on the dictionary page with each pair of guide words. Write those words in alphabetical order on the lines beneath the guide words.

osprey	rasp	moat	mirror	mixer	ornament
moist	ours	ought	rake	raft	ram

1. mineral · model

mirror

mixer

moat

2. organ · ounce

ornament

osprey

ought

3. radio · rank

raft

rake

ram

> Read the information in each exercise. Decide whether the word would appear **before, on,** or **after** the dictionary page with those guide words. Write your answer on the line.

4. You open the dictionary and see the guide words **firm · fixture.**
Would the word **fist** come *before, on* or *after* this dictionary page?

on

5. You open the dictionary and see the guide words **grief · grotto.**
Would the word **grew** come *before, on* or *after* this dictionary page?

before

6. You open the dictionary and see the guide words **code · comic.**
Would the word **collar** come *before, on* or *after* this dictionary page?

on

7. You open the dictionary and see the guide words **swell · swine.**
Would the word **sword** come *before, on* or *after* this dictionary page?

after

AUDITORY LEARNERS

LARGE GROUP

Materials: dictionary

Open a dictionary and read the guide words at the top of one page for students to copy. Then randomly read words on that page and the pages that come before and after it. Ask students to identify the words that would come between the guide words.

GIFTED LEARNERS

Challenge students to write as many more words as they can that belong on a page with each set of guide words on page 177. When they have finished, they could check the spelling of words they're unsure of in a dictionary.

LEARNERS WHO NEED EXTRA SUPPORT

Materials: tagboard strips

Suggest that students review each list on page 177 and cross out the words that won't fit in each set before they begin to alphabetize. Encourage them to make an alphabet chart on a tagboard strip to refer to as they work. See Daily Word Study Practice, page 207.

CURRICULUM CONNECTIONS

SPELLING

Materials: lists of the spelling words *third, knight, angriest, instrument, unusual, desert, soil, respell, employ, poisonous* numbered and scrambled

Divide students into teams lined up at the board. Give the first person in each team the scrambled list. That student unscrambles the first word, writes it on the board, and passes the list to the second student, and so on. The team that unscrambles all the words correctly first wins.

WRITING

Portfolio **Materials:** telephone directory

Have students use a telephone directory to do the following.

1. Identify the guide words on the page their name might be found.
2. Choose the name of a photographer from the yellow pages and write it, the telephone number, and the guide words on the page.
3. Make up a name for a kennel, and write the names of kennels that would appear before and after it in the yellow pages.

SOCIAL STUDIES

Materials: dictionaries

Ask students where they might look to find the correct spelling, date, and definition of familiar or not-so-familiar holidays. Then have them locate the following entries in a dictionary and write the guide words that appear on the page where each name is found: *New Year's Day, Valentine's Day, April Fools' Day, Arbor Day, Memorial Day, Flag Day, Independence Day, Labor Day, Halloween.*

LANGUAGE ARTS

Materials: dictionary, reference books

Encourage students to find out the history of the word *alphabet*, then compare the entire Greek alphabet with the one used in English. Discuss the similarities.

Entry Words and Definitions

Lesson Focus

INTRODUCING THE SKILL

- Explain that words in boldface on a dictionary page are entry words. The information about the word, abbreviation, or name found in a dictionary is called an entry.

- Write *largest*, *gathered*, and *rethink* on the board. Ask students to identify the prefix or ending in each word. Explain that many words that begin with *un-*, *re-*, and *dis-*, or that end with *-s*, *-es*, *-ing*, *-ed*, *-er*, and *-est* are not listed as separate entry words. Have students identify the base words they would look for. (*large, gather, think*)

- Tell students that when they find a word, they may see more than one meaning listed by number.

USING THE PAGES

- Be sure students understand what to do to complete pages 179 and 180.

- After students have completed both pages, ask a pair of students to model for the class the process of looking up a word in the dictionary.

Name _____

Many words that begin with **un, re,** or **dis** or end with **s, es, ing, ed, er,** or **est** are not listed as separate entry words in the dictionary. To find the meaning of these words, look up the base word to which the prefix or ending has been added. Abbreviations and contractions are listed alphabetically in the dictionary as though they were whole words.

> **DICTIONARY TIPS**
> The words shown in boldface print in the dictionary are called **entry words.** All the information about an entry word is called an **entry.**

Read each word. Then write the entry word you would look up in the dictionary. Remember that if a word has a common prefix or suffix, you may need to look up the base word to which the prefix or suffix has been added.

1. poodles	poodle		9. corrected	correct
2. wider	wide		10. darkness	dark
3. clouds	cloud		11. ivies	ivy
4. racing	race		12. omitting	omit
5. knitting	knit		13. rained	rain
6. angriest	angry		14. pennies	penny
7. permitted	permit		15. repack	pack
8. rewrap	wrap		16. dryly	dry

For each group, number the abbreviations and contractions in alphabetical order. Then write the word or phrase each stands for.

17.				18.		
5	M.D.	Doctor of Medicine		1	can't	cannot
4	lb	pound		3	they'll	they will
3	km	kilometer(s)		5	who's	who is
1	CA	California		2	here's	here is
2	Fri.	Friday		4	we've	we have

Lesson 82
Entry words

179

FOCUS ON ALL LEARNERS

ENGLISH LANGUAGE LEARNERS/ESL

Materials: dictionary

Show students entries in the dictionary, reading both the entry word and the definitions. Have each student name a word and locate it in the dictionary.

VISUAL LEARNERS

PARTNER **Materials:** dictionaries

On the board, write these sentences: *The <u>general</u> gave orders to the troops. The rock feels <u>rough</u>. We worked hard and got the <u>credit</u> for doing a good job.* Have pairs find each underlined word in the dictionary and write the meaning of the word as it is used in the sentence.

KINESTHETIC LEARNERS

SMALL GROUP **Materials:** dictionaries, index cards, markers

Have groups peruse the dictionary and find five new or unusual entry words and write each on a card with its meaning(s). Collect and shuffle the cards and let students draw one each day for "the word of the day."

Read the dictionary meanings. Then read the sentences below. Write the number of the meaning of each underlined word in the sentences on the lines.

> **HINT**
> Many entries in the dictionary list more than one meaning for an entry word.

1 **save** **1.** to rescue or keep from harm or danger **2.** to keep or store up for future use **3.** to keep from being lost or wasted **4.** to keep from being worn out or damaged

_4_ Jill plans to <u>save</u> her best shoes for special parties.

_1_ Paco was able to <u>save</u> his dog from drowning.

_2_ The squirrels <u>save</u> nuts and seeds so they will have food to eat during the winter.

2 **date** **1.** the time at which a thing happens **2.** the day of the month **3.** the words or figures on a coin or letter that tell when it was made

_3_ Marla needs a penny with the <u>date</u> 1964 to complete her coin collection.

_1_ The <u>date</u> of Martin Luther King, Jr.'s birth was January 15, 1929.

3 **glaring** **1.** shining so brightly as to hurt the eyes **2.** too bright and showy **3.** staring at in an angry way **4.** standing out so that it cannot be overlooked

_2_ I do not like the <u>glaring</u> color of those bright pink and green socks.

_1_ The <u>glaring</u> headlights hurt Mr. Day's eyes.

_4_ The accountant found a <u>glaring</u> mistake in the company records.

4 **instrument** **1.** a person or thing used to get something done **2.** a tool for doing exact work **3.** a device used in making musical sounds **4.** a legal paper by means of which some action is carried out

_3_ My sister plays an <u>instrument</u> in the school band.

_4_ A lawyer can prepare a legal <u>instrument</u> such as a deed or will.

_2_ A dentist uses a special <u>instrument</u> to clean teeth.

(180) Lesson 82
Definitions

SPELLING

Write the spelling words _third, knight, angriest, instrument, unusual, desert, soil, respell, employ, poisonous_ on the board. Have students see how many different words they can spell using some or all of the letters of each word. If a letter appears only once in the chosen word, then it can be used only once in any new word.

WRITING

Portfolio **Materials:** newspapers, magazines, dictionaries

Have students identify three new words in an article, copy the sentence for each, then look up the word in a dictionary and identify and write its meaning as used. Students can then write an article on a related topic using the three words.

ART/LANGUAGE ARTS

Materials: poster paper, markers, crayons

Students can work in small groups to make how-to posters explaining how to locate words in the dictionary. Posters should include alphabetical order, guide words, identifying entry words, and choosing the correct definition.

SOCIAL STUDIES

Materials: dictionaries with word histories

Tell students that long ago, news bulletins were posted in public places. Then came a time in Venice, Italy, when people paid one _gazeta_ to read the paper. Have students answer these questions about _gazettes_.

1. What is the entry word for _gazettes_?
2. What is its meaning?
3. What is the meaning of the Italian word from which _gazette_ comes?

AUDITORY LEARNERS

LARGE GROUP
Say each of these words in turn and have students name the word they would look for as an entry word: _knives, hope, blanketed, dissatisfied, stopping, standard, campaign, miserably, canteen, dried, pebbles, crazier._

GIFTED LEARNERS

Materials: at least two different dictionaries

Have students write a dictionary review that compares two dictionaries. Suggest that they look at what kind of information each contains, whether entry words are presented differently, and how definitions are worded. Ask volunteers to share their reviews with the class.

LEARNERS WHO NEED EXTRA SUPPORT

Materials: dictionary

Have students look up the words they have difficulty with in items 1–16 on page 179. Actually using the dictionary may help them better understand how to identify a base word entry. See Daily Word Study Practice, page 207.

Lesson 83

Pages 181–182

Definitions and Homographs

✳ ● ◦ ● ◦ ◆ ◦ ● ◦ ◆ ◦ ● ◦ ◦ ●

INFORMAL ASSESSMENT OBJECTIVES

Can students

✓ choose correct dictionary definitions?

✓ identify meanings of words that have like spellings?

Lesson Focus

INTRODUCING THE SKILL

Materials: dictionary

● Write this dictionary entry on the board.

grade 1. a school division **2.** test mark or score **3.** slope of a road

● Read aloud this sentence: *Jesse is in the fourth grade.* Ask students which definition of *grade* was used. *(1)* Discuss how dictionary meanings can be used to figure out the meaning.

● Next find the word *row* in a dictionary. Display the three entries. Point out the superscript numbers and explain that the numbers show homographs, or words that are spelled and often pronounced the same way but that have different meanings and origins.

USING THE PAGES

● Be sure students understand how to complete pages 181 and 182. When they have finished working, call on a volunteer to summarize what he or she has learned about homographs.

● **Critical Thinking** Have students read the question at the bottom of page 182 and discuss their responses.

181

Name _____

▶ Read the dictionary entries. Then choose one of the words to complete each sentence below. Write the word and the correct definition number on the line.

beyond 1 on the far side of: farther away than **2** later than **3** outside the reach or power of **4** more or better than
edge 1 the sharp, cutting part **2** the line or part where something ends **3** the brink
favor 1 a helpful or kind action **2** liking or approval **3** a small souvenir
groove 1 a long and narrow hollow, cut or worn in a surface **2** the track cut in a phonograph record for the needle to follow **3** a regular way of doing something as by habit

hutch 1 a pen or coop for small animals **2** a chest for storing things **3** a china cabinet with open shelves on top
level 1 with no part higher than any other part; flat and even **2** as high as something else **3** not excited or confused
paw 1 to touch, dig, or hit with the paws or feet **2** to handle in a rough and clumsy way
range 1 a row or line of connected mountains **2** open land over which cattle graze **3** a cooking stove

1. Dad was hanging a picture next to the ____hutch 3____ in the dining room.
2. He asked Dan to do him a ____favor 1____ and get a hammer.
3. There was a hammer in the kitchen next to the ____range 3____.
4. Before Dad hung the picture, he asked Dan if it was ____level 1____.
5. Dan set the hammer on the ____edge 3____ of the table, and it fell.
6. Dad tried to pick it up, but it was ____beyond 3____ his reach.
7. Dan was upset because the hammer made a ____groove 1____ in the floor.

Lesson 83
Definitions **181**

FOCUS ON ALL LEARNERS ✳ ● ◦ ◆ ◦ ●

ENGLISH LANGUAGE LEARNERS/ESL

To build background for the story on page 182, ask volunteers to share times when an older family member or friend helped them fix something, such as a bike, or plan something, such as a garden. Discuss things older people can teach young people.

VISUAL LEARNERS

PARTNER **Materials:** dictionary

Suggest that pairs look through a dictionary and find as many homographs as they can. Have them write the homographs and their meanings. Encourage students to add the homographs they found to their personal word bank, if they are keeping one.

KINESTHETIC/VISUAL LEARNERS

SMALL GROUP **Materials:** dictionary

On the board, write the words *pen, match, lap, jet, swallow,* and *tend.* Each group member, in turn, chooses a word and writes a sentence for it. Other group members look up the word and decide which meaning it has in the sentence.

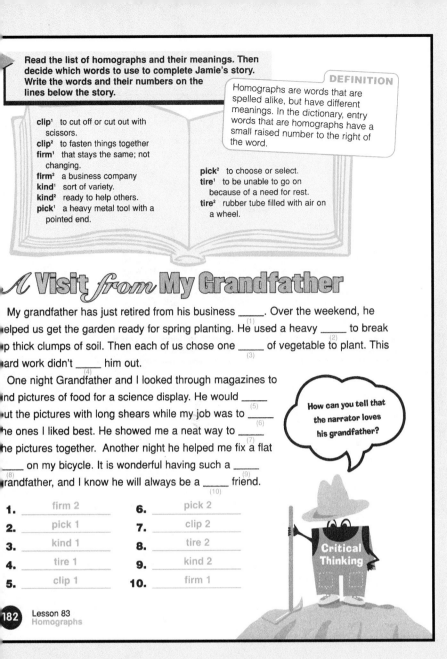

Read the list of homographs and their meanings. Then decide which words to use to complete Jamie's story. Write the words and their numbers on the lines below the story.

DEFINITION

Homographs are words that are spelled alike, but have different meanings. In the dictionary, entry words that are homographs have a small raised number to the right of the word.

clip¹ to cut off or cut out with scissors.
clip² to fasten things together
firm¹ that stays the same; not changing.
firm² a business company
kind¹ sort of variety.
kind² ready to help others.
pick¹ a heavy metal tool with a pointed end.

pick² to choose or select.
tire¹ to be unable to go on because of a need for rest.
tire² rubber tube filled with air on a wheel.

A Visit from My Grandfather

My grandfather has just retired from his business _____. Over the weekend, he helped us get the garden ready for spring planting. He used a heavy _____ to break up thick clumps of soil. Then each of us chose one _____ of vegetable to plant. This hard work didn't _____ him out.

One night Grandfather and I looked through magazines to find pictures of food for a science display. He would _____ out the pictures with long shears while my job was to _____ the ones I liked best. He showed me a neat way to _____ the pictures together. Another night he helped me fix a flat _____ on my bicycle. It is wonderful having such a _____ grandfather, and I know he will always be a _____ friend.

(1) (2) (3) (4) (5) (6) (7) (8) (9) (10)

How can you tell that the narrator loves his grandfather?

Critical Thinking

1. firm 2
2. pick 1
3. kind 1
4. tire 1
5. clip 1
6. pick 2
7. clip 2
8. tire 2
9. kind 2
10. firm 1

182 Lesson 83
Homographs

SPELLING

Materials: lists of the spelling words *third, knight, angriest, instrument, unusual, desert, soil, respell, employ, poisonous*

Provide pairs with a list of the spelling words and have them take turns quizzing each other on the spelling of each. Words can be spelled orally or written. Encourage the tester to use each word in a sentence.

WRITING

Portfolio Invite students to write about someone they know and admire very much. Encourage them to tell what they like about the person and what the person has done to win their admiration. When students have finished, suggest that they list any homographs they used.

LANGUAGE ARTS

Write the words *skirt, pants, tie, boot, coat, cap,* and *sweats* on the board. Have students make a chart listing each article of clothing in the first column, another meaning for the word in a second, and the part of speech of the new meaning in the third.

SCIENCE

Materials: levels, dictionary

Have students use the dictionary to find another meaning for *level,* different from the ones given on page 181. Then introduce them to the level and have them experiment to discover how it works. Have them speculate on how it could be used.

AUDITORY LEARNERS

LARGE GROUP Volunteers choose a homograph pair and say a sentence for each meaning, clapping instead of saying the word. Classmates guess what the missing word is; for example, *I (clap) tools carefully. This (clap) will help me break up hard earth. (pick)*

GIFTED LEARNERS

Challenge students to use both meanings of each homograph pair from the lesson (or others of their choosing) in the same sentence; for example, *The head of the firm spoke in a firm voice.*

LEARNERS WHO NEED EXTRA SUPPORT

Materials: dictionary

Locate entries for homographs in the dictionary with students. Point out the example sentences that can help them understand the meanings. See Daily Word Study Practice, page 207.

Lesson 84

Pages 183–184

Different Spellings for the Same Sound

INFORMAL ASSESSMENT OBJECTIVES

Can students

✔ recognize that the same sound can have different spellings?

✔ use the dictionary pronunciation key to identify correct pronunciation of entry words?

Lesson Focus

INTRODUCING THE SKILL

- Write *key, cab, chorus,* and *duck* on the board and invite volunteers to read the words aloud. Ask how the words are alike. (k *sound*) Have students tell how the sound of *k* is spelled. (*k, c, ch, ck*)

- Explain that dictionaries have a key showing how different sounds are spelled. Write this example, highlighting the boldfaced letters with a colored chalk: /k/ *kite, walk, can, account, luck, chrome, lacquer, biscuit, liquor.* Point out that students could use the different spellings for /k/ to figure out how a word such as *chorus* is spelled.

- Write *man' ij.* Have a volunteer read it. Explain that this respelling appears with the entry word *manage* to show how it is pronounced.

USING THE PAGES

- After students have finished pages 183 and 184, encourage them to discuss what they have learned.

- Make sure that students understand that if they learn to use the symbols and sounds in a pronunciation key, they can pronounce any word.

183

Name _____

The beginning sound in **choir** is **k** as in **keep**. Find **k** in the first column and look over to the next column to find words that have different spellings of the **k** sound. After you find the correct letter combinations for the beginning of a word, you should be able to find the word.

> **HINT**
> Every dictionary has a pronunciation key that shows various spellings for different sounds.

Pronunciation Key
consonant sounds

d	nod, ri**dd**le, calle**d**	l	leave, call, island
f	fix, di**ff**erent, lau**gh**, **ph**one, cal**f**	m	drum, dru**mm**er, lim**b**, hy**mn**, cal**m**
g	give, e**gg**, **gh**ost, **g**uard	n	near, di**nn**er, **gn**ome, **kn**eel, **pn**eumonia
h	her, **w**ho	n	long, think, tongue
j	jam, gem, exa**gg**erate, gra**d**uate, sol**d**ier, ju**dg**ment, a**dj**ust	p	hop, di**pp**er
		r	river, be**rr**y, **rh**yme, **w**rong
k	kite, wal**k**, **c**an, a**cc**ount, **ch**rome, lu**ck**, la**cq**uer, bis**c**uit, li**q**uor	s	sit, mi**ss**, **sc**ience, **c**ent, **ps**ychology, **sch**ism

▶ **Use the pronunciation key above to help you circle the correct spelling. You may also need to check a dictionary.**

1. Find a word that rhymes with **pail** and means "a small wild bird."
   (quail)   kwail   chwail

2. Find a word that rhymes with **ham** and means "a baby sheep."
   lam   (lamb)   lalm

3. Find a word that rhymes with **best** and means "a visitor."
   gest   thest   (guest)

4. Find a word that rhymes with **bat** and means "a small flying insect."
   (gnat)   nat   pant

5. Find a word that rhymes with **string** and means "to twist with force."
   rhing   (wring)   ring

6. Find a word that rhymes with **went** and means "a smell, an odor."
   cent   sent   (scent)

7. Find a word that rhymes with **craze** and means "disturb or upset."
   phase   (faze)   fase

Lesson 84
Different spellings for the same sound

183

FOCUS ON ALL LEARNERS

ENGLISH LANGUAGE LEARNERS/ESL

Because the riddles on page 184 rely on words or expressions with two meanings, students learning English may find them confusing. You may need to explain both meanings in each item before having students work independently.

VISUAL/AUDITORY LEARNERS

PARTNER   **Materials:** dictionaries

Invite partners to each choose ten words they have studied in this unit, find each word in the dictionary, and copy the respelling only. Then have them trade papers and use the pronunciation key to write the word for each respelling.

KINESTHETIC LEARNERS

SMALL GROUP   **Materials:** index cards, markers, bag

Make cards for several of the symbols in the pronunciation key. Place them in a bag and have students take turns drawing a card, saying a word that has that sound, and replacing the card in the bag.

The **respelling** that follows a dictionary entry shows you how to pronounce the word. The dictionary **pronunciation key** can help you pronounce each sound shown in the respelling.

Pronunciation Key

Symbol	Key Words	Symbol	Key Words	Symbol	Key Words
	bed	m	meat	y	yard
	dog	n	nose	z	zebra
	fall	p	put	ch	chin, arch
	get	r	red	ŋ	ring, drink
	help	s	see, circle	sh	she, push
	jump, gym	t	top	th	thin, truth
	kiss, call	v	vat	*th*	then, father
	leg	w	wish	zh	measure

Study the consonant sounds above taken from a dictionary pronunciation key. Then read each riddle. Use the pronunciation key to help you say each respelling that answers the riddle. Then write each word from the word bank on the line beside its respelling.

clock	glove	scales	comb	holes	crane
light	rose	fence	quick	lettuce	ice

1. What goes around a yard but doesn't move?

   a fens _____ fence

2. What can lie in a bed but can't sleep?

   a rōz _____ rose

3. What has two hands but no arms?

   a klok _____ clock

4. What bird can lift the most?

   a krān _____ crane

5. What can go through water without getting wet?

   lit _____ light

6. What is the hardest thing about learning to skate?

   the is _____ ice

7. What has teeth but no mouth?

   a kōm _____ comb

8. What has a head but no brain?

   letis _____ lettuce

AUDITORY LEARNERS

SMALL GROUP

Materials: index cards, markers

Make and display cards for the symbols *f, n, j, r, k, b, m, sh, z, ch, l.* Read these words aloud: *back, phone, giraffe, tobacco, enough, knife, mission, shameful, nose, cozy.* Have students take turns selecting the symbols for the consonant sounds in each word.

GIFTED LEARNERS

Materials: dictionaries

Have students look up these words and learn how to pronounce them correctly, using the dictionary's phonetic respellings: *cuisine, parquet, travois, meander, emirate, atrophy, campanile.* Have them make up and say a sentence using each word.

LEARNERS WHO NEED EXTRA SUPPORT

Students may be confused by the lesson's terminology, so be sure to make clear the differences among *sound, symbol,* and *letter.* For example: the symbol *k* stands for /k/; this sound can be spelled with the letters *k, lk, c, ck, cc, ch, cq, cu,* or *qu.* See Daily Word Study Practice, page 208.

CURRICULUM CONNECTIONS

SPELLING

Write these words on the board: *third, knight, angriest, instrument, unusual, desert, soil, respell, employ, poisonous.* Read these clues and have students orally spell the word that completes each set.

1. odd, strange, _____ (*unusual*)
2. warrior, soldier, _____ (*knight*)
3. spell over, spell again, _____ (*respell*)
4. first, second, _____ (*third*)
5. leave, abandon, _____ (*desert*)
6. dirt, earth, _____ (*soil*)
7. harmful, dangerous, _____ (*poisonous*)
8. angry, angrier, _____ (*angriest*)
9. tool, utensil, _____ (*instrument*)
10. engage, hire, _____ (*employ*)

WRITING

Portfolio Invite students to write their own riddles like the ones on page 184. First have the class brainstorm a list of words with more than one meaning. After each student has written a riddle, let the class compile them to make a riddle booklet.

LANGUAGE ARTS

Explain that many words have more than one correct pronunciation. Write the words *Caribbean Sea.* Have students read the words aloud and point out any inconsistencies in pronunciation. Have students locate the entry in a dictionary and note that there are two acceptable pronunciations: kar´ ə bē´ ən and kə rib´ ē ən. Then write *pajamas, catsup, Monaco, mobile, Colorado, lever,* and *Pakistan.* Have students locate each word in the dictionary and use the respellings to pronounce the words.

PHYSICAL EDUCATION

Write on the board the following sports terms: *soccer, high jump, marathon, ice skating, hockey, bicycling, gymnastics, boxing, equestrian.* Ask questions such as these: *Which words' respellings have the symbol ŋ?* (*skating, bicycling, boxing*) *Which word has /kw/?* (*equestrian*) *Which has /ks/?* (*boxing*) *Which word has the silent letters gh?* (*high*) Encourage students to add more sports words to the board. Let them challenge each other with questions about consonant sounds and spellings.

Lesson 85

Pages 185–186

The Pronunciation Key

INFORMAL ASSESSMENT OBJECTIVES

Can students

- recognize pronunciation symbols?
- identify correct pronunciation of words?

Lesson Focus

INTRODUCING THE SKILL

- Write these respellings on the board: *dēd, ded; rat, rāt; kit, kīt; kub, kyo͞ob; sak, sāk.* Point to the vowel in the first word. Tell students that this symbol over the vowel, a straight line, indicates a long sound.
- Then encourage students to pronounce each respelling and to name the word it represents. (*deed, dead; rat, rate; kit, kite; cub, cube; sack, sake*)
- Explain that a pronunciation key includes irregularly pronounced vowels, too. Write these examples: *er berry, care; ir mirror, here; ô law, horn; ou out, crowd; ur fur, fern.*
- Write these respellings and ask students to use the examples to identify the words they represent: *strô´ber´ē, stir, doun´fôl, kʉr´nəl. (strawberry, steer, downfall, kernel)*

USING THE PAGES

Make sure students understand how to complete pages 185 and 186. When they have completed the pages, review the pronunciation key with them and correct the papers together.

Name

Study the long and short vowel sounds from a dictionary pronunciation key. Pronounce each example word and listen for the vowel sound.

HINT In the last lesson you worked with the consonant section of a dictionary pronunciation key. Every pronunciation key also has a vowel section.

Pronunciation Key

Symbol	Key Words	Symbol	Key Words
a	cat	i	fit, here
ā	ape	ī	ice, fire
e	ten, berry	ō	go
ē	me	u	up

Read the respellings below. Each one contains a symbol from the key above. Beside each respelling, write the example words from the pronunciation key that show you how to pronounce the symbol. Write the entry word for each respelling.

1. (tīr)	ice, fire	tire
2. (grēt)	me	greet
3. (lāt)	ape	late
4. (mis)	fit, here	miss
5. (stōv)	go	stove
6. (plāt)	ape	plate
7. (pas)	cat	pass
8. (fus)	up	fuss
9. (bred)	ten, berry	bread
10. (mīs)	ice, fire	mice
11. (bluf)	up	bluff
12. (krēm)	me	cream
13. (stik)	fit, here	stick
14. (smel)	ten, berry	smell

© MCP All rights reserved.

FOCUS ON ALL LEARNERS

ENGLISH LANGUAGE LEARNERS/ESL

Before students begin working, say the key word on both pages and have students repeat them. Ask them to read the words in the word bank on page 186 aloud to be sure they are pronouncing them correctly.

VISUAL LEARNERS

LARGE GROUP

Materials: dictionaries

Write this question on the board: *Kan yo͞o i maj´ in a dī´ nə sôr in our sko͞ol?* Students use the pronunciation key to decipher the question. Encourage them to write other messages for classmates to decipher.

KINESTHETIC LEARNERS

SMALL GROUP

Materials: dictionaries, index cards

Each student chooses a word from the dictionary and copies its respelling carefully on a card. Collect the cards, shuffle them, and divide them equally among teams, who work together to identify the words. The team that finishes first with the most correctly identified words wins.

Study more vowel sounds taken from a dictionary pronunciation key. Pronounce each example word and listen for the vowel sound.

HINT
In addition to long and short vowel sounds, the pronunciation key also contains other vowel sounds.

Pronunciation Key

Symbol	Key Words	Symbol	Key Words
ä	cot, car	ʉ	fur, shirt
ô	fall, for	ə	a in ago
oi	oil		e in agent
ʘʘ	look, pull		i in pencil
ōō	tool, rule		o in atom
ou	out, crowd		u in circus

Use the pronunciation key to help you say each respelling. Then write each word from the word bank on the line beside its respelling.

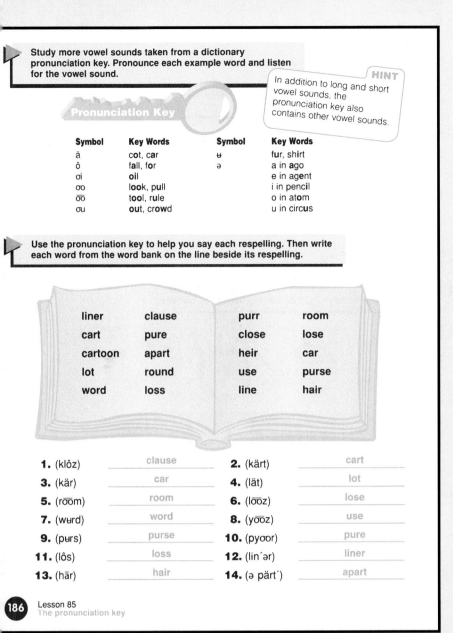

liner	clause	purr	room
cart	pure	close	lose
cartoon	apart	heir	car
lot	round	use	purse
word	loss	line	hair

1. (klôz) _clause_   2. (kärt) _cart_
3. (kär) _car_   4. (lät) _lot_
5. (rōōm) _room_   6. (lōōz) _lose_
7. (wʉrd) _word_   8. (yōōz) _use_
9. (pʉrs) _purse_   10. (pyʘor) _pure_
11. (lôs) _loss_   12. (lin´ər) _liner_
13. (här) _hair_   14. (ə pärt´) _apart_

186 Lesson 85
The pronunciation key

LARGE GROUP

AUDITORY LEARNERS
Materials: dictionary

Write these respellings on the board: kāk, tīm, hiz, wēp, hät, gum, bak, rōōt. Have students guess each word. Then, while a volunteer checks it in the dictionary, the group offers as many words that rhyme with the word as they can.

GIFTED LEARNER
Materials: dictionary

Introduce students to the term *diacritical marks*. Have them use the dictionary to discover what it means, then identify such commonly used diacritical markings as acute and grave accents, dieresis, circumflex, tilde, cedilla, macron, and breve.

LEARNERS WHO NEED EXTRA SUPPORT
Materials: dictionary

Help students name other words with the same vowel sounds as the examples given in the pronunciation key on pages 185 and 186. See *Daily Word Study Practice, page 208.*

CURRICULUM CONNECTIONS

SPELLING
Materials: a beanbag; list of the spelling words *third, knight, angriest, instrument, unusual, desert, soil, respell, employ, poisonous*

Have students stand in a circle and pass the beanbag. When you say *Stop,* the person holding the beanbag must spell the word you say. As soon as you say the word, the beanbag goes back into circulation. The speller must spell the word correctly before it returns to him or her.

WRITING
Portfolio **Materials:** dictionaries, posterboard, markers

Invite students to use the pronunciation key in the dictionary to encode their names and addresses as a respelling. Suggest that they encode other family members' names and make a name tag for each person with his or her name respelled.

SCIENCE

Write the following on the board: griz´ lē ber; bôld ē´gəl; grā hwāl; jī´ ənt pan´də; bäb´hwīt; kräk´ ə dīl. (grizzly bear, bald eagle, gray whale, giant panda, bobwhite, crocodile) Have students decode each, then relist the animals into categories and add the respellings of other animal names to each category.

SOCIAL STUDIES
Materials: posterboard, different-colored markers

The special characters in pronunciation keys are symbols, as words are. Ask students to make a poster of the symbols and signs used along streets and highways. Encourage students to include examples of different kinds of signs as well as an explanation of how their shapes are also symbolic.

Lesson 86

Pages 187–188

Accent Marks

INFORMAL ASSESSMENT OBJECTIVES

Can students

- understand the use of accent marks to indicate stressed syllables?

- recognize pronunciation symbols?

- identify the correct definition of words based on their pronunciation?

Lesson Focus

INTRODUCING THE SKILL

- Write *forward, forget,* and *formality* on the board. Have students say *forward.* Ask what syllable was said in a stronger voice. Say the word again, stressing the first syllable. Repeat these steps with *forget* and *formality,* stressing the second syllables.

- Have students look up the words in their dictionaries. Invite students to identify the clue in the respellings that shows which syllable is said more strongly. (*the accent mark*)

- Explain that in a word with two or more syllables, one syllable is accented more strongly than the others. In the dictionary an accent mark is placed after this syllable.

USING THE PAGES

Make sure students understand what to do on pages 187 and 188. After they complete the pages, invite them to discuss what they know about accent marks.

187

Name

For each word below, the respelling is shown. Place the accent mark where it belongs. You may check your dictionary, if necessary.

HINT
In a word with two or more syllables, one syllable is **accented** or **stressed** more than the others. In the dictionary, an accent mark (´) is placed after the syllable that is said with more stress.

da´ līt (daylight)

den´ tist (dentist)

i las´ tik (elastic)

1. iceberg (īs´ bʉrg)
2. event (ə vent´)
3. deny (dē nī´)
4. jacket (jack´ ət)
5. obey (ō bā´)
6. office (ôf´ is)
7. relieve (rē lēv´)
8. harvest (här´ vəst)
9. ruin (ro͞o´ in)
10. invite (in vīt´)

Read each sentence. Circle the respelling of the underlined word that makes sense in the sentence.

HINT
Sometimes a word can be pronounced in different ways depending on its meaning. In this case, the accent may shift to another syllable.

11. Olivia's favorite birthday <u>present</u> was a new bike.

prez´ ənt
pre zent´

12. She also liked the <u>record</u> of her favorite song.

re kôrd´
rek´ ərd

13. Her sister gave her a puzzle with a picture of a sandy <u>desert</u>.

də zurt´
dez´ ərt

14. Her big <u>project</u> now is to write thank you notes.

prä´ jekt
prə jekt´

FOCUS ON ALL LEARNERS

ENGLISH LANGUAGE LEARNERS/ESL

Pronounce the words in the first activity on page 187 for students before they begin. Make sure students see that for items 11–14 the look-alike respellings in each pair are actually two different words—the spelling is exactly the same but the pronunciations and meanings are different.

VISUAL LEARNERS

SMALL GROUP Write *1* on a pink card and *2* on a white card for each student. Display sentences like these, one at a time: *I object to your plan. Jesse set a world <u>record</u>. I won't <u>desert</u> you.* Ask students to read the sentence silently and then hold up the card telling which syllable in the underlined word is stressed—syllable 1 or 2.

KINESTHETIC LEARNERS

LARGE GROUP Write these words on the board: *present, project, desert, refuse, record, object.* Say a sentence using one of the words, and have a volunteer come up and place a colored accent mark on the correct syllable. Repeat until both pronunciations of each word have been used.

> **Read the passage. Choose the word from the word bank that will complete each sentence. Write the word on the line. You will use each word twice.**

"Just look at all the ___refuse___₁ in the park!" the ranger said. "Each ___object___₂ was carelessly thrown away by some litterbug. At ___present___₃ the park is dangerous and unhealthy. Does anyone here ___object___₄ to picking up trash?"

present	refuse
record	object

"No!" they said. "We won't ___refuse___₅ to help."

"Great!" said the ranger. "Let's try to set a speed ___record___₆ for cleaning up the park. The town will ___present___₇ prizes to the volunteers who collect the most trash. I'll ___record___₈ the number of bags each of you turns in."

> **Read the passage again. For each word you wrote, find and circle the correct respelling below.**

9		10		11		12	
refuse	(ref´ yooz) ri fyooz´	object	ob jekt´ (ob´jekt)	present	prē zent´ (prez´ənt)	object	(ob´ jekt´) ob´jekt

13		14		15		16	
refuse	ref´yooz (ri fyooz´)	record	(rek´ ərd) ri kôrd´	present	(prē zent´) prez´ənt	record	rek´ərd (ri kôrd´)

SPELLING

Write these words on the board, leaving random blanks for some of the letters: *employ, respell, desert, soil, poisonous, angriest, unusual, instrument, third, knight.* Use *employ* as an example and have a volunteer complete it: __ m p l __ __. Call on students to come to the board and fill in the missing letters to spell the other words correctly.

WRITING

Portfolio Have students imagine they have been presented with a wonderful present on their birthday. Have them decide what it is and who gave it to them. Then ask them to write a thank-you note for the present, using a few of the lesson words in their note.

SOCIAL STUDIES

Materials: dictionaries

Write *Oaxaca* on the board and explain that it is the name of a city in south central Mexico. Ask students how they think the name is pronounced. Write the respelling *wä hä´ kä.* Point out how the accent mark helps with the pronunciation. Invite students to browse through a pronunciation gazetteer in the back of a standard dictionary. Have them collect some interesting names of places and geographical features that they don't know how to pronounce and then write the names they chose along with their phonetic respellings.

MATH/SOCIAL STUDIES

Materials: plastic bags, chart paper, markers

Making a tally table is a good way to keep a record. Have students document the kinds of refuse they can find on the school grounds. Provide plastic bags and ask them to collect litter for 15 minutes. When the time is up, have them record each item they found in a table with the headings *Metal, Plastic, Paper,* and *Glass.*

AUDITORY LEARNERS

PARTNER Provide each pair of students with these words: *object, present, desert, refuse, record.* Have partners take turns pronouncing one of the words in one of its two correct ways. The other partner then uses that pronunciation of the word in a sentence.

GIFTED LEARNERS

Explain that respellings may include two kinds of accent marks—heavy and light. Point out that syllables with light marks are stressed too, but not as much. Have students use a dictionary to find ten words with more than one accent mark, write the words and respellings, and say the words.

LEARNERS WHO NEED EXTRA SUPPORT

Point out that all the look-alike words in this lesson that are accented on the first syllable are nouns and all those accented on the second syllable are verbs. Explain that knowing this will help them pronounce words correctly when reading aloud. See Daily Word Study Practice, page 208.

188

Lesson 87

Pages 189–190

 **R**eading  **W**riting

Synonyms, Antonyms, Homonyms, Alphabetical Order, and Dictionary Skills

Lesson Focus

READING

● Write on the board *reside, live* and *roasting, frigid*. Have students tell you the relationship of words in each pair. (*synonyms; antonyms*)

● Write the words *waste, waist*. Ask what these words are called. (*homonyms*)

● Write *desert (arid region) and desert (to leave behind)*. Ask what these words are called. (*homographs*)

● Write *saguaro, Sonoran, Papago, Kalahari*. Ask students how they can learn to spell and pronounce these words.

● Explain that as students read the passage on 189, they will be reading many more synonyms, antonyms, homonyms, and homographs.

WRITING

As students prepare to write their E-mail letter on page 180, refer them to the Helpful Hints.

 189

As students prepare to write their E-mail letter on page 180, refer them to the Helpful Hints.

Name _____

 Reading ▶ Read the passage. Then write your answer to the question at the end of the passage.

Deserts: HOT or COLD?

What do you think of when you hear the word *desert*? Probably you picture a hot, sandy, dry place with no water, not even a drop of dew. That describes some deserts, but not all.

The definition of a desert is an area that receives less than ten inches of rainfall a year. That includes the hot, arid reaches of the North African Sahara, where daytime temperatures reach 120°F. It also includes the frigid, icy continent of Antarctica, where winter temperatures drop to -70°F! Even deserts that are roasting during the day can be cold at night. A temperature drop of more than 60° between midday and midnight is not uncommon.

A desert is not a deserted place. Where there is even a small amount of moisture, cactus and other desert plants can grow. When the quantity of water is greater, animals live and flourish, too. Many kinds of snakes, lizards, small mammals, birds, and insects reside in the sandy wastes of deserts.

Deserts are also home to people. In the Sonoran Desert of the American Southwest, there is enough moisture for water-storing plants, such as the saguaro cactus, to thrive. For the Papago people who live there, the fruit of the saguaro is an important food source. In Tibet, the world's highest desert, the ground might look bare, but the soil can bear enough plants to feed the goats, sheep, and yaks kept by herders.

If you were going to spend time in a desert, what five things would you take with you and why?

_____

_____

_____

Synonyms, antonyms, homonyms, dictionary skills: Reading

Lesson 87 **189**

FOCUS ON ALL LEARNERS

ENGLISH LANGUAGE LEARNERS/ESL

To build background for students before they read the passage on page 189, ask if anyone has ever visited a desert or seen a television show about the desert. Invite students to imagine what it would be like in the desert.

VISUAL LEARNERS

PARTNER Write these words on the board and ask pairs of students to alphabetize them: *eight, every, full, empty, faith, fast, easily, frequently, east, extra, evening, fragile, filthy, expect, fried, friend, elephant, elegant, easel*. Have pairs share and compare their completed lists, using a dictionary to confirm accuracy.

KINESTHETIC LEARNERS

INDIVIDUAL **Materials:** drawing paper, markers, crayons

Have students draw and label pictures to illustrate the similarity or difference between each of these word pairs: *refuse, refuse; piece, peace; slow, fast; loves, adores*. Ask students to label their completed pictures *synonyms, antonyms, homonyms*, or *homographs*, as appropriate.

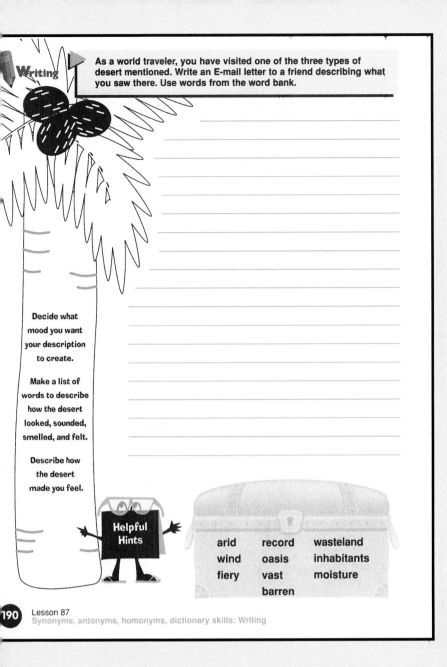

Writing

As a world traveler, you have visited one of the three types of desert mentioned. Write an E-mail letter to a friend describing what you saw there. Use words from the word bank.

Decide what mood you want your description to create.

Make a list of words to describe how the desert looked, sounded, smelled, and felt.

Describe how the desert made you feel.

Helpful Hints

arid	record	wasteland
wind	oasis	inhabitants
fiery	vast	moisture
	barren	

SPELLING

The following sentences can be used as a spelling posttest for synonyms, antonyms, and homonyms.

1. **desert** — I need you, so please don't **desert** me!
2. **instrument** — Jin plays a keyboard **instrument**.
3. **poisonous** — Some cleansers are **poisonous**.
4. **third** — Earth is the **third** planet from the Sun.
5. **angriest** — This is the **angriest** I've ever been!
6. **soil** — Rich **soil** helps vegetables grow.
7. **unusual** — Tilly found an **unusual** green stone.
8. **respell** — Let me **respell** my name for you.
9. **employ** — My bosses **employ** three workers.
10. **knight** — The **knight** wore a suit of armor.

SCIENCE

Portfolio

Materials: index cards, markers

Have students find out what kinds of creatures besides the antelope live in the Kalahari Desert (*giraffe, lion, impala, gemsbok, wildebeest, jackal, hyena,* and so on). Then invite students to create a trading card for each kind of animal, drawing a picture of the animal on the front and listing facts about it on the back of the card.

SOCIAL STUDIES

Tohono O odham means "Desert People." Ask students to research this Native American nation (called the Papago, Bean Eaters, by early explorers). How have they survived in the harsh desert environment?

AUDITORY/VISUAL LEARNERS

LARGE GROUP

Write on the board the following headings: *Synonyms, Antonyms, Homonyms, Homographs.* Say pairs of words from this lesson or other pairs that fit the categories and have volunteers write each pair under the appropriate heading.

GIFTED LEARNERS

Materials: identical dictionaries for each student, index cards

Have each student choose a target word at random in the dictionary. On a card he or she should write the two guide words on the word's page and also copy the word's phonetic respelling. Have students exchange cards and see who can find the target word first.

LEARNERS WHO NEED EXTRA SUPPORT

Ask students to paraphrase the information about each kind of desert and choose the desert they will write about before they proceed to write their E-mail messages. See Daily Word Study Practice, pages 206–208.

Lesson 88

Pages 191–192

Unit Checkup

Reviewing Synonyms, Antonyms, Homonyms, and Dictionary Skills

Name _____

Read each sentence. Decide whether the two underlined words are synonyms, antonyms, or homonyms. Fill in the circle beside your choice.

1. Tina <u>read</u> a book called The <u>Red</u> **Shawl** for school.
   ○ synonyms   ○ antonyms   ● homonyms

2. The story was about an <u>elderly</u> woman and her <u>young</u> granddaughter.
   ○ synonyms   ● antonyms   ○ homonyms

3. They <u>would</u> often sit on the <u>wood</u> porch swing and talk.
   ○ synonyms   ○ antonyms   ● homonyms

4. <u>Whether</u> the <u>weather</u> was cloudy or not, Grandma always wore a red shawl.
   ○ synonyms   ○ antonyms   ● homonyms

5. Grandma told Tina <u>amazing</u> stories about her <u>wonderful</u> life.
   ● synonyms   ○ antonyms   ○ homonyms

6. As a young woman, Grandma had gone to <u>sea</u> to <u>see</u> the world.
   ○ synonyms   ○ antonyms   ● homonyms

7. She had bought the <u>lovely</u> red shawl in a <u>beautiful</u> seaside town.
   ● synonyms   ○ antonyms   ○ homonyms

8. The red shawl helped her <u>remember</u> adventures she never wanted to <u>forget</u>.
   ○ synonyms   ● antonyms   ○ homonyms

Read each sentence. Fill in the circle next to the respelling of the underlined word that makes sense in the sentence.

9. The explorer looked out over the vast sandy <u>desert</u>.
   ○ di zûrt′   ● dez′ ərt

10. The searing hot <u>wind</u> scorched his face.
    ● wind   ○ wīnd

11. His research <u>project</u> had taken him to many amazing places.
    ● prä′ jekt   ○ prə jekt′

12. He had come <u>close</u> to danger many times.
    ○ kloz   ● klōs

Lesson 88   **191**
Synonyms, antonyms, homonyms, dictionary skills: Checkup

© MCP All rights reserved. Copying strictly prohibited.

Lesson Focus

PREPARING FOR THE CHECKUP

- Write on the board the word pairs *odd, strange; thick, thin; burro, burrow;* and *close (near), close (to shut).* Ask students to read each word pair aloud and tell what kind of words are in each pair. (*synonyms, antonyms, homonyms, homographs*) Have students define each term.

- Ask volunteers to find several words in a dictionary and name the guide words on the page, copy each word's respelling onto the board, and pronounce the words.

USING THE PAGES

- Make sure students understand what to do on pages 191 and 192. Before students begin to read the passage on page 192, talk about how Australia's isolation led to the development of animals unlike those anywhere else in the world.

- When students have completed both pages, call on volunteers in turn to tell what they learned about synonyms, antonyms, homonyms, homographs, and dictionary skills.

191

FOCUS ON ALL LEARNERS

ENGLISH LANGUAGE LEARNERS/ESL

Talk with students about the pictures on page 192 before reading "An Animal Oddity." If possible, show photographs of a platypus, duck, mole, and beaver to help students make comparisons. Explain vocabulary such as *rudder, burrow, shovel,* and *spur.*

VISUAL LEARNERS

PARTNER   Duplicate and distribute these analogies for partners to complete, using words with the same kind of relationship: *Nice is to pleasant as . . .; Depart is to leave as . . . ; In is to out as . . . ; House is to home as . . . ; Capture is to release as . . . ; Now is to later as . . . ; Huge is to tiny as . . . .*

KINESTHETIC LEARNERS

SMALL GROUP   **Materials:** index cards, markers

Make cards for these homographs (and perhaps others as well): *wind, tear, does, bow, wound, close, read, use.* Have students take turns drawing a homograph and then using each of its pronunciations in an oral sentence; for example, *I wind my watch. The wind blew.*

> Read the passage and answer the questions.

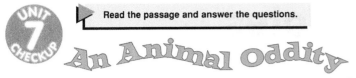

An Animal Oddity

When European scientists first saw the skin of an Australian platypus in 1797, they were convinced it was a hoax. They believed the skins of several different animals had been stitched together. It was no trick. The odd and amazing platypus really does look as if a number of animals have been sewn together to create this strange creature! Covered with thick fur as soft as a mole's, the platypus has the bill of a duck, webbed feet, and the tail of a beaver. Even more astonishing, this unusual mammal hatches from an egg!

At dawn and at dusk, the platypus emerges from its burrow near a stream to feed. Using its tail as a rudder, it swims close to the stream bottom. Employing its soft bill as a shovel, it probes in the mud for crayfish, worms, and other creatures to eat. To protect themselves, male platypuses are equipped with poisonous spurs on the ankles of their hind feet. Any animal chasing the small platypus through the water must avoid its poisonous kick. One scratch from a spur can kill a creature as large as a dog!

1. Which word in the passage is a synonym for *hoax*?

trick

2. Why did scientists think the platypus skin was a hoax?

Possible answer: A platypus looks as if several different animals have

been sewn together to make it.

3. Which two words in the passage are synonyms for *odd*?

strange, unusual

4. What meaning does the word *bill* have in this passage?

the horny part of the jaws of a bird

5. Which word in the passage is an antonym for *dawn*?

dusk

6. Find two antonyms in the last two sentences of the passage.

small, large

192 Lesson 88
Synonyms, antonyms, homonyms, dictionary skills: Checkup

Student Progress Assessment You may wish to review the observational notes you made as students worked through the activities in this unit. Your notes will help you evaluate the progress students made with synonyms, antonyms, homonyms, and dictionary skills.

Portfolio Assessment Review the materials students have collected in their portfolios. You may wish to have interviews with students to discuss their written work and the progress they have made since the beginning of the unit. As you review students' work, evaluate how well they use word study skills.

Daily Word Study Practice For students who need additional practice with synonyms, antonyms, homonyms, and dictionary skills, quick reviews are provided on pages 206–208 in Daily Word Study Practice.

Word Study Posttest To assess students' mastery of synonyms, antonyms, homonyms, and dictionary skills, use the posttest on pages 167g–167h.

Spelling Cumulative Posttest Review Unit 7 spelling words by using the following words and dictation sentences.

1. **knight** — Each **knight** bowed to his king.
2. **instrument** — A scalpel is a surgical **instrument**.
3. **respell** — Dictionaries **respell** each entry word.
4. **courageous** — Are you fearful or **courageous**?
5. **desert** — Many animals live in the sandy **desert**.
6. **unusual** — Snow in Florida is most **unusual**.
7. **threw** — We **threw** a party for Mei.
8. **bitter** — Our fight was **bitter**, but it's over now.
9. **poisonous** — Some snakes are **poisonous**.
10. **through** — The rain soaked **through** my jacket.
11. **weather** — How do you like this hot **weather**?
12. **whether** — I don't know **whether** to go or stay.
13. **angriest** — The **angriest** wasp stung my arm.

AUDITORY LEARNERS

LARGE GROUP Say pairs of sentences using homonyms. Have students name the homonyms and then tell what the two words mean, based on the context. An example is *Susan wore a plain dress. We took a plane to Toledo.* (*plain*—*simple*; *plane*—*flying vehicle*)

GIFTED LEARNERS

Materials: drawing paper, markers

Invite students to create silly rebus sentences using homonyms, homographs, and pictures. Brainstorm useful words such as *can, eye, ewe, bee, sea, dew.* Here are a few examples: *[Picture of eye] sea ewe have blew I's. [Picture of can] wee [picture of bee] friends? [Picture of lettuce] go 2 C a show.*

LEARNERS WHO NEED EXTRA SUPPORT

You may want to write the definitions of *synonym, antonym,* and *homonym* on the board for students to refer to as they complete the first activity. See Daily Word Study Practice, pages 206–208.

Teacher Notes

Daily Word Study Practice

Contents

UNIT 1 LESSONS 1–2, 8, 13
Short and Long Vowels

◆ Divide the class into two teams, one each for long and short vowels. Have each team go on a scavenger hunt to search for objects in the classroom whose names have long or short vowel sounds.

◆ Write the words *cap, cut, hop, hat,* and *pin* on the chalkboard. Have students add a silent *e* to change the short vowel sound to a long vowel sound.

◆ Students can create riddles with long or short vowel words. For example: *This word has the long* a *sound. It is a tool you use to put leaves in a pile.* (rake)

◆ Draw a hopscotch pattern on butcher paper and label the squares with long or short vowels. As students play, have them name words with the sounds written in the squares.

◆ Play a version of "Mother, may I?" If you say a long vowel word, have students step forward one step. If you say a short vowel word, have students step forward two steps.

◆ Write words on the chalkboard with long and short vowel sounds. Then have students sort them into two lists, one short and long. Ask them to circle the vowels that make each sound.

◆ Students can make paper chains for long and short vowel words. Have them write long vowel words on red strips and short vowel words on yellow strips and alternate colors.

◆ Make a word ladder and have students make new long and short vowel words by substituting vowels and consonants. Begin with a word such as *map.* (*mope, mole, mile, mail*)

◆ Have students sit in a circle. Say a long or a short vowel word and have students take turns saying words that rhyme with it. Use words such as these: *mail, lock, fit, cone, seal, cube.*

◆ Give students cards with long and short *a, i, e, o,* and *u* on them. As you say a list of words, have them hold up the card that names the vowel sound.

UNIT 1 LESSONS 3–4, 8, 13
Hard and Soft *c* and *g*

◆ Make a spinner with hard *c*, hard *g,* soft *c,* and soft *g* in four sections. Have students spin the spinner and then name a word that has the sound the spinner points to.

◆ Say words with hard and soft *c* and *g*. If you say a word with a soft sound, have students raise one hand. If you say a word with a hard sound, have them stand up.

◆ Have students make a list of words with either the hard or soft sound of *c* or *g*. Then have them create a tongue twister from their list.

◆ Make word cards for hard and soft *c* and *g*. Label bags for each sound and have students sort the words into the four bags.

◆ Students can play tic-tac-toe, substituting hard and soft *c* words for X and O.

Daily Word Study Practice

- Invite students to draw a circus scene, including as many objects as they can that have the hard and soft *c* and *g* sounds. Encourage them to write the words on the back of their papers.

- Make the day a soft *g* day. Have students write soft *g* words on the chalkboard throughout the day. Read their list at the end of the day. Repeat the next day with soft *c*.

UNIT 1 LESSONS 5–8, 13
Blends

- Write this tongue twister on the chalkboard. Challenge students to say it aloud. Then have them circle the consonant blends: *The sleek sled slides on the slightly slippery slope.*

- Say these words: *mask, skate, sink, bright, trip, roast, stripe, slap, coast.* Ask students to stand if the word begins with a blend and raise a hand if the word ends with a blend.

- Write the following words on the chalkboard and have students add a consonant to the beginning to make a new word with a blend: *rip (trip), rap (trap), rag (brag), pan, (plan), lad (glad), cab (crab), sick (stick), win (twin).*

- Scramble phrases with like blends and have students unscramble them and write them, for example, *mapst ytskic (sticky stamp)* or *elub locksb (blue blocks).*

- Write the following incomplete words on the chalkboard and have students fill in the blanks with consonant blends to make words: _ _ *ant,* _ _ *ack,* _ _ *ue,* _ _ *idge, a* _ _, _ _ *ow, de* _ _, *ha* _ _, *re* _ _, *la* _ _.

- Students can pantomime the following words for their classmates to guess: *cry, drag, clap, hunt, paint, wink, print, mask, smell, slam.* Write the words on the chalkboard after students make the correct guess.

- Write ten words on the chalkboard, seven of which contain blends. Then have volunteers circle and say the words with blends.

- Say a word with a blend, such as *desk* or *grape.* Have students name as many other words as they can that have the same blend.

UNIT 1 LESSONS 9–10, 12–13
Consonant Digraphs *sh, th, wh, ch*

- Say these words and ask students to tell if they hear a consonant digraph at the beginning, middle, or end of the word: *arch, switch, pitcher, washing, shell, that, whale, with.*

- Write words with missing letters and have students write a consonant digraph to complete the word. Use words such as: *pea_ _ (peach),* _ _ *eck (check),* _ _ *o (who), mu_ _room (mushroom).*

- On the chalkboard, write words that contain consonant digraphs. Have students circle the digraphs with another color of chalk.

- Invite students to raise their hands when you say a word with a consonant digraph. Then have them name another word with the same digraph.

◆ Play "twister." Draw large circles on butcher paper and put a consonant digraph on each circle. As you call out a word with a digraph, have a student put a hand or foot on the circle that has the digraph.

◆ Have students ask "Why?" questions. Direct students to include as many words as they can with consonant digraphs in their questions. Encourage silly questions. For example: *Why don't whales brush their teeth?*

◆ Have students brainstorm a list of ten words with *sh.* Then have students use as many as they can in a tongue twister. Repeat, using *th, ch,* and *wh.*

◆ Write these words on the chalkboard and tell students that they are spelled backwards: *hsup (push), elahw (whale), hcruhc (church), ohw (who), reehc (cheer).* Have students say the words and identify the digraphs.

◆ Play "I went to China and took ____." Fill in the blank with a word that begins with *ch,* such as *cheese.* As students take turns naming other *ch* words, they must name everyone else's words as well. Repeat with other digraphs.

UNIT 2 LESSONS 14–18, 27
r-Controlled Vowels *ar, or, ir, ur, er*

◆ Say a sentence in which one word is incorrect. Have students repeat the sentence, substituting a word that makes sense and that includes *ar, ir, or, ur,* or *er.* For example: *An elephant lives in a tree.* (bird) *There are steps in the sky.* (stars)

◆ Give students letter cards with *ar* and *or.* As you say the following words, have them hold up the card that has the same sound: *corn, hare, forty, store, rare, cartoon, March, horse, artist.*

◆ Write incomplete words on the chalkboard, such as *y__n, g__ment, st__e, b__n, c__d.* Have students complete them with *ar* or *or.*

◆ Write the following sentence on the chalkboard and have students underline the words with *er, ir,* and *ur: Because the girl in the purple coat had the upper berth on the train, she hurt her back falling to the floor during an emergency stop.*

◆ Invite students to unscramble letters to make words with *r.* Use words such as *erih (hire), nocr (corn), krad (dark).*

◆ Draw five large circles on butcher paper and put it on the floor. Inside each circle write *ir, er, or, ar,* or *ur.* Have students toss a beanbag on one of the circles and name a word that has that sound.

◆ Say groups of words like the following and have students tell which word has a different sound: *corn, farm, dark, harmful; hurt, turn, cart, curve; skirt, quirk, flirt, star.*

UNIT 2 LESSONS 19–22, 26–27
Words with the Sounds of *f, k,* and *s*

◆ Name the letter *f, k,* or *s.* Have a student name a word that begins with that letter, the next student names a word with the letter in the middle, and a third student names a word with the letter at the end.

Daily Word Study Practice

◆ Say this silly tongue twister and let students practice saying it as fast as they can: *Frantic Fred failed to telephone frightened Phyllis after the phony typhoon.*

◆ Have students brainstorm a list of words with the *s, z,* and *sh* sounds spelled as *s.* Then have them write a sentence using two or more of the words.

◆ Write sentences like the following on the chalkboard: *Each chord echoed quietly as the orchestra played the concerto.* Have students circle the letters that make the sound of *k.*

◆ Give students letter cards for *k, ch, ck, qu,* and *c.* As you say words with the sound of *k,* have students hold up the letter card that stands for the *k* sound. Then write the word on the chalkboard.

◆ Write "The Sounds of *k*" on the chalkboard. During the day have students find words in their textbooks that have this sound and write them under the heading on the board.

◆ Remind students of the different letters that can stand for the *k* sound: *c, ch, q, k.* Then have students fill in the blanks to spell words with the sound of *k.* Write the following incomplete words on the board: *_anopy, _uilt, lo_al, _opy, __orus, _oral, _ing, _angaroo, _uit, _onductor, s_ool, ar__itect.*

◆ Invite students to play "I spy" with objects or picture cards whose names contain the sounds of *f, k,* and *s.* For example: *I spy something that has the sound of* f *at the beginning of the word.* (phone)

◆ Ask students to write on slips of paper any word that has the *k* sound in the initial, medial, or final position. Collect the papers. Then write a sentence on the board with a missing word, such as *I see a _____ in the tree.* Have volunteers read the words on the slips to make silly sentences.

UNIT 2 LESSONS 23–24, 26–27
Silent Letters *gh, rh, wr, gn, kn, sc, st*

◆ Write the following words on the chalkboard: *wrong, fight, ribbon, rhino, wrinkle, actor, knee, ran, web, knickers, gnat, giant.* Have students read the words and identify which ones have a silent letter. Encourage students to identify the letter.

◆ Ask students to name words with *gh* or *wr* that are antonyms for these words: *right, unwrap, found, dropped, low, sold (wrong, wrap, sought, caught, high, bought).* Write the antonyms on the chalkboard.

◆ Write this tongue twister on the chalkboard and have students circle the silent letters: *Robby the Rhino ate rhubarb pies behind a rhododendron in Rhode Island.* Then have students say the sentence as fast as they can.

◆ Write these words on the chalkboard: *weigh, eight, dough, right, sought, mighty, bough, neighbor, daughter, brought, flight, mighty.* Have students erase the silent letters and write them in another color of chalk.

◆ Make word cards for *know, camera, gnome, knot, silent, scent, write, rhyme, poem, listen, quick, fought.* Ask students to sort the cards into words that have silent letters and those that do not.

◆ Have groups of students search for words containing *rh, wr, gh, gn,* and *kn* in books and dictionaries and list them. Then check how many words each group has collected.

◆ Direct students to write riddles for words with *rh*. For example: *It is not an island, but it is a state.* (Rhode Island) *It grows in the ground and is used to make pies.* (rhubarb)

UNIT 3 LESSONS 28–31, 38–39
Suffixes -s, -ed, -ing, -er, -est

◆ Write these words on the chalkboard: *boil, science, snowing, coats, printed, prints, walked, light, jacket, preparing.* Have students write *B* next to words that are base words and *S* next to words that have suffixes.

◆ Write the following words on the board and have students add *-er* and *-est* to each: *clean, dull, low, smooth, short.* Then have them find objects that they can compare by using each set of the three words.

◆ Print the following words on index cards: *printed, coats, walked, duller, snowing, painted, paints, highest.* Have students cut the base words apart from their suffixes. Mix up the endings and then have students add them to the base words to make new words.

◆ Have students stand up in the front of the room and display letter cards for *w, a, v,* and *e.* Call on other students to come up with letter cards for the suffix *-ing.* The student with *e* should sit down as the suffix is added. Repeat with *smile, dive, grade.*

◆ Invite students to write and read aloud sentences that compare two or more things. Have other students write the word that describes the comparison and circle the suffix.

◆ Read the following words and ask students to clap twice when they hear a word in which the final consonant is doubled when a suffix is added: *rest, nap, wish, hot, cold, fat, fit, swim, hope, run, plot, grin, wade.*

◆ On index cards, write words that end in *e,* and the suffixes *-ed, -er, -est,* and *-ing.* Have students make new words by taping the suffixes to the base words (and over the *e* as needed).

◆ Ask students to write the letter *S* on paper. Read the following sentences and have students hold up the letter each time they hear a word with a suffix: *The student was laughing and clapping at the trained dog. I picked up and cleaned off the biggest shell.*

◆ Write the following words on the chalkboard: *swim, hot, flat, drip, dark, act, fat, nap, sad, cute, rude, hike.* Have students choose a word and add *-ed, -er, -est, -ing,* or *-s* to see if the base word and suffix make a real word.

UNIT 3 LESSONS 32–33, 38–39
Suffixes -y, -ly, -le; Adding Suffixes to Words Ending in -y

◆ Have students write *-y* and *-ly* on two cards. As you call out each of the following words, have them raise the suffix that can be added to make a new word: *chill, rose, slow, quiet, luck, spice, flop, part.* (chilly, rosy, slowly, quietly, lucky, spicy, floppy, partly)

Daily Word Study Practice

- Write the following words on the chalkboard: *slow, fog, short, edge, dirt*. Have students use colored chalk to add *-y* or *-ly* to each word and to change the spelling of any base word.

- Give students letter cards for *r, o, s, e,* and *y*. Have them use the cards to make *rose* and then *rosy*. Repeat, using words such as *noise, noisy; spice, spicy;* and *ice, icy*.

- Write *nimble, feeble, pebble, tingle,* and *scribble* on the chalkboard. Have students use another color of chalk to make changes as they add *-ly* to each word.

- Invite students to draw pictures that show examples of things that are *pebbly, bubbly, scribbly, wobbly, crabby,* and *grubby*.

- Write these words on the chalkboard: *stubb_, wobb_, bubb_, hast_, loud_, ting_, ros_, luck_, loud_*. Have students complete the words with the suffix *-y* or *-ly*.

- Write the base words *enjoy, empty, rely, merry, happy, study, cry,* and *lucky* on the chalkboard and have students use different-colored chalk to add the suffix *-s, -ed, -er, -est, -ly,* or *-es* to make real words.

- Ask students to name the base words for *happily, dirtiest, shyly, studies, clumsily, busiest, bubbles, pried,* and *rosy*.

- Have students make word equation cards for base word and suffix combinations, such as *fly − y + i + es = flies*.

UNIT 3 LESSONS 34–39
Suffixes *-less, -ful, -ment, -ness, -able, -age, -ance, -en, -ity, -ive, -some, -ion, -tion, -sion, -ward*

- Invite students to look through newspapers and magazines to highlight words ending in *-less, -ful, -ment, -ness, -able, -age,* and *-ance*. Call on students to share the words they find.

- Write these suffixes and words on cards: *-less, -ness, -ful, -able, read, debate, brave, cloud, truth*. Have students choose a word card and a suffix card to make a new word.

- Write these suffixes on the chalkboard: *-less, -ment, -ness, -able, -ful, -en*. Name a suffix and let students write as many words with that suffix as they can.

- Say these words and have students stand when they hear a word with a suffix: *heavenly, weakness, enjoyably, football, forward, laughable, powerless, apartment, radio*.

- Write the following words on the board and ask students to identify the suffix(es) in each one: *thoughtfulness, surprisingly, sharpened, pretender, absolutely, impressive, education, admittance, available*.

- Encourage students to write riddles using definitions of suffixes and base words. For example: *This word means "without fear."* (fearless) Invite students to share their riddles with the class.

◆ Write the meanings of the suffixes *-less*, *-ful*, *-ment*, *-ness*, *-able*, *-age*, and *-ance* in one column on the chalkboard and the suffixes in the other. Have students draw lines to match them.

◆ Write words with suffixes on the chalkboard. Have students circle the suffix and write the base word.

◆ Create word cards for *mass*, *broke*, *quarrel*, *create*, *tire*, *awe*, *possible* and the suffixes *-en*, *-ity*, *-ive*, and *-some*. Mix up the cards. Then have students put the cards together to make words.

◆ Have students write on slips of paper any word with one of these suffixes: *-ly*, *-y*, *-less*, *-ness*, and *-able*. Collect the slips of paper. Then write the following sentence on the board: *The ____ crowd was ____.* Call on volunteers to fill in the blanks with their words to make silly sentences.

UNIT 4 LESSONS 40–42, 48, 55
Vowel Pairs *ai, ay, ee, ea, ei, ie, oa, oe, ow*

◆ On the chalkboard, write the following words with short vowels: *got, plan, pant, pal, ran, bed, net*. Ask students to add a vowel to make a vowel pair and a new word: *goat, plain, paint, pail, rain, bead, neat*.

◆ Write the following words on the chalkboard: *due, bowl, pillow, poach, cheap, lies, untied, daisies*. Have students circle the vowel pair in each word and tell what sound they hear.

◆ Write the following words on cards and have students pronounce them: *nail, toad, crow, raid, receive, fried, clue, keep, please*. Then encourage students to sort the words according to long vowel sounds.

◆ On the chalkboard, write a word with vowel pair letters out of order. Ask students to unscramble the letters, for example, *stoba* (*boast*).

◆ Invite students to make a list of rhyming words for *toe, float, boast, row, keep, speak, eat, neat, ties,* and *way*. Then have students circle the vowel pairs.

◆ Give a letter card for a consonant or a vowel to each student. Have students form groups to see how many words with vowel pairs they can make in a ten-minute period. Make sure there are students with vowel pair cards in each group.

◆ On butcher paper, write long *a, i, o, u,* and *e* on large circles. Have students take turns tossing a beanbag on one of the circles and naming a vowel pair word with that sound.

◆ Have students make word ladders with vowel pairs, for example, *toad, tied, ties, fries, fried, freed, bleed*.

UNIT 4 LESSONS 43–48, 55
Vowel Digraphs *ea, ei, ey, ie, oo, au, aw*

◆ Give students cards for *ea, ie, ey, oo, au,* and *aw*. As you say words with vowel digraphs, have students hold up the appropriate card.

Daily Word Study Practice

◆ Write these words on the chalkboard and invite students to circle the vowel digraphs: *cow, enjoy, boil, thread, grief, foot, boots, cautious, sprawled, gloomy, sleigh, new, yawn.*

◆ Write incomplete words on the chalkboard and have students fill in the blanks with vowel digraphs. Some examples are *shr_ _ d (shread), f_ _ cet (faucet), squ_ _ k (squawk), t_ _ (tie), v _ _ l (veil).*

◆ Have students stand when they hear the long *a* sound in the following words: *convey, head, reindeer, peach, eight, veil, neighbor, sweater, they, obey, leather.*

◆ On the chalkboard, write words with the long *i* and *e* vowel sounds spelled *ie* such as *brief* and *tied.* Have students sort the words in two lists, one for long *i* and one for long *e*.

◆ Invite students to unscramble letters to make words with the vowel digraph *ie*, such as *lifed (field), edi (die), ifreb (brief), hecif (chief).*

◆ Invite students to make two lists of words that have the digraph *oo*, one with words that sound like *look* and *good* and the other with words that sound like *too* and *moon.*

◆ Ask students to say the word *moo!* when they hear a word with the digraph *oo* as in *moo.* Say words such as *lagoon, loon, mourn, room, roost, roast, bone, crook, toadstools, mushroom.*

◆ Have students use the letter cards for *o, l, k, m, n, b, r, t, l,* and *s* to make words with the digraph *oo*, such as *room, soon, tool, noon, broom, loom, look, boom, boot, took.*

◆ Give students word cards with the digraphs *aw* and *au* and have them hold up the correct card as you say words such as *claw, pause, caught, haul, squawk, cautious,* and *scrawny.*

UNIT 4 LESSONS 49–52, 54–55
Vowel Diphthongs *oi, oy, ew, ou, ow*

◆ Invite students to pantomime or act out the following words with diphthongs: *cowboy, join, coin, point, coil, threw, blew.*

◆ Ask a volunteer to say a word with a diphthong. Write it on the chalkboard and have other students list words with the same diphthong. For example, if a student says *new*, other students may suggest *blew, few, stew,* and so on.

◆ For the following words, have students use antonyms with the diphthongs *oi, oy,* and *ew: please (annoy), old (new), fresh (spoiled), dry (moist), many (few), caught (threw), quiet (noisy).*

◆ Ask students to raise their hands when they hear a word that has the diphthong *oi* or *oy: royalty, ruin, voyage, postage, poinsettia, coin, package, noise, onion, broil.*

◆ Write words on the chalkboard with missing letters and have students fill them in with vowel diphthongs to make a word, for example, *n_ _ sy (noisy)* or *pr_ _ d (proud).*

◆ Write ten words on the chalkboard, seven of which contain the diphthong *ou* or *ow.* Have students circle the words with the *ou* sound.

◆ Make word cards for words with diphthongs. Invite students to choose a card, read it aloud, and then name the diphthong. Encourage them to use the word in a sentence.

♦ Make cards for rhyming words with diphthongs and pass them out to students. Have them find their rhyming partner and create a short poem with the words.

♦ Invite students to illustrate these words: *growl, enjoy, borrow, royal, coins, clown, bounced, fountain, crowd, loud, doused, jewelry.*

UNIT 5 LESSONS 56–58, 64
Plural Forms and Irregular Plurals

♦ Divide the class into two teams. List several nouns that end in *y* on the board, such as *cherry, bunny, monkey, donkey, baby, fairy, pony,* and so on. Have team members take turns writing the plural form of the words. Each team gets one point for each word written correctly.

♦ Give students letter cards for *w, i, f, e, v,* and *s*. Ask them to spell *wife* and then make the plural form. Repeat, using *loaf, thief, wolf, calf,* and *life.*

♦ Say these plural words and have students tell you the singular form: *feet, students, geese, mice, oxen, women.*

♦ Invite students to draw and label pictures that represent the plural form of these words: *tomato, calf, chimney, bush, pony, branch, grass, box.*

♦ In two columns, write at random singular words and their irregular plurals. Invite students to draw a line to each matching pair.

♦ Use a singular word in a sentence, such as *I see a. . . .* and have students change the sentence to its plural form: *I see some. . . .* Use words such as *ox, man, goose, mouse.*

♦ Write singular and plural forms of several words, including *sheep, salmon, deer, moose,* and *elk*. Have students tell if each word is singular, plural, or both.

♦ Students can create riddles for singular and plural words. For example: *It is more than one. It is an animal that swims in the sea. (salmon, fish)*

♦ Pick out several objects in the classroom such as a pencil, a box, and a watch. Have students write the object's name and its plural form.

♦ Invite students to open their math books to a page and make a list of all the singular and plural words they find.

UNIT 5 LESSONS 59–61, 63–64
Possessives and Contractions

♦ Give students word cards for singular nouns and cards for an apostrophe and s. Have students put the cards together to make the possessive form. Then have them use each word in a sentence.

♦ As you write several noun phrases on the chalkboard, such as *the girls' gloves* and *the boy's hat,* have students hold up one hand if it means one and two hands if it means more than one.

Daily Word Study Practice

- Write incomplete possessive phrases on chart paper and ask volunteers to fill in the blanks, for example, *the teachers'* _____ *(lounge)* or *the dog's* _____ *(leash)*.

- Write a list of singular and plural possessives on word cards. Have students sort them into groups for one or more than one.

- Give students letter cards for *l, e, t, u, s,* and an apostrophe. Have them form the words *let us* and *let's*. Repeat, using other contractions.

- On the chalkboard, write phrases such as *is not, we have,* and *they will* in white or yellow chalk. Have students use red chalk to make changes to create contractions.

- As you dictate simple sentences such as *That is my book,* have students rewrite them, using a contraction.

- Ask one student to name a contraction. Have the next student tell the words the contraction stands for.

- Write a mixture of contractions and possessives on word cards. Have students sort them into contractions and possessives.

UNIT 6 LESSONS 65–71, 75–76
Prefixes

- Write base words and the prefixes *un-, dis-, non-, il-,* and *ir-* on index cards. Have students put the word cards together to make new words. Then have them use the new words in sentences.

- Say sentences with base words. Then have students take turns adding a prefix to each base word to give the sentence the opposite meaning. For example: *I like carrots. I dislike carrots.*

- Write the prefixes *un-, dis-, non-, ir-, il-, im-, in-, en-,* and *em-* on the chalkboard. As you say base words such as *act, sense, fair,* and *moral* aloud, have students choose a prefix to turn each word into a new one. Have students define the new words.

- Invite students to choose a word that has the prefix *co-, com-,* or *con-* and draw a picture to illustrate it. Then have them use the word in a sentence that relates to the illustration.

- Ask students to write *ex-, re-,* and *de-* on three sheets of paper. As you read aloud *change, tie, part, tour, tend, write, face, press, plain, open, pay,* and *grade,* have students hold up the prefix that can be added to the word.

- Write the words *conspire, compete, contest, connect, conceal, cooperate, coexist, compose,* and *conductor* on cards. Have students identify each prefix and write a second word with that same prefix on the other side of the card.

- Form five teams and assign each team the prefix *super-, over-, sub-, under-,* or *out-*. Have them write as many words with those prefixes as they can in ten minutes.

- In two columns, write words with the prefixes *fore-, pre-,* and *pro-* and their meanings (for example: *preview* ("see ahead of time")). Have students match the prefixes with their meanings.

◆ Write words with the prefixes *bi-*, *tri-*, *semi-* and *mid-* on cards. Have students sort the words according to the prefixes and then use each word in a sentence.

UNIT 6 LESSONS 72–73, 75–76
Roots

◆ Write the following words on cards: *impose, dispel, oppose, compel, dispose, repose, repel.* Have students cut each word in half and then display the root and the prefix.

◆ Write words such as *import, eject, reject, project,* and *report* on cards. Have students choose one word and ask a partner a question using the word. Have the partner use the word in the answer. For example: *Is this radio portable? Yes, it is portable.*

◆ On the chalkboard, write words with the roots *pos, pel, port,* and *ject.* Have students circle the roots in each word and then give the meaning of the word.

◆ Invite students to draw a picture of a word with the root *duce, duct, tract, spec,* or *scribe.* Have them exchange their pictures with a partner and guess each other's word.

◆ Write these roots and prefixes on the board in two columns: *pos, pel, port, ject, duce, duct, tract, spect, scribe; in-, de-, com-, pro-, trans-, re-, im-, dis-, ex-.* Have students match the roots with prefixes to make words.

◆ Write roots and their meanings on separate index cards. Have students match each root with its meaning.

◆ Play a version of "Mother, may I?" Tell students that if you say a word with a prefix, they take one step forward. If you say a word with a root, they take two steps forward. If the word has both, they take three steps forward.

UNIT 7 LESSONS 77–79, 87–88
Synonyms, Homonyms, and Antonyms

◆ On the chalkboard, write ten words that are homonyms. Then have students draw a circle around the pairs and connect them with a line.

◆ On index cards, write synonym pairs, one pair per card. Mix the cards up and turn them face down. Have students turn the cards over in twos, trying to make a match.

◆ On the chalkboard, write words that have synonyms. Have students choose a word and write it on a card. Have them exchange cards with a partner who will write a synonym on the back of the card. Keep the cards in a file.

◆ On the chalkboard, write sentences such as *Luis <u>won</u> the race.* Ask a volunteer to read the sentence, substitute an antonym for the underlined word, and then reread the sentence. *(Luis lost the race.)*

◆ Divide the class into three groups for synonyms, homonyms, and antonyms. Say word pairs such as *slim, thin; smooth, rough;* and *see, sea* and have each group stand when they hear their category.

◆ Say the following words: *for, pour, bored, weather, bawl, made.* Call on volunteers to write each word on the chalkboard and then write a homonym next to each word.

◆ Write a list of homonyms on the chalkboard. Have students take turns changing the spellings of the words to make new words that sound the same but have different meanings.

◆ Ask students to brainstorm lists of homonym, synonym, and antonym pairs. Then have them choose one pair and use both words in the same sentence.

UNIT 7 LESSONS 80–83, 87–88
Alphabetical Order, Dictionary Guide Words, Entry Words, and Homographs

◆ On the chalkboard, write *enough, ending, enjoy, engage, ensure, encore, enlist,* and *energy.* Ask students to underline the letters they would use to put the words in alphabetical order. Then have them alphabetize the words.

◆ Give eight students cards for the following words and have them arrange themselves in alphabetical order: *justify, just, jurisdiction, junket, jury, June, judo, juvenile.*

◆ On the chalkboard, write the guide words *mouse* and *murmur.* Then write *mouth, mumps, mountain, much, mule,* and *muscle.* Ask students to alphabetize the list and cross out the words that would not be found on the same page as the guide words.

◆ Distribute dictionaries and ask students to open to any page and point out an entry word and the guide words. Then have them find a word that has more than one meaning and another word that is a homograph.

◆ Give meanings for the word *show: 1. to be seen 2. to guide or conduct 3. to display or exhibit.* Have students identify which meaning is used in this sentence: *We will show our rabbits at the county fair next month.*

◆ Ask students to find the homographs for *bill* in the dictionary. Then ask which entry is used for *bill* in each of these sentences: *The robin had a worm in its bill. A bill came with our order. Congress passed the tax bill yesterday.*

◆ Write words such as *absent, babies, noisiest, crucial, rotten, wolves,* and *sinking* on chart paper. Have students write *yes* next to each word they find as an entry word and *no* next to those that are not listed as entry words.

◆ Distribute dictionaries and have students find as many homographs as they can in a ten-minute period. Compile their lists on the chalkboard.

◆ Ask students if they would find these entries under the following guide words: *ill* under *illegitimacy, imaginary; scroll* under *screwball, scrub; butterscotch* under *bombard, boo; civilize* under *civil, clannish.*

◆ Say a word students are likely not to know. Write the definition on a slip of paper. Then have students make up definitions and write them on paper. Read each definition aloud and ask students to vote for the one they think is correct.

UNIT 7   LESSONS 84–88
Different Spellings, Pronunciation Key, and Accent Marks

◆ Write the respellings for *scene, missing, center,* and *psychology* on the chalkboard. Ask students to pronounce each word and write its correct spelling.

◆ In two columns, write the respellings and correct spellings for *section, session, success,* and *suction.* Have students match each respelling with its correct spelling.

◆ Have partners write a secret message, using respellings they find in the dictionary for each word. Have them exchange their sentences with a partner and then read each other's message.

◆ Invite students to write their own names with respellings and accent marks on the chalkboard.

◆ Write five words on cards and their respellings on five other cards. Place them face down and invite students to match the respellings with the correct spellings.

◆ Write the words *believe, pronounce, retell, story, pencil, diskette* on index cards. Have students cut the words between syllables. Then have them write an accent mark on each accented syllable.

UNITS 1–6   LESSONS 11–13, 25–27, 37, 53, 55, 62–64, 74–76
Syllables

◆ Label three bags 1, 2, and 3. Spread out word cards for one-, two- and three-syllable words. Invite volunteers to "bag" as many words as they can in ten seconds by reading a word, telling how many syllables it has, and putting it in the correct bag.

◆ Read aloud a list of words—such as *neighbor, clown, detour, wonderful, mantelpiece, umbrella, extend, officer*—and ask students to clap their hands for each syllable they hear.

◆ Have students play a game of "I spy." Invite them to take turns giving clues to objects in the classroom whose names have the number of syllables you designate. For example, Two! *I spy something you write on.* (chalkboard)

LEVEL D

PEARSON
Phonics

JANE ERVIN
Elwell - Murray - Kucia

Design: Bill SMITH STUDIO **Illustrations:** Andrea Barrett, Jenny Campbell, Chris Cantley, Daniel Clifford, Nelle Davis, Robin Dewitt, Pat Dewitt Grush, Estudio, Inc. , Janice Fried, Flora Jew, N. Jo Inc., Ron Jones, Fran Lee, Jane Manning, Mas Miyamoto, Roberta Morales, Hank Morehouse, Cary Pilla Lassen, Chris Reed, Margaret San Fillipo, Andrew Schiff, Stacey Schuett, Matt Straub, Brad Teare, Gary Undercuffler, Jessica Wolk-Stanley, Jerry Zimmerman .

Photographs: *All photographs by Silver Burdett Ginn & Parker/Boon Productions for Silver Burdett Ginn unless otherwise noted.* Cover: © Eric Isselée/Fotolia. Page 5: *Row1Column3.* © Ayupov Evgeniy/Fotolia, *Row2Column4.* © Jupiterimages/Thinkstock, *Row3Column1.* © Abderit99/Fotolia, *Row3Column2.* Yxowert/Fotolia, *Row5Column4.* © Eray/Fotolia, *Row5Column5.* © Gravicapa/Fotolia, *Row1Column1.* © Nbriam/Fotolia, *Row1Column2.* © Comstock/Thinkstock, *Row1Column4.* © Vasiliy Koval/Fotolia, *Row1Column5.* © Thomas Northcut/ Thinkstock, *Row2Column1.* © Ablestock.com/Thinkstock, *Row2Column3.* © PhotoGrapHie/Fotolia, *Row2Column5.* © Comstock/Thinkstock, *Row3Column3.* © Michael Gray/Fotolia, *Row3Column5.* © Michael Kempf/Fotolia, *Row4Column1.* © Olga Sapegina/Fotolia, *Row4Column2.* © Marietjie Opperman/Fotolia, *Row4Column3.* © Stockbyte/Thinkstock, *Row4Column4.* © Picture Partners/Fotolia, *Row4Column5.* © Hemera Technologies/Thinkstock, *Row5Column5.* © Andrew S./Fotolia, *Row5Column2.* © Thinkstock, *Row3Column3.* © Rtimages/Fotolia, *Row2Col-umn2.* © Iznogood/Fotolia, *Row3Column4.* © Elaine Barker/Fotolia. 6: *b.* © Glen Jones/Fotolia, 7: *mbl.* © Claudia Costa/Fotolia, *br.* © lithian/ Fotolia, *tl.* © Stockbyte/Fotolia, *tr.* © Jupiterimages/Thinkstock, *mtl.* © Valua Vitaly/Fotolia, *mtm.* © Getty Images/Hemera Technologies/ Thinkstock, *mtr.* © Joss/Fotolia, *mbm.* © Brand X Pictures/Thinkstock, *mbr.* © Iosif Szasz-Fabian/Fotolia, *bl.* © Mr Twister/Fotolia, *bm.* © Maksim Shebeko/Fotolia, *tm.* © Iznogood/Fotolia. 9: *tl.* © Jupiterimages/Thinkstock, *tmr.* © Anatoliy Meshkov/Fotolia, *bml.* © Ablestock.com/ Thinkstock, *br.* © Picsfive/Fotolia, *tml.* © Pavel Losevsky/Fotolia, *tr.* © Andrzej Tokarski/Fotolia, *bl.* © Cphoto/Fotolia, *bmr.* © Leonid Nyshko/ Fotolia. 13: *tl.* © Le Do/Fotolia, *tmr.* © Harris Shiffman/Fotolia, *bl.* © Michel Bazin/Fotolia, *bl.* © Esweet/Fotolia, *bmr.* © Jupiterimages/ Thinkstock, *tml.* © Marc Dietrich/Fotolia, *bml.* © Homydesign/Fotolia, *br.* © Michael Flippo/Fotolia. 15: *tmr.* © Comstock/Thinkstock, *ml.* © Tom Brakefield/Thinkstock, *mml.* © Shock/Fotolia, *bl.* © Hemera Technologies/Thinkstock, *br.* © Stockbyte/Thinkstock, *tml.* © Auter/Fotolia, *bml.* © Thinkstock, *tl.* © Hemera Technologies/Thinkstock, *tr.* © Hemera Technologies/Getty Images/Thinkstock, *mmr.* © Giuseppe_R/Fotolia, *mr.* © Efired/Fotolia, *bmr.* © Stockbyte/Thinkstock. 16: *tml.* © Hemera Technologies/Getty Images/Thinkstock, *bl.* © Stephen Finn/Fotolia, *br.* © Kraig Scarbinsky/Thinkstock, *tl.* © Getty Images/Comstock Images/Thinkstock, *tmr.* © Leonid Nyshko/Fotolia, *tr.* © Lamax/Fotolia, *bmr.* © Jaimie Duplass/Fotolia, *bml.* © Atropat/Fotolia. 17: *ml.* © Jupiterimages/Thinkstock. 19: *tl.* © Digital Vision/Thinkstock. 21: *tl.* © Roger Weber/ Thinkstock, *tm.* © Duncan Noakes/Fotolia, *ml.* © Thomas Moens/Fotolia, *m.* © Hemera Technologies/Thinkstock, *bl.* © Xavier Marchant/ Fotolia, *bm.* © Anyka/Fotolia, *tr.* © Terex/Fotolia, *mr.* © Hemera Technologies/Getty Images/Thinkstock, *br.* © Ugocutilli/Fotolia. 24: © Xuejun li/Fotolia. 27: *tr.* © Lisa F.Young/Fotolia. 33: *tl.* © Harris Shiffman/Fotolia, *bl.* © David De Lossy/Thinkstock, *bmr.* © Ecoview/Fotolia, *tmr.* © Comstock/Thinkstock, *tml.* © Sframe/Fotolia, *tr.* © Brand X Pictures/Thinkstock, *bml.* © Lasse Kristensen/Fotolia, *br.* © Atropat/Fotolia. 35: *tl.* © Jagi/Fotolia, *tml.* © Esweet/Fotolia, *tmr.* © Simone van den Berg/Fotolia, *tr.* © Mary Lane/Fotolia, *bmr.* © Hedgehog/Fotolia, *br.* © Anatoliy Meshkov/Fotolia, *bml.* © Thomas Northcut/Thinkstock, *bl.* © Bertold Werkmann/Fotolia. 37: *tl.* © Austinadams/Fotolia, *br.* © Jupiterimages/ Thinkstock, *bm.* © jirasak pakdeeto/Fotolia, *tm.* © HP_Photo/Fotolia, *bl.* © Pavel Losevsky/Fotolia, *tr.* © Bertold Werkmann/Fotolia. 38: *1bl.* © Alexford/Fotolia, *2bm.* © Jagi/Fotolia, *3tl.* © Tom Brakefield/Thinkstock, *3tr.* © Roger Scott/Fotolia, *3ml.* © Ecoview/Fotolia, *3br.* © Duncan Noakes/Fotolia, *4ml.* © Hemera Technologies/Getty Images/Thinkstock, *4br.* © Hemera Technologies/Thinkstock, *4tl.* © Terex/Fotolia, *4tm.* © Africa Studio/Fotolia, *4bl.* © Bruce MacQueen/Fotolia, *1tl.* © Thomas Northcut/Thinkstock, *1tr.* © Hemera Technologies/Thinkstock, *1ml.* © malgorzata bryndza/Fotolia, *1m.* © Alx/Thinkstock, *1mr.* © Andrew S./Fotolia, *1bm.* © Liron/Fotolia, *1br.* © Tommy/Fotolia, *2tl.* © Kasoga/ Fotolia, *2tm.* © Nymph/Fotolia, *2tr.* © Dleonis/Fotolia, *2ml.* © Thomas Northcut/Thinkstock, *2m.* © Ronen/Fotolia, *2mr.* © Hemera Technologies/Getty Images/Thinkstock, *2br.* © Ellypoo/Thinkstock, *3tm.* © Jeka84/Fotolia, *3m.* © HP_Photo/Fotolia, *3mr.* © Dleonis/Fotolia, *3bl.* © Ronen/Fotolia, *3bm.* © blue eye/Fotolia, *4tr.* © GIS/Fotolia, *4m.* © Hemera Technologies/Thinkstock, *4mr.* © Henryk Olszewski/ Fotolia, *4bm.* © Riverwalker/Fotolia, *1tm.* © Atropat/Fotolia, *2bl.* © Bertold Werkmann/Fotolia. 39: *tr.* © Paul Hakimata/Fotolia. 43: *mtl.* © Abderit99/Fotolia, *mtml.* © George Doyle/Thinkstock, *mr.* © Mark Scott/Fotolia, *mbmr.* © Garret Bautista/Fotolia, *mbr.* © Kitch Bain/Fotolia, *bml.* © Marcel Hurni/Fotolia, *mml.* © UZUMBA/Fotolia, *bmr.* © Elnur/Fotolia, *tl.* © Hemera Technologies/Getty Images/Thinkstock, *tml.* © Alexandra Karamyshev/Fotolia, *tmr.* © Iosif Szasz-Fabian/Fotolia, *tr.* © Kasoga/Fotolia, *mtmr.* © James Steidl/Fotolia, *mtr.* © MAXFX/Fotolia, *mmr.* © Brand X Pictures/Thinkstock, *mbl.* © Getty Images/Hemera Technologies/Thinkstock, *mbml.* © Graça Victoria/Fotolia, *bl.* © Borys Shevchuk/Fotolia, *br.* © Sharpshot/Fotolia, *ml.* © Anetta/Fotolia. 44: *b.* © Getty Images/Jupiterimages/Thinkstock. 46: *t.* © elcarli/Fotolia. 47: *r.* © © Graça Victoria/Fotolia. 49: *m.* © Matthew Grant/Fotolia. 52: *m.* © Gallas/Fotolia. 56: *tl.* © Stockbyte/Thinkstock, *ml.* © Marc Dietrich/ Fotolia, *bl.* © Trent Woods/Fotolia. 61: *tl.* © Paul Hakimata/Fotolia. 63: *tr.* © Louella Folsom/Fotolia, *mtr.* © John Holst/Fotolia, *mbr.* © Getty Images/Thinkstock, *br.* © PhotoObjects.net/Thinkstock. 66: *tl.* © Maxim Malevich/Fotolia. 69: *br.* © Vasiliy Koval/Fotolia. 71: *t.* © Lijuan Guo/ Fotolia, *b.* © Picture Partners/Fotolia. 72: *tl.* © Sursad/Fotolia, *mr.* © Tom Brakefield/Thinkstock, *bm.* © Tom Brakefield/Thinkstock. 73: *mr.* © Jupiterimages/Thinkstock. 75: *br.* © Maksym Gorpenyuk/Fotolia. 76: *tl.* © Diddy/Fotolia, *tr.* © Flavia Morlachetti/Fotolia, *bl.* © Getty Images/ Thinkstock, *br.* © Mark Markau/Fotolia. 80: *br.* © Getty Images/Hemera Technologies/Thinkstock. 82: *tl.* © Mates/Fotolia. 83: *tr.* © Mat Hayward/Fotolia. 89: *tr.* © Kushnirov Avraham/Fotolia, *bmr.* © Esweet/Fotolia, *tl.* © Lev Olkha/Fotolia, *tml.* © Ionescu Bogdan/Fotolia, *tmr.* © Mikko Pitkänen/Fotolia, *bl.* © Stockbyte/Thinkstock, *bml.* © Kelpfish/Fotolia, *br.* © Vladimir Chernyanski/Fotolia. 93: *br.* © Felix Gomes/Fotolia. 95: *tr.* © Philippe Leridon/Fotolia, *mr.* © Marcel Hurni/Fotolia, *bml.* © Mark Markau/Fotolia, *ml.* © Hemera Technologies/Thinkstock, *tl.* © Feng Yu/Fotolia, *tml.* © Elnur/Fotolia, *tmr.* © Berna Safoglu/Fotolia, *mml.* © NatUlrich/Fotolia, *mmr.* © Solodovnikova Elena/Fotolia, *bl.* © Yang Yu/Fotolia, *bmr.* © Ivan Gulei/Fotolia, *br.* © Getty Images/Zedcor Wholly Owned/Thinkstock. 99: *ml.* © Anyka/Fotolia, *bml.* © Dieter Spannknebel/Thinkstock, *bmr.* © Getty Images/Hemera Technologies/Thinkstock, *br.* © Eric Isselée/Fotolia, *tr.* © Andre/Fotolia, *tl.* © Hemera

Technologies/Getty Images/Thinkstock, *tml.* © Kasoga/Fotolia, *tmr.* © Picture Partners/Fotolia, *mml.* © VanHart/Fotolia, *mmr.* © Hemera Technologies/Thinkstock, *mr.* © Aleksandr Ugorenkov/Fotolia, *bl.* © Stockbyte/Thinkstock. 103: *tr.* © Lucy Clark/Fotolia, *tm.* © Haneck/ Fotolia, *m.* © Michel Bazin/Fotolia, *mr.* © Brand X Pictures/Thinkstock, *br.* © Paddler/Fotolia, *ml.* © Leticia Wilson/Fotolia, *tl.* © Dusan Zidar/ Fotolia. 107: *tl.* © John Holst/Fotolia, *tm.* © Arpad Nagy-Bagoly/Fotolia, *tr.* © Leslie Banks /123RF, *bl.* © Roman Sigaev/Fotolia, *bm.* © Jiri Hera/Fotolia, *br.* © Getty Images/Hemera Technologies/Thinkstock, *br.* © Stockbyte/Thinkstock. 109: *t.* © NASA/JSC, *m.* © NASA Human Spaceflight Collection, *b.* © NASA. 110: *t.* © Mariusz Blach/Fotolia, *b.* © Pix by Marti/Fotolia. 111: *bl.* © Terex/Fotolia, *br.* © Digital Vision/ Thinkstock, *tl.* © Route66Photography/Fotolia, *tm.* © Ivan Gulei/Fotolia, *bm.* © Tein/Fotolia, *tr.* © Andrew Johnson/Fotolia. 112: *t.* © David De Lossy/Thinkstock. 115: © Aaron Amat/Fotolia. 120: *tl.* © GOL/Fotolia. 126: *tr.* © Tyler Olson/Fotolia. 129: *tl.* © Eric Isselée/Fotolia. 131: *background.* © Siegfried Schnepf/Fotolia. 134: *bl.* © LuckyPhoto/Fotolia, *bm.* © Serghei Velusceac/Fotolia, *br.* © Stockbyte/Fotolia. 137: *tr.* © Michael Blann/Thinkstock. 143: *m.* © Pressmaster/Fotolia. 145: *br.* © Paul Moore/Fotolia. 148: *br.* © Superstock. 160: *tl.* © Vatikaki/Fotolia, *tm.* © Marie Stone/Superstock, *tr.* © Francois Jacquemin/Superstock, *bl.* © Kmit/Fotolia, *bm.* © Hemera Technologies/Thinkstock, *br.* © TheSupe/ Fotolia. 163: *tr.* © Andrey Danilovi/Fotolia. 171: *br.* © Joanna Zielinska/Fotolia, *bl.* © Tobias Kaltenbach/Fotolia. 173: *background.* © Getty Images/Jupiterimages/Thinkstock. 174: *tl.* © Jstock/Fotolia, *m.* © Jagi/Fotolia, *bl.* © Tony Campbell/Fotolia, *tr.* © Ernst Fretz/Fotolia, *ml.* © Feng Yu/Fotolia, *mr.* © Edyta Pawlowska/Fotolia, *bm.* © Stockbyte/Thinkstock, *br.* © By-Studio/Fotolia, *tm.* © Iznogood/Fotolia. 187: *m.* © Anik/ Fotolia, *BorderTop.* © Ablestock.com/Thinkstock, *BorderBottom.* © Getty Images/Ablestock.com/Thinkstock. 188: *tr.* © Jupiterimages/ Thinkstock. Back Cover: *bm.* © Steven Pepple/Fotolia.

Acknowledgments: Pearson gratefully acknowledges the following for the use of copyrighted materials: "Cricket" Copyright © 1991 by X.J. Kennedy. First appeared in The Kite That Braved Old Orchard Beach, published by Margaret K. McElderry Books. Reprinted by permission of Curtis Brown, Ltd.

Teacher Notes

Teacher Notes

Teacher Notes